JEWISH POLITICS IN SPINOZA'S AMSTERDAM

THE LITTMAN LIBRARY OF
JEWISH CIVILIZATION

Dedicated to the memory of
LOUIS THOMAS SIDNEY LITTMAN
*who founded the Littman Library for the love of God
and as an act of charity in memory of his father*
JOSEPH AARON LITTMAN
and to the memory of
ROBERT JOSEPH LITTMAN
who continued what his father Louis had begun
יהא זכרם ברוך

'Get wisdom, get understanding:
Forsake her not and she shall preserve thee'
PROV. 4: 5

The Littman Library of Jewish Civilization is a registered UK charity
Registered charity no. 1000784

JEWISH POLITICS IN SPINOZA'S AMSTERDAM

ANNE O. ALBERT

London
The Littman Library of Jewish Civilization
in association with Liverpool University Press
2022

The Littman Library of Jewish Civilization
Registered office: 4th floor, 7–10 Chandos Street, London W1G 9DQ

in association with Liverpool University Press
4 Cambridge Street, Liverpool L69 7ZU, UK
www.liverpooluniversitypress.co.uk/littman

Managing Editor: Connie Webber

Distributed in North America by
Oxford University Press Inc., 198 Madison Avenue
New York, NY 10016, USA

Catalogue records for this book are available from the
British Library and the Library of Congress

ISBN 978-1-789622-29-4

Publishing co-ordinator: Janet Moth
Copy-editing: Bonnie Blackburn
Proofreading: Philippa Claiden
Index: Francis Young
Production, design, and typesetting by
Pete Russell, Faringdon, Oxon.

Printed and bound in Great Britain by
TJ Books Limited, Padstow, Cornwall

For Tova and Mose

ACKNOWLEDGEMENTS

THE RESEARCH that ultimately made its way into this book had its origins in my doctoral dissertation at the University of Pennsylvania. I was supported there by a Benjamin Franklin Fellowship, while in Israel by funding from the Rothberg International School, and then later by grants and fellowships from the Mellon Foundation, the Woodrow Wilson Foundation, the American Association of University Women, the Memorial Foundation for Jewish Culture, the National Foundation for Jewish Culture, and the US Student Fulbright Program, which supported a crucial research year in Amsterdam. After completing my doctorate, I benefitted from the time and resources afforded by fellowships at Brown University and at the Herbert D. Katz Center for Advanced Judaic Studies at the University of Pennsylvania as I rethought and reworked the project.

The book was shaped by meaningful encounters with many individuals over the long period of its gestation and before, beginning with my teachers. My doctoral adviser, David Ruderman, welcomed me with generosity and curiosity to Penn and into his unparalleled network of scholarly friends. He taught me to think in terms of where my own perspective fits into a vast historiographical web, and his influence is present in large and small ways throughout this book. Earlier, my teachers at Reed College introduced me to the traditions and eras that have continued to drive my interests. David Sacks was my first instructor in early modern European culture, and Steven Wasserstrom introduced me to Jewish thought; both continue to teach the value of scholarly friendship.

Travelling to Jerusalem and Amsterdam to learn and do research was a privilege in itself, but the pleasure was compounded by the warm and helpful reception of Irene Zwiep, Emile Schrijver, and Odette Vlessing in Amsterdam, and of Israel Yuval, Ora Limor, Richie Cohen, and others in Israel.

Being first a student, then a fellow, and now a staff member at the Katz Center has afforded me countless stimulating conversations, whether about my own work or about others', with the latter finding its own magical way of coming back to affect my own. Katz Center fellows who had a particular impact on this project, whether by listening and nodding at the right times over coffee, or by popping into my office and offering unsolicited (but wholly useful) advice, include Lois Dubin, Elisheva Carlebach, Debra Glasberg Gail, Hadar Feldman Samet, Arye Edrei, Amnon Raz-Krakotzkin, Jesús de Prado Plumed, Theo Dunkelgrün, Pawel Maciejko, and Matt Goldish. Julie Cooper, Federica Francesconi, and Cornelia Aust additionally read drafts of various parts of the book at different stages. Their interventions, large and small, greatly improved the work. I am especially grateful to Menachem Lorberbaum for his early interest in the project.

Several readers in particular deserve special thanks for their efforts as this project was nearing completion. Francesca Bregoli and Joshua Teplitsky read my draft carefully and kindly. Arthur Kiron was extremely generous with his time and judgement and, happily, his efforts revealed the depth of our shared interests. I only wish that all readers could encounter my writing with his comment bubbles attached. I especially thank Natalie Dohrmann, a reader and editor of rare gifts. Seeing past innumerable infelicities, she sharpened my prose and perceived the project's overarching aims more clearly than I. In the end, defects remain, some of which I already recognize, and they are solely the result of my own limitations of ability or time. Speaking of time, I am exceedingly grateful to Janet Moth at the Littman Library for her superhuman efforts on the manuscript and tolerance with its author throughout the last few stages of editing. Sincere thanks, also, to Connie Webber for seeing the book's promise and remaining supportive when the demands of work and parenting during the Covid-19 pandemic introduced new delays.

I would like to specially acknowledge Miriam Bodian, on whose shoulders I stood most squarely in conceiving this book. One essay of hers opened a window onto the political ideas of Amsterdam's *nação*, and I enthusiastically jumped through it into my own world of interpretation. I am also grateful for early encouragement from Yosef Kaplan, who, among other insights, let me know that it wasn't wrong for me to prioritize family life over scholarly production for a time. I'm sure he won't remember the conversation, but it was the rare humane encounter that one hopes for in academe. My choices at that stage risked the book's ultimate completion but I have never regretted them.

My gratitude to my husband, JD, knows no bounds. It reflects the height of love (I assume) and forbearance (for certain) on his part that over these many years he has never suggested that I give up on this book, even while its costs, both material and personal, were real for both of us and I alone reaped the reward of intellectual satisfaction. All the while, he was building our house, a project of which he bore the burden and I share the beautiful result. We won't even mention the number of hours he spent cooking while I was 'working'. I am astonishingly lucky.

Finally, I dedicate this book to the lights of my life, my children. The project has been with me longer than they have and it has surely occupied a large space in their childhood. I hope that my preoccupation might convey the value of quixotic long-term pursuits—and, more fundamentally, the necessity of maintaining a rich and individual interior world even while devotedly caring for others. I wish for them the freedom to pursue their own projects, whatever they may be, with the support, connection, and understanding that I have enjoyed.

A.O.A.

CONTENTS

ILLUSTRATIONS

between pp. 128 and 129

NOTE ON
TRANSLITERATION AND
TRANSCRIPTION

Hebrew

The transliteration of Hebrew in this book reflects consideration of the type of book it is, in terms of its content, purpose, and readership. The system adopted therefore reflects a broad approach to transcription, rather than the narrower approaches found in the *Encyclopaedia Judaica* or other systems developed for text-based or linguistic studies. The aim has been to reflect the pronunciation prescribed for modern Hebrew, rather than the spelling or Hebrew word structure, and to do so using conventions that are generally familiar to the English-speaking reader.

In accordance with this approach, no attempt is made to indicate the distinctions between *alef* and *ayin*, *tet* and *taf*, *kaf* and *kuf*, *sin* and *samekh*, since these are not relevant to pronunciation; likewise, the *dagesh* is not indicated except where it affects pronunciation. Following the principle of using conventions familiar to the majority of readers, however, transcriptions that are well established have been retained even when they are not fully consistent with the transliteration system adopted. On similar grounds, the *tsadi* is rendered by 'tz' in such Anglicized words as barmitzvah. Likewise, the distinction between *ḥet* and *khaf* has been retained, using *ḥ* for the former and *kh* for the latter; the associated forms are generally familiar to readers, even if the distinction is not actually borne out in pronunciation, and for the same reason the final *heh* is indicated too. As in Hebrew, no capital letters are used, except that an initial capital has been retained in transliterating titles of published works (for example, *Shulḥan arukh*).

Since no distinction is made between *alef* and *ayin*, they are indicated by an apostrophe only in intervocalic positions where a failure to do so could lead an English-speaking reader to pronounce the vowel-cluster as a diphthong—as, for example, in *ha'ir*—or otherwise mispronounce the word. An apostrophe is also used, for the same reason, to disambiguate the pronunciation of other English vowel clusters, as for example in *mizbe'aḥ*.

The *sheva na* is indicated by an *e*—*perikat ol*, *reshut*—except, again, when established convention dictates otherwise.

The *yod* is represented by *i* when it occurs as a vowel (*bereshit*), by *y* when it occurs as a consonant (*yesodot*), and by *yi* when it occurs as both (*yisra'el*).

Transcription of Spanish and Portuguese

The idiosyncratic orthography typical of early modern texts in print and manuscript has been maintained here in all untranslated titles and quotations. As an exception to this rule, when the *ão* ending (as in *nação* or *oração*) appears as -*aõ*, it has been corrected in accordance with modern standards.

ABBREVIATIONS

EH	Ets Haim Library
Ros.	Bibliotheca Rosenthaliana
SA	Stadsarchief Amsterdam
TPT	Benedict de Spinoza, *A Theologico-Political Treatise; A Political Treatise*, trans. R. H. M. Elwes (New York, 1951)

INTRODUCTION

IN the politics-obsessed seventeenth century, Amsterdam's worldly and well-informed Spanish and Portuguese Jews followed the trends. Their identity as former conversos in the burgeoning Dutch Republic put an array of political perspectives at their disposal, and they deployed diverse ideas and practices in building a community and reflecting on various issues over time. But one period stands out as a time of particular urgency. At the start of the final third of the century, sermons, communal records, polemics, moral and legal tracts, commentaries, and more burst forth with political ideas and arguments. Discernible through the din over two decades is a shared effort to understand the Jewish community as a kind of state—a discourse that proved remarkably generative for Jewish thought broadly speaking, as well as for contested local affairs.

The idea that premodern Jewish communities were state-like is now so ubiquitous as to seem obvious. It forms part of a general impression that Jewish men and women lived in a less complicated social world, with an immutable sense of belonging to a unified Jewish body. The renowned historian Salo Baron painted an especially robust portrait of a close-knit society in which multiple factors—religion, economy, legal status, and more —operated in concert to set Jews apart, bind them together, and maintain norms. In his account, the community governed all aspects of Jewish life, enveloping court and market, council and guild, home and synagogue, law and awe. In 1942, Baron distilled his voluminous historical research into a generalized profile of Jewish society, ending with the remarkable statement that for the course of the long Middle Ages, the Jewish community 'was a sort of little state, interterritorial and non-political, but none the less quasi-totalitarian'.[1]

State-like and even totalitarian, but 'non-political'? The obvious dissolves into a puzzle. The most basic quality of a state is the political; what is a 'sort of little state' but a political entity? And yet both halves of the remark—that the Jewish community was state-like, and that Jews lacked true politics—were matters of scholarly consensus for many years. On one

[1] Baron, *The Jewish Community*, i. 208.

hand, it was common to describe Jews as forming as a 'corporate society', a unified body politic parallel to other groups. On the other hand, it was also nearly a truism in Jewish historiography that exilic Jews lacked politics. Ben-Zion Dinur, for example, took it as axiomatic that 'with the loss of their independence and the dispersion, the Jews ceased to constitute a political entity'.[2] Simon Dubnow saw the *kahal* (community) as state-like, finding in it evidence of the perennial Jewish impetus towards autonomy, and yet he still wrote that 'the originality of Jewish history', after the fall of the Second Temple, consisted of being 'the only history stripped of every active political element'.[3] Echoes of such attitudes are still felt in Jewish thought.

What is going on here? The question goes to the heart of the Jewish historical and political imagination, and the answer has two sides, one simple and one much more complex. The simple answer is that, in the main, 'politics' signified sovereignty to the above scholars. For Baron and other historians who lived through some of Jewish history's most intense moments of violent tragedy and political action in the form of Zionism and the Holocaust, it was crucial to distinguish between a 'semi-autonomous' community, subject to the whims of the majority, and a sovereign state possessing territory and the right to self-defence. The line such thinkers walked was very fine but clear as day. They took pride in a history of Jewish communal self-sufficiency and saw all forms of self-government as proof of Jewish normality. At the same time, they insisted that a community was the farthest thing from a real polity because it lacked ultimate self-determination, final control over its own fate.

A more complex account of the contradiction of the non-political polity focuses on the image of the 'sort of little state' rather than its 'non-political' nature, and will return us to the context of Spinoza's Amsterdam. How and why did Baron and others get the idea that the premodern community was like a state at all, and what did they mean by it? The notion is deeply ingrained but, if pressed, it becomes difficult to maintain that Jews lived apart in all-encompassing quasi-states across diaspora history. For one thing, actual arrangements and institutions varied tremendously and often lacked the structures, boundaries, and prerogatives that would amount to anything recognizably state-like. For another thing, the idea of the 'state' per se did not emerge until the seventeenth century, right at the end of the

---

[2] Dinur, 'Jewish History', 26.   [3] Dubnow, *Jewish History*, 18–19.

time period most historians once thought of as the long Jewish Middle Ages. The very concept of a state or polity that modern historians deployed was a product of early modern and modern European political culture. The quality of being state-like is not something medieval Jews would have recognized, much less sought, in their communities or anywhere else. The state-likeness of the medieval community was in the eye of the beholder— the historian.

It turns out, however, that at least one group of premodern Jews did describe their community as state-like, in terms that align remarkably well with Baron's account: the Spanish and Portuguese Jews of Amsterdam. The Kahal Kadosh Talmud Torah, as their community was called, became a wellspring of new interpretations of the community as a polity. These interpretations arose at a Goldilocks moment in the evolution of political thought, when the notion of the state was entering into common discourse but had not yet solidified into its modern incarnation entailing sovereignty. In fact, Baron's 'sort of little state' is an unintentionally apt way of paraphrasing the 'republic' or 'commonwealth' of seventeenth-century speech, referring to a generic polity or political collective irrespective of its hegemonic status. Amsterdam's Spanish and Portuguese Jews enthusiastically took up the conceptual apparatus of the republic or polity, along with the jumble of Christian European conversations and conflicts associated with it, as a fruitful way of approaching how groups of Jews belonged to each other and governed themselves. At this brief inflection point, Jews who were keyed into European political discourse could use the incipient idea of the state in concert with Jewish traditions to think about their own affairs, without the full accretion of specific qualities of statehood that would later make such analysis seem incongruous.

Unlike Baron and his contemporaries, the Jews of the Kahal Kadosh Talmud Torah did not shy away from the 'political' quality of the community. On the contrary, they described themselves as possessing and enacting their own fully realized Jewish politics, manifest in the setting of the local community seen as a polity. In this, the Spanish and Portuguese Jews' attitude was perhaps closer to that of twenty-first-century historians who perceive the exilic setting as a robust site of Jewish politics. However, in the age of Spinoza, Hobbes, and Sabbatai Zevi, to take up the mantle of politicality had different overtones and different stakes. Members of Amsterdam's Kahal Kadosh addressed questions that would become central to modern Jewish thought, but they did so from within a premodern practical and discursive context. Among the issues that arose were whether and how exilic Jewish politics were continuous with the biblical, how spiritual and worldly authority ought to relate within a Jewish polity, how Jewish politics compared to those of other peoples, what a messianic restoration would mean for a people that already had political institutions, and how to interpret Jewish political history—up to and including the present—as part of a divine narrative. The self-image of this particular group, which stood at the apex of transformative intellectual and social change in early modernity, provides a point of connection between the modern story of Jewish community and the premodern reality.

Religion and Politics

The way Amsterdam's Spanish and Portuguese Jews thought about their community was indelibly shaped by the cultures of the Anglo-Dutch Atlantic world in the seventeenth century and especially of Amsterdam in its second half. Tectonic shifts of society and ideas were at that time altering the landscape in myriad ways, in what is perennially—though not very precisely—understood as a 'general crisis of the seventeenth century'.[4] The end of the Thirty Years War, the English civil wars, and the explosion of overseas colonization all coincided with innovations in political philosophy regarding sovereignty, the rights of the people, constitutions, and more. At the core of many seventeenth-century European debates was the relationship between religion and politics. Religious conflicts had ravaged the European continent over the preceding century and longer, bringing desperate urgency to questions of how government ought to align with the dictates or institutions of any particular church, or religion in general. Early modern tumult brought new political threats, mob violence, and sharp economic turns, as well as new prominence to Holland. After decades of fighting for independence, it became an intellectual crossroads and an economic hub. The Dutch Republic positioned itself as a polar opposite to the Spanish Crown, with a commitment to individuals' freedom of conscience; and yet there, too, philosophers and pamphleteers alike disputed

---

[4] See Trevor-Roper, 'General Crisis'; Hazard, *La Crise de la conscience européenne*, and the recent English edition, *The Crisis of the European Mind*. See also the bibliography in Benedict and Gutmann (eds.), *Early Modern Europe*, 25–30; de Vries, 'Economic Crisis', 151–5; and Schöffer, 'Did Holland's Golden Age'.

the extent to which clergy should possess political power and religious minorities could be allowed to flourish.

Members of the Kahal Kadosh Talmud Torah were not passive observers of all this. They did not primarily react as objects of Christian toleration, or as stakeholders in a Dutch public sphere that might be starting to make space for them. Rather, they took up the questions of the day and applied them—rehearsing, enacting, and reflecting on them—within and about the community as their own public sphere.[5] Indeed, challenges to the status quo within the orbit of the Jewish community paralleled wider dynamics but had special bearing on their own perceptions of religion and politics. Between 1665 and 1685 alone, leaders of the Kahal Kadosh participated in the uproar of Sabbatai Zevi's messianic movement and its aftermath, witnessed the publication of Baruch Spinoza's *Theological-Political Treatise*, engaged in a massive and symbolic communal building project, and defended communal authority against internal rebellion and external sanction. All of these events they approached, one way or another, through the lens of contemporary European treatments of religion and politics. Amsterdam's Portuguese Jews asked themselves in these moments how to balance and harmonize the religious and political dimensions of a Jewish community.

Take, for example, a sermon delivered at a key moment in the life of the community. In August 1675, a young intellectual named David Sarphati served as the final speaker in a series celebrating the completion of a new synagogue complex, a grand edifice that marked the community's remarkable growth and success over just a few generations. Sarphati praised the lay leaders' skill in responding to a tumultuous world by comparing the governing council to a ship's captain. As he put it, the governors had navigated a stormy sea by strategic raising and lowering of sails, 'by sometimes celebrating politics and leaving religion aside, and other times elevating religion and dropping politics'. As he wistfully concluded, 'What can be done? The wind changes, and we would go straight.'[6] These comments were not

---

[5] This study owes an immeasurable debt to Miriam Bodian's initial recognition of these elements within the culture of the Amsterdam Kahal Kadosh and beyond. In her 1997 essay on the 'rhetoric of republicanism' she observed that some 17th-century Portuguese Jews 'depicted the autonomous Jewish community as a full-fledged commonwealth', and that their 'acquaintance with European republican values made them aware of a potential alternative to typical Jewish conditions of exile'; Bodian, 'Biblical Hebrews', 199–200, 221. She also offered initial reflections on a theopolitical stance among former conversos in 'Some Ideological Implications'.

[6] Sarphati, 'Sermão Septimo', 144–5.

casual kvetching. They formed the basis of an elaborate Baroque sermon on the Jewish condition that treated Jewish politics as a paradigm for politics in general. In Sarphati's presentation, Jewish leaders faced the universal quandary that even though 'politics are generally opposed to religion', they must nevertheless try to make the two cohere. His theme was not limited to how a religious minority must compromise within the wider political world. Nor did he address how a Christian state should relate to religious minorities like his own. Rather, he focused on the theopolitical balance within a Jewish community, seen as a polity: how a Jewish governor should relate to Jewish religion in his state.

Sarphati's exploration of the relationship between 'religion' and 'politics' signalled his participation in European Christian discourse by means of parallels between Jewish and Christian government. The approach, which he shared with many peers, was not unreasonable. After all, the Kahal Kadosh Talmud Torah was indeed a formal, institutionalized, and empowered entity that comprised both political and religious dimensions. Much like the kingdoms, republics, empires, and incorporated towns of Europe, Sarphati's community was governed by laymen with deep fidelity to their religion, and mandated a certain obeisance to religious authority.

That is not to say, however, that the application of Christian political ideas to a Jewish community was natural or unproblematic. When brought into the Jewish communal context, such discourse raised a special set of problems. The likeness Sarphati and his peers suggested between a Jewish community and a Christian state did not jibe with a common understanding of Jews as subjugated, dispersed, separated, and exiled—in other words, as politically erased or obviated. After all, modern historians' sense that Jews lacked politics, described above, did not come from thin air but recast some long-held ideas about exile. In addition, aligning Jewish politicality writ large with diaspora institutions ran counter to the monarchism of messianic expectation, setting up a clash between the two theopolitical frames of local lay-led republic and universal religious monarchy. Finally, the community, especially in the particular form it took in the Kahal Kadosh, as a lay-oriented administrative body, had to be both conceptually and practically reconciled with other potential forms of Jewish collective and Jewish government, namely, the congregation and the rabbinic court.[7]

[7] Here, as I do throughout the present volume, I distinguish between the proper name 'Kahal Kadosh Talmud Torah' and the general term *kahal*.

To say that the community was a locus of legitimate Jewish theo-politics was not, therefore, totally anodyne. Even less so was Sarphati's rather Machiavellian suggestion that Jewish leaders could freely 'drop religion' when politics made it strategic to do so. In that light, it is to be noted that Sarphati's political interpretation of the Kahal Kadosh, delivered in a situation of peak visibility, was not a provocation. The leaders who selected him for the honour knew the gist of his remarks in advance. Others—notably, those who opposed the lay leaders' policies or sought more power for rabbis within the communal system—may have disagreed with some of Sarphati's conclusions, but most accepted the underlying premiss that the community was, in a meaningful sense, a polity.

Examples abound among prominent members of the community. Abraham Pereyra (d. 1699), a wealthy merchant, scholarly patron, and amateur moralist, composed two books of pious advice, translating best practices for republics and individuals from general literature into the Jewish context. He addressed sections of his books to the 'governors' and 'subjects' within his community so that they could behave in ways that suited a well-run polity. The polemicist and self-styled 'politico' Isaac Orobio de Castro, for his part, took aim at the long history of the Jewish republic and other forms of self-rule. He constructed several innovative interpretations of the famous 'sceptre of Judah', a biblical phrase often used to represent Jewish sovereignty or political authority. A literato and former cavalry officer, Daniel Levi de Barrios tended towards the poetic and spiritual in contrast to Orobio's hard-headed philosophical and scriptural argumentation, but Barrios, too, explored the significance of the community as a polity. He glorified the Kahal Kadosh as a divine democracy and spun a tale of Jewish political history in which diaspora communities were a laudable component of God's universal plan.

Additional examples are found in a number of more minor figures—rabbis, teachers, and other thinking men. These figures were members of different generations and had different educational backgrounds and occupations. They had diverse ideological commitments and religious tendencies. They disagreed on serious issues. Still, each engaged with the way political conceptions of the community worked alongside religious concerns. Their writings, referring directly or obliquely to current events, in turn expose a wider conversation taking place throughout the community, including among members whose individual voices have not been preserved. Several of the above-mentioned texts implicitly acknowledged a lack of communal harmony, to put it gently. Most dramatically revealing in this regard is a pamphlet published by the communal rabbi Isaac Aboab da Fonseca in 1680, in which he urged members to abide by the rule of the lay governing council and drop their objections to the communal *ḥerem*, or ban of excommunication. Aboab's short but passionate treatise on the ban encapsulates the interplay of religion and politics in both ideas and affairs in the Kahal Kadosh and forms the basis of two chapters of the present volume.

At stake in the community's political discourse were multiple layers of concern. First, on the most granular and immediate level, members and leaders argued over the details of their own communal governance, questioning who had what authority over whom and why. What exactly was a Jewish community, according to the political categories of the new era? Who or what empowered Jewish leaders—whom were community members obligated to obey and why? What was the role of halakhah, rabbinic law? To what other types of community could theirs be compared? What were the standards by which governance could be judged or evaluated, and what recourse did members have if governors failed to meet those standards? Indeed, should Jews submit to the authority of other Jews at all? What was, in the end, the purpose of Jewish institutional belonging, and how far did it extend? Opinions about such issues were expressed in polemics and pamphlets, but also through lawsuits, petitions, and punishments.

Second, not only did members of the Kahal Kadosh explore political perspectives regarding the Jewish community, they also considered what it meant in Jewish terms for them to be doing so: they reflected as Jews on what I am calling their 'politicality', meaning their quality of being political—doing politics, existing in a polity, making political meaning. At a historical moment that has been recognized as the dawn of modern political thought, Spinoza's former peers identified the concept of 'politics' by name as an important dimension of Jewish institutions, laws, and identity. They implicitly acknowledged that such a self-description required some explanation; nevertheless, from rabbi to poet, the writers featured in this volume all expressed confidence, in one way or another, that Jewish life naturally and inherently included a political dimension. Some even suggested that Jews were *the* political nation par excellence, a model and a guide for all others, pushing back against the anti-Jewish polemics built into the Christian majority's view of Jewish history and political status. It was a way of inverting the emphasis on post-biblical Jewish subjugation, displacement, and political deficiency inherent in Christians' intense focus at the time on the biblical Jewish polity or 'Hebrew Republic' as a model for contemporary politics.

Third, and finally, the political activity of the Kahal Kadosh, whether discourse or practical negotiation, was a form of self-fashioning, as members self-consciously shaped their political selves through participation in a civic sphere of their own making. In addition to appreciating the fact of ongoing Jewish politicality, they took its existence as a starting point and employed it to make for themselves a political sphere that suited their unique sensibilities and circumstances. Seeing politics inherent in Jewish communities—republics unto themselves, set within the realms of the Gentile nations—instead of only in biblical history or messianic kingship allowed for particularism rather than oblivion in the diaspora. Unlike those who later sought enfranchisement through equal status as citizens in non-Jewish states, my subjects staked their considerable self-estimation on the ability of Jews to realize their political potential and wield their power through a separate Jewish polity, constituted and administered on their own terms, in a manner comparable to the doings of non-Jews. There is a clear affinity between their outlook in this regard and that which was imputed to medieval Jews by later historians, to be sure. But to say so risks losing sight of the remarkable specificity of the Kahal Kadosh Talmud Torah in the time of Spinoza and Sabbatai Zevi.

Culturally au courant, the elite among the Spanish and Portuguese Jews shared a contemporary desire to be men of action, engaged citizens, constituents of a *civitas*. Trying on the political ideas of the day during the epoch of the birth of the modern state, Sarphati and his peers imagined their community as a Jewish polity that was a commonwealth rather than a nation-state, self-ruled but not sovereign, and local but not territorial. Unlike those who shaped the drive to Jewish statehood in the nineteenth and twentieth centuries, members of Amsterdam's Kahal Kadosh did not conceive of the basis of a Jewish polity as either the entire Jewish people (or even the entirety of a national subgroup of Jews, the well-known Spanish and Portuguese Jewish 'nation') or a particular homeland (territory). Instead, they offered a Jewish politics based on mutuality and consent, of active Jewish self-determination in the sense of declared allegiance to a group with explicit and enforced boundaries, as well as local, differentiated Jewish identity. Their drive to constitute a Jewish polity had a complicated relationship to earlier forms of Jewish community, and may have done more to create the ideal of a diaspora quasi-state than to fulfil it.

Four Factors

This book delves into the contours of ideas and events over a short period within a small community. It draws on a range of textual, documentary, and material sources from two raucous decades between 1665 and 1685 to reveal a richly layered process of collective self-evaluation, internal strife, and cultural translation. The period treated here stands apart as a distinct moment in the history of the Spanish and Portuguese Jews of Amsterdam. It begins around the time the Sabbatian messianic movement took hold in Amsterdam and ends shortly after Sabbatai Zevi himself died. The period also aligns chronologically with the Dutch reception of Hobbes and the time of Spinoza's first meteoric impact on European thought. The era's distinctiveness can be organized into four interrelated factors that, together, pressed the issue of Jewish politics to the fore and shaped the resultant discourse: the background of this particular community and its members; the new political thought of the Anglo-Dutch Atlantic world and Christian interest in biblical politics; the publication of Spinoza's *Theological-Political Treatise*; and the Sabbatian messianic movement.

Communal History: Conversos and the Kahal Kadosh

Amsterdam's community of Spanish and Portuguese Jews was famous in its own day, and its unique qualities have continued to fascinate over the centuries. It was made up of people whose ancestors had converted to Catholicism sometime before or during the 1492 Spanish expulsion or the 1497 compulsory conversion of the remaining Jews in Portugal. Beginning around the turn of the seventeenth century, fleeing the persecutory atmosphere of Iberia, these conversos, as descendants of such converts are often called, began settling in Amsterdam.[8] There, they enjoyed relative social and economic freedom at an early date—though the extent, nature, and tenor of the famed Dutch toleration are matters for debate.[9] At first, they

[8] Converso is a more neutral term, replacing the pejorative 'Marrano' of older usage.
[9] On Amsterdam's toleration of the Jewish community, see Swetschinski, *Reluctant Cos-*

balanced between hidden and open expression of Judaism as they met for prayer inside private homes. Neither denying nor flaunting their Jewish identity, as foreigners they could just as well appear to native Amsterdammers as Iberian Catholics.[10] Over a couple of decades the newcomers coalesced into three formal congregations, and then continued to undergo institutional consolidation, culminating in 1639 with official unification into a single overarching community with a new name: the Kahal Kadosh Talmud Torah.

The community's culture was undeniably shaped by its origins—members called themselves members of the Portuguese 'nation', Portuguese was the language of communal archives and many inward-facing publications, and Iberian mores and ideals determined many of their religious and social choices.[11] Indeed, in later decades when Jewish immigrants from Germany and Poland began arriving, the Portuguese Jews aided the newcomers but did not welcome them into their congregation, since its identity was conceived in these national terms. Members of the Kahal Kadosh also saw themselves as (or aspired to be) particularly genteel—in the sense of being refined in manners and civility, and also implicitly in the sense of being at home among the Gentiles. After all, they or their ancestors had lived as Christians in Spain and Portugal for generations. Many worked as global traders; some made names for themselves in the Christian republic of letters or served Christian nobles, government agencies, and armed forces as procurators, financiers, or diplomatic agents. Their converso origins could also be a source of tension, as leaders tried to both educate and legislate members into full commitment to their new Jewish affiliation and compliance with the community's particular regulations.[12]

mopolitans, 8–53, and Bodian, *Hebrews*, 53–75. On Dutch toleration in general, see Israel, 'Intellectual Debate', and B. Kaplan, '"Dutch" Religious Tolerance', among many treatments; more studies are cited in Ch. 1.

[10] On this phenomenon in other contexts, see Wilke, 'Semi-Clandestine Judaism' and the other essays in Part I of Y. Kaplan (ed.), *Religious Changes*. See also Y. Kaplan, 'Concealed and Fluid Identities' (Heb.).

[11] On their famous self-identification as a 'nation', see Bodian, '"Men of the Nation"'. On how the culture of the Kahal Kadosh was shaped by that of Spain and Portugal, see, among many studies, Bodian, *Hebrews*; Méchoulan, 'The Importance of Hispanicity'; and Gutwirth, 'Penso's Roots'.

[12] Some have seen them as plagued by inner conflict; see e.g. van Praag, 'Almas en litigio'. Swetschinski, however, observed that the conflict is in the eyes of the historical observers: 'to everyone but themselves, it would seem, the Portuguese Jews of seventeenth-century Amsterdam were living a contradiction' (*Reluctant Cosmopolitans*, 315).

Later on, because of this background, Enlightenment-era Jews admired
Amsterdam's culturally open Sephardim for having bypassed what they saw
as the 'ghetto mentality' of the later Jewish Middle Ages in central and eastern Europe.[13] Historians in the nineteenth and twentieth centuries, too,
emphasized the cosmopolitanism and mercantile bent of the Portuguese
Jewish 'nation' in Amsterdam, detecting precociously or prematurely modern qualities in their ability to bridge cultural contexts and in the scepticism
or spiritual alienation expressed openly by some among them.[14] On the
other hand, having experienced great discontinuity in the past, the Spanish
and Portuguese Jews made every effort to project continuity despite the
need for innovation. They neither blindly adhered to a status quo nor intentionally broke with tradition, in the historian Yosef Kaplan's fine formulation.[15]

Although the enduring connection to Iberian and converso heritage
undeniably shaped the culture of the Kahal Kadosh, its members were also
affected by wider trends among early modern European Jewish communities and by the unique setting of Amsterdam. Early leaders brought rabbis
from other Jewish communities to Judaize newcomers and educate their
children, and they carried out their institution-building with the structures
of existing communities across Europe very much in mind. Jews across
Europe in the seventeenth century increasingly pursued arrangements
featuring powerful lay leadership and a limited, professional role for rabbis.
The specific way the Kahal Kadosh Talmud Torah adopted such models
bore the marks of Dutch and English traditions of contract and constitution.

The connection with local political and intellectual culture deepened
over the years. By the time of Sarphati's sermon in 1675, thirty-six years
after the unification of the three congregations, among the successes signified by the grand new synagogue complex he commemorated was the
community's deep physical and metaphorical embeddedness in Amsterdam's cityscape. The combination of Portuguese identity, early modern

[13] See Sutcliffe, 'Sephardic Amsterdam' and 'Imagining Amsterdam'.
[14] Yirmiyahu Yovel found in them a modernity before modernity, suggesting that their experience hiding their Jewishness made them acutely aware of the malleability and instrumen-
tality of religious identity. Yovel, *Other*. See also Israel, 'Orobio de Castro'. On Spinoza, see
D. Schwartz, *The First Modern Jew*.
[15] Y. Kaplan, 'Alternative Path', and cf. J. Katz, *Tradition*, as a representative articulation of
the older view.

Jewish institution-building, and Dutch republicanism was a unique brew that stimulated new Jewish political ideas.

The 1639 unification was key to the fermentation. In a founding document best described as a constitution, members of three congregations founded a new shared community. The constitution established a seven-member council of rotating lay leaders called the Mahamad to govern nearly every aspect of communal life. Rabbis—called ḥakhamim, in typical Sephardi parlance—were named to permanent salaried appointments as teachers, preachers, halakhic decisors, and advisers to the Mahamad, lacking independent authority in the government. The Kahal Kadosh was a lay entity in that it was governed by laymen according to lay (not primarily halakhic) rules, and in that the scope of communal government went beyond ritual, spiritual, or halakhic affairs to promote a general common good. On the other hand, the constitution made clear that government should be guided by religious values, and the very authority of the lay leadership was based rabbinic principles.

The Kahal Kadosh was truly a *community*, and not only a congregation, meaning that it was a collective in many ways beyond the religious, based on mutual obligation and shared self-preservation. On the other hand, its entire raison d'être was the promotion of Judaism and Jewish interests. The Kahal Kadosh did not sharply diverge from Jewish traditions, but imposed a newly systematic and rational differentiation between lay and rabbinic authority, assigning each its place in a hierarchical and ramified administrative entity. The founders took communal dynamics that had usually been fluid and concretized them.

The shape the community thereby took on was a result of the very particular setting of Amsterdam's politics, including the evolving terms of toleration of religious minorities and a strong valuation of local collectives that was part of emerging Dutch republicanism. Such adaptation, in turn, set the stage for the charged theopolitical discourse that emerged several decades later, and which occupies most of the present book. At that time, as members of the community engaged with the thinking that transformed medieval kingdoms into modern states—early modern ideas that addressed the nature and purpose of political society, and new practices that subtly altered the dynamics of governance—they thought about the Kahal Kadosh in a new way. Many of its features were readily interpreted as those of a polity—a republic, or commonwealth.

The adoption of aspects of Dutch republicanism marked a distinct shift away from the affinity for monarchy and monarchism that had characterized medieval Jewish political ideas, especially in Spain and Portugal. But this does not mean all of the community's cultural inheritance was shed. Alongside Dutch-inflected ideas were long-held Iberian attitudes, including a valuation of nobility and genealogical purity, an interest in genteel appearances, an autocratic leadership style, and an intolerance of dissidence and religious nonconformity.[16] Indeed, throughout the seventeenth century, leaders of the Kahal Kadosh continued to make liberal use of a wide range of texts and concepts that made up the Iberian Catholic monarchist intellectual landscape, translating them into approaches that suited their present circumstances. They also maintained that especial interest in status that is often attributed to pre-expulsion Spanish Jews, who took great pride in their access to the halls of power, their familiarity with kings. Now it was translated into pride in their own separate republic.

Converso (as opposed to Jewish) identity also helps to explain the readiness of some in Amsterdam to embrace the community as a site of politics. Converso and crypto-Jewish life was marked by exclusion, persecution, and disenfranchisement: despite conversion, New Christians were often prevented from fully exercising their membership in the body politic.[17] The humiliation that most conversos were subjected to in the political sphere was countered by intense pride in the new ability to participate openly in a collectivity or polity once they entered Jewish life.[18] That the Kahal Kadosh was a lay-governed entity allowed Judaizing conversos not only to enter into a new community of religious practitioners, but also to join a community in the sense of a political or civic body. In contrast to the ethnic and religious ambiguity of converso identity, open communal affiliation and institutional legitimacy offered something new: politics in a commonwealth of their own.

Sometimes such a move meant leaving behind positions of influence

---

[16] Y. Kaplan, 'Political Concepts' and '*Gente Política*'. See also Méchoulan, 'The Importance of Hispanicity'; id., 'Abraham Pereyra'; and van Praag, 'Almas en litigio'.

[17] As Stuczynski has shown, conversos could have corporate status in political terms, and some figures envisaged a special theopolitical role for conversos. Such a positive sense of political identity shows their appreciation for belonging to a collective. See Stuczynski, 'From Polemics', 'Harmonizing Identities', and 'Toward a Repoliticization'.

[18] 'Returned' Jews expressed tremendous pride in their new status. See Rosenstock, 'Abraham Miguel Cardoso's Messianism', 97, and the bibliography listed there.

within Christian politics and society. Isaac Orobio de Castro is an example. Here is a man who moved within the highest circles in the courts of Spain and France before moving to Amsterdam in the 1660s.[19] To embrace Judaism and a new life in Amsterdam required him to renounce that position, but his sacrifice allowed him to find self-realization. As a converso in the Christian political world, he had reached the limit of his access and influence. Further, he had experienced a disjunction between his own beliefs and the religious basis of the general political discourse, a disjunction that made full intellectual participation difficult. Like many former conversos, he expressed a sense that life prior to open Judaism was a life of pretence. He wrote: 'in Spain I presented a Christian appearance, since life is sweet; but I was never very good at it'.[20] Writing about Jewish politics as a Jew, Orobio was also able to invert the anti-Jewish trope of the dissimulating converso (also applied to the politico[21]) and fight against the very idea of Jewish subjugation. After turning to Judaism, Orobio's position may have been lower in the Christian political hierarchy, but it was much higher within a Jewish political sphere.

The paradox of finding greater political legitimacy as a Jew than as a Christian within Christian Europe contributed to the positive embrace of exilic life that is so evident in the Amsterdam sources from the time of Spinoza and Sabbatai Zevi. Members of the Iberian Jewish diaspora were preoccupied with exile and its meanings, ranging from the historical to the metaphorical, often expressed as a deep longing, search for consolation, or messianic expectation.[22] However, the way the members of the Kahal Kadosh related to exile was different during the time of Sabbatianism and Spinoza: as the historian Harm den Boer noted, the 'nostalgic, plaintive tone' was absent in most of their cultural production.[23] They claimed a

[19] On Orobio, see Y. Kaplan, *From Christianity to Judaism.*

[20] Y. Kaplan's translation, in *From Christianity to Judaism*, 329. See further sources and the bibliography listed in Albert, 'Return'.

[21] As in the words of Fray Juan Marquez: 'Let the *políticos* take off their masks; let those who follow them speak clearly.' Quoted in Magnier, *Pedro de Valencia*, 354. See Shoulson, *Fictions*, 1–39.

[22] Exile is central to Gershom Scholem's interpretation of Lurianic kabbalah, Sabbatianism, and Jewish modernity. Y. H. Yerushalmi and Amos Funkenstein are also among those who discussed premodern views of exile. Funkenstein, *Perceptions*, 203–8; Yerushalmi, 'Clio', and id., *Zakhor*.

[23] 'Quite the contrary, their literature . . . celebrated many aspects of religious and social life in the Dutch Republic'; den Boer, 'Exile', 187.

political home where they were, reinterpreting exile as a component of ever-changing history, and the diaspora as a site of Jewish success.

Christian Politics

Staking a claim to open and legitimate politicality ran against the grain of most contemporaneous views of Jewish status in exile. Since at least the Middle Ages, most Christians and Jews had agreed that the lack of a king or kingdom set Jews apart in some fundamental way.[24] According to a widely shared narrative, the Jewish experience of perpetual exile was exceptional among nations. It was marked by subjection to the rule of others, a condition that would only be remedied with messianic restoration in an unknown future. The lack of self-rule after the destruction of the Second Temple need not be seen as absolute. Some sources treated rabbinic or lay leaders as inheriting biblical authority one way or another, and Jews could indeed wield various forms of power within their diaspora worlds.[25] Still, few in early modern Europe would have disputed that exile was defined as much by politics as by geography: Jews were not only dispersed but also deprived of sovereignty.

In the seventeenth century, some Jews even treated the lack of Jewish politics as a virtue. Writing in Verona during our period, the former converso Isaac Cardoso suggested that the reason for exile was that it enabled Jews to teach divine law to Christian kings and thereby reform the governments of the nations in the absence of their own.[26] Another writer, Simone Luzzatto in Venice, had gone so far as to deny that Jews possessed *virtù*, Machiavelli's term for the political drive, in order to emphasize Jewish loyalty to host states.[27] Even in Amsterdam, in the middle of the seventeenth century, the rabbi Menasseh ben Israel portrayed Jews as fundamentally loyal to Gentile regimes due to the lack of any foreign state to which Jews would owe natural allegiance.[28] To be sure, these were apologetic works designed to facilitate Christian acceptance of Jews, and so they may be read with some scepticism as to the true feelings of their authors. Nevertheless,

---

[24] The theological significance of Jewish political status seems to have been expanded in medieval Jewish–Christian polemics. See Funkenstein, 'Basic Types'.

[25] See Biale, *Power and Powerlessness*.   [26] Cardoso, *Excelencias*, 20a.

[27] Septimus, 'Biblical Religion', 402. See Luzzatto, *Discorso*, and the recent edition, ed. and trans. Veltri and Lissa, and the scholarly essays appended there.

[28] See Ravid, 'How Profitable'; Menasseh, *Humble Addresses*.

together they show how the question of Jewish politicality was culturally present, with Jewish political self-denial reflecting either a fully internalized sense that Jews naturally lacked independent political will, or perhaps some wider anxiety about the Jewish potential for political activism.

In contrast to all that, the approach taken by members of the Kahal Kadosh Talmud Torah in Spinoza's time was to portray Jews as active members of a separate Jewish republic within the Christian one. They treated the Jewish polity as parallel or equivalent to Christian polities. Conceptually, they built upon the traditions of Jewish governance that had long formed a grey area between sovereignty and total domination, an act of reinterpretation made possible by new Christian discourse that spoke less of kingdoms and more of commonwealths. This stance made Jews politically normal without suggesting that they would disrupt Christian affairs. It also allowed members to repurpose for themselves quite neatly a whole area of European political thought focused on Jewish theopolitics.

Central to the new republicanism of the seventeenth century was a turn to the Bible's account of ancient Jewish history as a source of political ideas and examples. Christian thinkers made copious use of whatever they could glean about the government and laws of the Jewish state in biblical times— what they commonly referred to as the 'Republic of the Hebrews' or the 'Republic of Moses'.[29] They treated the Bible as a source of divine instruction for government, analysing the circumstances of Moses' government as well as the periods of judges and of kings as models for combining religious and political authority.[30] As Petrus Cunaeus wrote, 'Moses . . . was the first to write and publish laws so that the people might learn what was right and what was wrong, and which sanctions might steady the state Almighty God had ordered to be set up . . . He wanted to found a republic that would be the most sacred in the world.'[31] Making sense of the way this 'most sacred' law and government operated was, however, no simple matter, and, like many other early modern Christians, Cunaeus read not only his Bible but also his Talmud, his Rashi, and his Maimonides for help. In privileging the ancient Jewish state as the most perfectly divine one, early modern

[29] See Nelson, *Hebrew Republic*, and Dunkelgrün, '"Neerlands Israel".

[30] Classic works on Christian political thought focusing on Jewish sources include Hill, *English Bible*, and Oz-Salzberger, 'Jewish Roots'. A subfield was spawned in the area of Jewish sources in early modern political thought, reflected in the journal *Hebraic Political Studies* (2005–9). [31] Cunaeus, *Hebrew Republic*, 12.

Christian political thinkers spent a lot of time reading and thinking about
Jews and Judaism.[32]

In fact, this intellectual arena entailed a particular relationship to Judaism and Jews that demanded a response. Despite taking Jewish texts seriously, Christians rejected the relevance of contemporaneous Jewish life to
politics. The tenet of supersession—the idea that Christianity had replaced
Judaism as God's word, Christians had replaced Jews as the 'true Israel',
and the laws and predictions given to ancient Israelites (including chosenness and sovereignty) now rightly belonged to Christendom—supported
treating biblical politics as the purview of Christians and Christians alone.
Therefore, the discussions of the Mosaic republic that peppered much
seventeenth-century political thought depended not only on the idea that
the Bible offered a relevant republican model, but also on the premiss that
the specific historical republic described there was disconnected from contemporary Jewish life because Christians had superseded it politically and
religiously. Of course, Jewish thinkers could not accept that premiss, and in
rejecting it, the Spanish and Portuguese Jews reappropriated Jewish politics from a majority culture that was obsessed with them.

Christian intellectual treatment of the properly religious republic was,
despite being Christian, readily adaptable to a Jewish republic—an exilic
community—because it had developed with reference to Jewish sources.
Christian interpretations lent contemporary utility and new layers of meaning to elements already present in Jewish thought and practices. Accordingly, the writings of the Spanish and Portuguese Jews are replete with
references, explicit and oblique, to the ideas of Hobbes, Locke, John
Selden, and Samuel Pufendorf; to Niccolò Machiavelli, Juan Marquez, Jean
Bodin, and Jacques-Bénigne Bossuet; Johannes Althusius, Hugo Grotius,
Justus Lipsius, Petrus Cunaeus, and many more. Fully participating in the
cultural and literary forms of their era as they did, they used political images
and tropes in works that were at the very heart of Jewishness: sermons for
the inauguration of the synagogue, funeral orations for dearly loved parents
and spiritual leaders, conversionary tracts. Since Jewish theopolitics were
already woven into Christian political thought more or less across the

---

[32] They also turned to Jews as teachers, by no means limited to the context of political
thought. Studies include: Katchen, *Christian Hebraists*; Coudert and Shoulson (eds.), *Hebraica
veritas*; Grafton and Weinberg, *I Have Always*; Mandelbrote and Weinberg, *Jewish Books*; and
Dunkelgrün, 'Christian Study'.

board, it was relatively straightforward—and deeply meaningful—for Jews to pick up the threads for their own purposes.

Such wide-ranging engagement was stimulated not only by Christian interest in Judaica, but more fundamentally by key features of the new republicanism of the seventeenth century, particularly in the Anglo-Dutch or Atlantic world. As first illuminated by the watershed historiography of J. G. A. Pocock, Quentin Skinner, and others, it was in this era that the generic concept of the polity first emerged. Classical and humanistic republican traditions combined with local ideas regarding associations, rights, and self-rule, and were adapted to the setting of the English monarchy. Once the concept of the 'republic' was freed from its particular meaning as not-monarchy, it became something more generic: as Pocock explained, it meant simply a polity, a political entity. Now it was a categorical concept that could and did include the whole range of political arrangements. Theorizing the polity was the start of what would become political science, and the concept of the polity was what would become the idea of the state.

So it was newly the case that there was a word and an accompanying discourse for the affairs of any state-like entity—any self-governed collective or society—and even a new vogue for thinking in such terms. As this innovation took hold in Holland in the 1660s, it deeply affected Amsterdam's Spanish and Portuguese Jews. The non-specificity of the 'polity' as opposed to categories such as kingdom, bishopric, or city-state made it applicable to the Jewish self-governed collective. This generic idea of the polity, though distinct from the more specific classical meaning of 'republic', was still expressed by most writers in seventeenth-century Europe by means of the Latin *res publica* and its cognates, and it was thus that members of the Kahal Kadosh referred to their community when discussing its politics.[33]

English-speakers of the age often used the word 'commonwealth' alongside or in place of 'republic'. Thomas Hobbes wrote of the 'commonwealth' in his *Leviathan*, and though members of the Kahal Kadosh probably did not read it in English, they absorbed its impact. Following Pocock, 'commonwealth' is often used as a convention of European historiography to avoid conflation with the modern connotations of either 'republic' or 'state',[34] and modern English translations of Spinoza's *Theological-Political Treatise*, first written in Latin, often use 'commonwealth'. It is accordingly

---

[33] See Bodian, 'Biblical Hebrews'.   [34] See Skinner, *Foundations*, i, pp. ix–x, xxiii.

well suited to the mental world of Amsterdam's Portuguese Jews, and serves as a reminder that the community-focused republicanism of the Kahal Kadosh was of the seventeenth-century English variety, rather than the classical or Renaissance variety.

With the community now interpreted as a commonwealth, it was easily subject to the same kinds of analysis as Christian polities. And Jews in Amsterdam began to use it for thinking about their affairs—for example, about how to justify leaders' authority, what rights individuals might have, and what structures and practices would constitute the best Jewish government. It is worth pointing out that such engagement was not limited to intellectual circles. Rather, as in the Christian world, the new politics evolved simultaneously in popular attitudes and concrete actions.

If the wider backdrop for the Jewish politics of Spinoza's cohort was the new republicanism, the local scene in Amsterdam from the 1660s to the 1680s also conditioned Jewish affairs. It was a time of marked instability —the year 1672 is known as the 'year of disaster', featuring government change, military defeat, and a sharp economic downturn—matched by an intense culture of polemicizing and theorizing about what a state should be and do. Amsterdam's reputation for intellectual freedom and its place at the centre of a global network of trade and colonization made it a locus for the new, exciting, extreme, and illicit. It was not merely an empty junction; during precisely this time, the Dutch began to develop their own local flavour of republicanism, having absorbed Hobbesian thought, newly translated from its original English. Local Dutch thinkers like Jan and Pieter de la Court theorized Holland's independence.[35] In short, the political language that the Spanish and Portuguese Jews used to speak about their affairs was inflected by the Dutch setting as well as being connected to a wider web of late seventeenth-century conversations.[36]

In the Jewish politics of Spinoza's Amsterdam, I argue, can be located the first entrance of the incipient idea of the state into the heart of Jewish theopolitics. The subjects of the present study were the first to fully explore a vision of the exilic Jewish community as state-like in the terms of modern political thought. The combination of Bible-focused politics, the new

---

[35] On the de la Court brothers, see Israel, 'Intellectual Origins'; Price, *Holland*; Kossmann, 'Course'; and Weststeijn, *Commercial Republicanism*.

[36] I am intentionally echoing J. G. A. Pocock's discussion of political languages. See Pocock, *Politics, Language, and Time*.

republicanism, the reception of Hobbes, and local factors produced a lasting image of Jewish self-government. It reappeared in later Jewish thought like that of Baron, whose impressions were mediated through the same central political traditions of the modern West and influenced by the legacy of the Kahal Kadosh itself.

Spinoza

Spinoza's *Theological-Political Treatise* was a third main factor shaping the political discourse of the Kahal Kadosh. In that famous work, Spinoza proffered a provocative interpretation of Jewish history that took the early modern European political engagement with Jews, Judaism, and Jewish history to a new level by embracing Jewish politics but also enacting a profound betrayal of his former community on a widely visible stage. If Sabbatai Zevi stands among the most famous Jewish messiahs, Spinoza is certainly one of the best-known excommunicates in Jewish history. The son of a former converso, Spinoza was born into Amsterdam's Portuguese Jewish community and educated alongside some of the writers discussed in this book. In 1656 the Mahamad excommunicated him for 'evil opinions' and 'abominable heresies'. In its harsh curses and reference to heresy, Spinoza's ban was atypical; most were relatively mundane affairs, imposed for disobedience of the Mahamad or infractions of communal laws.[37] Though no more specific account of his crime survives, clearly something about Spinoza's ideas offended. It is likely that he was already beginning to think through the ideas at the heart of his later works, including his *Ethics* and his *Political Treatise*, both published posthumously in 1677, and his *Theological-Political Treatise*, published (anonymously) in 1670. As these works were read and digested, Spinoza became 'the supreme philosophical bogeyman of Early Enlightenment Europe', in the words of the historian Jonathan Israel.[38]

Among the best-known claims in the *Theological-Political Treatise* was that Judaism was formed as the civic religion of the Mosaic republic: it was

---

[37] The power of the *ḥerem*, or ban of excommunication, was its ability to cut a member off from his local familial, commercial, and religious networks, and in the blow to an individual's honour that it represented. On the ban in the Kahal Kadosh see Y. Kaplan, 'Social Functions', as well as id., 'Deviance'. On Spinoza's ban, see Méchoulan, 'Le *Ḥerem*'; Kasher and Biderman, 'Why Was Baruch de Spinoza Excommunicated?'; Vlessing, 'The Excommunication of Baruch Spinoza'; and Nadler, *Spinoza*, 116–54 and the bibliography there.

[38] Israel, *Radical Enlightenment*, 159.

for a particular people in a particular historical time and place.[39] The conclusion Spinoza drew from this claim was that Judaism (specifically, Jewish law) was both essentially political and also by definition obsolete after the republic's loss of political independence. He argued that Jews were only 'chosen' in a political sense, meaning that God led them to geopolitical power: the Jewish nation was 'chosen by God . . . in respect to its social organization and the good fortune with which it obtained supremacy and retained it so many years. . . . Their election and vocation consisted only in the material success and prosperity of their state.'[40] Later he called this 'their temporal physical happiness and freedom, in other words, autonomous government'.[41] When their success as a state waned, in Spinoza's view, the Hebrews were no longer chosen.

This argument went against contemporaneous Jewish perspectives in multiple ways. As others have noted, it denied the validity of post-biblical Judaism by indicating that once the political purpose of what he called 'ritual and ceremonial' observance had ended, there was no point in maintaining it. This challenge aligned with Christian polemical views and also with a predilection towards anti-rabbinism or religious scepticism among former conversos, against which some Amsterdam Jewish thinkers, including Isaac Orobio de Castro and Abraham Pereyra, mounted responses. Still, considering Spinoza's direct confrontation with the very idea of rabbinic law, little reaction to the 1670 treatise has been marked among his former fellow members of the Kahal Kadosh—or among Jewish writers at all, in its wake.[42]

Another, more complicated, challenge presented by Spinoza's political assessment of Judaism had to do with its implications for the idea of Jewish community, rather than for Jewish law or religion. In this arena, it offered useful avenues for thinking about a Jewish polity at the same time as it undermined the basis for a lay-controlled exilic Jewish community exactly like the Kahal Kadosh. The same position regarding the political nature of Mosaic law that obviated post-biblical Jewish religion in his eyes also meant that there was no basis for Jews to govern themselves apart

---

[39] e.g. *TPT*, 8, 63–4, 69. See Levene, *Spinoza's Revelation*, 6.   [40] *TPT*, 46.
[41] *TPT*, 48. He describes the opposing view near the end of ch. 3: 'It now only remains to us to answer the arguments of those who would persuade themselves that the election of the Jews was not temporal, and merely in respect of their commonwealth, but eternal; for, they say, we see the Jews after the loss of their commonwealth, and after being scattered so many years and . . . still surviving' (*TPT*, 54).   [42] D. Schwartz, *The First Modern Jew*, 18–19.

from others in contemporary life. Although Spinoza's ideal Christian commonwealth was a religiously tolerant one in the sense of allowing for diverse individual beliefs, it did not allow for religion to constitute political bodies apart from the commonwealth as a whole. Nor did it allow for religious leaders to wield temporal power over members of their communities of faith. Spinoza's preferred arrangement in a Christian commonwealth would have allowed some version of Judaism but only with Jews integrated into the larger body politic.[43] Such a prospect invalidated the most basic idea of the Kahal Kadosh, as it was being discussed among Spinoza's former peers in Amsterdam at the very time the *Treatise* was published.

On the other hand, the treatment of Jewish law as political that underlay Spinoza's theoretical threat could not be dismissed easily; it shared a great deal with perspectives that were central to the internal politics of the Kahal Kadosh. Spinoza insisted that the Jewish loss of independence meant the loss of a civic arena in which politics by definition took place, and hence denied both Jewish religion and Jewish politics after the biblical era. But in the minds of Jews who saw themselves as possessing just such a civic arena, things looked different. The *Treatise*'s political ideas spoke to them as members of a Jewish polity rather than as (or in addition to) Jews within a Christian polity, and therefore they found intriguing ideas in the work about how to organize their civic affairs, account for religious authority within lay-run institutions, and accommodate intellectual freedom. Although Spinoza's positions undermining rabbinic law, Jewish communal legitimacy, and conventional concepts of Scripture as revelation were roundly rejected, some of his views about the politics of commonwealth were similar to those espoused by Jewish community members in good standing.

Examples of such engagement are found throughout this book, as thinkers like Pereyra, Orobio, and Barrios saw the community not as a continuation of the ancient Hebrew commonwealth but as its analogue—as parallel, too, to Spinoza's ideal republic. They connected with specific components of Spinoza's thought, including the logic behind individuals' participation in a polity or society, the roles of covenant or contract and of sovereignty in setting the limits of government authority, and the status of Jewish law understood as divine political instruction. The ideal Christian commonwealth that he advocated was actually very much like the Kahal

[43] See S. B. Smith, *Spinoza*.

Kadosh in that it was governed by lay people on the broad basis of religious and political principles, employing but not directly empowering clerics.[44] The correlation suggests a deep relationship between Spinoza's politics and the politics of Jewish communities, to complement the connections that have long been studied between his thought and Jewish theology, law, and philosophy.[45]

The *Treatise* also suggests that Spinoza shared his former peers' pre-occupation with Jewish politicality, though his conclusions were different. He went further than any other writer in theorizing politics at the core of Judaism—a stance with which some of the Amsterdam Sephardim, especially David Sarphati, showed real affinity—while at the same time demolishing its legitimacy in the present. His famous remark about restoration, that 'if the foundations of their religion have not emasculated their minds they may even, if occasion offers . . . raise up their empire afresh, and that God may a second time elect them', echoes Luzzatto and Menasseh's earlier disavowal of the political drive (mentioned above) by impugning Jewish manliness.[46] And yet it does not quite do the same thing. It also has a flavour of the historical realism and ongoing sense of possibility that Kahal Kadosh members showed in the Sabbatian era. Aside from the insult it contains, ironically, the statement reads as a suggestion that Jews are like all other peoples, with political fortunes subject to the same ups and downs as others. Spinoza's presentation of the politics of the ancient Hebrew republic had the same quality. Instead of elevating Moses' republic as a special geopolitical scenario in which actors and actions were privileged and distinct from all others due to chosenness, Spinoza instead lowered the biblical republic to the level of normalcy. The message that 'the ancient

[44] Spinoza excoriated Jews for their lack of tolerance. One can see how the model of the Jewish commonwealth almost, but not quite, lived up to his religio-political ideal. See S. B. Smith, 'Spinoza's Paradox'.

[45] Whereas the *TPT* was explicitly both theological and political, the theological (or religious) dimension has overwhelmingly dominated research on Spinoza's relationship to Jewish tradition. See Ravven and Goodman (eds.), *Jewish Themes*; Nadler, *Spinoza's Heresy*; Leo Strauss, *Spinoza's Critique*; Y. Melamed, *Spinoza's Metaphysics*; and D. Schwartz (ed.), *Spinoza's Challenge*. Studies of Spinoza's political ideas, on the other hand, have mainly not engaged with their relationship to Jewish traditions and practices. For example, Y. Melamed and Rosenthal (eds.), *Spinoza's Theological-Political Treatise*, includes three essays devoted to political topics, none of which engages with Jewish contexts. Levene, *Spinoza's Revelation*, is an exception.

[46] *TPT*, 56. See D. Schwartz, *The First Modern Jew*, 113–53; Adler, 'Zionists'; and Harvey, 'Spinoza's Counterfactual Zionism'.

Israelites were just like us' supported a Christian view that Europeans could be just like the ancient Israelites; in Spinoza's account, it also made Jews just like everyone else. Members of the Kahal Kadosh thought the same way.

Much later, Spinoza's comment about chosenness was read by early Zionists as a sign of his proto-Zionism, as he seemed to foretell the return to Jewish world-historical relevance; and for different reasons, Gershom Scholem read it as a reaction to Sabbatianism.[47] Both readings acknowledge his making Jewish politicality seem less transcendent and unique. This is what seems so modern about it, and it is precisely what he shared with his former co-religionists. Their views of Jewish politics stemmed from the same conditions.

Sabbatianism

The final factor that shaped the discourse of Jewish politicality was Sabbatianism, which, I argue, sharpened the interest of members of the Kahal Kadosh in the possibilities of Jewish politics in their own time. Sabbatianism primed Jewish minds with robust and imminent political ambition that was easily converted into, or counteracted by, a non-monarchical mode in the light of contemporary republicanism. Sabbatai Zevi was a Turkish Jew whose claims of messiahship were, for a time, backed by most Jews in Europe and the Ottoman empire, including the Sephardi and Ashkenazi Jews in Amsterdam. His stated worldly intention—to take over the Ottoman empire, delivering control of Jerusalem as well as the rest of the empire's vast territory to him as a Jewish king—was dramatically frustrated at the end of 1666 when the Ottoman sultan instead compelled Sabbatai to convert to Islam, first installing him within the sultan's own court and eventually sending him into isolation in a remote location, where he died in 1676.

These events had a long and notable aftermath. Most Jews eventually gave up on their Sabbatian belief, but not all. A set of followers within the Ottoman empire chose to follow Sabbatai into Islam and maintained a secretive society of believers into the twentieth century. Another, more widespread, phenomenon was the conversion of Sabbatian expectations

---

[47] Scholem, *Sabbatai Ṣevi*, 544. On the former point, see Harvey, 'Spinoza's Counterfactual Zionism', 241 n. 16; Septimus, 'Biblical Religion', 402; and Lazier, *God*.

into a kind of mystical antinomianism, spearheaded by the likes of Nathan of Gaza and Abraham Cardoso. This later form of Sabbatianism had its roots in various strange and transgressive acts of Sabbatai himself, but it truly found its footing only in the 1680s after Sabbatai's death eliminated hope of his near-term return to geopolitical influence. Accusations of illicit Sabbatian leanings featured centrally in bitter disputes that played out on institutional, halakhic, and personal levels among prominent rabbis from the 1690s to the eighteenth century.[48] Antinomianism and spiritual messianism feature prominently in the popular and scholarly imagination of Sabbatianism—understandably, since their impact was unique and long-lasting. Indeed, Gershom Scholem focused on ritual transgression as a key component of the Sabbatian movement and portrayed messianic disappointment following Sabbatai's conversion as a key transformation in the history of Jewish spirituality.[49] Generally, we are given to understand that followers quickly turned to mystical explanations as a way of resolving the cognitive dissonance induced by the would-be messiah's failure to ascend a literal throne.

However, in the period studied here—the two decades beginning with Sabbatai's rise to prominence—the more realistic, geopolitical dimension of the movement had not yet been entirely supplanted. Although it is marginalized in Jewish life today, belief in an actual future messianic king was the norm for premodern Jews. Historians agree that Sabbatian messianic expectation included an expectation of realistic political change, that this expectation related to seemingly mundane matters, and that such expectations and hopes continued into the 1670s and even early 1680s, well after Sabbatai's apostasy. As Yehuda Liebes wrote, Sabbatianism at the time of the mass movement was 'predominantly a belief in earthly and political redemption' for most people.[50] Scholem, too, paid plenty of attention to the various ways in which Sabbatai claimed kingship or impending king-

[48] See Carlebach, *The Pursuit of Heresy*; ead., 'Sabbatianism'; Goldish, 'Orthodoxy', and id., 'Jews, Christians and Conversos'.

[49] Scholem, *Sabbatai Ṣevi*; id., 'Sabbatianism'; id., 'Redemption'.

[50] Liebes nevertheless discounted the importance of such a belief in favour of the mystical interpretations of Sabbatian believers over the ensuing decades. He contrasted spiritual messianism, which he attributed to thinking elites, with the expectation of political restoration, which he saw as limited to the simple masses, citing the need to counter a negative view of Jewish messianism as overly earthly; Liebes, 'Sabbatean Messianism', 93–5. Carlebach discusses in detail the role of Sabbatianism in Jewish–Christian polemics in 'Sabbatianism' and in *Divided Souls*, 76–87.

ship.[51] In fact, it was precisely because the earlier form of expectation had been literal that Scholem saw the disappointment as causing wholesale messianic disenchantment, arguing that modern Jewish (mystical) consciousness had sublimated, internalized, and spiritualized messianism so that it lost all connection with political expectations.[52]

The question, then, is only when the practical expectation that messianism would entail Jewish kingship faded away. Most historians have agreed that the closer one gets to 1666, moving back in time, the more literal the Sabbatian movement appears to have been. At the height of the movement before the apostasy, it was common to acknowledge that the world might be about to change dramatically. Sabbatian leaders articulated the expectation in political terms in countless symbolic and literal acts. The 'prayer for the king' typically recited in exilic communities at the time was adapted to praise Sabbatai instead.[53] The very story of Sabbatai's confrontation with the sultan, central to the way the Sabbatian tale was told then as well as now, turns on the expectation that Sabbatai would acquire the sultan's temporal rule.[54]

Political realism was clearly present in the kind of Sabbatianism that was reported by eyewitnesses of Jewish activity during the peak years before the disappointment: it was the stuff of newspaper reports and epistolary rumour-mongering about massing armies and imminent seizure of power,[55] as Jews, but also many Christians, reported the upcoming

[51] In *Sabbatai Ṣevi* Scholem documented the intertwined expectations of spiritual and political redemption, in support of his wider preoccupation with their disentanglement in modernity. While he thus did not deny the literal politicality of early Sabbatianism—on the contrary, he illustrated it copiously—he also set it squarely in a mental world to which, he said, moderns no longer have access. Pawel Maciejko revisits Scholem's project and makes important correctives. See his introduction in Maciejko (ed.), *Sabbatian Heresy*.

[52] See Dan, *Gershom Scholem*, 287–8; Biale, *Gershom Scholem*; Albert, 'On the Possibility of Jewish Politics in Our Time'.

[53] In Amsterdam the rabbi Isaac Aboab da Fonseca reworked the prayer to apply to Sabbatai Zevi as the new Jewish king (Scholem, *Sabbatai Ṣevi*, 424 and 533). The old version had been translated into English by Menasseh ben Israel in his *Humble Addresses*, 12, to show the fidelity of Jews to their rulers. On the prayer in general, see Sarna, 'Jewish Prayers', esp. 205–7, and B. Schwartz, '*Hanoten Teshua*'.

[54] As one historian summarized the last stages before the apostasy, when an imprisoned messiah awaited his climactic audience with the Turkish leader, 'Sabbetai lived like a king in captivity, receiving embassies and assigning the provinces of his future kingdom to his relatives and friends'. Werblowsky, 'Messianism', 42.

[55] The Dutch writer Thomas Coenen wrote the fullest Christian account at the time. See *Ydele werwachtinge* and the Hebrew edition, *Tsipiyot shav*. It is discussed in Scholem, *Sabbatai*

'Restauration of the Jews, or true Relation of their Progress and Proceedings in order to the regaining of their ancient Kingdom', as a 1665
pamphlet announced in London.[56] A rabbi who vehemently opposed the
movement, Jacob Sasportas, later reported that 'there was a great commotion in the city of Amsterdam . . . They rejoiced . . . in all the streets . . .
without considering the possible danger . . . They publicly proclaimed
[the news] and informed the gentiles of all the reports'.[57] Overturning the
usual protocols of submission through acts such as boastful street processions or selling off real estate at a loss is a theme that often appears in
accounts of the time. One of the most important believers in Sabbatai
among the Portuguese Jews of Amsterdam was Abraham Pereyra, the
merchant turned moralist mentioned above. He left Amsterdam to go and
meet the rising messiah, apparently to use his vast wealth to support the
new regime. According to an admittedly sensationalist report written by
an Englishman in Amsterdam, before his departure Pereyra specially went
to the city magistrates to express his gratitude 'for the favour he and his
Nation in their dispersion had received here', suggesting he saw no need for
such favour anymore; and further: 'It's said he offered to sell a Countrey-
house of his worth Three thousand pound *Sterling*, at much loss, and on
this Condition, That the Buyer should not pay one farthing till he be convinced in his own Conscience, That the *Jews* have a King.'[58]

In a separate incident, Sasportas's old friend, a supporter of the movement despite the rabbi's warnings, taunted him: 'What will you say when
you shall hear in three or four weeks from now . . . that the Grand Turk has
placed the royal crown on his [the messiah's] head and given him the whole
land of Judah and Jerusalem?'[59] In another street-level view of messianic
expectation, an administrative document arranging a new burial ground for

Ṣevi, 424–5. The Dutch scholar Peter Serrarius also took particular interest in these messianic
doings as he had millenarian interests of his own. See Scholem, *Sabbatai Ṣevi*, 333.

[56] This is only one of the many accounts mentioned by Scholem. See *Sabbatai Ṣevi*, 335.

[57] Quoted ibid. 521. Sasportas's letters from the Sabbatian era were published in a shortened
version in the 18th century and then in full in the 20th. Sasportas, *Tsitsat novel tsevi*. On Sasportas, see Dweck, *Dissident Rabbi*.

[58] Scholem, *Sabbatai Ṣevi*, 530, citing Wilensky, 'Four' (Heb.), where the letter appears on
pp. 167–8. Of course, Christian accounts cannot be assumed to accurately reflect Sabbatian
attitudes and actions, but Jewish contemporary reports are scarce (Scholem, *Sabbatai Ṣevi*,
762–3). See also Popkin, 'Three English Tellings' and 'Two Unused Sources'.

[59] Scholem, *Sabbatai Ṣevi*, 523. The writer was Aaron Sarphati, who Scholem says was also a
rabbi, originally from Morocco.

the Ashkenazi Jews of Hamburg included a clause indicating how the deal would be affected by the redemption, should it occur shortly. Strikingly, it states that 'if the redemption in the World to Come arrives' before a certain time, money should still be paid to the Altona community, which would then donate it to the Temple in Jerusalem.[60] A typical feature of old-fashioned Jewish messianism was that it envisaged geopolitical change within an otherwise continuous world. Here, the deal-makers did not even imagine redemption as an end to the diaspora, but rather as a change in relations within it.

Furthermore, such considerations did not disappear overnight when Sabbatai converted to Islam. From the time that word of his apostasy reached communities throughout Europe, North Africa, and the Middle East, most Jews with formal leadership roles withdrew their support from Sabbatai, as they did in Amsterdam.[61] But it was by no means obvious to everyone that the hoped-for alteration would not still take place.[62] Specific ritual and spiritual innovations connected with the Sabbatian movement also continued while Sabbatai was alive. Within the Kahal Kadosh, those who continued to believe in his return were rarely prevented from continuing their devotions privately, or even in groups, one of which was funded and attended by Pereyra, and later by Barrios, in Amsterdam.[63] Multiple sources report the ongoing, open belief in Sabbatai during this period in Holland.[64] In fact, in the years 1674–5 and again in 1683, small revivals of Sabbatian support took place, the latter as a final wave of hope for his return centred on the seventh anniversary of his death.[65] In short, despite

[60] Brilling, 'Umbekanter Document'. I thank Joshua Teplitsky for this reference; see Teplitsky, 'Messianic Hope', for discussion of the document.   [61] Y. Kaplan, 'Attitude'.

[62] For example, the extraordinary 17th-century female diarist Glikl of Hameln recorded that her father-in-law prepared a trunk filled with dry goods for shipping to the Holy Land. Four years passed before the family gave up and retrieved the goods. See Turniansky (ed.), *Glikl*; Carlebach, 'Sabbatian Posture'.

[63] See Scholem, *Sabbatai Ṣevi*, 749–92, esp. 754–6 and 785–6 on Amsterdam.

[64] However, the Mahamad of the Kahal Kadosh Talmud Torah did react strongly with the excommunication of a Sabbatian rabble-rouser from out of town during the High Holy Days of 1667, in an incident that highlighted differences between the Sephardi and Ashkenazi communities and the fragility of the ban, since the Ashkenazim sought to have the Amsterdam city magistrates overturn the Sephardi expulsion of their Sabbatian hero. See Scholem, *Sabbatai Ṣevi*, 785–7.

[65] Scholem reported that there was a profusion of predictions about the second coming, to follow seven years after the first—which would be somewhere between 1672 and 1674, depending on how exactly one timed the beginning of Sabbatai Zevi's first coming. *Sabbatai Ṣevi*, 898.

the official stance of lay leaders, uncertainty about Sabbatai's messianic prospects continued to exert influence during this time, as average community members experienced various degrees and stages of ongoing expectation.

Of course, the movement's appeal was far from limited to the political, but Sabbatianism raised the public spectre of Jewish kingship and the end of the exile as it was then experienced, and many reasonable people took the possibility of Jewish political restoration seriously. At a minimum, it was prevalent as the language in which messianism was expressed, and this observation is critical to understanding how it helped to catalyse new political thinking of a non-monarchical variety among the Amsterdam Sephardim. There had already been a tendency among conversos to think messianically about world affairs, as for example in Sebastianism, a movement focused on the predicted return of a lost Portuguese king.[66] For former conversos who had become openly practising Jews, steeped in European culture, an innate political sensibility was aroused, leading them to focus not only on the possibility of Jewish kingship but also more generally on the prospect of Jewish politics within the world they knew.

The vision of Jewish political vitality did not immediately fade when the success of Sabbatai himself appeared less and less likely. On the contrary, facing the failure of Sabbatai in particular, some community leaders and members converted their hopes for Jewish politics into a new perspective on the community, finding there a stable and legitimate Jewish political arena worthy of the same pride. They replaced the global messianic or theocratic empire with a local, lay-led commonwealth, and some members of the Kahal Kadosh saw fit to strengthen and entrench the Mahamad's authority. Not everyone agreed, of course. Part of the complexity of the religio-political moment was that some drew different conclusions, whether adhering to the messianic tradition, pushing for a more rabbinically oriented community, or looking to weaken the Kahal Kadosh. The very possibility of Jewish rule entailed a new attention to Jewish politicality, particularly the place of religion in Jewish politics and vice versa.

[66] See Hermann, *No reino*; Goldish, 'Patterns'; id., *Sabbatean Prophets*, including pp. 48 and 190; and Yerushalmi, *From Spanish Court to Italian Ghetto*, 306–13. See also Moreno-Carvalho, 'Yaacov Rosales'. Sebastianism was only one component in a wider common zone between Jewish and Christian messianism and millenarianism in early modern Europe. See Popkin and Goldish (eds.), *Millenarianism*; Y. Kaplan, 'El mesianismo'; and Goldish, 'New Approaches'.

After all, Sabbatian messianism spoke of an alternative political regime. As the case of the Hamburg cemetery exemplifies, power dynamics would be altered, not erased, by Sabbatian success. In the scenario of a new Jewish empire, what would become of the Mahamad and the extensive structure of local administration that claimed its own authority, quite differentiated from kingship? Soon after Sabbatai's failure to take the sultan's crown, a public discourse developed regarding the Jewish community and its meaning in a universal divine narrative, including the eschatological. Such a conversation was a reasonable response to Sabbatianism, both as a prospect and as a disappointment. The well-known religious antinomianism of Sabbatianism is thus shown to have been accompanied by a threat to existing Jewish political structures. The sources in this book illuminate how Sabbatian fallout had to some extent always played out on the communal level as well as in the spiritual or rabbinic domain, filling a gap in our knowledge about the early reception of Sabbatianism and specifically about its impact on communal politics.

Paths Forward

Beyond their immediate impact on the members of the Kahal Kadosh, the movement of Sabbatai Zevi and the writings of Benedict Spinoza were both critical loci of change in Jewish early modernity. With Spinoza seen by historians as a paragon of secularization and Sabbatianism as a massive spiritual folly, the two had intertwined afterlives in the Jewish imagination; the apparent clash between the paths of the rationalistic assimilationist and the mystical traditionalist informs the fault-lines of Jewish culture up to today. We may—we should—take issue with both of these characterizations, questioning the accuracy of such a vision of bifurcated modern Jewish life, and also complicating the relationship of seventeenth-century events themselves to the broad new directions of Jewish modernity. Still, the very power of their paradigmatic pairing calls attention to the common point from which they both began. They were experienced by the same early modern Jewish people, especially in Amsterdam, where Spinoza had particular impact. Those people's direct experience has receded in the historical imagination and until now their reactions to each have seemed to have little to do with each other. As it turns out, it is political ideas that bind Spinozism and Sabbatianism together.

In 1665 the community was confidently run by its strong-handed lay leaders, in the manner set out in its constitution. By 1685, nothing had changed on the surface: the community's constitution was still in place, and so was the Mahamad. But a transformation had taken place underneath, in the world of ideas, with subtler effects on social organization. Christian political ideas, the converso experience, Sabbatianism, and Spinoza's *Theological-Political Treatise* together created a perfect storm stimulating Kahal Kadosh members to consider very carefully the nature of their community, its authority, its future, and its ultimate purpose. The Sabbatian movement raised the possibility of an imminent end to the status quo, while also stoking a desire for earthly Jewish politics—forcing a complex confrontation with the idea of local communal authority. Similarly, Spinoza's views of the ideal relationship between religion and politics threatened the basis for the existence of a Jewish polity within the Christian one even while elevating Jewish politicality to a central place in human history. Meanwhile, other forms of Christian thought offered a new way of thinking about local communities that explicitly politicized what the Kahal Kadosh already possessed, and for former conversos the prospect of immediate, concrete political participation had particular appeal. All of these factors peaked between the 1660s and the 1680s.

Together with the contexts of early modern political thought and converso background that disposed community members to serious engagement with the idea of the exilic community, the Sabbatian and Spinozistic contexts brought into sharp relief questions about what such an entity was and what it ought to be. Members of Amsterdam's Kahal Kadosh sought to make sense of the community's institutional and legal coherence and its relationship to external authorities, seeking a stable conception of a community that was not fully sovereign and yet still politically distinct. Revealed through these discussions is an overarching interest in the meaning of Jewish politics in the diaspora: what did it mean for Jews to have a form of political self-rule that was neither biblical nor messianically restored, but that was also divinely ordained and religiously significant? From one perspective, this was a Jewish theological question, falling wholly within the purview of rabbinic traditions; from another, it was very much of a piece with early modern political thought, trying to understand present-day political circumstances in terms of God's intentions, especially as revealed in the Bible. It was the theological-political problem applied to Jews; or, put differently, an inside-out version of the 'Jewish question', treated by means of a serious, self-reflective, sometimes surprising public political discourse.

Amsterdam's Spanish and Portuguese Jews addressed these questions out loud and in depth for just two decades, but they show the generative potential of committed Jewish thought in conversation with the political thinking that modernized the West. The close look at their theological-political moment offered here opens out to a broad view: the microhistory exposes a hidden complexity in the ways premodern Jews thought about their communal organizations. It serves, then, as an intervention in the historiography of Jewish community, an area of inquiry that has used the 'social' rather than the 'political' as its primary frame of reference for at least a century. In the outlook of the founders of modern Jewish social history, exilic Jews by definition lacked 'politics' since they lacked a state, even though their 'social' life mimicked political life in many respects. For the seventeenth century and before, we can now see, such a distinction is anachronistic. Our Amsterdam thinkers may have been the first Jews to openly and self-consciously call their community a 'polity' in the sense of being state-like because they were the first to be deeply touched by the new discourse of politics in the West. Among other things, this observation calls for a re-evaluation of what Jewish communities were in the minds of premodern Jewish people, taking a more sophisticated approach to terminology and intellectual context. I return to this point below in Chapter 1 and again, in relation to modern Jewish historiography, in the Conclusion.

But neither modern historiography, nor the premodern Jewish community writ large, is the subject of this book. Here, the focus is on the re-conceptualization of the community specifically within the orbit of the Spanish and Portuguese Jews in Amsterdam in the middle of the seventeenth century: first, through the creation of a new Jewish political order in the 1630s, and then in the form of public discourse and political activity in the 1660s, 1670s, and 1680s—the time of Spinoza's intellectual production as well as Sabbatai Zevi's messianic movement. Unfolding against the backdrop of Hobbesian political thought and Christian discussion of the biblical political model, a public discourse emerged to address universal political questions in Jewish terms and the Jewish political condition in universal terms. To examine this discourse, *Jewish Politics in Spinoza's Amsterdam* unfolds in three parts, looking first at shared assumptions about the community, next at points of conflict within it, and finally at how members reflected on the community's politics on a broader scale. Each chapter supports the propositions that I have laid out here by means of close readings and deeper contextualization.

Chapter 1, 'Community', offers a new interpretation of the early history and 1639 constitution of the Kahal Kadosh to argue for a different impression of its structure and status than has been given before. The founders established a system based on office-holding, contract and agreement, fiscal collectivity, clear boundaries, and public order guided by religious precepts and a strong sense of ethnic and religious conformity. It was a distinctly civic entity—a commonwealth—justified by rabbinic law. As such it was continuous with traditions and practices already existing in Jewish communities, but it put them to a new use that uniquely suited the political and religious codes of Holland during the Revolt. Reflecting on such an entity leads to observations about administrative, executive, or corporate models for Jewish communal self-rule as opposed to the judicial or legal model that typically dominates discussion of Jewish autonomy. The values and practices that shaped the community in the first place then served as a seedbed for the new flowering of political discourse, beginning in the 1660s.

Chapter 2, 'Republic', shows that a new conception of the Jewish 'republic' was born after 1665, equating it with a local self-governing community instead of the global diaspora. Careful attention to terms of self-reference used before and after that time reveals a conceptual shift expressed in linguistic terms. Ruminations on the Jewish republic, including those of Abraham Pereyra, provide examples of how the commonwealth model was applied to the community on a granular level, adapting governmental terms and concepts to communal affairs with self-awareness in acts of cultural translation.

With Chapter 3, 'Civitas', the book begins to address differentiation and conflict within the community, showing how lay leadership, constitutionalism, Jewish law, rabbinic authority, and the ban were particular foci of unrest and of creative synthesis. This chapter offers a reading of the 1675 synagogue as an intentional embodiment of the Mahamad's rule and simultaneously a response to a Sabbatian messianic politics that would have disrupted the exilic status quo. Analysis of the synagogue's architecture and its representation in image and text from the time shows what the building signified at the moment of its construction: inherent in its architecture was a message about enduring diaspora institutions as opposed to messianic ingathering. Its walled enclosure created a space, if not a territory, to match the community's self-image as a commonwealth, establishing a civic sphere that emphasized the community's overall lay orientation and especially the rule of the Mahamad. The Mahamad's simultaneous moves to consolidate and entrench its own rule, and several discussions of the building, affirm this intention. They also attest to the existence of meaningful opposition to such framing, as not all members of the community went happily along with the Mahamad's efforts, for both pragmatic and ideological reasons.

Chapter 4, 'Covenant', analyses a defence of the Mahamad's excommunicatory authority written by the senior rabbi of the community, Isaac Aboab da Fonseca. He published a pamphlet in 1680 answering members who advocated secession on the basis of arguments that undercut the community's hold on them—an episode that was unknown until this rare text came to light. Aboab's pamphlet shows how various factions battled over interpretations of the founding document, in aspects that engaged its terms in detail and recapitulated contemporary debates on constitution and covenant, including those of Hobbes and Spinoza among others.

Chapter 5, 'Rabbis', looks at the same text alongside Orobio's discussion of the 'sceptre of Judah' to ask how members accounted for the place of rabbinic authority and Jewish law in the Kahal Kadosh. Aboab defended the unlimited right of the lay leaders to wield the *herem*, whereas others demanded that a rabbi be involved. They took up questions about religious and political authority that, once again, closely traced parallel debates about excommunication and civic authority among Christian contemporaries. As those debates made use of biblical models, they stimulated questions about the legitimacy of Jewish law in exile.

The final two chapters step back to look at broader ways in which ideas of the Kahal Kadosh aided its members in reflecting on Jewish status in the world and the place of diaspora communities in Jewish history. Chapter 6, 'Politics', faces head-on community members' embrace of Jewish 'politics' by name, showing the ramifications of such a move for their understanding of exile and Jewish particularity. Through the lens of Abraham Pereyra's pious works and Sarphati's sermon, it shows up close how the new conceptions of 'religion' and 'politics' provided an opportunity for new Jewish self-reflection but also presented new problems. Pereyra and Sarphati both conceived of politics in terms of the 'reason of state' as a necessary but low worldly activity in some ways inherently opposed to purely religious behaviour, but at the same time identified Jewish law and/or lay communal rule as divine politics. These stances and contradictions paralleled those of Christian thinkers but dealt with factors particular to Judaism such as the challenges of free political and religious action in exile. Both saw Jewish politics as politics par excellence.

Chapter 7, 'History', turns the spotlight on Orobio's discussion of biblical history and Barrios's all-encompassing communal history to explore how they treated the exilic Jewish community in the light of a divine narrative of universal history. They both made use of conceptions of popular rule, employing historiographical and philosophical contrasts between monarchy and republicanism to tell new stories of the Jewish past and future. Orobio did so by identifying in the tribe of Judah a biblical republic apart from that of Moses, providing a more apt analogue to the Kahal Kadosh. In a twist on a Sabbatian messianic vision, Barrios interpreted the community's politics, which were based in halakhic terms on the underlying authority of its members to govern themselves, as a step in the divinely ordained progress of Jews through history towards democracy, and thereby towards divine union.

The perspectives explored in Chapter 7, wherein Jews not only had politics in exile but also considered it part of a universal political history, bear on a central thread of modern Jewish historiography that attributes a perceived lack of historical thinking among premodern Jews to their lack of an authentic or fully realized political existence in exile. Historians like Yosef Hayim Yerushalmi, Amos Funkenstein, and others zeroed in on the seventeenth century as a time of transition in this regard. The Conclusion brings the voices of Amsterdam's Kahal Kadosh into conversation with ones that have become central to Jewish thought in our times. Their embrace of both worldly politics and the religious historiography of remembrance sets them as a bridge between approaches seen as typically medieval and typically modern. Amsterdam's Portuguese Jews were able to position themselves at the centre of world history, rather than on its margins, in part because Jewish politics were not yet shaped by the modern dilemmas that defined them for the likes of Yerushalmi or Baron.

The particular way of conceptualizing diaspora community that was put forward by Spinoza's Jewish peers was unknown a generation earlier, and it was no longer current a generation later. Nor could it have arisen anywhere else, having been stimulated by a unique matrix of local conditions and communal traits. Before the end of the century, new themes took hold in European politics, Sabbatianism moved definitively away from geopolitical realism, and the Kahal Kadosh began to decentralize and diversify, with the Mahamad becoming less powerful. Religious toleration became a byword. The 1688 Glorious Revolution put the Dutch William III on the English throne, leading to the decline of Amsterdam in favour of London as an international mercantile and intellectual hub. As time went on, power shifted in the Atlantic in the age of revolutions, and Jewish Enlightenment thinkers deliberately dismantled the ideal of a community with independent political authority. The notion of a Jewish commonwealth in exile would be derided as a 'state within a state'. However, the full flowering of such a vision over two critical decades had a lasting impact. It had set up a new ideal image of Jewish self-government, thereafter perceived as traditional, and against which later transformations would be judged.

ONE

COMMUNITY

THE CONSTITUTION OF
THE KAHAL KADOSH

IN THE AUTUMN OF 1638, soon after the High Holy Days had passed, a
committee representing the three Jewish congregations in Amsterdam
drafted articles of unification. The document was titled *Acordos*, or 'Agreements', in their lingua franca of Portuguese. The forty-two proposed articles laid out a system of government for the new community, which was to
be called the Kahal Kadosh Talmud Torah. The committee agreed that
the document should be read aloud in all three existing synagogues on the
following sabbath, initiating a public discussion period. Five months later,
in time for Passover 1639, the articles (with one minor amendment) were
'approved by all the people' and duly ratified. According to the closing
words of the document, it was signed by the 'heads of households' of 'the
entire nation', signifying that they accepted the agreements.[1] Pages filled
with personal signatures follow the text (see Fig. 1) in a striking record of
individual commitment and group accord.

Less than two decades earlier, the Mayflower Compact famously
cemented the will of some Puritans arriving in Massachusetts to 'covenant
and combine ourselves together into a civil body politic for our better
ordering and preservation'. The *Acordos* reflected a similar intent. Although
the Amsterdam Jewish agreement lacked the explicitly political framing
of the Mayflower pact, the founders of the Kahal Kadosh Talmud Torah
also fashioned a unified civic body to order and govern themselves by common agreement. The *Acordos* established the formal lay government of a
society based on shared interests and mutual commitment, undergirded by

---

[1] SA 334, 19, fo. 5ᵛ (dated 28 Adar II 5399). At the beginning of November (6 Kislev 5399),
one of the original articles was amended. *Acordos* is a direct Portuguese translation of the
Hebrew *haskamot*, a typical name for communal enactments in the Sephardi diaspora.

religious authority. As such, the Kahal Kadosh was legible to its members and others as an association both religious and political in nature.

What models, traditions, and concepts did the founders of the Kahal Kadosh deploy in creating this new entity? What does it say about the nature and status of Jewish community in the Dutch context? And how did the leaders and members understand the significance of this agreement? A close reading of the *Acordos* will show what its authors gleaned from traditions of Jewish self-government and European collectives alike. It will reveal the material, religious, and political aims of the founders. The community that they designed had as much in common with local polities (such as incorporated towns and Puritan 'godly republics') as with other forms of community (such as confraternities, guilds, companies, or even churches) in early modern Europe. The *Acordos* and the community they established were shaped by Jewish traditions crossed with patterns of community-building common to the new Protestant republicanism, which the Spanish and Portuguese Jews were now absorbing.

Formative Years

It was not obvious or automatic that the Spanish and Portuguese Jews in Amsterdam would organize themselves in the way they did. The system codified in the *Acordos* did not adhere unquestioningly to existing models; it wholeheartedly embraced some traditions but it also made some pointed changes to the status quo. Nor did the Kahal Kadosh Talmud Torah emerge whole-cloth. On the contrary, the document was the result of decades of evolution, experimentation, negotiation, and intentional self-fashioning, as the population grew from a few crypto-Jews and private prayer groups into a single, organized, empowered body.

Nearly all of the Jews in Amsterdam up to the 1630s were converso emigrants from Spain and Portugal, who had little direct experience of lived Judaism before their arrival. Though some had observed crypto-Jewish practices, almost none had participated in an open Jewish community. Furthermore, Amsterdam lacked an existing Jewish population. The newcomers did not lack help; they worked with experienced leaders such as Joseph Pardo from Salonika (via Venice), the German Jew Saul Levi Morteira, and, at the very start, Uriel Halevi from Hamburg-Altona, so their activities were not wholly improvised or uninformed. Still, whatever

Jewish life the new Jews would build in Amsterdam, they would build from scratch.

The first to arrive were tentative, unsure whether or how they would be permitted to establish Jewish worship. If Amsterdam had been a different place, their community might have looked much like the ones in southern France, which remained for generations in a limbo of unstable and partial recognition of their Jewishness. But Amsterdam during the time of the Dutch revolt against Spain received the new Jews differently. A foundation myth of the community, recorded in a member's chronicle much later, tells of a Jewish prayer group being denounced to the police by its Dutch neighbours. According to the story, the Calvinists were delighted to find that the pious Iberians were Jews—in their eyes, bearers of true witness to Scripture—and not secret Catholics, whom they feared and detested on both religious and political grounds.[2]

As others have pointed out, like any myth this tale reveals more about later attitudes than about actual historical events;[3] but it does encapsulate the dynamic atmosphere of Amsterdam during this era. Dutch citizens actively remade and negotiated their social and political culture, which included communities and authorities ranging from local trade unions, churches, and towns to patrician family networks and international churches —not to mention the separate provinces, their evolving alliance in the new republic, and the effort to secure independence from the Spanish, which was not concluded until 1648. Throughout the period in which the Jewish community was growing and evolving, therefore, so were Amsterdam itself—even literally, with the construction and expansion of urban infrastructure—and the Dutch Republic.

Accordingly, permission to reside and openly practise Judaism was relatively ad hoc at the start.[4] Those Jews who gained admission to nearby cities around the same time did so by negotiating official agreements with the local governments, in the manner of most early modern Jewish settlers. Such agreements in localities surrounding Amsterdam were informed by

---

[2] The story appears in Daniel Levi de Barrios, 'Casa de Jacob', an essay within his *Triumpho*.

[3] See Bodian, *Hebrews*, 20–2; Swetschinski, *Reluctant Cosmopolitans*, 169–72; and Vlessing, 'New Light'.

[4] On Amsterdam's toleration of the Jewish community overall, see Swetschinski, *Reluctant Cosmopolitans*, 8–53, and Bodian, *Hebrews*, 53–75. On Dutch toleration, see Israel, 'The Intellectual Debate', and B. Kaplan, '"Dutch" Religious Tolerance'; for a comparison with toleration of Portuguese Jews elsewhere, see Cooperman, 'Amsterdam'.

the (mainly theoretical) recommendations that the Dutch legal scholar Hugo Grotius (1583–1645) put forth for the basis of Jewish toleration. In Alkmaar Jews were granted only private worship. In Hamburg, Jewish negotiators rejected a charter offering those same limitations.[5] In Amsterdam, on the other hand, no such permission or set of terms was ever officially set down and, instead, a de facto toleration evolved, as local laws and rulings on specific cases increasingly acknowledged open Jewish practice.[6]

Diverging from centuries of tradition regarding Jewish residence in European locales, Amsterdam's leaders apparently saw Jewish membership in Christian society in new terms, essentially rejecting the premiss that Jews could only reside there as a distinct group and by special agreement. Although they were not totally unconstrained, Amsterdam's Jews enjoyed a high degree of social and economic acceptance, a circumstance that, along with the lack of a conditional residence permit, has made their status appear precociously modern.[7]

Despite such potential for integration, the Spanish and Portuguese Jews gravitated towards discrete social organization and strong self-government. In the thirty or so years from the start of the seventeenth century, the immigrants organized themselves into two, and then three, formal congregations, connected by kinship or class. These congregations began as prayer quorums meeting in private homes, eventually taking on a more formal institutional structure and coalescing into organizations with dedicated communal spaces, property (books, furnishings, etc.), paid rabbis, elected lay leaders, and by-laws. In 1622 the three institutions established a central council, forming a confederation. Continuing the tendency towards centralization and systematization, the confederation gradually gained power relative to the individual congregations, a process that would culminate in total unification as a single congregation when the Kahal Kadosh Talmud Torah was established in 1639.[8]

---

[5] Haarlem then offered them public worship but only if fifty families would relocate there, a condition that never materialized. See de Wilde, 'Offering Hospitality', 401–2 and 424, and Huussen, 'The Legal Position'.

[6] See Swetschinski, *Reluctant Cosmopolitans*, 10–15.

[7] On prejudicial treatment, see Swetschinski, *Reluctant Cosmopolitans*, 20–4. Adam Sutcliffe questions the 'quasi-utopic inter-ethnic social ease that is so widely associated with Sephardic life in seventeenth-century Amsterdam' ('Imagining Amsterdam', 89). On the perception of their status as modern, see Y. Kaplan, 'An Alternative Path', 3–8.

[8] Much more detail about the era of early congregational establishment is laid out in Bodian, *Hebrews*, 44–9, and Swetschinski, *Reluctant Cosmopolitans*, 172–87. The first congregation, Bet

A closer look at the period of evolution leading up to 1639 gives a more detailed sense of how and why unification was achieved. The central council was first formed in 1622 with the specific charge of administering an import tax (*imposta*) across the three congregations. This fiscal role was justified in terms that made clear a wider intent. The preamble of the board's charter cites 'affairs that are common and necessary for the nation and its preservation [*conservação*]', with lay leaders agreeing that 'the income would go towards the common good and general benefit of the nation . . . for the greater glory and praise of our Lord'.[9] Thus the establishment of a confederated structure was described in grand terms as supporting the 'common good' and 'preservation' of the entire 'nation', using key words in early modern political speech.[10]

Further on, the *imposta* board by-laws clarify that the common good was especially connected to social welfare: 'the principal intent and foundation of this *imposta* is for us to relieve ourselves of the excessive expense that we have with the poor of our Portuguese and Spanish nation'.[11] Its authority in this regard was not limited to collecting and spending funds for poor relief; since a significant method for dealing with poor migrants was to prevent them from settling there by forwarding them on to other communities, the arrogation of poverty amelioration to the central council also gave it de facto authority over admission to the community, at least for people without means. This process, which was called *encaminhamiento* and occupies Articles 22–9 of the *imposta* board's by-laws, would have been impossible without an overarching entity able to speak for the entire local population.[12]

Jacob, named after Jacob Tirado, received donations of ritual objects and, at least in 1610, services were apparently held in Tirado's home. In 1612/13 he was referred to as a '*parnas* of the Portuguese Nation' (Bodian, *Hebrews*, 45).

[9] SA 334, 13, fo. 1 (24 Shevat 5382/4 Feb. 1622).

[10] See Y. Kaplan, 'Political Concepts', who noted that 'preservation' (or 'conservation', *conservação*) was part of Iberian political discourse; the equivalent term was also used in English, French, Latin, etc., as in the Mayflower Compact quoted above. The 'common good' was, of course, an analogue of the 'commonwealth', on which more below. Later in the document the intended usage of the funds is defined similarly broadly: 'From the income of this *imposta* all of the common matters of the nation for its good conservation will be attended to' (Article 19; SA, 334, 13, fo. 2ᵛ).

[11] Article 22; SA, 334, 13, fo. 3. Article 21 also set a monthly contribution to the almsmen of Amsterdam in support of the non-Jewish poor, 'in the name of the entire nation'.

[12] Levie Bernfeld, *Poverty*, 14–15, 41–6, 78. Poor relief justified the creation of the *imposta* board not only pragmatically but also increasingly rhetorically. See ibid. 158–86, esp. 175–7.

Similarly, the council enforced regulations that were being flouted by members who could move freely among congregations to avoid punishment. The board could also choose whether to intervene with Dutch authorities in the case of a member's arrest, if it was found to 'harm the nation' and hence to be a shared concern.[13] Although the board's authority was ostensibly fiscal, in reality it was an umbrella government, albeit a limited one that left most administration to its constituent congregations. It is worth noting that these documents variously use the terms 'congregation' (*congrega* or *congregação*), 'synagogue' (*sinagoga*), and *kahal* to refer to a member organization.

Over time, the power of the *imposta* board expanded yet more, and along with it, questions about its use of Jewish, mercantile, and Dutch law. In 1633, a new juridical system was drafted to handle disputes between individual members uniformly across all three congregations, aiming to 'make a compromise as much as possible between our law and the judgement of the nations' and also 'admitting the mercantile style inasmuch as it does not expressly contradict our holy law'.[14] At the same time, a committee was formed to revise the by-laws of the *imposta* board itself.[15] Neither plan appears to have been formally implemented. However, the lay board's records for the same year reveal a new insistence on its authority to impose a *ḥerem*, or rabbinic ban of excommunication, for violations of its rules;[16] and around the same time they record discussions among themselves and

---

Cf. Swetschinski, *Reluctant Cosmopolitans*, 19. On provision for charity as an exercise of authority, see D. Kaplan, *Patrons*.

[13] Article 31: 'And no person who is excluded from any one of the synagogues will be admitted to another without entirely satisfying the penalty that he owes to the *imposta* in his *kahal*; or if he leaves of his own accord, without first paying everything he owes.' SA 334, 13, fo. 4. Article 19: 'Private [i.e. individual] cases that arise and harm the nation may also be held to be common.' On Jewish communities practising diplomacy, see Mittleman, *Scepter*, 42 n. 1; Graff, *Separation*; and Biale, *Power and Powerlessness*, 56. On the authority to speak for the community arrogated to the Mahamad in Venice and the communities that followed it, see Israel, *Diasporas*, 78–9.

[14] The quotations are from Articles 6 and 9 of the proposed system; SA 334, 13, fos. 89–90. As reasons for the creation of the system, it lists promoting the observance of the holy law and avoiding 'continually molesting the *Senhores* of this city with such prolix disputes'. SA 334, 13, fo. 88. The adjudication system as a whole is in SA 334, 13, fos. 88–91.

[15] The committee formation is recorded at SA 334, 13, fo. 111.

[16] The *imposta* board by-laws claim the right to punish by means of exclusion anyone not on the council who purports to speak for the nation (Article 30, SA 334, 13, fo. 4). However, the punishment is called a *berakhah*, rather than *ḥerem*, here and in some other places. The change in terminology might, I suggest, reflect a new, stronger, claim of religious authority.

with Dutch authorities about how to handle criminal or troublesome activity among their members.[17] These are the documents of a government
working to set the extent, boundaries, and terms of its authority along with
its relationship to religious law.

These formative years set the stage for the ratification of the *Acordos*
in 1639 and reveal issues that the new constitution tried to solve. A few
themes from this period would define the system established in the *Acordos*
and remain central in communal affairs for most of the century. First, communal affairs exhibited a tension between multiplicity and unity, especially
in the tug of war between individual congregations and the ties that bound
them, including their shared sense of ethnicity as the *nação* and their collective practical needs. Despite the legalistic by-laws and clear statement of
the powers of the *imposta* board, a clear distinction between the umbrella
government and the congregations was elusive. Was there one community,
or were there three? In rabbinic terms, were they all together one *kahal*
(assembly or congregation) or *tsibur* (public body), and what was the relationship between a *kahal* and a lay council? Could individuals move freely
between congregations? Who would be held responsible for the poor, or
for troublemakers, vagrants, or heretics—one person, one congregation, or
the entire population of Jews? How?[18]

Inherent in this tension—and explicit in the documents—was a second
question: that of who might wield the power to discipline in the form of the
ḥerem. The *ḥerem* is a halakhic construct typically understood as excommunication, and deployed in many premodern Jewish contexts in the form
of social exclusion. Individuals in good standing were not permitted to
interact in any way with a banned person, causing personal and economic
embarrassment and difficulty. As such it was a social matter, and in Amsterdam, as elsewhere, a *ḥerem* would often be imposed only temporarily, to
impel a person to cease his or her transgression and make amends.[19] On
the other hand it also had—or could have—a spiritual dimension whereby

---

[17] For 1636 the records include talks with city magistrates about young Jewish men disturbing the peace. SA 334, 13, fo. 123ff.

[18] The uneven distribution of the burden of the poor on the different congregations was
cited more than once as a reason for unification, including by the burgomasters of Amsterdam
when they affirmed the Kahal Kadosh Talmud Torah's authority in 1670. See Levie Bernfeld,
Poverty, 14–15, 78; ead., 'Financing Poor Relief'; and Swetschinski, *Reluctant Cosmopolitans*,
187.

[19] The *ḥerem* was a blunt tool, as likely to alienate already marginal members as to pull them
in. See Y. Kaplan, 'Social Functions'.

the ban was pronounced together with dark curses on the violator's soul and ritual removal not only from the living social body but also eternally from the Jewish people.[20]

In Amsterdam and in the affairs of early modern European Jews more generally, the ban was often a flash point among rabbis, lay leaders, and communal affairs. As the most severe punishment a Jew could impose on another Jew in most places, it was natural that it would appear frequently in an age of increasing differentiation, encounter, and social and religious transformation. It was particularly prone to dispute because of the way it straddled rabbinic and lay domains, and also because it embodied the dual binds of semi-autonomy and dispersion, representing totalizing authority within a particular Jewish realm, and yet ultimately subject to external limits. In the particular context of the Spanish and Portuguese efforts to govern themselves in Amsterdam before 1639, the issues that arose concerning the *ḥerem* included whether and on what basis lay leaders—be they leaders of a congregation or members of an overarching council—could make use of this sanction. What rabbinic authority was needed, and which individuals were obligated to comply?

The third theme of note in the pre-unification period is attention to ownership and provision of property. That includes buildings and spaces, fittings and paraphernalia, and money (taxes, dues, and fines), along with a more general sense that economic mutuality justified and scaffolded the collective. Even before the *imposta* board was formed in 1622, shared property marked each congregation's boundaries, and a universal tax assessment in 1614 to purchase ground for a cemetery was one of the first organized population-wide efforts; this tax applied even to those who were not officially members of any congregation, establishing concretely that members of the nation were, like it or not, part of a collective.[21] Property was a significant marker of community both in Jewish tradition and in the Dutch political context. Taxes, fines, damages, and the like were the driving factors in some of the most important rabbinic precedents for thinking about lay rule. On the Dutch side, the right to amass and spend funds was critical to Dutch legal distinctions between a religious corporate society (at that time forbidden) and a minority church (allowed if understood as private).

---

[20] Spinoza's ban is recorded with such curses. See Introduction, n. 37.

[21] The assessment suggested that the population as a whole had the authority to tax its members. See Swetschinski, *Reluctant Cosmopolitans*, 12, and Bodian, *Hebrews*, 47.

One Nation, One Congregation, One Community, One Ban

A new communal system was established in 1639, and the same three inter-related issues that had driven earlier developments—multiplicity and unity, the use of the *ḥerem*, and fiscal affairs—lay at the heart of the unification. Most glaringly, the *Acordos* upended the arrangement that had been in place since the establishment of the *imposta* board in 1622. Instead of a confeder-ated structure of three individual synagogues under a central council, the new constitution established one single body and government. It elim-inated the inconsistencies and complications of the old decentralized system, incorporating control over the ban, fiscal affairs, and religious assembly into one lay-led body.

The *Acordos* enumerated the aims, boundaries, and fundamental prin-ciples of the new community, beginning with a preamble citing the author-ity on which it was based.[22] In it, the drafting committee recorded that it had been 'authorized' by a document written by the rabbi Joseph Pardo and 'signed by the nation, approving its union and that of the congrega-tions'. The committee also noted its intent to consult with the magistrates of Amsterdam during the discussion period.[23] The *Acordos* thus indicated from the outset that communal authority was based on a combination of the inherent authority of its members as a group, the consent of a higher political authority, and some form of rabbinic guidance. The structure that the *Acordos* established was consistent with such an understanding.

The first article of the *Acordos* addressed the consolidation of property, declaring: 'First, in unanimous agreement we resolve and order that all of the property owned at present by the three *ke[h]ilot K* [pl. of *kahal kadosh*], Bet Jacob, Neve Shalom, and Bet Israel, will be common, and from all [there will be] one, without division or any separation.' This first sentence prioritized common ownership as a, if not the, defining principle of the

---

[22] SA 334, 19, fo. 1. This is the first paginated folio page but it appears after more than fifty pages of indexes. The book in which the *Acordos* and the Mahamad's subsequent decrees were recorded provides a clear example of an organized system of record-keeping maintained by each successive recording secretary over many decades, complete with cross-references and evidence that earlier decisions were edited when directly affected by later ones. It thus has char-acteristics of a book of laws as much as a book of minutes.

[23] The reference to the magistrates reveals a little-noted element of Dutch involvement in the unification of Amsterdam's three Jewish congregations, a process that has mainly been seen as independent and inward-facing.

new body. Although the language emphasized consensus and cohesion, the unification of membership (as opposed to assets) was only stipulated in the second article.[24] The attention to property perpetuated the conceptual basis for the confederation that had existed from 1622 to 1639, revolving around taxation and poor relief, and expanded it to convey a sense of shared wealth. The common holding of property was a vital component of an institutionalized community as they construed it.

Pointing out that material interests were central to the *Acordos* does not reduce community-building to a mere matter of mercenary utility. On the contrary, fiscal concerns dovetail with the legal and social priorities that have long been understood as constitutive of meaningful community and of Jewish governing authority. Rabbinic precedents from the Talmud through medieval responsa connected the authority to govern with the authority to impose fines and levy taxes. The oft-cited talmudic statement 'the residents of a city may fix weights and measures, prices and wages, and inflict penalties for the infringement of their rules'[25] anchored such political logic. Financial interdependence was an important component of much medieval and early modern Jewish communal organization, and medieval communities have sometimes been compared to guilds, monopolies, and tax farms.[26] The growth of medieval Jewish communities has likewise been connected to the commercial dimension of medieval cities.[27] Certainly, the acquisition and regulation of shared material necessities, including kosher meat, matzah, and *mikveh* (ritual bath), formed a symbolic framework for Jewish collectivization and cooperation. Poor relief was another pillar of communal activities. In the Kahal Kadosh, it was also explicitly recognized as a core principle underlying the need for unity among Jews, including in the form of obedience to communal regulations and leaders.[28] The phrases 'the unity and conservation of the *kahal*' and 'the feeding of the poor'

---

[24] SA 334, 19, fo. 1. Perhaps because of this, the first scholar to analyse the document called it a 'merger agreement'. Wiznitzer, 'Merger Agreement'.

[25] BT *Bava batra* 8b, Tosefta *Bava metsia* 11: 23. See, among many other discussions, Kanarfogel, 'Unanimity', 79. These sources and others are published in translation with brief commentary in Walzer et al. (eds.), *The Jewish Political Tradition*, i. 386–98.

[26] Zimmer, *Jewish Synods*, 84–8, for example, and Simonsohn, *History of the Jews*, 322–4.

[27] Baer, 'Origins', 28–9. See also Woolf, *Fabric*, 24 n. 8, and Rabinowitz, *The Herem Hayyishub*. Social historians of early modern Jewish life have also emphasized the importance of the fiscal responsibilities of the community. See Zimmer, *Harmony and Discord*, 4, 30–66.

[28] This came to be part of the community's renown, and it was a central focus of rhetorical and practical efforts to foster intracommunal charitability. Levie Bernfeld, *Poverty*, 159–86.

became almost interchangeable shorthand for the essential mission, boundaries, and good government of the community: in other words, they denoted the community's common good and its common wealth.

Article 1 of the new constitution continues: 'Nevertheless, in this book where these agreements of unification are written, an inventory will be made of the property of each one of the congregations separately, so that we will know what belonged to each one in case we should ever be compelled to leave this land, may God prevent it.' Such an inventory was indeed inscribed in the record book, giving it pride of place as one of the first acts of the new administration,[29] poignantly expressing the sense of uncertainty that Portuguese Jews still felt in Amsterdam in 1638. Their failsafe plan not only acknowledged the potential impermanence of communal arrangements but also reveals a cognizance of the independence that existing communities were giving up, even at the moment of unification. Such loss, like unity, was couched here in terms of property.

The pooling of resources formalized a perceived (if fragile) sense of mutuality, recognizing and deepening the way members depended on each other and inherently affected each other. Article 2 reflects the same principle, now expressed in the setting of institutional boundaries. It begins by declaring 'that only one single congregation will be made in this city of Amsterdam, into which will be gathered and reconciled all three of the present ones'.[30] The creation of an altogether new collectivity instead of new rules for the existing ones reflected a practical need for clear boundaries and strong discipline. A single organization would be more easily managed by a centralized authority,[31] and it also served other immediate pragmatic ends, including the elimination of disputes among congregations.[32]

In order for these aims to be fully realized, the community needed to be able to wield the ban (ḥerem). Article 2 goes on:

And that with all the punishments or bans [pennas o Heremse] that are appropriate, following the style of Venice, it is prescribed that at no time may there be in

---

[29] As time went on, the original divisions became less visible, but in the Sabbatian era they came to haunt the community, as disputes of that era were based, again, on property, fiscal affairs, and taxation. See Chapter 3 below.   [30] SA 334, 19, fo. 1.

[31] Many placed themselves in marginal positions with respect to the Jewish community. See Y. Kaplan, 'Social Functions', and id., 'Deviance and Excommunication', 103–4. This problem by no means disappeared with the new arrangement, but it became more straightforward.

[32] Swetschinski, Reluctant Cosmopolitans, 15; Wiznitzer, 'Merger Agreement', 110.

this city or in its district any [other] congregation, nor may people who are separated or who desire to separate themselves from the congregation meet together to pray in a minyan, with the exception of those who pray in the houses of newlyweds or mourners, or those who in other respects remain subjects [*sujeitos*] and continue in the congregation, and for whom it is necessary to pray together one or more times; and those who are separated from the congregation who desire to meet with a minyan will be understood as going against this Article and they will be proceeded against with all the appropriate punishments and rigour for what they committed, and will be placed under the ban [*porpostos em Kerem*[33]] and separated from the nation [*apartados da nação*].

The urgency of Article 2's tone testifies to the perceived perils of separatism—particularly the separatism of groups, not of recalcitrant, heretical, or otherwise marginal individuals. The framers defined the unity they prescribed simultaneously in religious and political terms. Identifying the collectivity as a congregation, indeed as the sole congregation allowed in Amsterdam, Article 2 emphasizes that the congregation as a whole was the only setting in which group prayer should be organized. It also called members of such a congregation 'subjects', and in the same breath announced the community's authority to punish, articulating the authors' sense that belonging in this 'congregation' was as much a matter of political belonging as religious participation.

Article 2, banning separate congregations and even prayer quorums, effected a distinct and deliberate change from the confederate model that had governed Amsterdam's Spanish and Portuguese Jewish community organization since 1622. In fact, it was a departure from the common practice of most European Jewish communities, among which it was not the norm to insist on a single unitary synagogue and or to prohibit private regular prayer quorums. In most large urban locales, multiple Jewish congregations or synagogues existed side by side, usually with some overarching structure, just as they did in Amsterdam until 1639.[34] In both large and small populations, it was also common for regular prayer services to take place in various domestic and other spaces as needed. Even though such

---

[33] So *ḥerem* is spelled in this document.

[34] Livorno was an exception, as community members were prohibited from forming separate prayer groups, though in actuality such groups met informally. I know of no study of this question across communities, but it is widely acknowledged in passing that Amsterdam's unitary system diverged from the norm. See Swetschinski, *Reluctant Cosmopolitans*, 174; Wiznitzer, 'Merger Agreement', 110; and Israel, *Diasporas*, 77.

groupings could lead to conflict over access, belonging, and ownership, they were not treated as an inherent threat to the unity of the whole body of Jews as suggested by the strong language of Article 2 of Amsterdam's *Acordos*.[35]

How can this innovation be explained? A clue lies in the way Article 2 cited the *ḥerem*, twice. Such prominence of the ban at the start of the constitution speaks to the particular way collective authority was understood to function in this community. The *Acordos* relied on a typical halakhic distinction between individual and group prayer that gives a special status to a group of at least ten qualified people, understood as a *kahal* or *tsibur*—technical categories with bearing on the authority of a group to coerce an individual or a minority.[36] The political meaning of such a group as it operated in Amsterdam's Kahal Kadosh followed the views of the medieval Spanish rabbi Moses Nahmanides, who grounded communal government in a theory of collective oaths combined with the authority of townspeople to enforce decrees made among them.[37] He theorized the *ḥerem* not specifically as a punishment of exclusion but, in line with its biblical and earlier rabbinic origins, as a kind of oath or vow. For Nahmanides, a *ḥerem* was a *kahal*'s collective vow to comply with ordinances, a commitment made sacrosanct and inviolable by its parallel to the divine covenant. Those who violated this imagined vow could then be subject to the punishment of exclusion. In this view, a group of at least ten halakhically eligible people were able to 'create a *ḥerem*', meaning, as a group they acquired the authority to enforce a decree applying to all of them. A decree created by such a group would become binding on individuals as though each one had personally sworn an oath to follow it.[38]

Nahmanides' treatment is relevant because in this framework the *ḥerem* was an underlying pact of obedience and collectivization. It was a proactive

---

[35] See Liberles, 'On the Threshold of Modernity', 71–2, and D. Kaplan, 'Communal Places', 328. In the Ottoman empire, prohibitions on synagogue-building often dictated that congregations and their prayers had to be located inside private homes. See Arad, 'When the Home Becomes a Shrine', 59–68.

[36] A systematic account of rabbinic thought about the conditions that allow a group to compel an individual or minority is found in Elon, 'On Power and Authority'.

[37] Based on Tosefta *Bava metsia* 11: 23: 'Townspeople can compel each other to build a synagogue and to purchase scrolls of the Torah and the prophets for themselves. Townspeople are authorized to stipulate regarding prices, measures, and the pay of laborers. . . . And they are authorized to enforce their decree.' Translation in Walzer et al. (eds.), *The Jewish Political Tradition*, i. 388.   [38] See Zohar, 'Civil Society'.

form of general authority rather than a reactive punishment. And it was based, at least theoretically, on mutual agreement—exactly like the agreement expressed by the members of the Kahal Kadosh in signing the *Acordos*. It offered a conception of how a *kahal* could also be a political body, a group of members whose collective will could be enforced through sanctions, as the collective was constituted by the aggregation of individuals sworn to unanimity. Admittedly, the *Acordos* themselves do not contain any explicit reference to a halakhic basis for the communal system. However, Isaac Aboab da Fonseca, one of the four rabbis appointed to serve the community upon unification in 1639, and certainly involved in the founding, later made this justification clear. In 1680, writing in response to a debate that was then raging about communal authority, Aboab referred to the signatures on the *Acordos* as oaths that collectively constituted a communal *ḥerem*.[39] With explicit reference to Nahmanides and a few other rabbinic authorities, the Amsterdam rabbi's comments strongly suggest that a medieval Sephardi justification of lay rule was operative in the founding.[40]

The inner logic of the *Acordos* was that the authority of the Kahal Kadosh depended on the community (in the political sense, the body of members) and the congregation (a religious body) being coterminous. The authors of the *Acordos* therefore only permitted separate group prayer in certain temporary ritual situations, such as those surrounding a funeral or a wedding. Article 2 specifically emphasized that, even in those situations, group prayer must take place in a private home—following the Dutch distinction between public and private worship—and that those who formed such a minyan nevertheless agreed to 'remain subjects' of the wider community.

The threat inherent in separate group prayer, to which Article 2 responded, was not merely that of social splintering and infighting. It was recognized as a politically existential threat, since a quorum also had the potential to constitute a new community by authorizing a new *ḥerem*. From the perspective of the founders of Amsterdam's Kahal Kadosh, the previous (confederative) structure had complicated a simple halakhic model in which a *kahal*/congregation could enact rules that obligated all of its members, by virtue of being a *kahal*. In a confederation, was there one *kahal*

---

[39] Aboab, *Exortação*.

[40] Menachem Lorberbaum has argued that the views of Nahmanides and some others near his historical milieu facilitated a distinctly political arena within the community. See Lorberbaum, *Politics*, 106–11.

or were there several? If the former, then what authority, if any, did the individual congregations or synagogues have? If the latter, then on what basis could the community (as a confederation of *kehilot*, rather than a *kahal* in and of itself) punish using the ban? In resolving this quandary, Amsterdam's leaders moved away from the usual model. In its first two articles, the constitution enacted more than a simple merger: its transformation of the communal structure from multiplicity to unity was crucial because it enabled a newly strict one-to-one correlation between the domain of the lay council and the halakhically significant domain of the quorum or *kahal*.

One city with a confederated model similar to Amsterdam's between 1622 and 1639 was Venice. In fact, Venice's Jewish community is often seen as a kind of elder sister to that of Amsterdam, as two of its early rabbis, Joseph Pardo and Saul Levi Morteira, had lived there, and the more established community continued to offer guidance. Seeming to suggest that the Kahal Kadosh was thus modelled after the Venetian Jewish system, Article 2 prominently cites the 'style of Venice'. And yet this reference comes in support of the very move that caused Amsterdam to diverge from the Venetian model. The mention of Venice cannot be read as supporting the communal structure laid out in the *Acordos* as a whole. Instead, it refers only to the use of the *ḥerem* established by this specific article. In fact, it invoked a controversial stance only recently adopted by Venetian Jewish lay leaders, that the Small Assembly—the umbrella governing council— had the authority to set rules for the use of the *ḥerem*, superseding the authority of the individual synagogues and rabbinic academies within the community.

Jewish Venice in the 1620s and 1630s had been plagued by internal conflict over the ban, rabbinic authority, and the extent of Jewish communal autonomy with respect to the Venetian state. In the midst of an investigation by Venetian officials into Jewish self-government, some Jews banned and denounced others, at times even reporting them to the Christian authorities for claiming undue authority. As David Malkiel showed in his reconstruction of this episode, at stake for the lay leaders of the Small Assembly was not a denial of rabbinic authority per se, but rather a distinction between communally authorized rabbis and those affiliated with some subgroup like a synagogue or academy within the community.[41] The Venetian innovation, and the backlash to it, must now be acknowledged as

---

[41] See Malkiel, *A Separate Republic*, 38ff., 168–85.

part of the background of the formation of Amsterdam's Kahal Kadosh. It reflected competition between community (as a whole) and congregations (individually) just as much as between lay leaders and rabbis. Similarly, here in Article 2 of Amsterdam's new constitution, the *ḥerem* is claimed in no uncertain terms as a prerogative of the indivisible community. In fact, Article 2 does not mention either rabbis or lay leaders. Instead, the main thrust here is to specify that the *community as a whole*—the newly formed Kahal Kadosh Talmud Torah, and not any subgroup or external body of Spanish and Portuguese Jews—could wield the *ḥerem*.

Next, the *Acordos* specify exactly who would make up the population of members, or subjects, of the new community. Article 3 stipulates 'that this congregation is for Jews of the Portuguese and Spanish nation who are at present in this city and who newly arrive here, and that any Jewish people of other nations who come here may be admitted if the reason seems good to the Mahamad at the time'.[42] In other words, even though the *Acordos* were ratified by a particular group of members present at the moment of unification, the Kahal Kadosh was meant to automatically incorporate future members of the *nação* in Amsterdam as well.[43] Clearly, the role of ethnicity or nation is central here, as we would expect for a group that is known for emphasizing its distinctive identity.[44] At the same time, with the formation of the Kahal Kadosh, national identity became merely one component part. Instead of being purely a matter of national origin, membership in the formal collectivity now also signalled physical, geographical locality and other forms of mutuality.

In addition, Article 3 stipulated that Kahal Kadosh members would be 'Jews of the Portuguese and Spanish nation'. It says 'Jews', not 'men' or 'Hebrews', clearly connoting religious affiliation and not only ethnic identity. On the other hand, membership was not solely a matter of voluntary enrolment, but rather included all such people in the area. Articles 2 and 3

[42] SA 334, 19, fo. 1. The phrasing here elides a difference that we might seek between 'Jews of the Portuguese nation' and 'Jews who come from the nation of Portugal'.

[43] The prohibition on extraneous prayer quorums and new congregations was made even more clear in the first set of revised by-laws produced about six months after the *Acordos* were ratified. SA 334, 19, fo. 21. Article 3 of the *Acordos* leaves open the possibility that it might include other kinds of Jews on demand. In contrast to the fear of internal division evident in Article 2, the possibility of including other Jews seems not to have been on the founders' minds here, so it should not be read primarily as an assertion of ethnic separation. On the contrary, the impact in context is inclusive rather than exclusive.

[44] See Bodian, '"Portuguese" Dowry Societies'.

tie together the nation, the congregation, and the community. Immediately afterwards, the text of the *Acordos* mentions both *kahal* and nation in one breath: 'the *kahal* and the nation shall be governed by [the new regulations]' (Article 4) and a Mahamad shall be elected 'for the administration and government of the *kahal* and nation' (Article 5). The rhetorical and in-stitutional conjoining of *kahal* and nation did away with ambiguity about belonging among a population known for its mixed identities, unstable reli-gious status, and marginal figures. Before 1639, the relationship between congregation, nation, and community—between religious ritual and law, ethnic or national identity, and formally constituted local body—was fluid. The unification brought these three circles of identity into alignment. After the *Acordos* were signed, one government was unequivocally in charge of a population defined in all three ways at once.

Leadership and Authority in the Communal System

To summarize, the first three articles of the *Acordos* collectivize congrega-tional property and worship, set the relationship between individuals and the whole as one of subjection and obedience, and name the population to which this arrangement applies. They address fundamental components of the Kahal Kadosh: property, religion, ethnicity, and authority (in the form of *ḥerem*). Next, Article 4 establishes a governing body, the all-powerful lay leadership council called the Mahamad, a group of seven men. The first group of seven was to be selected by the constitutional committee, which consisted of representatives of the original three congregations; thereafter, half of the council would be replaced semi-annually, as new members were chosen by the Mahamad then in office.[45]

Subsequent articles prescribe various dimensions of the Mahamad's activities and its powers. Among them is Article 12:

The Mahamad will have authority and superiority over everything, and no per-son or persons may go against the resolutions taken by said Mahamad, nor sign or publish papers to oppose them, and those who do so incur the punishment

[45] Article 6: 'It will proceed in this manner, that every half year they will elect a new Mahamad to succeed them and this way each Mahamad in turn will elect the next, and all of the elections must be carried out according to the resolved practices, and done by box and ballot with five out of seven votes. And all of them must consent and sign with the majority, that which is decided by the five votes, without any opposition or contradiction.' SA 334, 19, fo. 1ᵛ.

of the *ḥerem*; because it is finally ordered and understood that the Mahamad must be supreme in the government of the nation, the community, and its dependencies.[46]

This sentence is one of the most frequently reproduced passages of any Amsterdam Sephardi text from the first half of the seventeenth century, contributing to a reception of the lay leaders as fearsome, omnipotent, and even tyrannical. It seems to grant the Mahamad unfettered authority —a move that is only compounded by the fact that this body was self-perpetuating (with each cohort of officers choosing the next) and generally populated by the moneyed elite. It seems indicative of an authoritarian, autocratic, and oligarchical regime.

However, the strict obedience due to the Mahamad obscures the place of such authority in the wider system of the Kahal Kadosh. First, it is worth reiterating that this passage is part of the document that individual members signed. When they did so, they knowingly took on an obligation to obey and respect these leaders. In the matter of free expression as in many other matters, they agreed via the *Acordos* to subsume their will within that of the group, a will that would from then on be embodied in the new leadership. For example, in Article 14 (regarding a certain tax), the *Acordos* note that 'the *kahal* gives [the Mahamad] full authority and power, submitting itself to obey it'.[47]

Further, this was not unusual, nor was it necessarily a recurrence of a Spanish and Portuguese taste for autocracy, despite a popular conception of these Jews as mired in such ancestral custom. Consensus was an important early modern political value despite, or perhaps because of, a constant chorus of disruption across communities of many types and periods. The modern notion that open, vocalized dissent is an essential right and an inherent political good was not yet on the horizon. Instead, even those who theoretically prized the active consent of the governed tended to express such consent in terms of unanimity and harmony. While individuals sometimes needed to be convinced or compelled, the assumption was, ultimately, a polity should speak with one voice and act as one body.

Thomas Hobbes wrote that to create a commonwealth is

to appoint one Man, or one Assembly of men, to beare their Person . . . and theirin to submit their Wills . . . This is more than Consent, or Concord; it is a

---

[46] Article 12. SA 334, 19, fo. 2.   [47] SA 334, 19, fo. 2ᵛ.

reall Unitie of them all, in one and the same Person, made by Covenant of every man with every man, in such manner, as if every man should say to every man, *I Authorise and give up my Right of Governing my selfe, to this Man, or to this Assembly of men*. . .[48]

The establishment in the *Acordos* of the Mahamad's superiority in every-thing reflected just such a notion of the fundamental order of a civic body in relation to its government. The idea was visually expressed in Abraham Bosse's famous 1651 cover image for Hobbes's *Leviathan* (see Fig. 2). This image was published a dozen years after the signing of the *Acordos*, but drew on elements of political culture that were common earlier in England and increasingly shared in the Dutch Republic. The frontispiece shows a giant person—the embodiment of the 'commonwealth'—made up of many smaller people. The Leviathan is not a mob but a single entity. Its voice is not a chorus in unison but rather a discrete individual voice, one that is sup-ported and empowered by the collectivity within it—but, crucially, one that surpasses and replaces it in terms of agency and government action.

Although the men of the Mahamad were the sole holders of authority, they were office-holders, not aristocrats.[49] Certainly, leadership usually fell in practice to an elite subset of community members, and tensions of class, clique, or kinship were part of the communal experience. But the Kahal Kadosh was not set up functionally as an aristocracy or even formally as an oligarchy. Rather, it asked private members to take their turns serving as officers of the community and then pass on the same responsibility. The expectation of submissive behaviour with respect to the members of the Mahamad related to the office, not the man, at least in theory.

In fact, not solely the Mahamad but the entire government of the Kahal Kadosh made ample use of offices and committees, a signature characteris-tic of many local polities and small communities in early modern Europe.[50] The Mahamad stood at the top level of an administrative structure with bureaucratic processes and departments, and though its centrality as the highest council was undeniable, its role was also normalized and mitigated by its embeddedness within that structure. The Mahamad as a body was established with explicit standards and aims; it set eligibility rules and a

---

[48] Hobbes, *Leviathan*, 120 (ch. 12).

[49] It is perhaps unnecessary to point out that the leaders were presumed to be male, and that the Kahal Kadosh as a whole was patriarchally structured. Indeed, it may have been more so than some parallel Christian civic entities. See Withington on the 'patriarchal commonwealth' in *Politics*, 195–229.   [50] Goldie, 'The Unacknowledged Republic', 153–94.

mechanism for self-perpetuation, so that the office was understood to stand in continuity, irrespective of the particular men who would fill it. After noting that the Mahamad is the final authority, Article 12 goes on to symbolically subject it to the sacred purpose of the community, stipulating that each new office-holder should take an oath of office in the direct presence of Torah scrolls, in front of an open ark, 'promising to serve in their position with truth and justice and to fear God without self-interest or spiteful damage'.[51]

It was the offices, departments, and committees of the Kahal Kadosh, and not individual leaders in a personal capacity, that constituted the communal government. The articulation of the Mahamad's superiority in Article 12 appears only after eight full articles devoted to processes, standards, qualifications, and limitations related to the council. Many of the remaining articles of the *Acordos* treat the establishment of offices beneath the Mahamad and further administrative rules and processes. As a whole, the document is occupied with the rules and procedures to be followed by the Mahamad and other officers and subcommittee members. (A set of by-laws promulgated by the first Mahamad six months later further elaborated on the system.[52]) The *Livro dos Acordos* itself, the book in which the constitution and the Mahamad's ensuing rules and judgements were recorded, became an archive, physically manifesting political structures as had become the norm among early modern states and other communities.[53] The *Acordos* also included a process by which the constitution could be amended: a committee was to be made up of six members, two deputized from each original congregation, and maintained in perpetuity, with each member who passed away or departed being replaced with another member associated with the same original congregation.[54]

---

[51] SA 334, 19, fo. 2.

[52] In compliance with Article 5 of the *Acordos*: 'Said Mahamad will then give orders, so that from the *haskamot* of the 3 congregations [*congregaconis*] and of the *imposta* they will choose as they see fit, reducing some and increasing the ones that seem better to them, so that the community [*kahal*] and nation are to be governed by them [the *haskamot*].' Ibid. 21.

[53] On changing attitudes and practices in early modern communal record-keeping, see Carlebach, 'The Early Modern Jewish Community', 176–9; Litt, *Pinkas*; and Bell, *Jewish Identity*, 45–8. Record-keeping in early modern Europe has been seen in political terms at least since Michel Foucault's *The Order of Things* and *The Archaeology of Knowledge*, and Jacques Derrida's *Archive Fever*. For an account of this literature, including on early modern religious polities and the Low Countries, see Walsham, 'The Social History of the Archive'.

[54] SA 334, 19, fo. 2.

Clearly, the communal system set in place by the *Acordos* was over-whelmingly oriented towards lay leadership. However, rabbis had their own unique and crucial place within it. Unlike the members of the Mahamad, the rabbis were not installed as office-holders, temporary and unpaid, but rather as career workers, salaried with permanent (if contin-gent) positions of employment. Therefore, they could not be seen as gover-nors or rulers of the community but rather teachers, spiritual leaders, and judges in certain types of conflict, primarily in terms of halakhic questions. There was no *office* of communal *hakham* or chief rabbi, no department of the rabbinate created in the *Acordos*; no official qualifications, term limits, or other conditions listed—and, in fact, little explicit or specific im-brication of their roles with respect to the rest of communal government. The *Acordos* treat rabbinic activity either negatively (e.g. rabbis may not contradict the Mahamad) or as quite limited and instrumental (e.g. they will give sermons and read certain halakhic decisions in the synagogue as instructed).[55] Even in the area of halakhic rulings, the Mahamad was given a tie-breaking vote.

Most striking is that control over the *herem* was absolutely in lay hands, despite the fact that the *herem* had a strong traditional association with rabbinic and religious authority. In fact, it is commonly claimed that the power of excommunication was exclusive to rabbis in premodern Europe.[56] Although that is clearly not the case here, it is significant that, in Amster-dam and in other places, rabbis were often tasked with announcing bans even when they themselves were not responsible for the decisions to im-pose them. This practice reflected a sense that the punishment of the ban, however temporal—however 'social' or 'political'—was strongly associated with religious authority.

The conclusion we may draw, as far as the *Acordos* are concerned, is that the rabbis represented the religious dimension of the *community*'s authority. The *herem* was a communal instrument: the temporal powers of lay leaders were legitimated in halakhic terms even though their deliberations, regula-

[55] Article 20: 'If any of the *hakhamim* say, maintain, or write anything in opposition to that which is resolved, with two witnesses to condemn him, he will be removed from his salaried position in the congregation and will never again be readmitted to that position'; and Article 19.

[56] See Bonfil, *Rabbis and Jewish Communities in Renaissance Italy*, 67–75, 112–15, and J. Katz, *Tradition and Crisis*, 84–6. See also Albert, 'The Rabbi and the Rebels', 173–6.

tions, and decisions were not carried out in a halakhic mode.[57] The authority of the community so drawn borrowed selectively and symbolically from the authorizing vocabularies and traditions of rabbinic authority, but never put itself under its jurisdiction. That, in itself, was not new; it is merely an example of the rabbinic justification of the authority of 'townspeople' to govern. What was innovative, I suggest, is the way the *ḥerem* was deployed to hold together a formal, institutionalized collective. The Kahal Kadosh's system harks back to medieval Spanish Jewish halakhah, but updates it for a world tending towards bureaucratic, systematized, and constitutional polities.

That clerical authority would be subsumed within a lay government may have been new for Jewish communities, but it was patently normal from a European political perspective. There, political rule had long been allied with and justified by, but not directly administered by means of, church authority, doctrine, and law. The extent to which lay rulers ought to behave in accordance with Christian principles was the central argument at the heart of Machiavellian and anti-Machiavellian debates in the sixteenth and seventeenth centuries; this debate was so much a part of early modern European culture that Amsterdam's former conversos would have understood it innately. Later on, in the time of Sabbatianism and Spinoza, community intellectuals like Abraham Pereyra and David Sarphati would take up such debates explicitly. Some heated disputes that took place in those same years are typically viewed in terms of the decline of halakhah as a binding code in Jewish life, as they addressed the use of mercantile versus rabbinic law in communal arbitration.[58] However, the question of which type of law to use should be distinguished from the question of communal structure. Halakhah was central to the Kahal Kadosh in that it legitimated the community's structure. But the *Acordos* established an administrative government, not a legal system.

---

[57] Many rabbinic authorities held that a rabbi's approval was necessary for communal decrees. The *Acordos* do not even come close to suggesting this; such a view seems totally contrary to the way the Kahal Kadosh was set up. However, it is true that the records of the Mahamad over the ensuing decades do indicate the participation of rabbis in many decisions. See Albert, 'The Rabbi and the Rebels', 183–5. A systematic look at which of the Mahamad's decisions make reference to rabbinic consultation remains a desideratum.

[58] A dispute about this issue spanned the communities of Livorno and Amsterdam as the rabbi Jacob Sasportas objected to communal legitimization of mercantile law (see Ch. 4 below). See Toaff, 'The Controversy' (Heb). Some excerpts of texts in that dispute are translated in Walzer et al. (eds.), *The Jewish Political Tradition*, i: *Authority*, 424–9.

The only early sign of dissent against the system of the *Acordos* appears in one particular incident in 1640, when Menasseh ben Israel, one of the four rabbis then employed by the Kahal Kadosh, was briefly banned. Menasseh was perhaps the best-known Jewish intellectual in Europe at the time, but was not always aligned with communal leadership. Since Menasseh had disobeyed the Mahamad's direct instructions and behaved in a disorderly manner, raising his voice and pounding on the table while complaining about a perceived slight, the Mahamad exercised their prerogative as outlined in the constitution, and excommunicated him—imposing a temporary, punitive *ḥerem*. In an angry moment of confrontation with the lay leaders in their chambers, the rabbi declared that it was he who could ban them, and not the other way around.[59] As an idiosyncratic matter of honour and bad temper, the incident can hardly be called a real act of ideological rebellion; anyway, it was quickly quashed and papered over.[60] But it was also bigger than that, as it touched on who was in charge, and why. And it does emphasize that the arrangement established just the year before was not automatically or universally accepted.

In fact, the authority of the Mahamad in relation to the rabbis in the Kahal Kadosh presents a rather extreme example of an early modern trend towards the subordination of rabbis to lay leaders. In this period a new phenomenon emerged, that of the rabbi as a communal professional. Increasingly, rabbis were appointed and paid as employees of particular communities, rather than serving as teachers, preachers, decisors, or scholars, either independently or within an academy or school.[61] Communal rabbis of the new type lost independence but gained influence, at least in some ways, as they became enmeshed in the communal machine.

The *Acordos* clarify this dimension of rabbinic emplacement within a community: even though the rabbis of the Kahal Kadosh were subordinate to the Mahamad in day-to-day affairs, they were also uniquely privileged

[59] 'He responded in a loud voice that he could impose the *ḥerem* on them, and not the above-mentioned Senhores on him, and other similar disorderly acts [*discomposturas*].' SA 334, 19, fo. 70. The encounter is discussed in Nadler, *Menasseh ben Israel*, 101–5.

[60] I am indulging in a bit of speculation that the physically papered-over page immediately preceding the record of Menasseh's discomposure is related to that event. The folio in SA 334, 19, that would be numbered 70 is covered with a sheet of paper, on which is written a note that on 8 Elul 5407 (8 Sept. 1647) the Mahamad agreed to cover this page out of respect. Whoever later added the page numbers in ink skipped this page.

[61] Teller, 'Laicization'; Bonfil, *Rabbis and Jewish Communities in Renaissance Italy*, introduction and ch. 5.

in an underlying way. Details regarding their roles—not only who in particular was employed, but their salaries, precise division of labour, and seniority—were laid out in the constitution itself, and not, as might be expected, in the first set of regulations put forth by the first seated Mahamad. According to the *Acordos*, the Mahamad could censure and silence rabbis for specific causes, including direct disobedience and failure to uphold their duties, but they could not fire them. Changes to the terms of their employment amounted to changes to the *Acordos*, and required the approval of the external constitutional committee. On a symbolic level, the approval of such a superior body represented recourse to the original authority of the membership from before their collective subjection to the community. The same was true even in practical ways, as the makeup of the committee in question was explicitly tied to the originally separate three congregations. The rabbis' position was therefore integral to and firmly ensconced within a broadly lay system, but it also transcended the system. Their status connected outwards to sources of authority that pre-dated and underlay the establishment of the community, and simultaneously imbued the community with sacrality.

The *Acordos* thus established a system that enmeshed the rabbis, the Mahamad, and the members in a close society with a web of interrelated forms of authority, carefully setting the web within an external framework. The approval of the city of Amsterdam, the sacrality of rabbinic law, and the agreement of the assembled individuals justified and supported the Kahal Kadosh as a unified and integrated whole.

The Kahal Kadosh as a Polity

The tools and offices of government were not in the hands of the clergy of the Kahal Kadosh, and the institution's modalities were lay. The community was grounded in and justified by religiously defined ideals, identities, and authority, but these stood alongside other aims and other sources of authority including those of the people and the city of Amsterdam. The two dimensions, the *kahal* ('assembly') and the *kadosh* ('holy'), were inextricable in the Kahal Kadosh and, though not coequal in temporal power, both were fundamental to the self-understanding of the community's creators. In this, the Kahal Kadosh Talmud Torah echoed the makeup of most early modern Christian kingdoms and commonwealths. However, while historians of Amsterdam's Kahal Kadosh have compared it to a church, a confraternity, a 'factory' or foreign 'nation', and a company, they have not described it as a polity.[62]

The default avoidance of political models is understandable. To describe the community of former conversos in tolerant Amsterdam as a polity seems to go against a common view of the history of Jewish communal life and the place of this particular community within it. It is a truism in Jewish historiography that modernity brought an end to Jewish social and legal separation, including the breakdown of the self-governing community, or *kehilah*. A prototypical image of the *kehilah* would feature a population of Jews accommodated by special charter, strictly set apart socially and religiously, and governed according to rabbinic stricture. Such a vision of the 'traditional' Jewish community does not match Amsterdam's Kahal Kadosh in the seventeenth century. The high degree of cultural integration and religious fluidity among members of this population, along with the lack of a set charter as discussed above, make the Kahal Kadosh appear to have already diverged from traditional forms of Jewish collectivity.

The very word 'community', often used with little reflection in Jewish historiography, requires some attention. The framers of the Kahal Kadosh themselves did not use the label 'republic', nor indeed 'civic' or 'political', in the text of the 1638 *Acordos*. But neither did they call it a church, confraternity, factory, or company, so there is no immediate reason to choose those labels over any other. Nor does even *kehilah* appear in the *Acordos*, highlighting the fact that a generic and timeless understanding of Jewish community should not be taken for granted. The realia of Jewish organization varied immensely across chronological, geographical, demographic, national, and religious distance.[63] For some Jews it may not have been an

---

[62] For a comparison to resident 'nations' of foreign merchants, see Spaans, 'Religious Policies', and Swetschinski, *Reluctant Cosmopolitans*, 184–7, where he determines that the community was a hybrid of a voluntary religious association and a mercantile colony. Yosef Kaplan has pointed out a deep similarity to Protestant churches in terms of social discipline, treating the activities of the Kahal Kadosh as an example of confessionalization. See e.g. Y. Kaplan, 'Preface', pp. xviii–xxii.

[63] Dean Phillip Bell has noted the inadequacy of the term to reflect the diverse realities of 16th-century Ashkenazi society; this is even more true from a perspective that includes the converso diaspora in the Atlantic and Ottoman worlds. Bell, 'Jewish Communities', 144–6; id., *Sacred Communities*, 149–70, esp. 150–3. See also Carlebach, 'Between Universal and Particular'.

active component of life at all: not all Jews had wanted or thought about being part of a Jewish-run entity, as opposed to merely following Jewish law and local custom or identifying with some national or religious subgroup of Jews. Those who did specifically value organized belonging, whether in a *kehilah*, a *kahal*, or some other named body, did not necessarily share the idea of a 'community' as such.[64] With regard to Jewish life in Amsterdam, the simple notion of community is inadequate on its own to account for the complex coexistence of an overall local Jewish population, various substructures defined around worship and ethnicity, and superstructures created through agreement and other legal means.

'Community' is also an anachronistic term that stands in for a wide range of words used in early modern Europe including *republica*, *universitas*, *sociatio* or *consociatio*, *civitas*, and others. As a general term for such associations, 'community' is simultaneously a key to early modern European culture and so variable as almost to elude definition—as it is in Jewish historiography. A recent treatment defines one expansively as 'a group of people who perceived themselves as having common interests and, thus, a common identity or self-understanding'.[65] From the widest possible perspective, a community might be anything along a spectrum from people with shared interests or characteristics, to a legally recognized church or guild, to a sovereign republic. Since such a definition is so broad as to lose its usefulness, we might prefer a closer definition of community, requiring some formal or discursive recognition of aggregation.

Within that frame, some communities could be meaningfully classified as political and others not. Let us take a political community to be one where politics—understood as the art or science of government, including power relations and allocation of resources among members of a group —constituted a central element of its purpose and self-definition. Such a definition accords with the way 'republic' and 'politics' were used in the context of statecraft. To say that a community was political in orientation is not to deny the role of religion, ethnicity, or material interests within it. On the contrary, it was normal for a polity to reflect and promote such ties: the early modern Christian commonwealth and the emerging idea of a 'nation-state' exemplify the way religion, peoplehood, and economy could

---

[64] Siegmund, 'Communal Leaders', esp. 333–43; D. Kaplan, 'Communal Places'; Ray, *The Sephardic Frontier*, 99.

[65] Spierling and Halvorson, 'Introduction: Definitions of Community', 1–2.

be intertwined in the identity of a polity. At the same time, the political was not limited to contexts of state sovereignty. A 'republic' was a form of association that could be found among diverse groups and within wider hierarchies.[66]

I suggest that the Kahal Kadosh fitted the profile of such a political community, or polity according to the standards of the time. It was not just any community but a formal, contractual, bureaucratic, lay, and centralized self-governing society. It combined Jewish legal tools and concepts like the *kahal* and the *ḥerem* with practices like office-holding, procedural rules, consensus, and contracts to create careful policing of internal order and external boundaries that purported to control most aspects of a member's life. Its particular nature as a polity comes into focus despite the fact that such an entity should not have been allowed to exist according to today's prevailing narratives.

Approaching without preconceptions the self-fashioning of members of the *nação* as they forged a new collective Jewish life, their own self-presentation offers the best evidence of the kind of community they envisaged. The terms for community that they used in these documents were primarily *kahal* and *congrega* (equivalent to each other) and the phrase *kahal kadosh* (often capitalized). These word choices were not neutral but instead recognized the nature of the entity as a holy assembly. I would even argue that *congrega* was not only an analogue of *kahal* but also held within it some of the particular resonance of the word 'congregation' in the early seventeenth-century Protestant context, where congregationalism emphasized local lay self-rule and common consent.[67]

With the ratification of the *Acordos*, the same three issues that had propelled affairs in the period before 1639 also marked the established Kahal Kadosh as a polity. Its use of excommunication to enforce regulations, its focus on shared economy and assets, and its emphasis on unity expressed as a relationship between the whole and individual members, were all elements of the way polities were commonly organized and conceived.

Beginning with the most surprising of these markers, excommunication was a key temporal power in Christian thought of the era. In fact, the

---

[66] 'Commonwealth had become a keyword because its ambiguities gave it a creative adaptability'; Knights et al., 'Commonwealth', 671; see also p. 666.

[67] English Presbyterians with such attitudes were present in Amsterdam. See Ha, *English Presbyterianism*, esp. chs. 4 and 7.

ban was a central component of Christian debates about the proper extent of clerical authority with respect to the state, and within those debates (ancient) Jewish excommunication figured prominently. Thomas Erastus (1524–83), for whom the anticlerical political stance called Erastianism was named, had written about the need for civil authorities to be the sole bearers of temporal authority, based largely on an analysis of excommunication. Treatments of ancient Jewish laws of the *ḥerem* continued into the seventeenth century as a common ingredient in church–state debates across Europe. The influential Dutch figures Petrus Cunaeus and especially Hugo Grotius published similar conclusions in their respective works *De republica Hebraeorum* and *De imperio* (finished in 1617). In fact, in his *Remonstrantie*, proposing (theoretical) conditions for Jewish settlement in Holland, Grotius signalled a clear perception that the ban was not only a matter of religious freedom but also constitutive of political authority. He advocated giving Jews the right to excommunicate but only if it was limited by appeal to city magistrates, in order to prevent Jews from 'usurping among them a too extensive and exorbitant authority'.[68]

Such precedents point to a mutual understanding among Dutch Christians and Amsterdam's Portuguese Jews that excommunication was a constituent piece of governance—thus, political—rather than being primarily a matter of spiritual status. In Jewish historiography, the *ḥerem* is now widely understood to have had a 'social' function, at least in Amsterdam.[69] Reframing it as political is only a matter of recognizing it as a component of political discourse and practice writ large. Its position in the *Acordos* should be read in the context of early modern political concepts: the framers understood the *ḥerem* as a marker of political authority both within the community and with respect to the regime(s) within which the community was embedded.

Second, ownership and distribution of communal property were also elements that particularly marked a public, civic, or government entity. In fact, they were seen as having the dangerous potential to undermine the state's own authority. The principle of freedom of conscience, enshrined in Dutch legal culture from the time of the Union of Utrecht in

---

[68] De Wilde, 'Offering Hospitality', 426. See Meijer, 'Hugo Grotius' "Remonstrantie"', 100–1.

[69] Yosef Kaplan showed this beyond doubt, and very much against assumptions that were then prevalent, in 'The Social Functions of the Herem'.

1579, guaranteed individual religious freedom but did not necessarily extend to collective worship, and Dutch law in the first half of the seventeenth century forbade any religious group other than the state church to worship publicly or administer charity. The legal reasoning had to do with collective ownership of money and property, since such ownership would establish the collective as an intermediate entity positioned between the family and the sovereign entity (city, republic, kingdom, empire) in which it was situated. As others have argued, the policy applied a distinction from Roman civil law between a voluntary association organized solely for worship and a corporate entity that could amass wealth and hence take on separate power.[70]

The distinction between 'public' and 'private' worship, then, was in Holland in this era less a matter of separate spheres—as they were not yet fully distinct in modern terms—and more a matter of the nature of the group that gathered for worship. The technical meaning of 'public' was not necessarily that worship took place in plain sight, or among a certain number of people—though these elements were at play as well—but that the activity was facilitated by a formal entity that surpassed the domestic unit, a society or collectivity with full legal standing in fiscal terms.[71] The fact that the Portuguese Jews could exercise monopolistic control over the provision of meat; collect taxes, fines, and charity; employ paid officials; and administer funds for their own poor were distinct markers of an entity with tangible—material—temporal power.[72] The Kahal Kadosh was public rather than private, a corporate society rather than a loose religious, national, or familial association, hence in this particular sense political rather than (solely) religious.

The community's ownership of a synagogue reflects the same fiscal conception of a public, or corporate, entity. The 'private' worship permitted to religious minorities was technically understood to take place domestically, meaning that people were free to manifest their piety however they

---

[70] Grotius used this logic in his recommendations regarding the admission of Jews. Spaans, 'Religious Policies', 79. See Frijhoff, 'Religious Toleration', 34; Parker, 'Paying for the Privilege'; and Kooi, *Calvinists and Catholics*.

[71] For an account of these traditions as an organizing principle for understanding the interconnection between theories of local and state politics, see Black, *Guilds and Civil Society*.

[72] The establishment of a separate meat market was not a politically neutral act. Grotius treats it in his *Remonstrantie*, arguing that it should be allowed. The exclusive use of the Kahal Kadosh's meat market as opposed to that of the Ashkenazi Jews was also hotly disputed within the community in the 1670s; see Ch. 3.

wished, including with texts and religious paraphernalia, but forbidden to gather in groups larger than one family (understood broadly to include a household, dependents, and relatives).[73] Essentially, prayer gatherings were legal, but not under the auspices of an association; instead, as the purview of a family, they were to take place in a private space. The structure had to be owned by an individual rather than by the church or congregation—which did not (and could not) exist as a legal entity.[74] It was, of course, the case that some such churches grew to occupy spaces that were relatively grand despite being nominally 'private'; enforcement was lax as long as the group avoided any impression of disruption of the wider body politic.[75] In the Kahal Kadosh, the ban on separate group prayer except in 'private' homes where the worshippers remained 'subjects' of the community, articulated in Article 2 of the *Acordos*, has to be understood in the context of this particular legal culture: it prohibited activities that could constitute a second or subsidiary Jewish community. Within the community the Kahal Kadosh recapitulated standards of the Dutch polity.

The same logic that underlay the toleration of minority churches defined the initial terms of Jewish worship. Citing Roman law regarding synagogues, Grotius had recommended that Jews be permitted to have designated private houses (of limited size) for their worship,[76] and in the charters granted to Jews in surrounding cities, such terms were a central component.[77] When one of the first three Amsterdam congregations, Neve Shalom, hired a carpenter to build a dedicated building in 1612, the city regents, prodded by fierce objections from church leaders, prohibited its use as a synagogue in no uncertain terms.[78] However, when ownership of the building was transferred to a (Catholic) member of the council, who then rented it to the Jewish group for the same purpose, the issue was resolved. The obvious legal fiction was an elegant solution if the issue revolved around religious minorities' property ownership as a group and not their presence or religious practices per se. Catholics used similar legal fictions to establish spaces for worship, so the problem did not stem from any unique problematic of Jewish toleration, but rather from this idiosyncrasy of Dutch pluralism.[79]

---

[73] See B. Kaplan, *Divided by Faith*, 179.   [74] Ibid. 181.   [75] Spaans, 'Religious Policies'.

[76] De Wilde, 'Offering Hospitality', 423; Meijer, 'Hugo Grotius' "Remonstrantie"', 99.

[77] B. Kaplan, *Divided by Faith*, 189–91; de Wilde, 'Offering Hospitality', 401–2.

[78] Bodian, *Hebrews*, 59.

[79] Catholics used the same strategy (Bodian, *Hebrews*, 59) and, in general, their position

The tacit permission to build a synagogue is often characterized as a feature of the new brand of toleration in Amsterdam, a pragmatic approach on the part of mercantilist Dutch leaders overruling an old-fashioned, religious prejudice.[80] From this perspective it was a pivotal moment, as the Jewish presence began to be legally acknowledged without a charter or residence agreement, allowing Jews to slip organically into the fabric of Dutch civil society on more or less the same terms as non-Jews, organized like other minority religious groups. Indeed, it is a special feature of Amsterdam's approach at first that there was no special niche carved out for Jews in particular. City leaders evidently saw their political culture as capable of accommodating them. As with other groups, the city council sought a balance between giving Jewish leaders free rein to keep their own membership in good order and insisting that Jews were still subject, as individuals and as a collective, to the city's political order. It is a significant episode in the story of the gradual opening up of European states to Jews as full members and citizens.

However, as the *Acordos* reveal, at least by the 1630s Jews were telling themselves a different story, deriving a different meaning out of the status they had in Amsterdam. They actively pushed towards strong lay government over a defined population. Although the Dutch system theoretically dictated that the synagogue should operate along the lines of a private church, the *Acordos* leaned in the other direction. As a matter of fact, the corporate nature of the Kahal Kadosh as established in 1639 was no secret, as we have already seen that magistrates were notified of the unification and *Acordos*, which included the use of the ban and the collectivization of property. Additionally, in the same year, one congregation (Bet Israel) built a new synagogue large enough to accommodate the soon-to-be-unified population, without known interference.[81] Did city leaders, then, condone the establishment of a Jewish community as a corporate society and share

during the first half of the century was similar. See Kooi, 'Paying off the Sheriff', and van Nierop, 'Sewing the Bailiff in a Blanket'. Notably, the Jewish position became more stable fairly rapidly, whereas Catholics continued to face unpredictable conditions. See also Parker, 'Paying for the Privilege'.

[80] For Swetschinski, the episode highlights the extent to which Dutch Jewry policy was not ideological but rather improvised, pragmatic, and bent on compromise; for Bodian, it exemplifies the city government's willingness to accommodate a Jewish community over the objections of the Calvinist clergy. Swetschinski, *Reluctant Cosmopolitans*, 11–12. See also Bodian, *Hebrews*, 47 and 59; Hsia, 'Introduction', 3–4; and Stiefel, 'Architectural Origins', n. 35.

[81] See Stiefel, 'Architectural Origins'.

the framers' political conception of it? The answer need not be clear-cut. Amsterdam officials understood the need for internal order and framed the community from the outside in the terms that worked for them. The Dutch government never did create any kind of charter for Jews, but it quietly allowed Jews to constitute a society for themselves.

Further, from the start, the Jewish population was expected to take care of its own poor, setting it apart from the rules applying to other distinct groups, including Christian religious minorities, groups of resident foreigners, etc.[82] Eventually, this expectation came to be mandated for all minority churches: in the second half of the seventeenth century, the Dutch embraced a system in which each religious community was responsible for its own poor, universalizing the status Jews had already been granted.[83] The fact that Jews were the first exceptions may be explained by perceptions of thoroughgoing Jewish difference,[84] as well as by European traditions of Jewish communal organization and Jewry law, which certainly shaped the inner dynamics and external legitimacy of the new Kahal Kadosh. In that regard, the Amsterdam situation was not as novel as it sometimes appears. In addition, the legal distinction between public and private was not as tidy in practice as it appears in theory. Minority churches, too, were run by lay elders who carefully kept social and religious order within their ranks so as to avoid unwanted intervention from without. And by the last few decades of the century, those leaders, like the Mahamad, had their influence magnified by fiscal responsibility. Simultaneously, the clear delineation of a 'public' church or corporate society was fading.

The similarities between the Kahal Kadosh and other religious minorities that emerged later therefore do not imply that the Jewish community was understood as a purely religious entity in the modern sense of a church (as opposed to a state), even though Dutch writers often referred to it as a *kerk*. Far less did either Jews or Christians see the Kahal Kadosh as a voluntary association of the type advocated by Jewish Enlighteners

---

[82] I thank Hans Cools for fruitful conversation about Italian semi-permanent residents in Amsterdam, who were denied the possibility of corporate existence.

[83] See van Rooden, 'Jews and Religious Toleration'; Groenveld, 'For the Benefit of the Poor'; Spaans, 'Religious Policies', 80; and Catterall, *Community without Borders*, 28 n. 9.

[84] The Jewish community was most likely exempt from the prohibitions applied to other religious groups because it was not seen as a threat to the state or its church. Unlike other churches or foreign nations, they had no empowered institution to support them or subvert the Dutch.

and advocates of emancipation a century and more later. On the contrary, the parallels rather remind us that churches, too, could be conceived in corporate and political terms. The very lines that were drawn in the terms of Dutch toleration, to prevent churches from becoming polities that might compete with the overarching polity, reveal the political as a critical dimension of religious organization. And churches—especially those in or influenced by the increasing 'communalization' of the church in Reformation Germany[85]—were important sites of innovation in theopolitics.

A Hobbesian Microcosm

The third quality that marked the Kahal Kadosh as a polity was its corporate nature in another sense: in terms of its make-up as a whole and unified body of individuals subjected to common authority. The idea of a polity within a polity would eventually become problematic in the light of Hobbes's theorization of a commonwealth as an entity that could suffer no internal division. He railed against the 'many lesser Commonwealths in the bowels of a greater, like wormes in the entrayles of a naturall man'.[86] The disintegration of medieval systems and the transformation of Christian nations into unified bodies politic necessarily entailed the disruption of Jewish collective separateness. But meanwhile, as an intermediate step, the Jews of Amsterdam's Kahal Kadosh embraced internally those very same politics of wholeness, treating themselves as a civic body and aiming to eliminate subgroups in the form of congregational bodies (corporate entities) within their community. They created a microcosm of the Hobbesian state within the nascent Hobbesian state.

Of course, the Kahal Kadosh existed within the legal and governmental systems of Amsterdam, Holland, and the United Provinces. It was not fully autonomous, and the *Acordos* do not claim that it was. A word about autonomy is therefore in order. Often, Jewish autonomy is understood juridically, to mean that Jews had a separate system of law and some ability to enforce compliance. Theoretically, a fully autonomous community would be empowered to judge disputes among its members without any recourse to external courts, but such a situation rarely existed. The semi-

---

[85] The idea of communalization is from Blickle, *Communal Reformation*. For an overview, see von Greyerz, *Religion and Culture*, 113–18, and the references there.

[86] Hobbes, *Leviathan*, 230 (ch. 29).

autonomy of the Kahal Kadosh is thus not unusual. The *Acordos* did require members to initiate litigation of property disputes internally, but they allowed members to pursue justice elsewhere if they remained dissatisfied.[87] Regarding marriage and divorce, which might be expected to fall within a religious (and hence communal) purview, members of the Kahal Kadosh had to abide by Dutch law, conforming to Dutch legal standards of consanguinity and registering all marriages with the city.[88] Later on, in 1683, Amsterdam officials would clarify that the ban had always been intended for enforcing internal regulations, at which it was 'as effective . . . as the strictest political laws'; whereas justice in general had always been the purview of the state.[89] And recall that the comprehensive juridical system designed in 1633 was not implemented, suggesting that the founders knowingly chose a different path to political separation. They framed a community in administrative rather than judicial terms. The lack of autonomy does not detract from the fact that members of the Kahal Kadosh saw themselves as members of a body with a government that had real (if ultimately limited) authority over them.

The United Provinces consisted of many small bodies claiming both rights and duties, demanding their say as collectives in public political discourse. It was not uncommon for local collectivities to claim authority deriving from their members and at the same time remain fully embedded within a wider system of entities with competing and overlapping claims to rule. The origin of the Dutch Republic as a loose confederation united primarily by shared resistance to the Spanish monarchy defined both its workings and its developing political ideas. In early modern Europe in general, intermediate bodies often claimed broad, but not ultimate, authority over their members; such societies included, in the words of one historian, 'corporate boroughs, towns, cities, companies, and hospitals that made up the larger "common weal"'.[90] Among them were free or incorporated cities or city-states such as the Venetian Republic, Tuscan communes, cities that had vied for independence in Iberia, and even Amsterdam itself, which had a high degree of independence from the state of Holland.[91] Indeed, Dutch

---

[87] Article 33. According to Article 20, matters of rabbinic law (*dinim*) were to come before the rabbis, who were empowered to decide by majority vote, but in case of a tie the Mahamad would rule.   [88] Swetschinski, *Reluctant Cosmopolitans*, 18–19.   [89] Ibid. 16–17.

[90] Turner, *The Corporate Commonwealth*, 34.

[91] Geoffrey Parker highlights these three, among many others, in his overview of semi-autonomous local polities in *Sovereign City*, 78–91, 151–82.

cities existed almost as states—certainly as corporate entities—within their provinces and then within the union.[92]

In both England and Holland, the high politics and new republicanism of the seventeenth century emerged from and relied on traditional practices and codes of local people-powered collectivities that were not sovereign but still political in nature. In many such polities, the 'people' were understood to have freely chosen to participate, at least in some original sense. It was common to emphasize active constitution of authority by consent of the subjects and through negotiation with higher levels of government—just as the *Acordos* show the Spanish and Portuguese Jews doing. The election and installation of lay leadership in local congregations was a central fight in battles over the relative power of state, church, and citizens.[93] English city commonwealths of the same era typically claimed legal personhood and paid for the privilege.[94] The Mahamad's arrogation to itself of the right to speak on behalf of the community reflects this impulse.[95]

The political theorist Johannes Althusius, a contemporary of Grotius and native of Germany who was active in Dutch circles in the 1630s, explained how a political community or association (*consociatio*) was made up of, but also transcended, the aggregation of individual members:

Even though the individual persons of a community may be changed by the withdrawal or death of some superiors and inferiors, the community itself remains. It is held to be immortal because of the continued substitution and succession of men in place of those withdrawing. Whence it appears that the community is different from the individual persons of a community, although it is often considered to be a representational and fictional person.[96]

---

[92] 'The city of early modern times was viewed in the first place as a community regulated by public law, a *corporation* with its own statutes, rights, and duties. The city was an institutionalized, self-governing community that promoted the specific interests of its members. It had acquired certain rights and some degree of autonomy for the governing of this microcosm and for its role in the outside world.' Frijhoff and Spies, *Dutch Culture in a European Perspective*, i. 179–80.

[93] See Winship, *Godly Republicanism*, esp. chs. 2 and 4.   [94] Withington, *Politics*, 8.

[95] The Kahal Kadosh's regular contributions to the city's poor relief fund, over and above providing for its own poor, are perhaps an analogue to such payment, making use of a particular political language centred on charity that prevailed in Calvinist Holland. The articles of confederation in 1622 also set a monthly contribution to support the non-Jewish poor, 'in the name of the entire nation'. SA, 334, 13, fo. 3 (Article 21).   [96] Althusius, *Politica*, 41.

Althusius described what Article 3 of the *Acordos* accomplished by declaring that the Kahal Kadosh automatically incorporated newly arriving Spanish and Portuguese Jews: the polity remained in place despite the movement into or out of it by individual people.

Put differently, the reference to future immigrants suggests that members saw the *Acordos* not as a contingent or narrowly legal personal contract among the signatories as individuals, but rather as an abstract contract binding upon a changing population across time: in other words, a constitution. Critically, this makes the Kahal Kadosh more like a political entity, a commonwealth or state, and less like a company or corporation, or even like a guild or trade union, which would require new members to proactively join or be admitted. Here, too, the interpretation of the rabbi Isaac Aboab da Fonseca several decades later provides a helpful guide to the implicit logic of the *Acordos*, as he defended the authority of the *Acordos* over newcomers in constitutional terms. His discussion (see Chapter 4 below) opens up much more fully the conception of government authority that prevailed in the Kahal Kadosh.

Althusius emphasized the necessity of theorizing distinctions between the polity in itself, the orders that made up its government, and the individuals that constituted its subjects.[97] While such distinctions were not always well marked in casual speech, they certainly informed the general understanding, even as they do now: most people would acknowledge that the acts of a state are not identical with the acts of its citizens. A distinction between an organic, felt community that inhered in the people and the formal institution that the people created was critical to conceptions of political authority. They have come down to modern thought in a distinction between 'community' and 'society', or *Gemeinschaft* and *Gesellschaft*, so named by the early twentieth-century sociologist Ferdinand Tönnies, who in turn derived his *Gemeinschaft* from what Hobbes called 'concord'—an underlying, 'preexisting consensus or prepolitical social integration'.[98]

The same distinction operated within the Kahal Kadosh, with the people-level community located in the nation and congregation (*kahal*), and the formal society they instituted being the Kahal Kadosh. The latter's authority relied on and derived from the rabbinically constructed authority of a *kahal*, i.e. a local assembly of individuals, also understood as a

---

[97] See Dauber, *State and Commonwealth*, 1, and Brett, *Changes of State*, esp. 112–34.
[98] Hont, *Politics in Commercial Society*, 6–8; Tönnies, *Community and Society*.

congregation. But in *relying on* and *deriving from* the *kahal*, the Kahal Kadosh also transcended it. It was not coincident with the simple assembly itself but with its wholeness, its unity; its existence was not an automatic result of such a grouping but rather the result of an explicit, legally contracted, mutual agreement. The whole—now concentrated in the authority of a designated government—relied upon and incorporated the authority and consent of the many.

The Kahal Kadosh, then, was no generic community—no group of people with a loose 'common identity or understanding'—though that phrase might indeed accurately describe the population of converso immigrants in Amsterdam before the *imposta* board and confederation were established. Rather, a community of the sort the framers of the Kahal Kadosh envisaged was a component of what would become modern Western political theory.

Tradition and Innovation

My claim here is not for uniqueness but for particularity: this community, in this time and place, used ideas, practices, and structures that were locally legible as public, civic, and governmental—in short, political. Elements of the communal system such as lay governing councils, salaried communal rabbis, and the understanding of the *ḥerem* as constitutive of collective authority were not in themselves new. The *Acordos* remained continuous with Jewish traditions even as it pressed them into a new mould. One example is the way the Kahal Kadosh used the ban. It relied on Iberian Jewish traditions of rabbinic thought about the *kahal* and the *ḥerem*, traditions with which other communities in the Sephardi diaspora were similarly in conversation, in what may have been a distinct stream of rabbinic thought about self-government. This was received in Amsterdam via the writings of Nahmanides and others, as well as sixteenth-century Ottoman responsa. The Kahal Kadosh also shared with its Iberian predecessors comfort with lay, non-halakhic adjudication and even a sense of the community as a lay sphere.[99]

[99] Aboab's 1680 *Exhortation* makes these sources visible (see Chs. 3 and 4 below), as he made reference in his 1680 treatise to the works of several Sephardi rabbis from 16th-century Salonika, suggesting a shared halakhic or communal culture with these other descendants of Iberian Jews. On the medieval Sephardi context, see Lorberbaum, *Politics and the Limits of the Law*; Klein, *Jews, Christian Society, and Royal Power*, 26–51; and Ray, *The Sephardic Frontier*,

The Kahal Kadosh inherited Jewish communal practices from Ash-kenazi lands as well, where a conception of the *kehilah* was key from the late Middle Ages onwards, and where looser forms of organization were co-alescing into more bureaucratic and unified systems by the end of the six-teenth century.[100] Many Ashkenazi communities featured an emphasis on assembly and majority rule, as well as, according to Dean Phillip Bell, an adaptation of certain Christian models in which the civic body was sacred and the sacred community was civically organized.[101] Some dimensions of the Kahal Kadosh's distinctive structure also have parallels among com-munities in Italian lands. The community of Spanish Jews in Rome granted 'absolute' authority to the lay leadership and prohibited disobedience on pain of minor and major bans, with rabbis as communal officials.[102] Various Jewish communities in Italy also sometimes had formal, written agree-ments, signed by the members.[103] In general, Jewish communal institutions have often mirrored surrounding governments,[104] and various forms of local associations, republics, and commonwealths proliferated in early modern Europe. Other Jewish populations reconstituted their communities in the sixteenth or seventeenth century to suit local modalities, too, and further research may uncover more precedents for the elements of the *Acordos*.

On the other hand, the ways in which the Kahal Kadosh founders introduced innovations are telling. Prohibiting multiple prayer groups was not usual; nor was it typical to eliminate direct government by the mem-bers of the *kahal* in favour of full and permanent transference of power to a self-perpetuating central council. While lay councils of various kinds had

104-11. On later Sephardi rabbinic political thinking, see Lehmann, *Ladino Rabbinic*; see also Ray, *After Expulsion*, with the idea that early modern Sephardi culture was more a product of post-expulsion conditions than a reconstruction of the pre-expulsion world articulated con-cisely on p. 7.

[100] Carlebach, 'The Early Modern Jewish Community'; Israel, *European Jewry*, 151-69; Ruderman, *Early Modern Jewry*, 57-98.

[101] See Bell, *Sacred Communities*; Woolf, *The Fabric of Religious Life*; and Lifshitz, *Rabbi Meir*.

[102] Cooperman, 'Ethnicity', 139, translating a document from the 1490s published in Espos-ito, *Un'altra Roma*, 267ff. There was also a move towards greater lay authority, creating a board of seven officials, in 1470.

[103] Rome had them as early as the late 15th century. Cooperman, 'Ethnicity', 119. Simon-sohn (*History of the Jews*, 324-7) also uses the word 'constitution' to describe the documents that established communal authority in early modern Mantua. Malkiel, writing about Venice, correctly differentiates between such documents and charters. *A Separate Republic*, 19.

[104] See e.g. Bonfil, *Jewish Life in Renaissance Italy*, 179-81, 190-3; Siegmund, *The Medici State*; Bell, *Sacred Communities*.

long held charge of European and Ottoman Jewish communities, such councils commonly had some accountability to the wider congregation. In German and eastern European lands communal structures varied tremendously, but whole communities regularly assembled to vote, whether on specific measures or to select new leadership cohorts.[105] In early modern Italy—in Rome, Mantua, Venice, and Florence, at least—there was a 'large assembly' or its equivalent, an assembly of all adult men eligible to vote —with an active role in communal affairs.[106] Such practices allowed the whole body of eligible adult male members to participate in government, whereas in Amsterdam's Kahal Kadosh the signing of the *Acordos* was the last exercise of communal authority permitted to individuals except as officers of the government. Members did not vote on communal affairs, or even in elections to fill the Mahamad, as the lay council chose new half-cohorts semi-annually.

The contrast with these norms highlights how Amsterdam's Spanish and Portuguese Jews put a stronger emphasis on the Kahal Kadosh as opposed to the *kahal*, on the whole polity as opposed to the aggregated individuals it comprised. The *Acordos* harnessed individuals into a collective, such that their original authority was given over to a governing body with broadly defined authority. The Kahal Kadosh as it was established in 1639 not only perpetuated existing norms but captured and radicalized them, pushing the form of the *kehilah* towards something new and fitted to its particular environment at the dawn of modern politics. Strong, centralized leadership fused with an emphasis on the consent and authority of members to create a new valuation of uniformity and unanimity, where the people were treated as constitutive subjects of government authority rather than as active citizens. This combination was not only a synthesis of the Iberian and northern European Jewish traditions; it also adapted these traditions to fit a powerful Christian discourse about religio-political bodies as well as particular features of Dutch politics. The key to the adaptation overall was the exacting requirement that the congregation, the population, and the polity be coterminous and indivisible.

The Kahal Kadosh was constituted in a vital new way that reflected

[105] See Bell, *Sacred Communities*, 156.

[106] Cooperman, 'Ethnicity', 131; Malkiel, *A Separate Republic*, 61, 213, and *passim*; Simonsohn, *History of the Jews*, 324–7; Siegmund, *The Medici State*, 252–3; and Bonfil, *Jewish Life in Renaissance Italy*, 190–2; though in general the tendency from the late 16th to the 17th century was towards less general participation and a smaller, tighter governing elite.

the age. A few conclusions are worth stressing. First, my close reading of the *Acordos* revealed a Jewish corporate society. The community as corporate society is an image that has been used to emphasize Jewish cultural separateness, whereas the Spanish and Portuguese Jews of Amsterdam were more culturally integrated than many Jews of their age. The premodern Jewish collectivity is often envisioned as a world unto itself and, at least in its ideal, as 'autonomous': aspiring, and at the same time relegated, to self-rule against a hostile Christian backdrop. In Amsterdam, it appears, it was possible to define a political modality that demanded obedience without demanding legal or cultural separation. The government of the Kahal Kadosh was understood as serving the common good, particularly in terms of material assets as well as civility, which included good morals, orderly behaviour, and religious conformity. Such independent self-government did not have to be absolute in order to be strong and meaningful. Of course, the same is true of other modes of partial autonomy, including legal ones, but it bears emphasis here because the very idea of a corporate society so strongly connotes separateness.

In addition, we have seen here an example of Jewish self-government not based primarily on legal or judicial modalities. In general, scholarship on Jewish communities overweighs judicial autonomy as the main mode in which a Jewish community can be understood as a separate body. To some extent that is understandable, since courts and legal decision-making were constitutive of much government authority in premodern Europe. What we see in Amsterdam's Kahal Kadosh Talmud Torah is something quite different: it is the constitution of a political entity based not on judicial process, but on executive or administrative process and authority. The Kahal Kadosh had a relatively light and lenient rule requiring only an attempt at internal arbitration before seeking justice in other courts. The power of the Mahamad to act as arbiter was not a central component of the communal structure; it lent little to the logically coherent, clearly bounded, and cohesive Jewish political society of the Kahal Kadosh. This community was a highly ramified institution built not on decisions but on decrees.

With that distinction in mind, the Kahal Kadosh also speaks to a perceived competition or tension between lay leaders and rabbis, or lay and rabbinic authority. The simple notion that premodern European Jewish communities were run by rabbis in a primarily halakhic mode has mostly been retired. Still, old assumptions about rabbinic leadership and halakhic governance still exert influence. In reality, across many medieval and early modern contexts, Jewish self-government comprised some combination of lay and rabbinic leadership. It combined Jewish law with what Ephraim Shoham-Steiner and Elisabeth Hollender call 'Jewish tradition and common sense'—thinking that was informed, in most cases, by the social and political habits of the surrounding culture.[107] The constitution of the Kahal Kadosh is an unusually fulsome source of information about exactly how the community was made up: what traditions and what forms of 'common sense' were in play. It shows an understanding of government and political bodies shared with the Christian world, carefully adjusted to Jewish needs and legitimated by halakhah.

Hollender and Shoham-Steiner's observation highlights another dimension of the novelty of the Kahal Kadosh: the 1639 constitution systematized and rationalized a mixture of elements that had more often coexisted organically and unevenly in the past. It had not been uncommon for a prominent rabbi to be a prominent executive as well; or, on the other hand, for lay leaders to be invested with informal but nevertheless quite strong authority. Ordinances, or *takanot*, straddled lay and rabbinic spheres. Such arrangements apparently had not appeared inconsistent to other Jewish leaders in the way that they did to the framers of the *Acordos*. In their hands, however, order was imposed—much in the style of many early modern transformations. Indeed, there are precursors of such ordering among Jewish communities in Italian lands, as Christian rulers investigated, reformed, and/or constructed Jewish community, including in the emergence of the Jewish ghetto and the creation of the Florentine Jewish communal structure.[108] We see an explicit echo of the Italian developments in the way the *Acordos* cited the 'style of Venice' at a critical juncture. In their shift from a confederation of synagogues to the Kahal Kadosh, and in their highly specific positioning of rabbinic authority, the Spanish and Portuguese Jews tightened up relationships that had been loose and variable. They assigned strict and clearly defined boundaries to members, rabbis, office-holders, rules, record-keeping, and more.

In all, a close reading of the *Acordos* offers a corrective to some pervasive narratives about cohesion and religion in premodern Jewish society and illuminates some early modern communal dynamics. The Kahal Kadosh's

---

[107] See Shoham-Steiner and Hollender, 'Beyond the Rabbinic Paradigm', abstract (online only), doi:10.1353/jqr.2021.0010.   [108] D. Schwartz, *Ghetto*; Siegmund, *The Medici State*.

particular conception of community as corporate was part of an emergent political discourse adapted to Jewish life. The system as elaborated in the *Acordos* matched trends in the surrounding political culture, and with that context in mind, it is possible to say that the community was conceived as a polity, as opposed to other possible forms of association. In fact, I suggest that the very notion of Jewish community as a semi-autonomous, state-like 'corporate society' derives, in some measure, from the legacy of the self-understanding of this highly visible and culturally influential community. I return to this point in the Conclusion.

This chapter began with the Mayflower Compact, calling the reader's attention to the flavour of contemporaneous agreements and civic participation.[109] The Mayflower pilgrims saw fit to create the Compact because they had found themselves suddenly, perplexingly, free of any political belonging, free of the rule of any established law. The same cannot be said of the Amsterdam Jews—but, on the other hand, perhaps there is something akin to the pilgrims' experience among the early Jewish settlers in Amsterdam who found themselves subject to at least three forms of law and several varieties of group identity, none of which coincided precisely with the boundaries of a political community to which they belonged unequivocally. The Puritans drew on a rich culture of political 'covenants' and local compacts to form a polity, as did the framers of the Kahal Kadosh. All of them described the purpose of their polity as their own 'preservation' along with the pursuance of godliness as a collective. For both groups, a formal agreement among peers to voluntarily subject themselves to a new authority was a way to create order and pursue shared aims, spiritual and material.

Eventually, the Mayflower Compact led to the foundation of free communities that would become states. For Jews it was the opposite; their community would gradually lose its state-like characteristics. But we ought not to let the end of the story cloud our view of the start of it. In this chapter I have read the *Acordos* and other sources to reveal what I see as a fundamental orientation towards establishing the community in political form, despite the fact that—unlike the Mayflower Compact—the *Acordos* do not use the terms 'civic' or 'body politic' or 'republic'.

That came later. Beginning in the 1660s, community members would fully activate the language that informed their political community and fol-

---

[109] They also shared a discursive environment in Holland. See Sprunger, *Trumpets from the Tower*, and Winship, *Godly Republicanism*, ch. 4.

low this thinking as far as it could take them. They embraced the language of the Jewish 'polity' as an apt descriptor of communal ideals, terms, and priorities. The emergence of such language some twenty-five years after the *Acordos* only reinforces the more essential point that I have made about this community's constitution, namely, that it established an association whose resemblance to the core concept of a polity was not merely superficial. It was a polity, I have argued, not only in the generic sense that it accomplished aims that we might define as political, but also in that the principles underlying its construction were the very principles that underlay new conceptions of the polity in their own world.

In Christian polities of the seventeenth century, the notion of a social compact or constitution that established government authority was never entirely free of the authorizing power of the sacred. The same holds true for the Kahal Kadosh. What the *Acordos* established had certain features that made it literally a Jewish commonwealth—a religious commonwealth that was Jewish. With such a move came a whole new problematic of Jewish politicality. In turning to the era of Spinoza and Sabbatianism, as I shall now do, it is important to have established that such ideas did not spring out of nothing. Those later claims for the Jewish commonwealth were not thin or faddish; they were not mere posturing. They grew organically from both a self-image and an institutional structure that had been carefully constructed in the 1630s as a Jewish civic body, a form of godly republicanism.

TWO

REPUBLIC

THE COMMUNITY AS A COMMONWEALTH

SAUL LEVI MORTEIRA (1596–1660), one of the founding rabbis of the Kahal Kadosh Talmud Torah, stated an apparently obvious fact when he wrote that Jews were 'split up and dispersed here and there among all peoples. They do not have a republic, land, or government like other peoples do.'[1] With this formulation, Morteira articulated a common perception of Jewish exceptionalism defined by political status. Subjugation and dispersion, without a kingdom to return to or a king for protection, were indisputable facts of Jewish existence. And yet Morteira's own student, Moses Raphael d'Aguilar (d. 1679), who served the community after Morteira's death, ceased to treat this apparently universal assumption as plain truth. Aguilar rhetorically placed the claim that Jews lack a republic into the mouth of a polemical opponent, a hypothetical Christian, as an accusation to disprove.[2] In doing so, he opened up a striking new possibility: perhaps dispersed Jews *did* have a republic?

In fact, according to Aguilar and many others after 1666, Jews did. And

---

[1] Morteira, *Obstaculos*, MS EH 48 D3, fo. 45. Morteira echoes the terms of the evil royal adviser Haman's denigration of Jews in Esther 3:8.

[2] Aguilar, *Breve explicação*, MS EH 48 A 11, §3, fo. 33. The manuscript is undated, but it must have been written after 1654. If it dates from the 1650s it would be the earliest example of the new perspective. Actually, Aguilar first echoed and then contradicted Morteira's statement. While stationed in the Brazilian colonies (that is, before 1654 and during Morteira's lifetime), he wrote, following Morteira closely: 'In the world today, [the Jewish] people alone lacks the form or appearance of a people, dwelling together like other peoples do; nor does it have a republic, or leader, or government, or land.' Aguilar, *Explicação*, MS EH 48 A 11, §14, fo. 429ᵛ. Back in Amsterdam, Aguilar revised his view in a newer exposition on the same biblical passage (Isa. 53), now criticizing the claim of Jewish political dispossession. One wonders if the question also echoes the one put in the mouth of a fictional king in Judah Halevi's *Sefer hakuzari* (Essay 2), when the king asks the rabbi if Jews are 'a body without either head or heart'. See Halevi, *Kitab*, 106, and Shear, *The Kuzari*.

the Jewish republic he referred to was not a restored messianic kingdom populated by a nation gathered in from exile across the globe; nor did he mean Moses' biblical republic. Rather, Aguilar saw something that fitted the profile of a republic in his own local, self-governed community: a polity, just 'like other peoples' had. Examples of similar thinking abound: the moralist Abraham Pereyra wrote about how lay leaders and rabbis should govern the Jewish republic. The new constitution of the Spanish and Portuguese community in London, composed in 1664 under the tutelage of Amsterdam leaders and following its example, explicitly named the community a republic.[3] The poet Daniel Levi de Barrios wrote about the history of Jewish communities as separate republics unto themselves. The homilist Abraham Gomes Silveira called the members of the Mahamad 'suns who illuminate this Kahal Kadosh, and hearts who give life to the body of this republic'.[4] These men did not accept that Jews were unique in lacking politics because they lacked a sovereign king or state, but rather adjusted their focus to the circumstances and qualities that they shared with other organized collective societies in their orbit, which were understood as 'republics'—or, to use the English term of the day, 'commonwealths'.

Thus, whereas Morteira had observed that the Jewish people lacked any 'republic, land, or government', perpetuating a common assumption of his time, Aguilar and his peers reconsidered the case. Aguilar altered Morteira's phrasing in a critical way, asking whether Jews formed 'a people or republic in *any*' place, not whether the Jewish people as a whole formed one in one place, as his teacher had put it. Further, Aguilar dropped the word 'land'.[5] He was able to envisage the diaspora as a series of individual Jewish polities, rather than as a global nation broken into shards, or a destroyed/lost common republic. His innovation had far-reaching implications in Jewish thought and polemics—and also in communal affairs—as the bald claim of having a republic was fleshed out through a profusion of sources treating the Kahal Kadosh as one.[6]

---

[3] See Bodian, '*Escamot*', where the text of the constitution in Portuguese is published. Likewise, the *Acordos* were not themselves labelled as a 'constitution', but in 1680 the rabbi Isaac Aboab da Fonseca used that very word for it. See below, Ch 4.

[4] Gomes Silveira, *Sermones*, 31.

[5] He wrote that a Christian would say that 'Israel is so dispersed in all parts of the world that they do not take the form of a people or republic in any of them'. Aguilar knew his teacher's words well and distinctly echoed them even as he offered a different perspective.

[6] See Bodian, 'Biblical Hebrews', for the first recognition of such discourse.

In this chapter, I trace the conceptual and linguistic shift that took place between the time of Morteira and that of Aguilar, a chronological frame that also maps onto the time span separating the *Acordos* from Spinoza and Sabbatai Zevi. The contrast between Morteira's unquestioning acceptance of Jewish political absence and Aguilar's strategic assertion of presence reflects the emergence of a new understanding of the exilic community, expressed through a new way of using the word 'republic' that blossomed in the era of Spinoza and Sabbatianism.

The change in perspective can be traced in two ways. First, Jewish political writing in Amsterdam centred on a new way of using the word 'republic' that was then current in the wider context of Protestant northwest Europe. The Kahal Kadosh's 1639 constitution had already pressed the community into the mould of a political body in the terms of its immediate Dutch locale. In turn, those very conceptions of the polity that were in play in Holland in the first half of the century were squarely at the heart of new Atlantic republicanism in the second half of the century, on their way to becoming ideologies of the state, and central to a new general understanding of the 'political'. Community members were then positioned both pragmatically and conceptually to take the obvious leap of calling the community a republic by name. New, in other words, was not only that Aguilar and others applied the word *república* to the Jewish community, but also, more subtly, what the word meant in Amsterdam by the 1660s and beyond, when it was often closely aligned with discourses around the 'commonwealth' in the Anglo-Dutch Atlantic.

Secondly, having made the move to thinking of the community in republican terms, community members deepened their existing understanding of the Kahal Kadosh as a political body. Jewish thinkers recalibrated their focus from a global perspective on the Jewish people as a whole to their own locality, from authority based on privilege and permission to that based on contract and consensus, and from kingdoms to republics. In doing so they followed the zeitgeist, adapting their existing language of communal organization to a new political discourse. The lexical shift opened the community to a world of now explicitly 'political' interpretation, and invited comparisons, even a sense of equivalence, between Jewish and Christian governments. Careful adaptation of Christian political thought followed, so that a seemingly superficial moniker came to inform

Spinoza's peers' discussion of internal Jewish communal dynamics as well as a far-reaching evaluation of Jewish status.

Menasseh vs. Pereyra on the Jewish Republic

In the first half of the seventeenth century, Amsterdam's Jews, like most literate Europeans, were familiar with this range of meanings, and made use of many of them in both Jewish and non-Jewish contexts. Members of earlier Jewish generations, too, especially those in the converso diaspora and others who were steeped in Latin and European vernacular learning, had been aware of the European revival of republicanism and civic humanism from the Renaissance on. Most famously, Isaac Abravanel, the Spanish Jewish philosopher who settled in the city-states of northern Italy following the expulsion of Iberian Jewry, had valorized the political form of the republic—meaning, in this case, the specific form of government without a king—by arguing that it was just such a government that Moses established for the biblical Israelites.[7]

Over the following two centuries, European thinkers across the Christian religious spectrum, especially those interested in the place of religion in government, increasingly agreed that the Mosaic polity, often called the 'Republic of the Hebrews', was organized according to God's direct instruction and thus served as the best political model for their own religious nations. The Dutch and English were not uniquely, but were especially, enthusiastic in their adoption of the badge of the 'new Israel' to express national pride and claim themselves as the true inheritors of the spiritual and political covenants of the Hebrew Bible.[8] In addition to an idealized image of the biblical Jewish republic that came to be taken as a given, Jewish sources regarding biblical politics also became important to Christian thought about the place of religion in the ideal state.[9] Expositors like Petrus Cunaeus and Hugo Grotius in the first half of the seventeenth century, and then Samuel Pufendorf and John Selden later on, are only among

[7] See Cohen-Skalli, *Don Isaac Abravanel*, 138–55; A. Melamed, *Wisdom's Little Sister*, 230–43; Netanyahu, *Don Isaac Abravanel*, 150–94; and Kimelman, 'Abravanel'.

[8] Bodian, 'The Biblical "Jewish Republic"'; Boralevi, 'Classical Foundational Myths'; Hill, *The English Bible*; Dunkelgrün, '"Neerlands Israel"'; Eyffinger, 'How Wondrously'.

[9] Oz-Salzberger, 'Jewish Roots'; Nelson, *Hebrew Republic*; Dunkelgrün, 'Christian Study of Judaism'; Remer, 'After Machiavelli'; Neuman, 'Political Hebraism'; Schochet et al. (eds.), *Political Hebraism*; Fukuoka, *The Sovereign*.

the best-known of a large array of intellectuals who engaged with Jewish texts to inform their Christian politics.[10]

The widespread attention to the 'Republic of the Hebrews' was, for Christians, one dimension of their complex renewal and iteration of classical republicanism in dialogue with contemporary church–state relations, in both theory and practice. A critical component of the formative sixteenth- and seventeenth-century interpretations of the Jewish (or Hebrew, or Mosaic) republic was that the Jewish action was entirely limited to the biblical period. Indeed, any Christian self-image as inheriting biblical theopolitics was inherently supersessionist, built on the premiss that the *Jewish* 'Hebrew republic' was a thing of the past, obliterated with the fall of the Temple and Jewish loss of land and government. Thus despite its centring of Judaism, it was oddly tangential to any impression of post-biblical Jews; insofar as it took account of them at all, it framed their existence in terms of the loss of their republic.

Morteira, then, was already keyed into a convention of his age when he updated the trope of Jewish dispersion and fallen polity to speak of the fate of the 'republic of the Jews' instead of the biblical monarchy or some other form of sovereignty. For example, in answer to the question 'For what sins has God ruined the Republic of the Jews [*La Republica de los Judios*] for so many centuries?' he wrote that the Jewish republic had not been eliminated, but rather subjected to an elongated captivity, like 'a criminal who deserves death, and out of pity the punishment is changed to long imprisonment'.[11] He also used the word 'republic' to address the utility of Jewish law for governance—but he only did so in reference to the ancient Jewish state or the global population, ignoring the diaspora community as an institution.[12] A generation later, Aguilar and his compatriots noticed that the newest way of thinking about the republic—especially now that it was translated into the political language of the 'commonwealth'—was indeed applicable to Jews on the local communal level.

A second contrast, this one between the rabbi Menasseh ben Israel and his student Abraham Pereyra, is parallel to the one between Morteira and Aguilar. It further illuminates the difference in perspective between early

[10] I name these four in particular because they appear in connection with the writings of members of the Kahal Kadosh discussed below.
[11] It is possible that this particular phrasing was chosen by the questioner, not Morteira himself, but he does not reject the premiss in his answer. Morteira, *Preguntas*, MS Ros. 127, fos. 8–9.   [12] Morteira, *Providencia*, MS EH 48 B 16, fo. 365ᵛ.

members of the Kahal Kadosh Talmud Torah and their successors after 1666. Menasseh was, like Morteira, a rabbi employed by the Kahal Kadosh Talmud Torah at the time of its formation in 1639. He was a generation younger than his senior colleague (and former teacher) Morteira and, famously, did not get along well with him.[13] But Menasseh died relatively young—within a few years of Morteira's own passing—and neither of the two men lived to witness the new developments of the 1660s and 1670s. In addition to being a printer and a self-appointed diplomat on behalf of his nation, Menasseh was also a consummate scholar, engaged in correspondence with members of the European republic of letters such as the above-mentioned Hugo Grotius.

Pereyra, for his part, was not a rabbi or scholar per se but a successful mercantile agent who became a patron of Menasseh's scholarship and eventually a moralist writer in his own right at the start of the Sabbatian years. He was a prominent figure in Amsterdam's Kahal Kadosh, with a high profile in business and communal government as well as charitable and religious pursuits. He had arrived in Amsterdam in 1646 as a new Jew, already possessing status and fortune, which were to grow exponentially by the end of his first decade in the city, and he served for the first time on the Mahamad in 1651. Deeply invested in the idea of learning as a source of spiritual improvement, Pereyra founded a yeshiva in Amsterdam in 1656 (Tora Hor, headed by the rabbi Isaac Aboab da Fonseca), and another in 1659 in Hebron, in the land of Israel.[14]

Pereyra was also the author of two books, published in 1666 and 1671.[15] Both were compendia of wise advice culled from diverse sources, Jewish and non-Jewish, ancient and modern.[16] In the first, *La certeza del camino* (The Certainty of the Path), he stated his aim as helping to guide others who came late to the path of salvation, as he had. Notably, he referred not to his midlife adoption of Judaism, since he recalled his early years in the Kahal Kadosh Talmud Torah as a period of gross materialism and sceptical scoffing at the pious, but rather to a religious transformation that took place sometime after that, and before the time of Sabbatian excitement. Although Pereyra appears to have been philanthropically active

---

[13] Nadler, *Menasseh ben Israel*, and Roth, *A Life*.   [14] Pereyra, *Certeza*, 288.

[15] He may also have produced a third book in 1672: a manuscript titled *Discursos legales sobre la verdad de la Ley* is mentioned in Kayserling, *Biblioteca*, 87.

[16] Méchoulan, in *Hispanidad*, published *Certeza* in a modern edition with a historical introduction and identified many of the sources that go unnamed in that work.

from the moment he arrived in Amsterdam, he recounts how in his youth he would mock virtuous and charitable people, calling them *misvoteros*.[17] His second book, *Espejo de la vanidad del mundo* (Mirror of the World's Vanity), appeared five years later, a greatly revised and expanded version of the first book, including many more Jewish sources and more of his own contributions.

As Aguilar did with his teacher Morteira, Pereyra echoed the work of Menasseh but introduced a critical difference, in fact inverting the original in order to turn a site of Jewish political emptiness into one of fullness. In this case, where Menasseh used the idea of the republic metaphorically, Pereyra embraced it literally. Menasseh's 1642 book *De la fragilidad humana* (On Human Frailty) was composed for the edification of his Jewish readers, but also with an eye towards the international community of scholars among whom he cherished a reputation.[18] In this book he wrote about the republic as one of the nesting circles that make up a Neoplatonic cosmos. Man, the polity, and the universe all reiterate each other's structures, each entity a coherent whole and yet also a constituent part; all interconnect in systems of influence and imitation. With characteristic eclecticism Menasseh brought such disparate sources as the Talmud, Aristotle, and the Renaissance man Giovanni Pico della Mirandola into accord with each other in his exegesis of Ecclesiastes 9: 14 ('There was a little city, with few men in it; and to it came a great king, who invested it and built mighty siege works against it'). Menasseh explained the city as a macrocosm of man: 'The men who inhabit the city, the political city-dwellers and courtiers, are . . . the interior senses with all the faculties. The "great king" who comes to the city . . . against whom they fortify their resistance, is the appetite, trying in every way to subject the man, and dominate him.'[19]

Menasseh's interest in this humanistic trope was intellectual, spiritual, and perhaps ecumenical. He used the correspondence between the human and the polity in order to elucidate the internal workings of a person's mind, spirit, and will. And he used a range of sources about the 'city' and the 'republic', both Jewish and Christian, as a way of finding exegetically neutral ground. Menasseh's highly learned world was full of classical and Renaissance republics, and he was confident of his readers' comfort with

---

[17] Pereyra, *Certeza*, 103; and id., *Espejo*, 100.
[18] Ben Israel, *De la fragilidad humana*. See Nadler, *Menasseh ben Israel*, 63–90, 115–19, and *passim*.   [19] Ben Israel, *De la fragilidad humana*, 28.

that language. The 'republic' there, though explicitly 'political', has nothing to do with Jewish politics and everything to do with piety and ethics on the part of individuals and a universal conception of man, with the soul mimicking an idealized republic.

Pereyra, a generation later, inverted the logic of the same analogy, now using the correspondence between man and republic to elucidate not the man but the republic: not just any republic, but a Jewish one, and not just any Jewish republic, but in particular his very own community. In *Certeza del camino*, in a section that he subtitled 'De la fragilidad humana' in a nod to Menasseh, Pereyra wrote:

> Just as man is composed of body and soul, the republic is composed of a body, which is the people, and a rational soul, which is the prudence of the governors. The republic must act like the perfect man who conquers his passions by subjecting the earthly to the spiritual. If the people are not obedient subjects of the government, sin will win the mortal struggle and reign in the republic.[20]

Pereyra's attitude was consistent with Menasseh's teaching. It even shared in his teacher's project of Judaizing ideas from the learned Christian world, as this interpretation, too, was drawn from a well of common political aphorisms. But Pereyra directed his comments at political rather than spiritual behaviours. The people, he argued, must humbly submit to the leadership of the governors, just as—his readers would agree, self-evidently—a man must subjugate his passions to his rational will. Pereyra's 'republic' was the Jewish community, congregants were the 'people' (ideally, 'obedient subjects'), and the leaders were 'governors'. His purpose in writing, he said, was 'that we shall know the obligations we have in our state [*estado*], and the governors shall know what they must do'. It is abundantly clear from the context that he was not referring to participation in a non-Jewish state, as he prescribed harmony between lay and clerical leaders in administering the republic according to true, i.e. Jewish, divine law.

The difference is all the more striking in the light of the two men's intellectual profiles, which ought to have produced the opposite results. Pereyra's books were oriented above all towards the spiritual health of his peers, seeking to inculcate in them a shared devotion to moral uprightness

---

[20] Pereyra, *Certeza*, 164. I have translated both *plebe* and *pueblo* as 'people' in this passage. Dauber points out that a 17th-century attitude like this has roots in Renaissance humanism. See *State and Commonwealth*, 2, 87–93.

and Jewish ideals, creating a truly religious community with frequent calls to repentance and more sincere observance. If he is known for anything, it is his anti-heretical efforts and his enthusiasm for the Sabbatian movement—which seem on their face to have more to do with sin and redemption than with politics. Menasseh, in contrast, was oriented towards politics, at least in the conventional outward-facing sense of premodern Jewish interests in diplomacy, seeking to secure a place for Jews among sovereign nations. Menasseh offered himself as an ambassador to the English government on behalf of his Jewish 'nation' and in his books *Piedra gloriosa*, *Hope of Israel*, and *Humble Addresses* he expressed Jewish hope for a restored Jewish monarchy, the 'nobility' of the Portuguese Jewish nation or Jews in general, and the contributions of Jews to the states they lived in.[21] And yet Menasseh developed a spiritual interpretation of the republic whereas Pereyra focused on the governance of the community, making the Jewish communal context political.

The differences between them reveal the extent to which discourse had shifted in the short time between the composition of the two men's oeuvres. Despite his supplications to Christian leaders and politic engagement with Christian *érudits*—or perhaps precisely because those men were his audience—Menasseh would not claim that Jews possessed a republic of their own. His *república* or *res publica* was the republic of letters, or perhaps the City of God in the Augustinian tradition. Morteira and Menasseh clashed personally, professionally, and intellectually, but they stand on the same side of this divide. Like Morteira, Menasseh started to think in terms of Jewish politics, but did not connect them to the community. For these two men and indeed for most in their time, Jewish politics were still assumed to be a matter of the past or future, in the form of ancient biblical or future messianic statehood, or a matter of realpolitik in order to smooth the way for the bare necessities of Jewish existence. Preoccupied by precarity, a tradition of Jewish engagement with European political ideas and practices had grown up around the practice of intercession.[22] It tended to position Jews as specially connected with monarchs, reflecting the reality of most communities relying on the personal magnanimity of

---

[21] Menasseh ben Israel, *'Even yeqarah* and *Hope of Israel*; see Méchoulan and Nahon (eds.), *Menasseh ben Israel*.

[22] See Guesnet, 'Politics of Precariousness', esp. around n. 4, and the bibliography on intercession cited there.

individual rulers and possessing a status as the particular pets of those rulers.[23] Menasseh, in other words, paid a great deal of attention to *Christian* politics and their impact on Jews.

Pereyra, on the other hand, was preoccupied specifically and primarily with the Jewish commonwealth and wrote about it as such. As his books combined elements of classical, Christian, and Jewish traditions, his mind was, like Menasseh's, deeply enmeshed in Christian politics; but unlike Menasseh he saw the Jewish community as analogous to other republics and he used his knowledge to offer his co-religionists advice on how to behave, on the communal as well as the individual level. In both books he devoted significant space to the ordering of political affairs in their republic, as a natural way of importing a central part of their ambient culture into a particularly Jewish idiom.

The Language of Commonwealth

Morteira and Menasseh wrote before mid-century about 'republics'—the republic of the Jews, the republic of letters, Plato's republic. In each case a republic was a general or faraway concept, or in fact pointedly something that Jews did not have. For Aguilar and Pereyra just a short time later, the idea of the Jewish republic was specifically and literally political, local and self-empowered, pragmatic and presentist, as it referred to the Kahal Kadosh. Why the change? If Morteira had already been comfortable with the idea of a theoretical Jewish republic but—like Jewish republican thinkers before him—did not see exilic communities in such terms, how should we explain Aguilar's new perspective? If Menasseh was just as involved in Christian intellectual and political culture as Pereyra, why did Pereyra alone apply its insights to the workings of their community?

An intellectual watershed separated the two different generations, as a new political discourse flooded their environment. Beginning in the 1660s, new arenas of republican and constitutionalist thinking facilitated what can be seen as a Hobbesian moment, with the minds of intellectuals and laymen alike fixed on the ideal qualities of a republic, now meaning 'polity' in a generic sense rather than specifically a polity without a monarch. Having been founded on principles of unanimity, fiscal collectivity, and Jewish civic

---

[23] See Yerushalmi, *Servants of Kings*, and Walfish, *Esther*, 191–5. See also Baron, "'Plenitude'"; Kisch, *The Jews in Medieval Germany*; Dubin, 'Yosef Hayim Yerushalmi'.

order, within the very political culture that gave rise to the new common-wealth discourse, the Kahal Kadosh was easy to discuss using the new terminology.

When early modern Jews spoke of themselves as a 'nation', a 'congre-gation', or a 'republic', they meant something in particular, and their self-descriptions are revealing.[24] Critical to understanding the Sabbatian-era innovation in the Kahal Kadosh is to trace the language that the Spanish and Portuguese Jews used to refer to themselves. Earlier, their self-referential monikers had primarily captured ethnic or religious soli-darity (as in 'the nation') or religious practice (as in 'congregations'). The *nação* ('nation' in Portuguese) was an ethnic category central to the self-understanding of the diaspora of Jews and conversos from Portugal that differentiated them from Jews of other heritage and connected them with Jews of Iberian origin across the globe, even those with divergent religi-ous and political allegiances.[25] The ethnic category was well suited to the conditions of early Jewish settlement in Amsterdam since the first social and religious groupings were oriented around kinship networks and geo-graphical origins. Secondarily, the term evoked another meaning of the 'nation' in early modern Europe, referring to groups of foreign merchants with a collective resident alien status, often housed together and granted a special legal position with reference to their nation of origin. Those con-ditions did not apply to Jews (or indeed other foreigners) in Amsterdam, as foreign groups of merchants were not allowed to organize formally there, and resistance to such bodies was part of what made the seventeenth-century Dutch political culture distinctive.[26] Still, the resident foreign 'nation' was a widely recognized model that probably informed the use of this term, such that it evoked translocal identity in contrast with the notion of a commonwealth, which emphasized discreteness, intentional or consent-based unity, and physical proximity.[27]

Another way the Portuguese Jews in Amsterdam had often referred to

[24] See Withington, *Politics*, 13.
[25] The authoritative articulation of the ethnic understanding of the *nação* is in Bodian, *Hebrews*. On the uniqueness of the self-conception of members of the converso diaspora in the Atlantic world, see Bodian, 'Hebrews'. The *nação* crossed institutional and political boundaries to include those of a certain background, sometimes even when they did not clearly identify as Jewish. See Bodian, '"Portuguese" Dowry Societies'.
[26] See Swetschinski, *Reluctant Cosmopolitans*, 184–5.
[27] On Jews and other foreign nations in Livorno, for example, see Trivellato, *Familiarity of Strangers*, 73–84.

their community over much of the seventeenth century was with the word
congrega, or congregation. It indicated a well-defined local group, specifically one that was united through collective worship. In this way it was
similar to *igreja* (or the Spanish *iglesia*, 'church'), deriving from the Greek
ekklesia and at least theoretically possessing the same sense of gathering
or assembly as the Latin-derived *congrega*. However, *congrega* connotated
primarily people and did not share *igreja*'s additional usage to refer to a
structure that might contain them. The way members of the Kahal Kadosh used it in their records and other writings, *congrega* was approximately
equivalent to the rabbinic concept of the *kahal*—an assembly of Jews who,
by assembling, create the conditions for certain ritual and legal actions,
including group prayer and binding collective agreements or decrees.
(*Kahal* is, of course, related to *kehilah*, the modern Hebrew word for 'community'. *Kehilah* appears in many premodern contexts, but infrequently in
our subjects' texts.) That the biblical book Ecclesiastes is named *Kohelet* in
Hebrew gives a sense of how these terms were related. *Congrega* entailed
some essential conceptual relationship between religion and polity—as an
assembly for prayer that becomes a body—but it did not necessarily involve
formal or enduring aggregation. It was, in that sense, not a republic; in
addition, 'congregation' leaned to the religious while 'republic' leaned to
the political.

The word 'republic' had great semantic elasticity in the early modern
world, just as it does today. In its broadest usage, it could refer to all kinds
of collectivities composed of conjoined parts in a mutually committed
system. The independent polity without a monarch, like the Republic of
Venice or the ancient Roman republic, comprised its citizens. But the concept of the republic also extended far beyond the context of governments
and states. The kind of political body it could describe was quite flexible—
as in the case of referring to native peoples in the Americas as republics.[28]
Even farther afield, there could also be a heavenly republic, referring to
the order of celestial bodies and beings; a republic of the passions within an
individual, needing to be piously governed; or of course a republic of letters, an imagined community or network of relationships among scholars.
Still, the term retained a dominant political connotation, as the Latin analogue to the Greek *polis*.[29]

[28] See Deardorff, 'Republics', 174 and *passim*.
[29] See e.g. Gil, 'Republican Politics', 263–5.

The shift to the use of the word 'republic' among members of the Kahal Kadosh in the 1660s, then, represented a sharpening of the political awareness of members of the community. It subsumed both the ethnic and the religious dimensions of identity within the political or institutional: it did not do away with those categories by which Amsterdam Jews had defined themselves since they started arriving in the early seventeenth century, but rather incorporated them into a new frame. If members of the Kahal Kadosh saw their community as a republic along the lines of a state, it was as a religious nation-state: obviously it was not a 'nation-state' in the modern sense, but the familiar phrase reminds us that there was nothing inherent in religion, nationality, or politics that excluded the others. Religion and ethnicity defined the *population* of the Kahal Kadosh, as it was designated for Jews of the Spanish and Portuguese nation, but their *community* was defined by its politics. Above all, thinking of themselves as part of a republic—instead of only a congregation or nation—emphasized that what bound them together were organization and order, institutions and common agreement, rather than a pre-existing shared identity. 'Republic' invoked law, government, and civic affairs, amounting to a view that the community was constituted by political authority and worked in significantly, if not primarily, political ways.

Reference to a Jewish community as a republic may, in itself, not have been unprecedented. After all, among its meanings was the sense, shared with 'university', of a world unto itself, including an administrative or governmental sense, used for bodies of merchants, artisans, or students.[30] The term *università* was used in Italian to refer to Jewish communities, derived from its application to Jewish status in the Roman empire.[31] Stefanie Siegmund reports that some residents of the Florentine ghetto in the late sixteenth century referred to their community as a 'republic'; there are even some government records using that word, although in one place it is crossed out and replaced with 'university'.[32] Siegmund indicates that the choice of words does not signify much in this context; it is likely that 'university' represented a similar conception of corporate structure but lacked the political connotation of 'republic', and was therefore preferable in the eyes of whoever made that change. I would imagine that similar examples of flirtation with the term exist, not yet flagged by historians.

[30] See Simonsohn, *History of the Jews*, 322.

[31] See Cooperman, 'Ethnicity', 131. On *universitas* in the Roman empire, see Baron, *The Jewish Community*, i. 108.   [32] Siegmund, *The Medici State*, 253 and 501 n. 50.

Beyond uses of the word itself, it is clear that Jewish communities could and did structure themselves along the lines of 'republics' in various local senses throughout Europe. In this characteristic, Amsterdam's Kahal Kadosh was not unique but it was particular. In Renaissance Italy Jews absorbed many aspects of the humanist revival of republicanism and the myths of the great republics of Florence and Venice, structured their communities using aspects of the republican model, and applied republican politics to biblical history. Medieval Spanish Jews enjoyed self-government along the lines of a city within a state.[33] Generally, Jews and Christians alike shared at least a trope that Jews governed themselves according to a separate law. Despite it all, a full-fledged discourse of the community as a republic per se did not emerge in any of those contexts.

Such a discourse did emerge in Amsterdam, and its immediate context was the period after the successful mid-century conclusion of the Dutch struggle for independence from Spain, and the second wave of European republicanism wherein Italian civic humanism was translated into a new Anglocentric politicism. The word 'republic' and its cognates were on everyone's lips—Jews' and Christians' alike—in cosmopolitan Amsterdam, and beginning in the 1660s it came to possess a new sense particular to the age, aligned with the English word 'commonwealth' and the customs and codes that informed it. It was about this very context that J. G. A. Pocock illuminated the way transmission and transformation of language is a central component of the historical process: as he wrote, for Machiavellian and republican ideas to be deployed in England, they 'had to become domiciled in an environment dominated by monarchical, legal, and theological concepts apparently in no way disposed to require the definition of England as a polis or the Englishman as a citizen'.[34] Likewise, with the English commonwealth were imported to Holland and the Kahal Kadosh the specific values and resonances of early modern English political culture—ready to be redeployed in a different landscape.

On the other hand, the 'commonwealth'—or 'republic' used in the same way—came to denote a polity in the most generic sense, becoming

[33] In fact, Jewish communities in pre-expulsion Spain are another example, as the terms under which Jews enjoyed legal jurisdiction have been interpreted as a cultural forerunner to 16th-century Spanish thinking about colonized peoples in terms of republics. Deardorff, 'Republics', 177–8.

[34] Pocock, *The Machiavellian Moment*, 334; more generally, see id., *Politics, Language, and Time*.

disconnected from its earlier more specific meanings. With such trans-position came abstraction, and this historical moment formed the back-ground in which 'politics' emerged in the European imagination as a discrete mode or zone of human activity, and 'political science' developed as a field of analysis.[35] Attention to commonwealths—theorizing them, arguing over them, legally constituting them—formed the discursive realm in which the modern state and its theory was able to take shape. It was thus both universalizing, beginning to speak of politics as something shared by all peoples, and very particular, enmeshed and embodied in local politi-cal practices and concepts. As we shall see, the Amsterdam Jewish attention to the community as commonwealth was similarly expressed in a combina-tion of universals and careful adaptations to their own domicile.

Commonwealths of the type elaborated in the Anglo-Dutch context were commonly understood to rely on the voluntary subjection of individ-uals to a common governing authority for their collective good. 'Com-monwealth' connoted locality, unity, lawfully constituted government, and especially mutual economic and other interests; the word was 'tightly bound with a network of related words, such as '"the common good", "common weal", "community", "the common interest", and their virtues'.[36] A com-monwealth was discrete and unified, defined by a consolidation of assets, a shared legal status or jurisdiction, and subjugation of its members, whose participation was based on an original consent or contract, also understood as a 'constitution'.[37] One sixteenth-century Englishman described a com-monwealth as 'a society or common doing of a multitude of free men col-lected together and united by common accord and coveanauntes among themselves, for the conservation of themselves as well in peace as in warre'.[38] In uniting, the individuals who formed such a 'common doing' agreed to be a part of something larger than themselves, even to put the common inter-est ahead of their own. The sense of agreement, the basic concept that a group of people could form a government by agreeing to act with a single will and voice, was critical to this vision and, ultimately, fundamental to social contract theory.[39] It also was increasingly bureaucratized and, like

---

[35] See Skinner, *Foundations*, i, pp. ix–x, and 'Hobbes's Changing Conception'.

[36] Knights et al., 'Commonwealth', 661.

[37] See Lee, *Popular Sovereignty*, and Dauber, *State and Commonwealth*.

[38] T. Smith, *De republica anglorum*, 10, cited in Knights et al., 'Commonwealth', 660 n. 1.

[39] The volition of subjects to go along with the actions of a state is a perennial problem in the political theory of the 17th century. See Brett, *Liberty*, and Lee, *Popular Sovereignty*.

other types of early modern community or association, featured office-holding, regulations or by-laws, and careful record-keeping as important elements of its legitimacy.

The idea of a 'commonwealth' differed from the looser concept of a republic in that it tended to be understood in terms of physical proximity in community, and hence also in terms of shared material property and interests. A commonwealth can be seen as analogous to a city, in the city's sense as a *civitas* or civic realm—in the words of Annabel Brett, a 'civic not a stone structure'[40]—whose foundation was association and not territory. Indeed, the state (or city) had to be abstracted from physical territory in order to constitute its own authoritative sphere. Brett writes that 'the local fixity that marks this kind of city challenges the juridical self-definition of the commonwealth, which must transcend place if it is to constitute itself as a self-sufficient or sovereign juridical structure'.[41] A city was not different in essence from a state, as each was the product of the joining together of a group or groups of people, constituting a sphere of mutuality and authority through agreement on fixed laws.[42] One of the salient characteristics of the idea of a commonwealth, at least at first, was that it could be used for a range of institutions and collectives at various levels. Residents of an English town might call themselves a 'community', a 'society', or a small 'commonwealth';[43] English colonists in seventeenth- and eighteenth-century New England also actively constituted their communities in these terms.[44] Such self-identified polities were often proudly urban and bourgeois, possessing a strong public political discourse, as Withington put it: 'The ideal of community lay at the heart of city commonwealth; likewise, the ideal of communication lay at the heart of community.'[45]

Using a term from Protestant England to discuss Spanish and Portuguese Jewish thinkers located in Holland emphasizes their participation in what is widely acknowledged as a paradigm shift in Western intellectual

[40] In fact, the relationship between state authority and territory was not imagined to be simple, and it was the object of sustained direct attention during the 17th century. See Brett, *Changes of State*, 2.   [41] Ibid., 7.

[42] Citing Hobbes, Brett notes that this sense of the city was, for some, 'nothing other than the state' or 'commonwealth' (ibid. 2).

[43] Withington quotes Thomas Wilson in 1600: 'every city being, as it were, a Common wealth among themselves' (*Politics*, 11).

[44] See Winship, *Godly Republicanism*; Demos, *A Little Commonwealth*; and Zuckerman, *Peaceable Kingdoms*. I thank my colleague Arthur Kiron for pointing me in the direction of the colonies.   [45] Withington, *Politics*, 127.

traditions regarding government. Thomas Hobbes, the prototypical theorist of the early modern state, used 'commonwealth' throughout his English masterwork *Leviathan*, and in recognition of the shared conversation, 'commonwealth' is frequently used as the best translation for incidences of (cognates of) 'republic' in Latin and European vernaculars during this era. For example, in a standard translation of Spinoza's *Theological-Political Treatise* his Latin *res publica* is rendered 'commonwealth', as in: 'We have now seen how religion was introduced into the Hebrew commonwealth.'[46] The broad acceptance of 'commonwealth' in wider historiography today is a marker of the extent to which those traditions came to dominate the world of ideas in the heady atmosphere of north-west Europe in the age of social and religious crisis, and it was particularly influential in the decades leading up to what has been called 'the Anglo-Dutch moment' of the Glorious Revolution in 1688 and beyond.[47] At the height of its golden age, Amsterdam served as a hub for printing and other forms of intellectual intercourse and provided a haven for writers whose controversial ideas were dangerous to them elsewhere.

On the other hand, it was also during this time that the Dutch began to develop a full-blown political discourse of their own, interconnected with but differentiated from the English commonwealth thinking. Although they fought against the rule of the Spanish Crown for decades and thus had a healthy strain of anti-monarchical sentiment, earlier Dutch efforts to theorize a mixed constitution based on the model of Venice were minimal, and there was little high intellectual intercourse between England and Holland until the 1660s.[48] Dutch republicanism in the wake of the translation of Hobbes into Dutch and Latin (in 1667 and 1668)[49] differed from forms that had developed during the Dutch Revolt, and put a unique spin on the wider Atlantic republicanism of which it was a part.[50] It featured an interest in commerce and economy, strong anti-monarchism, centralized versus

---

[46] *TPT*, 236.

[47] Israel (ed.), *The Anglo-Dutch Moment*.

[48] Haitsma Mulier, 'A Controversial Republican', 263; Haitsma Mulier, 'Language', 183–8; and Weststeijn, 'Why the Dutch Didn't Read Harrington'. See also van Gelderen, 'Machiavellian Moment'; Haitsma Mulier, 'Controversial Republican'; and Pocock, 'Dutch Republican Tradition'.

[49] Hobbes's *Leviathan* was first published in English in 1651; it was translated into Dutch in 1667, and into Latin (published in Amsterdam) in 1668. Newey, *Routledge Guidebook*, 317–18.

[50] Israel, *Monarchy*, 5. Several have pointed out that Pocock did not include the slightly different Dutch modes. See Boralevi, 'Classical Foundational Myths', 247; Kossmann, 'Dutch Republicanism'; and Velema, '"That a Republic Is Better than a Monarchy"'.

confederated models, and the emphasis on individual and group rights and privileges. Dutch republican discourse emphasized war and the military as signs of independence, along with attention to sovereignty and the authority of the people, but evinced less interest in either land or the bearing of arms.[51] Many of these elements, especially anti-monarchism, commerce, the authority of the people, and the deprioritization of land and arms, were particularly ripe for adaptation in a Jewish communal context.

Although the Dutch political culture was distinct, the thinkers that theorized it—primarily Spinoza, the Stadtholder Johan de Witt, and Jan and Pieter de la Court—were universally aware of, and spurred on by, Hobbesian thought. They were part of a widespread movement to develop politics and political science around a generic understanding of the proto-state, or commonwealth. Amsterdam's Portuguese Jews received the earlier European republicanism that had idealized classical republics in an embrace of civic humanism, filtered through later seventeenth-century treatments, and they reinterpreted it in turn to suit their own particular political circumstances.

It is not hard to see why members of the Kahal Kadosh adapted the notion of the commonwealth to their internal affairs. Many of the qualities that particularly characterized commonwealths were shared by the Kahal Kadosh as it had been set up at the time of the *Acordos*, as I discussed at length above in Chapter 1. The communal system was based on a collective agreement to abide by a common set of rules and obey an established government, and the signatures on the *Acordos* visually demonstrate the centrality of the original consent of the people. The Jewish community also possessed the in-person, spatially localized interactions that characterized a political society for many early modern thinkers.[52] The internal logic justifying communal order revolved to a great extent around the idea of shared material interests, the literal common wealth, and provision for the needy among their members. Rhetoric about unity reinforced a halakhic justification of all-encompassing authority on the part of the lay Mahamad. Notably, it did not centre on legal autonomy or separate jurisdiction as the main principle that set Jews apart, but rather utilized administrative, lay, and agreement-based modes of collectivization. That shift—moving away

[51] See Prokhovnik, *Spinoza and Republicanism*; Kossmann, *Political Thought*; Velema, "'That a Republic Is Better than a Monarchy'"; and Weststeijn, *Commercial Republicanism*.
[52] See Sacks, *The Widening Gate*, 5–7.

from medieval Spanish models as well as common conceptions of Jewish separateness—set up this particular community as a polity rather than as a court, further aligning it with extant commonwealth discourse.

In other words, the community had already been fashioned as a polity within the logic and codes of the Dutch system. Only now, members of the Kahal Kadosh began to interpret those qualities as elements of the community understood as a 'republic' with the particular qualities of commonwealth politics, and to fit such an interpretation into Jewish thought. This act of translation and adaptation was made possible by the combination of two fortuitous but seemingly opposing circumstances: first, that the community already existed in a form consistent with the particularity of the new, commonwealth-like, idea of the 'republic'; and second, that the new discourse included within it a universalizing dimension that saw 'political' behaviour and institutions in many forms and contexts. In parallel to the way that English and Dutch Christians translated civic humanism and classical political thought into their local codes and modes, the Spanish and Portuguese Jews who lived among them translated the translation into Jewish discourse.

Unity and Order in the Ideal Jewish Commonwealth

Pereyra frequently referred to the republic, the community-as-commonwealth, as a body politic. In addition to his discussion of the celestial hierarchy quoted above, he wrote:

The senses are the professors and judges in our republic by whose doctrine we govern, and thus must see and observe the actions of all, hear all parties equally, smell good and bad reputation, take with gusto and zeal the charges of the people and touch important cases with their own hands. The heart is the beginning of life and the distribution of blood. . . . Who is the heart of the republic, if not the professors and governors of it? The blood, which it so carefully guards, is the temporal wealth of the subjects that they must defend as their own; the preservation of natural heat is the zeal for the common good. . . . In the two arms we see reward and punishment; in the bones and nerves, the weapons and letters that sustain the peoples; in the stomach we see distributive . . . [and] commutative justice.[53]

Pereyra touched on a number of themes that would come to dominate

---

[53] Pereyra, *Certeza*, 164.

communal discourse during these two decades, including the relationship
between lay and rabbinic leaders (the 'professors and governors'), the importance of shared and distributed wealth, and the role of the community
in arbitrating justice.[54] Compare his analogy to Hobbes's:

By Art is created that great LEVIATHAN called a COMMON-WEALTH, or
STATE (in latine, CIVITAS), which is but an Artificiall Man . . . The *Magistrates*,
and other *Officers* of Judicature and Execution [are] artificiall *Joynts*; *Reward* and
Punishment . . . are the *Nerves*. . . . The *Wealth* and *Riches* of all the particular
members, are the *Strength*; *Salus Populi* (the *peoples safety*) its *Businesse*; *Counsellors*,
by whom all things needfull for it to know, are suggested unto it, are the *Memory*;
Equity and *Lawes*, an artificiall *Reason* and *Will*; *Concord*, *Health*; *Sedition*, *Sicknesse*;
and *Civill war*, *Death*.[55]

Pereyra's exposition of the community as a body politic had more in common with that of Hobbes, a Christian Englishman, and in turn with a widespread discourse of political thought within the Christian West, than with
that of his co-religionist, the ostensibly politically active Menasseh ben
Israel.

The classical republic was a union of the people, and this quality was
key to much seventeenth-century analysis of polities,[56] even when the precise mechanism of political constitution or the relationship between people
and government might be debated. Brett writes about the commonwealth
or state as a *civitas*, or civic realm, that 'both medieval and early modern
legal and scholastic discourse is saturated with the idea that the city is a
unity. *Civitas* was even defined, in a pseudo-etymology, as *civium unitas*,
a unity of citizens . . . The dominant interpretation of this unity is the unity
of *one body*'.[57] This was the tradition on which Abraham Pereyra drew when
he wrote of the Kahal Kadosh as a body politic consisting of individual
members conjoined in divine order, imitating the celestial republic or a
perfect man and making the community into a Leviathan.

Others echoed the sentiment. In his sermon celebrating the opening of
the community's new synagogue in 1675, the young intellectual and physician David Sarphati elaborated on the theme of multiplicity in unity as

[54] For example: 'In the head, superior to all of the members, is encoded the necessary love,
veneration, and support for the Law and its professors that are the head and crown of the
republic, because the lights of reason and the eminence of virtue are resplendent in them'
(Pereyra, *Certeza*, 164).   [55] Hobbes, *Leviathan*, 9.
[56] Dauber, *State and Commonwealth*, 2.   [57] Brett, *Changes of State*, 122.

follows: 'Like a part that encompasses the whole, we offer the whole of this small part. And to the Noble Listener, as the whole is distributed into parts, we dedicate the part to celebrate this whole. . . . As we all participate in the whole, so the part that by chance we play is like a motif contributing to this glory.'[58] Sarphati also noted that the Mahamad, made up of illustrious individuals, acted as one body, and he described the roles played by various segments of the congregation who had joined together to erect the synagogue in a unified act of piety: 'The lords of the Mahamad worked laboriously on this building, and the administrators and treasurer laboured on it with equal workmanship; our Lord *Hakham, morenu u-rabenu*, zealously persuaded everyone to do it, and the holy Kahal acted with equally persuasive zeal.'[59] In this short passage Sarphati's Baroque-inflected inversions—'working laboriously' and 'labouring with workmanship', 'zealous persuasion' and 'persuasive zeal'—poetically evoke a similar structural reciprocity in the community, whereby the members, rabbis, and lay leaders at various levels are seen as inextricably connected in a harmonious web of mutual engagement.

Other writers, too, lauded reciprocity, perpetuating a common ideal of republican harmony ultimately headed by the Mahamad. Pereyra used a common musical metaphor to illustrate the importance of individual contributions to the common good: he wrote that harmonious music, representing 'rectitude in the republic', was produced by the controlling judgement of the player, i.e. the governor, in *Certeza*,[60] and elaborated on similar themes in *Espejo*.[61] The poet Daniel Levi de Barrios used a harp as a model to illuminate the value of strong leadership in a republic: 'The key to its pleasantness', he wrote, 'lies in tempering the strings of different wills' and 'bringing together distant tensions'.[62]

[58] Sarphati, 'Sermão Septimo', 139. This is a loose translation of a particularly ornate passage.   [59] Ibid. 138.   [60] Pereyra, *Certeza*, 168–9.

[61] Paraphrasing the 16th-century Francesco Giorgio's *De harmonia mundi*. Pereyra, *Espejo*, 144, 406.

[62] Barrios, *Triumpho*, 4. He may be intentionally echoing Pereyra, as in the following pages he offers several paraphrases of Pereyra or his sources that appeared in Pereyra's political chapters, including the assertions that a governor must first learn to govern himself and that the 'governor is a law that speaks'. See Pereyra, *Espejo*, 152, and Barrios, *Triumpho*, 5–6, though Pereyra attributes it to Plato and Barrios to Cicero. An intellectual accord between the two dissimilar men is also supported by the fact that a sonnet of praise written by Barrios is printed at the beginning of *Espejo*. Presumably Barrios was aided by the wealthy Pereyra's patronage; they were also fellow Sabbatian thinkers in the years after the apostasy.

The ideal harmony Kahal Kadosh members spoke of was especially relevant to the relationship between two essential facets of the Jewish commonwealth, the sacred and temporal, and reinforced the primacy of the lay leadership, lending it a civic quality. Pereyra, for example, affirmed the necessity of a strong lay government even as he infused his discussion of it with religious justification. God, Pereyra wrote, 'wanted to show us that not only the terrestrial republics need governors: even the celestial republic cannot prosper without princes who take charge of its decisions'.[63] The successive celestial hierarchies were, according to him, recapitulated in the way the lay leaders governed the Jewish community: 'It would not be possible to preserve a republic without a head to correct vices and foster virtues.'[64] Pereyra thus prescribed an ordered society in which lesser subjects would obey their superiors: 'If the people are not obedient subjects of the government, sin will win the mortal struggle and reign in the republic.'[65]

Pereyra's justification of strong lay leadership here introduces a long prescriptive discussion of political affairs, leaving no uncertainty about his meaning: all republics instantiate universal order, and a Jewish republic guided by Jewish law all the more. Likewise, Pereyra indicated, excommunication could be understood as the amputation of a limb, necessary to prevent the spread of a dangerous cancer. More than some others in the Kahal Kadosh, Pereyra thought that halakhah ought to be integrated into communal law, and he tended to refer to rabbis as having a kind of authority of their own; but he did not go so far as to suggest that rabbis should rule. For example: 'The divine majesty granted power (*imperio*) and rule (*mando*) to the princes and legitimate governors in republics, and [did so] with much more authority in those [republics] of his beloved people because he constituted, by affirmative precept, obedience not merely to kings but even more to the Judges and teachers of the Divine Law.'[66] This passage simultaneously suggests that Jewish republics possess *imperio* and *mando* analogous to Christian republics and emphasizes that the source of that power is religious. Within that framework, excommunication is clearly portrayed as a tool of the republic and the prerogative of its lay leaders. He generally followed the pattern of his peers in referring to lay leaders as governors or

---

[63] Pereyra, *Certeza*, 163.   [64] Ibid.

[65] Méchoulan cites Marquez's *El governador christiano* as the source for this passage. Pereyra, *Certeza*, 164.   [66] Pereyra, *Certeza*, 163.

judges and to rabbis as teachers, emphasizing harmony through hierarchy. He insisted that communal leaders must follow general principles of good political behaviour, as they were part of a divinely arranged system of rule and subjection, and that communal members must, for their part, practise obedience.

Top-down order was not the only harmony described and prescribed within Amsterdam's Kahal Kadosh. The early seventeenth-century Dutch political theorist Johannes Althusius's view of a city, community, or commonwealth had it consisting, like Aristotle's *polis*, of civic structures (councils, guilds, etc.), jurisdictions, and neighbourhoods, and households[67] in a nested structure similar to the one Pereyra described on a universal scale. In reality, the seventeenth-century incorporated city was not as tidy as a pre-Copernican system of heavenly orbs would suggest, as other powerful bodies existed within and above city institutions, in a horizontally segmented quasi-order formed by negotiation and competition by means of petitions, appeals to 'rights', and public complaint.[68] Likewise, empires and kingdoms were themselves 'composite realms', made up of sub-units with complex and often contentious relations to each other and the whole —leading historians to call the Spanish system in the sixteenth century a 'republic of republics'.[69] The Kahal Kadosh, too, was embedded within a wider legal and economic system but set apart in a relationship of constant negotiation, check, and balance; in turn, it contained multiple societies, offices, hierarchies, and departments within it.

Daniel Levi de Barrios's systematic account of how the Jewish polity operated painted it very much in this style. Born a converso in Spain, Barrios left to convert to Judaism, briefly residing in Tobago and Livorno before making his way to the Low Countries. In Amsterdam he married a member of the Kahal Kadosh in 1662 but continued to serve as a captain in the Spanish army, publishing panegyrics and occasional poems in Brussels under the name El Capitan Miguel de Barrios for some time.[70] In the first half of the 1670s, Barrios began to stay permanently in Amsterdam—a decision that may have been related to a newfound religious enthusiasm sparked by Sabbatianism. Literarily, Barrios is known for his ornate, highly allusive, and sometimes opaque Baroque style, full of complex schemes of

[67] Withington, *Politics*, 10.   [68] Frijhoff and Spies, *Dutch Culture*, 179–80.

[69] Deardorff, 'Republics', 172–4, and Herrero Sánchez, 'Monarquía Hispánica'.

[70] He resigned his commission in 1674. Scholberg, 'Miguel de Barrios', 121.

correspondence and linguistic derivation, in works devoted to Jewish and general history, current affairs, and ideas.[71] His *Triumpho del govierno popular* (composed in multiple parts and editions, first appearing in 1683) is a chronicle and memorial of the institutions of the Kahal Kadosh, written as a bid for patronage from the communal elite. It opens with an abstract discussion of government forms, moves on to a specific discussion of the nature and origins of the present government of the Kahal Kadosh, and then in a section called 'Govierno popular judayco' discusses in detail the various branches and sub-organizations that made up the communal administrative structure—first schematically, and then through detailed histories of each branch, committee, brotherhood, society, and yeshiva.[72] Barrios aimed to flatter, but in many places his tone was matter-of-fact. His work served in part as a guide to Jewish communal and political affairs, parallel to the many guides to Jewish religious observance that were created in this era as part of the 'rejudaization' of former conversos.[73] Like many chronicles and histories of the day, it thus also justified and supported an existing political regime.[74]

According to Barrios, 'The Popular Jewish Government of Amsterdam is divided into 4 governments: Political, Rabbinic, Charitable, and Academic. . . . The Political Government has jurisdiction over the Rabbinic Government in the Synagogue, and in the Treasury.'[75] He further described intracommunal organizations, vividly portraying a thriving commonwealth in which the needs of the people were met by a variety of institutions that all had a part in self-governance. The multiple 'governments' with different sources and mandates, including brotherhoods, academies, charities, and councils, look much like the messy polities that surrounded Barrios in the Christian world. His depiction of the Kahal Kadosh as ruled by a 'popular' or 'democratic' government, as reflected in the title and subtitle as well as in other portions of the text, emphasizes that the people (the members of the *kahal*) were the ultimate source for the authority of the government of the Kahal Kadosh, building on Spinozistic and contemporary Dutch interest in the power of the people.[76]

---

[71] Some untanglings of Barrios's ideas include: den Boer, 'Literature'; den Boer and Israel, 'William III'; Díaz Esteban, 'Fanciful Biblical Etymologies'; Wilke, 'La *Trompette du jugement*'; Lieberman, *El teatro alegórico*; and Oelman, *Marrano Poets*.

[72] Barrios, *Triumpho*, 25.   [73] See Bodian, *Hebrews*, 96–131.   [74] See Ch. 7.

[75] Barrios, *Triumpho*, 38.   [76] And reflecting the precedent of the *Acordos*.

Isaac Orobio de Castro (1620–87) was a contemporary of Barrios, and similarly engaged in using mature cultural tools to make sense of a Jewish community adopted midlife. Intellectually and temperamentally, however, they were polar opposites. After arriving in Amsterdam (only in 1662) Orobio made a name for himself as a defender of Judaism through oral and epistolary debates as well as manuscripts that circulated widely.[77] He also participated in actual governance to a limited extent, serving on the board of a couple of 'societies' within the community and then on the Mahamad in 1669–70.[78] Like Barrios, Orobio appreciated the new flavour of Jewish communal republicanism; he deployed it to think in a new way about analogies between biblical and exilic Jewish polities. He addressed Genesis 49: 10 ('The sceptre will not depart from Judah, nor a lawgiver from beneath his feet, until Shiloh comes'), a verse that served as the linchpin for centuries of vociferous Christian–Jewish disputation throughout the Middle Ages and into the early modern period, with both Jewish and Christian thinkers grappling with how the prophecy could be understood as having been fulfilled historically.

Orobio's multidimensional treatment (discussed more fully below, in Chapter 7) included an argument that the prophecy referred to the tribe of Judah alone rather than to all Jews. Investigating their politics, then, Orobio wrote that Judah's descendants were 'set apart from the rest of the tribes ... constituting a different house from all of Israel, as a republic unto itself [*república de por sí*]'.[79] Of course, everyone knew that the Judites did not constitute their own kingdom. Orobio clarified that the Hebrew *shevet* in the verse need not be translated as a (royal) sceptre but rather a more generic and not necessarily sovereign, but still actualized, 'rule' (*mando*), and he described in detail the workings of Judah's ancient republic. His rejection of kingship as the only form of politics updated a minor thread of rabbinic interpretation of the passage to reflect the new republicanism. It offered a biblical alternative to the Mosaic republic as a model for a polity like the Kahal Kadosh, since the republic of Judah was characterized not by religious law but by lay self-rule, and it was distinctive genealogically, economically, and geographically within the Jewish people rather than being identified with the entire people.

---

[77] On Orobio, see Yosef Kaplan's erudite biography, *From Christianity to Judaism*.
[78] He served as an official in the Bikur Holim society, 1664–5, and the Ets Hayim society, 1668–9.   [79] Orobio, *Prevenciones*, MS Ros. 631, p. 76.

Cultural Translation

Discussion of the political nature of the Kahal Kadosh Talmud Torah was
not limited to the above brief comments by Aguilar, Pereyra, Barrios, and
Orobio. In multiple works over two decades members expanded on themes
of exile and sovereignty, history and politics, contract, constitution, unity,
and division. In doing so, they adapted and updated older traditions of
Jewish politics and of republicanism to fit their particular circumstances.
The terminology that the Spanish and Portuguese Jews of Amsterdam employed opens a window on their self-understanding, as they not only rhetorically claimed a commonwealth but actively treated their community as
one, in all its complexity. Their use of 'republic' beginning in the 1660s
came along with other words that reflected the same political turn: terms
like government, constitution, sovereignty, authority, law, rights, judge,
subject, tribunal, democracy, and politics—all in reference to Jewish self-
government. Amsterdam's *nação* used this kind of political language literally and metaphorically, with subtlety and self-awareness, in relation to
things that mattered to them—issues with direct impact on their affairs and
deep resonance with Jewish intellectual and practical traditions. Community members saw in it some key characteristics of commonwealths as they
knew them: collectivity and aggregation, unity in multiplicity, consensus
and agreement, and the incorporation of religious authority and principles
into a civic realm.

Abraham Pereyra's books offer material for an exceptionally clear case
study of how such adaptation was carried out. He articulated commonplace
themes and tropes from a wider non-Jewish political world that reached
beyond contemporary sources from Protestant north-west Europe. He
drew largely on late sixteenth- and early seventeenth-century Spanish
writings, like those of Saavedra Fajardo, Claudio Clemente, Francisco de
Quevedo, Juan Marquez, Fray Luis de la Puente, Diego de Estella, and
Pedro de Ribadeneira,[80] as well as many classical sources. Extended passages are copied verbatim or paraphrased and strung together; they are
bridged by passages apparently penned by Pereyra himself, and the whole
thing hangs together according to a loose organizational framework. It is

[80] On his use of particular sources, see Méchoulan, 'Abraham Pereyra'; 'Diego de Estella';
'La Pensée'; *Hispanidad*; and Robles Carcedo, 'Abraham Pereyra'.

no wonder that he has mainly been seen as rooted, or even stuck, in a conservative Iberian mindset.

But Pereyra did more than merely collect and summarize: he interpreted, harmonized, and adapted these sources into something new: something Jewish, and something quite contemporary, reflecting the new availability of the concept of a polity for a Jewish community. Into his text he wove works of Jewish writers such as Menasseh ben Israel, Immanuel Aboab, David Cohen de Lara, and more, drawing from the many guides to Jewish dogma and practice that were published in Spanish and Portuguese during the first half of the seventeenth century. Pereyra's remark that *Certeza* was for those who came late to the path meant not only that he hoped to inspire repentance, but also that it would bridge a twofold gap by offering Jewish wisdom in Spanish, and Spanish wisdom made appropriate for Jews. Moses Raphael d'Aguilar confirmed this intent in his approbation to the book, writing that many who had thankfully been delivered from tyranny and Inquisition still had trouble understanding and studying divine letters: as he wrote, there was a need for pious Jewish writings in 'our language'.[81]

In a twist on the same idea, Hakham Isaac Aboab da Fonseca explained that Pereyra's book met an urgent need since many zealous members of the nation, unable to read Hebrew moral tracts, turned instead to 'profane books, the least damaging of which are still full of vanity and lies'. Aboab may be interpreted as saying that his congregants were reading the very works that Pereyra paraphrased, thus exposing themselves to the sharp Catholic apologetics they contain, or as saying that they were shying away from books of Christian piety and were thus left with more unsavoury selections. Probably both. A glance at the few libraries that are known from the seventeenth-century Sephardim confirms that they were enthusiastic consumers of European history, geography, and politics,[82] and that they valued a wide range of Iberian literary works.

Pereyra was creating a sanitized version of non-Jewish writings at the same time as offering a culturally (and linguistically) Spanish translation of

---

[81] Pereyra, *Certeza*, 98–101. Aguilar's approbation is in Portuguese, while Aboab's is in Spanish. There is also one from Isaac Naar, who partnered with Pereyra in Sabbatian activities.

[82] Including works like Jose de Acosta's *Historia natural y moral de las Indias*, Pedro Mexia's *Historia imperial y cesarea*, and Pedro Teixeira's *Relaciones . . . de los reyes de Persia*. See Swetschinski, 'Portuguese Jews'; Y. Kaplan, 'Perfil Cultural'; and id., 'Preface'.

Jewish works—and putting them all into the context of life in an exilic Jewish commonwealth. The translation effort was typical of the Sephardi Jews of Amsterdam, who produced many volumes of texts newly translated into Spanish from Hebrew in order to educate and Judaize new immigrants, making the major texts of Jewish ritual and thought available to those who might never learn the holy tongue. Many of these were not merely translations of extant works in Hebrew, but codifications and commentaries in their own right, anthologies attempting to encapsulate the most essential Jewish knowledge. Pereyra's books undertake a parallel project for non-Jewish sources. There was thus nothing surreptitious or psychologically problematic about Pereyra's use of Catholic writers: his books reflect not a tragically 'divided soul'[83] but a man actively fashioning not only himself but his community, and mustering an intellectual armoury with which to protect and refine it.

After all, such anthologization was not limited to Jews who used it to straddle discursive worlds. In early modern Europe, it was common to translate, rewrite, reframe, or adapt existing sources for new contexts, with or without attribution.[84] A prototypical example of such work is that of Justus Lipsius, whose *Six Books of Politics*, one of the most widely read books in seventeenth-century Europe, was constructed out of political material gleaned mainly from classical sources. As Lipsius put it: 'I have taken the stones and rafters from others; but the construction and shape of the building are mine entirely. I am the architect, but I have collected material from everywhere around.'[85] Pereyra echoed Lipsius's sentiment when he compared himself in the prologue of the *Certeza* to the author of the biblical book *Kohelet* (Ecclesiastes), itself a collection of sayings regarding piety, proper behaviour, and common wisdom, with authorship traditionally associated with the kingly line of David and Solomon.[86] Pereyra wrote:

I was motivated by the sage saying, 'authors of collections were made by one governor' [see Eccles. 12: 11, 'The sayings of the wise are like goads, like nails fixed in prodding sticks. They were given by one Shepherd'[87]], meaning that

[83] Van Praag, 'Almas en litigio'.   [84] Burke, 'Cultures'.   [85] Lipsius, *Politica*, 55.
[86] See Eccles. 12: 9–10: 'Because Koheleth was a sage, he continued to instruct the people. He listened to and tested the soundness of many maxims. Koheleth sought to discover useful sayings and recorded genuinely truthful sayings.'
[87] Pereyra renders *ro'eh* as governor instead of shepherd in his paraphrase ('The wise one inspired me when he said, "Authors of collections were given by one governor"'), a translation that is not supported by the Ferrara or Reina-Valeria Spanish versions. Pereyra, *Certeza*, 104.

even if the writers have done nothing more than collect and summarize what older ones had said, they deserve praise and reward because everything good has its origin in the single governor who is God.[88]

The encyclopedic or aggregatory quality of these books should not be seen as a failure on the part of Pereyra as an original author. On the contrary, they reflect his clear vision.

Lipsius's *Politica* is believed to have originated as a commonplace book, as its author wrote down wise sayings according to a thematic framework of his own construction and then connected them.[89] Pereyra's *Certeza* may very well have taken shape in the same way, as he noted passages of his favourite moral works and his new-found Jewish books, 'ancient and modern examples, some for their authoritativeness [*autoridad*] and others because they are more persuasive',[90] and organized them into categories, like with like, into a kind of encyclopedia of wisdom. Like Lipsius, he then cemented the passages together, paraphrasing, changing syntax, and even altering significant details when necessary to make a continuous text with its own argument.

Such reworking was typical. Daniel Levi de Barrios, too, paraphrased liberally from countless sources, playing with the linguistic and religious perspectives of author and reader. Isaac Aboab da Fonseca's *Parafrasis comentado sobre el pentateuco* (1681) is an extremely free narrative retelling of the Hebrew Bible, incorporating a wide range of commentaries without explicitly acknowledging its sources or even marking its many divergences from the sacred text itself. Aboab described the work as a new Targum, the ancient vernacular version of the Hebrew Bible that was more of a paraphrase than a translation:

The censure and calumny of others will be reduced if I tell you that the greater part [of this work] is taken from the most famous Authors in my library . . . In this I was led by the great historian of antiquity Josephus, who wrote as if for the Romans, and I write as if for my brothers . . . One is obliged to read the *parashah* every week, each verse twice, and once in the Chaldean paraphrase, and it is also said that whoever reads the commentary of Rashi (our great Commentator) will have satisfied this obligation . . . Other sages agree with me that reading this translation and commentary will have the same effect if you are unable to read either one or the other.[91]

---

[88] Ibid.
[90] Pereyra, *Certeza*, 103.
[89] Moss, 'Politica', and Waszink, 'Introduction', 55–79.
[91] Aboab, *Parafrasis*, unpaginated prologue.

Aboab positioned his Bible version as a translation, such that reading it would be equivalent to reading the original. But in comparing himself to the ancient historian Josephus and the medieval commentator Rashi, he acknowledges that his text is an amalgam. Indeed, he not only acknowledges it but legitimates his innovation on that basis.

Like Lipsius, Barrios, and Aboab, Pereyra did not shrink from redirecting a text, removing it from its context to make it support an idea that its original author most certainly would not,[92] as, for example, when Fray Luis de Granada's advice on regular examination of one's conscience comes to support the observance of Jewish religious commandments at specifically appointed times.[93] Lipsius filtered Tacitean aphorisms into a Christian intellectual milieu where Stoicism was taboo by association with Machiavelli. Pereyra may well have seen his work as a counterpart to Lipsius's, translating Christian and classical commonplaces into the Jewish political world in order to similarly rehabilitate ideas tainted by their expression in Christian texts.

But Lipsius is only one example of this widespread literary technique. Most writers sprinkled their narrative stream with a liberal dose of quotations or allusions, and in the seventeenth century a text was not yet conceived as the unbreakable intellectual property of its author.[94] A translation with more regard for the new target reader than for fidelity to the source even has a name: a *belle infidèle*,[95] or 'unfaithful beauty'. One's political and religious enemies were often good sources for an argument or a turn of phrase; the acknowledgement of that fact, and willingness to use it, was hardly unique to those, like former conversos, who had crossed a confessional or national divide. It is most likely that Pereyra and his readers were aware of the kaleidoscopic nature of his text and of their lives, without being disturbed by it.[96] Pereyra knitted together sources and styles that included but were not limited to Iberian ones; the rabbis who wrote approbations for him, and presumably many readers, understood the value of such a craft.[97]

[92] Jones, 'Aphorism', 64.   [93] Pereyra, *Certeza*, 310.
[94] Burke, 'Cultures', 30–4.   [95] Bastin, 'Adaptation', 5.
[96] Swetschinski, *Reluctant Cosmopolitans*, 315, and the entire chapter, 'A Patchwork Culture: Iberian, Jewish, and Dutch Elements in Peaceable Coexistence'.
[97] In such a context, there are no clear lines distinguishing translation, adaptation, 'tradaptation', compilation, and appropriation. On 'tradaptation', see Bastin, 'Adaptation', 8, citing Michel Garneau's coinage.

In his work of cultural translation in a political sphere, it is unusually visible which elements were difficult to reconcile and why. Pereyra carefully adjusted terms to make his text work for his readers, even when both source and 'translation' were in the same language. His methods reveal much about his way of thinking as he transposed political ideas from Christian contexts and, often, sovereign monarchical ones, into that of a Jewish commonwealth. Pereyra used specific terms—*mando, gobierno, gobernador, sujeto, justicia, pueblo,* and *autoridad,* for example—that could fit a Jewish communal context and yet retained their governmental or political feel.

His word choice was often quite shrewd. For example, when describing the correct punishment for those who disturbed the peace of the commonwealth, he called for 'banishment'. In both Jewish and Christian traditions, banishment was connected thematically with two other forms of punishment: excommunication and execution.[98] All of them represented the essential right of a ruler to completely remove a person from the body politic, but they have subtle differences. Excommunication is read as more religious, the purview of the rulers of a spiritual body. Execution, on the other hand, came to represent sovereignty, and was thus implausible for the context of the Jewish commonwealth. These were distinctions that were very much present in the general politics of the day, and were discussed by other members of the Kahal Kadosh, exploring the limits of the analogy between excommunication and the death penalty. Aboab da Fonseca adapted the Hebrew word *ḥerem* into Portuguese to describe a banned person as *enhermado*; Isaac Orobio de Castro described excommunication as a penalty of 'civic death'.[99] In choosing the word 'banishment' Pereyra portrayed the *ḥerem* in plainly political terms, as the exclusion of a person from the polity, with no halakhic or spiritual overtones, but also in a way that was true to the realities of Jewish communal authority. He chose the term that made the Jewish context sound most like a political republic, without overreaching to the absurdity of claiming a sovereign state.

Another example is 'professors' for rabbis. Here the word was sometimes carried over directly from Iberian sources, where it referred to a specifically Catholic figure of a priest or theologian, but it was well suited to the actual role of rabbis in the Kahal Kadosh, emphasizing their function as teachers and spiritual guides. (Similarly, rabbis appear throughout

---

[98] See below, Ch. 5, where conceptions of excommunication as a penalty of death or banishment are discussed at length.   [99] See below, Ch. 5.

Orobio de Castro's work as 'doctors of the Law'.) It also evokes the locally dominant title of *ḥakham*, literally 'wise man', though it is not a direct Spanish translation of it like *sabio* (sage or wise one), which was sometimes used by Pereyra's contemporaries. 'Professor' instead connoted the learned quality of the person and some kind of institutional standing—but also, tellingly, set rabbis apart from juridical roles that might be implied by calling them judges or lawyers. Actually, Pereyra did sometimes call them 'judges', a fact that is revealing of his uncertainty about the extent to which the rabbinic law about which they were qualified to issue judgment was integrated with, or tangential to, communal government. In that he was not alone.

Likewise, the term 'governor' often appears in place of the 'prince' or 'king' of his sources. This choice was natural since 'governor' was already present in some of them, like Marquez's *El gobernador Christiano*. The term's use in Spanish literature reflected a turn towards the art and practice of governing throughout the bureaucratic or court hierarchy, rather than focusing exclusively on the monarch, and it suited Jewish communal office-holders as well. Increasing discussions of 'government' represented the opening up of a cultural space for the political nature of non-sovereign (and non-state) leaders. Just as it could be used for the governor of a province or colony, or indeed a company, it could easily be used for a member of the Mahamad. Politics emerged as a neutral sphere in which diverse states, systems, and governments were newly understood to participate. The story of the commonwealth in European thought is the story of the rise of the idea of the state and of an independent area of human activity called politics. It is this that the Amsterdam Sephardim were ultimately adopting.[100]

Pereyra also sometimes replaced *principe* or *monarca* with *pueblo*, a democratizing move that reflected the people-powered conception of the Kahal Kadosh.[101] Moving in this direction took Jewish politics out of the monarchical context and capitalized on new conceptions of popular sovereignty in early modern Europe, and especially in the Dutch Republic. Pereyra was here retrofitting both Jewish and contemporary Christian politics onto the Spanish sources that he and his peers knew intimately. The same emphasis on the people is found in metaphorical form in the

[100] See Ch. 6 for more on the implications of the adoption of the generic idea of politics.
[101] See Robles Carcedo, 'Abraham Pereyra', 328.

discussions of communal harmony in multiplicity cited above, as well as in Barrios's explicit and even provocative claims that diaspora Jewish communities were divinely ordained democracies. Likewise, when Isaac Orobio de Castro wrote about the biblical tribe of Judah as an autonomous 'republic unto itself' (*república de por sí*) as against other tribes, he emphasized that the members of the tribe ruled themselves. These particular adaptations reveal the double move that Pereyra and his peers were making: they took account of new political discourse and brought it into the Jewish community, to which it was particularly well suited.

⁂

The way members of the Kahal Kadosh characterized their Jewish polity in the 1660s and 1670s was deeply indebted to the European political discourse that had received, revived, and adapted the republican ideal for new settings that were not obviously 'republics'. It was the concomitant formation of a flexible and universalizing approach to the concept of a 'polity' that enabled Pereyra, Aguilar, and others to apply the concept to the Jewish community—and in doing so they maintained the spirit of the new politics by drawing from and adapting ideas from a wide variety of contexts. That Amsterdam's Spanish and Portuguese Jews looked not to Abravanel but to Hobbes, Spinoza, and, yes, even Marquez, and that they wrote so realistically about the community, shows that the model they had in mind was not the classical republic or the biblical republic but the early modern European commonwealth.

As we shall see, along with this wider political discourse they also adopted some of the tensions inherent within it. Their designation of the Kahal Kadosh as a commonwealth was more than a game of dress-up. The widely circulating commonwealth-centred discourse of the 1660s, 1670s, and 1680s offered the members of the Kahal Kadosh a rich lexicon from which to build their own form of Jewish republicanism. The notion of the Jewish community as commonwealth would soon become problematic— not because of outside pressures for political integration, but because members began to question the meaning of a Jewish polity, viewed from within. The new moniker reflected not necessarily a change to the fundamental principles underlying the community, but a new drive to address those principles: to think about and rethink them, to argue about them, re-legislate and renegotiate and reinterpret them, in terms that emphasized political identity and confronted questions of exile and the Jewish fate.

THREE

CIVITAS
CONSOLIDATION AND STRIFE IN THE SABBATIAN ERA

I N 1675 the Kahal Kadosh completed the construction of a new synagogue compound, grand and distinctive. The 'Esnoga', as members came
to call the physical space at the symbolic centre of their community, is often
seen as a culmination of the community's golden seventeenth century.[1]
Overshadowing the stately Ashkenazi synagogue that had just been built
across the way and rivalling the landmark Dutch churches of the era in size
and monumentality, the synagogue proper boasted sumptuous furnishings,
an ornate wooden ark, and two large balconies for women.[2] With enormous
multi-storey interior columns, seventy-two windows, and a footprint encompassing over 1,000 square metres, it was the largest and most opulent
Jewish worship space in seventeenth-century Europe. This sanctuary building, in turn, was set within a courtyard bounded on three sides by lower
structures housing communal functions and functionaries, and on the
fourth side by a fence. As Daniel Levi de Barrios described the complex
in 1684, 'in the western side of the courtyard are the spaces for the Political Government, six Colleges, two houses of the Chazzanim or cantors,
and one of the Guardian'.[3] The overall effect was of a separate and walled
Jewish communal space, within which the synagogue was ensconced.

This extraordinary compound was completed only after years of
setbacks and delays, and the achievement was widely recognized as an
impressive feat of fundraising, organizing, motivation, and management—
in short, of governance—on the part of the Mahamad. David de Castro

---

[1] For recent general overviews of the Esnoga and its significance, see Vlaardingerbroek
(ed.), *The Portuguese Synagogue*; Belinfante et al., *The Esnoga*; and Perelis, 'Jewish Sacred Architecture'.

[2] The new Esnoga was 38 × 26 metres at the base, as opposed to the Ashkenazi shul's 16 × 18
metres. Stiefel, 'Architectural Origins', at nn. 40 and 49.   [3] Barrios, *Triumpho*, 38.

Tartaz, the editor and printer of a lavish volume commemorating the
Esnoga's construction, included a triumphant account of communal tribulations in his introduction, noting that wars with Great Britain and France
as well as a destructive storm had nearly defeated them—until, he wrote,
the community's 'spirits were resuscitated, the state began to open its eyes,
and the nation to lift its head'.[4] He noted that 'all these impediments' could
not 'cool the ardent zeal with which [the community] longed to possess
such a fine thing', as members anticipated the day when the Esnoga would
be 'made public'.

Expressing the collective joy of commencing to inhabit the space,
the community put on an eight-day inaugural celebration during the week
following the fasting and lamentations of the Ninth of Av. The festival
included a torchlit procession of Torah scrolls, musical performances, and
daily speeches delivered by the 'most learned lights of our congregation'.
In Castro Tartaz's words, the celebration was as hearty as 'the modesty of
our captivity permitted',[5] with the eight days seeming 'more like a Passover
in a liberated Temple than a festival of captivity in a synagogue'.[6] Castro
Tartaz's words hint at the multiple levels of meaning the project held for
members of the Kahal Kadosh and capture the ambiguity of laying new
foundations of diaspora community in the shadow of Sabbatian messianic
expectation. After all, Sabbatai himself was still alive, writing letters to his
followers from exile, and although the congregation as a whole had ceased
to formally support his pretensions, his fate was still an open question in
the minds of many.

Like the editor and publisher Castro Tartaz, several speakers at the
celebration made explicit comparisons between the Esnoga and the biblical
Temple.[7] In itself, such comparisons are not surprising. As is well known,
the layout and some architectural elements of the sanctuary building bore
a striking resemblance to images of Solomon's Temple that were produced
mid-century in Amsterdam, including a scale model made and displayed
by a member of the Kahal Kadosh who thereby acquired some fame under
the name Leon Templo (Figs. 3 and 4).[8] In an era of shared Christian and

[4] Castro Tartaz, 'Prologo'.
[5] Ibid., reverse of first (unpaginated) leaf of text.   [6] Ibid., third (unpaginated) leaf of text.
[7] Including that of Isaac Aboab da Fonseca and Selomoh de Olivera, not discussed here.
Vlaardingerbroek (ed.), *The Portuguese Synagogue*, 127–30, contains a brief summary of each
sermon.
[8] On Templo, see Offenberg, 'Jacob Jehuda Leon', and Fisher, *Amsterdam's People*, 7.

Jewish interest in biblical history both for its realia and for reproducible typologies, it makes sense that the Jewish building, designed by the Christian architect Elias Bouwman, would make the most of the Temple imagery —after all, some churches of the same era had already done the same.[9] The symbolism deployed in the Esnoga, particularly numerological symbols in the dimensions and layout of the sanctuary building, has been well analysed, as it diverged from Jewish traditions differentiating between the Temple and synagogues; this symbolic erasure of exilic difference has been contextualized in terms of messianism and millenarianism.[10]

Speakers at the inaugural celebration, however, had an unexpected take on the Esnoga's parallel with the Temple: Isaac Vellozino, David Sarphati, and Isaac Netto rhetorically connected both edifices, ancient and contemporary, to lay temporal rule rather than sacred rites alone.[11] They remarked that the Mahamad had imitated King Solomon in their skilled governance and praised the alignment of religion with politics that had made such a construction project possible. Their comments suggested that reference to Solomon's Temple had as much to do with Solomon the king as with the holy Temple he built. Their portrayal of the Esnoga complex in these terms aligns with the unusual setting of the synagogue within an enclosure. The layout of the complex was such that the vaunted sanctuary building was only part of a wider space bounded and defined by a walled courtyard, just as the Temple appeared in Templo's model and other contemporary depictions (Figs. 3 and 4). As I suggest below, the layout recapitulated the vision of the community as a religious polity, a bounded society centred on—but not limited to—religious pursuits; indeed, the enclosure itself was distinctly lay in orientation.

Castro Tartaz's commemorative book includes the text of the seven speeches, each one introduced by a dedicatory preface composed by Castro Tartaz himself. The speakers were a mixture of rabbis and learned lay

[9] See Vlaardingerbroek (ed.), *The Portuguese Synagogue*, 64–72.

[10] Virtually every treatment of the Esnoga deals with its similarity to Solomon's Temple. In addition to the above-cited sources, see especially Offenberg, 'Dirk van Santen', which carries the reception of Templo's scholarship and model up into the 1680s; Rosenau, 'Jacob Judah Leon Templo's Contribution to Architectural Imagery', and Leibman, 'Sephardi Sacred Space'.

[11] Vellozino and Sarphati are quoted below. Netto was a student of Aboab, preacher in the Brotherhood of the Orphans, and *rosh yeshivah* of the Temime Dareh society. See Isaac Netto, 'Sermão Quarto', 61.

people; all of the speeches were dedicated to lay leaders or significant donors.[12] The first sermon was delivered by the pre-eminent rabbi of the Kahal Kadosh, Isaac Aboab da Fonseca, and Castro Tartaz's dedication of Aboab's sermon to the Mahamad was filled with praise for both. Castro Tartaz began by describing the ideal harmony that existed between the rabbi and the lay leaders, whose leadership was perfectly complementary, mutually beneficial, and even mutually dependent:

There is such great proportionality between spiritual and temporal government that it is impossible for one to exist without the other. The former delivers the spiritual laws to the people for the observance of divine rites, and it is impossible for them to be observed if the temporal government does not obligate their observance. Nor is it possible for the human government to be perfect if it is not guided by the divine government.[13]

He then connected this relationship with the particular sermon the dedication introduced:

The author [i.e. Aboab] is the one to whom the administration of the Holy Law belongs; it falls to you, Lords [*Senhores*, i.e. members of the Mahamad], to make its observance inviolable. The sermon is the word of God, which the Lord Hakham explains to the people; and you, Lords, must hold the people in obedience to the word of God. It is just that the word should be dedicated to the one who holds the office of guarding it; thus, the Spiritual Government of the Doctrine offers its hand to the temporal government to conserve it.

In this depiction, Castro Tartaz presented rabbis as spiritual leaders without temporal authority of their own, and the Mahamad as temporal rulers seeking divine guidance for their government. The rabbi's role was not only to offer spiritual advice and halakhic instruction to members, but also, significantly, to support ('conserve', a word that connoted statecraft) the rule of the Mahamad, which governed many activities beyond religious observance. According to Castro Tartaz's careful rhetoric, the two needed each other in order to carry out their respective aims, but the spiritual component was subsumed within the temporal. This was, in fact, an accurate depiction of the institutional and political relationship between rabbis and lay leaders in the communal system of the Kahal Kadosh. Lay leaders were

[12] The dedicatees listed are the Mahamad, the building committee, Isaac Penso, Isaac Gabay Henriques, Jacob de Pinto, Jacob Telles da Costa, and Isaac Orobio de Castro.

[13] Castro Tartaz, 'Prologo'.

the ones empowered to legislate and compel members' actions, as had been the case at least since the 1639 unification. Castro Tartaz treated the Kahal Kadosh as an ideal civic entity where different leaders and members had various roles to play in enacting a combination of spiritual and temporal authority.

At a defining moment in communal life, Castro Tartaz chose to focus on the nature of the Kahal Kadosh as a combination of religious and political elements, where spiritual leaders showed deference to political ones in an immediate sense but the politics as a whole relied on religious authority and supported a religious mission. He saw these religio-political characteristics of his community recapitulated and reflected in the Esnoga, lending a concrete and localized dimension to its characterization in civic terms. As he wrote:

And since this whole discourse is in honour of God and his Palace, the whole discourse is owed to you, Lords, who sought the honour of God and the sumptuous building of his palace with such zeal that it would achieve ultimate perfection and the admiration of the nations. It is without a doubt God himself who built this house, but who could doubt that he chose you, Lords, as the instrument to build it?

Castro Tartaz reflected on the compound not only as a sacred place in which to conduct spiritual activity, a transcendent site of ritual, prayer, or legal observance, but also as a palace—and one sumptuous enough to impress the nations. His introduction of such a metaphor reflects his interest in emphasizing the worldly—temporal and lay—dimension of what the community had achieved.

One speaker whose sermon is included in the volume, Isaac Vellozino, similarly connected spiritual and political aims in the Mahamad's work, with attention to the act of building. He declared that in creating this new edifice the Mahamad had enacted a 'divine politics' (*política divina*) modelled on God's creation of a world to govern, and on Moses' building of a tabernacle to solidify his position as governor of his republic. Vellozino began by asking why the first words of the Bible, *bereshit bara elohim*, 'in the beginning God created', put the verb 'created' (*bara*) before the name of God (*elohim*), which seems as if it should come first because God existed first. Vellozino's answer was that the 'sacred history' reflected a logical order not of ontology but of hierarchy:

First [God] had to produce those creatures of whom he would be called lord and judge. Until then, he had the power to create them; but it was impossible for him to rule over them until he had created them, or to call himself [their] judge before having produced them. . . . Until he had given them existence, he did not have this holy name. It was necessary to build in order to have dominion and to judge as a higher authority in his edifice.[14]

According to Vellozino the synagogue reflected divine order above all by being a worldly site in which proper rulers could enact their rule. If the Esnoga was, to paraphrase Castro Tartaz, a castle, for Vellozino the members of the Mahamad were its lords. As he commented: 'One cannot title himself with the name of Lord without having subjects to dominate.'[15]

Vellozino's vision shared much with Pereyra's discussion of celestial imitation (discussed above), but emphasized that all rulers required material realms to instantiate their authority. Thus, he wrote that the lay leaders of the Kahal Kadosh imitated the divine politics 'of God and ancient princes alike', and that 'those who govern the Israelite Congregations in this dispersion and captivity . . . build a house of God according to the possibilities of the time'.[16] Vellozino was not straightforwardly describing the synagogue as a site of religious ritual that echoed the function of the ancient Temple. He was, rather, playing on that notion by reframing it in terms of the temporal authority that such buildings concretize. Vellozino also compared the Mahamad to King Solomon, noting that David accumulated riches through military victories while Solomon, 'admired for his governmental judgement', used them to build the Temple—perhaps a nod to the mercantile and financial talents of the community's elite. In comparing the Esnoga to the Temple he focused on the political acumen of the leadership.

Communal Space and Civic Order

Vellozino's lionization of the Mahamad was not only praise intended for the ears of the *parnasim*. It was also a message to the members. He presented the lay leaders' relationship to the people as one of lordship and superiority: like God, Moses, and the biblical kings, the lay leaders had to build an edifice in order to solidify their rule. And solidify their rule they indeed had, in another way: in the same year that they decided to undertake

---

[14] Vellozino, 'Sermão Sexto', 104.   [15] Ibid. 103.   [16] Ibid. 104–5.

the building project, they also moved to re-establish and rearticulate the Mahamad's position in the communal system. In a dramatic move in 1670, they asked both community members and Dutch authorities to affirm the 'manner and form of government of the synagogue and Hebrew Portuguese nation in Amsterdam'.[17] They demanded that all members of the community sign a document recognizing the Mahamad as the sole governing body in the community. It reinforced the structure of the community as it had been established in the *Acordos*, with even greater emphasis on lay rule over the rabbis. The document included a statement that the rabbis were employed (*asalareados*) by the *parnasim* (members of the Mahamad), and 'hence they are subject to said *parnasim* and to their orders in everything'. In effect, the Mahamad had its subjects renew their vows.

If the Kahal Kadosh was being contractually renewed as a civic sphere, it would soon have an expanded physical instantiation to match. The synagogue had long stood as a locus of the community, as much in its civic nature as its religious activity. The very fact of a dedicated synagogue owned by the Kahal Kadosh instead of by private individuals was a marker of identification as a body politic, a kind of discrete public within Amsterdam; with unification in 1639 had come the establishment of a fiscal and material body, concentrated in one single synagogue, to mirror the one single congregation. From that time onwards, the leaders of the Kahal Kadosh had striven to enact its civic ideals and communal structure within the space of the synagogue.[18]

The synagogue was not a political space in a parliamentary sense, as the lay leaders' deliberations took place in separate chambers, but in a structural and social sense. The sanctuary was the place of assembly for the *kahal*, and hence a place of physical order corresponding to social and political order. Rules regarding authority, gender, civility, and class were set down in the text of the *Acordos*, with the inside of the synagogue serving as a space where hierarchies could be displayed and enacted. The rabbis were placed in a certain order on a certain bench, and the same for the lay

---

[17] The document, titled 'Declarasao do modo e forma que se observa no governo da sinagoga e naçao ebrea Portugueza em Amsterdam', in SA 334, 119AA, 21, contains pages of members' signatures, 754ff. On the outside cover of what was clearly a folded document it is labelled with the words 'Paper signed by the nation in declaration of the form of the government of this congregation and its confidence in the Mahamad'. On the episode overall, see Hagoort, 'The Del Sottos', 44–5, and Y. Kaplan, *From Christianity to Judaism*, 196.

[18] See Siegmund, *The Medici State*, 247, on Florence.

leaders.[19] The Mahamad was tasked with assigning seats to all individual men; women's places were separate and not fixed, a normal circumstance that also, in this case, represented their exclusion from the order of communal citizenship along with their traditional absence from public prayer.[20] The boundary of the synagogue, symbolizing the boundaries of the *kahal* or *congrega*, was marked in the ritual of excommunication, as a banned person could be made to lie down on the threshold of the synagogue while the members passed over him into the space.

In the set of regulations enacted by the first Mahamad, this ordering received even more attention than it had in the *Acordos*, with a number of rules devoted to comportment within the synagogue space and empowering the Mahamad to command members to leave the synagogue or stay quiet within it.[21] The attention to such behaviour in part reflected anxiety about how the community would appear in the eyes of non-Jews, and as such it also shows an internalization of shared standards of civilized behaviour— not only in the sense of manners, but also in the sense of civic hierarchy. In gentility and Gentiles' acceptance, politeness and politics, civilization and civic ideals, shared linguistic roots highlight shared meanings.[22]

With this culture of spatial ordering already in place, and an existing sense that the synagogue was a sphere in which political order was enacted (though not legislated), the Esnoga recapitulated and recast that order at the height of the Sabbatian era. The Kahal Kadosh built literal new foundations in a striking extension of its long-standing use of space to define itself—now in a way that clarified its self-understanding as a commonwealth or *civitas*, setting the rooms devoted to everything except full ritual assembly in a circle around the central sanctuary so as to define and bound the communal sphere and mediate, like city walls, between it and its surroundings. The Kahal Kadosh had already been its own sphere of authority

---

[19] Articles 4, 9, and 18. SA 334, 19, fos. 1ᵛ–3.

[20] Article 13. SA 334, 19, fo. 2ᵛ. See Amussen, *An Ordered Society*, 138ff., on seat placement in church as part of the 'ordering of society'.

[21] On comportment, see Articles 1, 9, 16, 19, 20, 22, 24, 25, 26, and 28 of the *haskamot*— though the essential logistics are all contained in the *Acordos*. SA 334, 19, fos. 21–6. They also set the precise arrangement of drawers containing names to be pulled for honours within the synagogue, embodying the hierarchy between men with different levels of wealth and marital status (Article 25 and its amendment on the signature page, SA 334, 19, fos. 3ᵛ, 5). On the Mahamad's control over behaviour in the synagogue, see *Haskamot*, Article 1. SA 334, 19, fo. 21.

[22] On the valuation of manners as a matter of gentility and social discipline, see Y. Kaplan, '*Gente Política*', id., 'Order', and id., 'Discipline'.

with clear boundaries and internal order, embedded in a wider civic landscape, and the new communal complex completed in 1675 gave it a corresponding physical structure within the public cityscape.

In general, spaces and places—buildings and monuments, burial and festival grounds, chambers and offices, boundaries and bulwarks—have been recognized as deeply important components of local, professional, confessional, and other identity groupings in early modern Europe.[23] Civic dynamics and political authority were embodied in a sense of place, not necessarily marking the boundaries of sovereign or even jurisdictional territory but rather reflecting and enforcing the civic sense, including internal hierarchies and a sense of good social order. One's 'place' had the sense of both absolute geographical location and relational location, often not physical but rather institutional or familial. In incorporated cities, physical offices and zones reflected the offices that were held by leaders and the legal and political jurisdictions over which they held sway.[24] In terms of architecture, the religious and civic buildings constructed in the seventeenth century communicated their meaning in elaborate fashion with classical and biblical references and spiritual and political symbolism. In Holland in particular, public churches displayed urban and civic iconography, reflecting the way they were understood to be integrated into the political fabric.[25]

The situation of a synagogue and other Jewish spaces within this physical and conceptual landscape was not simple. The spaces and places of Jews as 'others' interrupted those of local Christians. The quest for a Jewish burial ground, for example, had immediate practical implications, of course, but also far-reaching symbolic ones regarding permanence, land, and the relationship between a Christian state and its territory.[26] The Jewish tradition of being buried in the land of Israel after a life lived elsewhere attests to the elementality of the relationship between body and land, especially in the premodern imagination, as does the affective power of medieval and early modern Jewish cemeteries still extant throughout the diaspora. The establishment of a cemetery was an early component of community-building for many Jewish populations, and not always an easy

---

[23] See e.g. Tittler, *Architecture and Power*.
[24] I owe this formulation to Withington, *Politics*, 86–8.
[25] Such images might be surprising in a Reformed (anti-iconographic) context; Spicer explains it by the fact that they were owned by the parish and not the church. Spicer, *Calvinist Churches*, 155.   [26] See Swetschinski, *Reluctant Cosmopolitans*, 12, and Bodian, *Hebrews*, 47.

thing to accomplish. Anecdotally, accompanying the body of a deceased colleague or relative to a place where it could be buried appropriately appears at two prominent moments in the history of the Kahal Kadosh.[27] Jewish funeral and other processions—in which Jews participated in a ritual that, among Christians, demarcated and enacted dominion in certain spaces —could also be fraught with tension. Certainly, Jews worried about Christian reactions to such public displays, and sometimes imposed strict controls on them.[28]

Constructed space was also a central focus of the conditions of Amsterdam's toleration of religious minorities, detailed in Chapter 1, as it distinguished between the state church, with public worship, and private worship that was at least nominally limited to the private or domestic sphere. 'Private' religious practice, a concept that was also key to de facto accommodation of religious minorities across early modern Europe,[29] was supposed to be limited to members of a household (however broadly defined).[30] A 'public' church, on the other hand, was owned by a non-familial association and was a meeting space for multiple families.[31] As such, it took its place within the streetscape of the city and was, theoretically, open. The Dutch Reformed Church was understood to have a monopoly on such status.

In practice, the private worship of tolerated minorities did involve group gatherings, but congregations were expected to be small and discreet, with worshippers arriving and departing through side doors or interior rooms, physically enacting the legislated sense that the building was not public, that is, open to free entry and hence recognized as part of the interwoven religious, economic, and spatial domains of the Dutch polity. Thus, the famous 'secret' Catholic churches, ostensibly prohibited spaces that were hidden in plain sight, were distinguished by a lack of

[27] The rabbi Saul Levi Morteira first arrived in the Low Countries when he brought the body of Elijah Montalto out of France; and Menasseh ben Israel left England after his failed mission there, in order to bring his son's body back to Amsterdam.

[28] See Horowitz, 'Procession'; Y. Kaplan, '*Gente Política*', 36. Wiznitzer (*Jews in Colonial Brazil*, 74) notes that Jewish and Catholic street processions were banned in Dutch Brazil.

[29] B. Kaplan, 'Fictions of Privacy', 1050–5, 1056–7, 1061–2, notes that the same standard allowed other forms of private or ostensibly clandestine religious nonconformism such as manorial chapels, court chapels, and embassy chapels. The distinction was critical to the formulation of a conceptual distinction between public and private.

[30] See B. Kaplan, *Divided by Faith*, 179.

[31] Ibid. 181, and B. Kaplan, 'Fictions of Privacy', 1043.

monumentality or other forms of architectural marking as churches on their exteriors, no matter how grand or opulent they might be inside.[32]

The Kahal Kadosh constituted itself as an exception to many of the rules governing Christian minorities, and it clearly saw its possession of a dedicated and commonly owned worship space as a key aspect of its corporate structure in contrast to such churches. The synagogue that had been built for the unified congregation back in 1638 had suited its moment. It was styled to look like a residence, in nominal conformity with the rule against 'public' worship, but within those restrictions it nevertheless attracted attention by imitating one of the era's finest private mansions.[33] Its finery was not typical of synagogue architecture at the time, which generally adopted humble and inconspicuous external styling in accordance with Jewry laws and/or for practical reasons.[34] In the particular context of Amsterdam's new Jews in the first half of the century, hiding a synagogue could also play into perceptions of Jewish dissimulation, which were particularly strong with respect to conversos and connected to Dutch historical mistrust of the Spanish.[35] The prominent, even immodest appearance of the building, and yet on the other hand its intentionally domestic styling, says much about the position the newly constituted community was in.

The new Esnoga completed in 1675 departed from the model of its predecessor in style and in approach to architectural representation of Jewishness. It stood, in fact, in stark contrast to minority churches and the Kahal Kadosh's own previous synagogue alike. It was part of a wider early modern trend that began to buck the tradition of inconspicuous synagogues with larger and more architecturally significant structures. Within the Kahal Kadosh, however, the immediate contrast was not between inconspicuous and grand but between the architectural styles of a domicile and a church.

The Ashkenazi community had already moved in the same direction with its 1670 Grote Sjoel (Great Synagogue; see Fig. 5), suggesting that the two groups shared a common perception of what was newly possible for Jews within the particular political circumstances of Amsterdam. In

---

[32] B. Kaplan, *Divided by Faith*, 173.   [33] See also Lipis, *Symbolic Houses*.

[34] See Stiefel, 'Architectural Origins', at n. 38, and Mann, 'Synagogues'. For a few examples of synagogues across Europe constructed within or behind homes, or meant to appear like a typical building, see Goldman-Ida, 'Synagogues', 184–7.

[35] See Lipton, *Dark Mirror*, 272–4, and Shoulson, *Fictions of Conversion*.

contrast, in nearby Hamburg, an effort to build a more distinctive synagogue in 1672 was quickly shut down.[36] In fact, the Grote Sjoel imitated
Amsterdam's Oosterkerk of the same era, employing a notable Dutch architect, Daniel Stalpaert, who had assisted in the design of that prominent
church. The Kahal Kadosh Talmud Torah, in turn, hired Stalpaert's assis-
tant on the Grote Sjoel, Elias Bouwman, to design the Spanish and Portuguese community's own—larger, grander—project.[37] Once the Esnoga
was built, the two synagogues stood as monuments to open Jewish presence, to their rather unusual freedom to exist as 'publics'. For the Spanish
and Portuguese Jews, at least, as we have already seen, their status as a
public, or corporate, society was innately tied to their internal civic bond.

The Esnoga itself was the subject of much analysis and depiction in
Jewish and Christian sources alike, seen as the greatest synagogue in all of
Europe until the nineteenth century.[37] Castro Tartaz's commemorative
book included not only the text of the seven speeches but also detailed
images and descriptions of the Esnoga itself, including a floor plan and elevation, with the stated aim that the reader would not only see the building
but also 'understand its architecture'.[39] Indeed, its architecture spoke volumes about the edifice's meaning. Like the community, the new compound
had both sacred and secular components, where the secular encompassed,
defined, and protected the sacred and the sacred lent meaning and legitimacy to the whole. The central sanctuary space, towering above the rest of
the complex, projected a sense of grandeur from the outside and of transcendent elevation from within. It was also enveloped within a protective
boundary that allowed it to be seen, but not accessed, directly from the
street. From the inside of the sanctuary, large clear windows made the surroundings visible, contributing to a sense of being enclosed within a dedicated space and removed from the wider world. Such enclosure should not
be read as a reflection of a practical requirement to make the space 'private'
by preventing direct access from the street, since the Great Synagogue
already existed without such a barrier. The fact, too, that the outbuildings contained residences for communal employees should not be seen as

[36] See B. Kaplan, 'Fictions of Privacy', 1054–6.
[37] Stiefel, 'Architectural Origins', 123–4, and Paraira, 'A Jewel in the City'.
[38] See Sutcliffe, 'Boundaries', 20–2; Stiefel, 'Architectural Origins', 126.
[39] Castro Tartaz, 'Prologo'. The Dutch architect's intentions and instructions are not
directly known. See Vlaardingerbroek (ed.), *The Portuguese Synagogue*, 68–72; Fuks and Fuks-
Mansfeld, 'Inauguration', 492 ff.; and Fuks, 'Inauguration'.

signalling a kind of domesticity that mattered to the public/private or civic/familial distinction, because the complex contained multiple households as well as offices, storage rooms, meeting spaces, and other facilities. If anything, it was more of a city than a house.

The outbuildings, low and long, sometimes only one narrow room across, were continuous with the wall that enclosed the entire complex. The walled area approximated a rectangle (allowing for the odd angles of the building lot and the necessity of an eastward face for the sanctuary), with a grand main opening for direct entrance and egress, emulating a city wall with a formal gate (Fig. 3, bottom left, and Fig. 6, background).[40] An open area inside the gate and surrounding the synagogue served as a kind of plaza, a public space within the boundaries of the complex (Figs. 6 and 7). There was also an informal rear entrance of some kind near the women's entrance to the sanctuary, perhaps implying once again the exclusion of women from the 'public' or civic display of the main gate and courtyard (Fig. 7).[41] In several contemporary depictions the whole complex is shown, with the outer annex buildings along the busy street and the inner sanctuary building visible behind, as in Figure 8 and the top right corner of Figure 9. Sacred and worldly activities were distinctly separated, with the sacred in a privileged and cocooned central position whereas the boundaries, and the interaction with the rest of the city, were given over to the worldly.

The sense that the outbuildings were critical to the overall composition of the complex appears to have been shared by the architect, the community's lay leaders, and the Dutch artist Romeyn de Hooghe, who produced

[40] See Jütte, *Strait Gate*, 209–30.

[41] De Hooghe's plan of the complex's footprint (Fig. 3) shows a wall along the east side, enclosing the space as a whole, with his attached drawing showing that wall as an open colonnade. His view of the courtyard interior (Fig. 6) shows it as a wooden fence with a service entrance. The east side of the sanctuary building itself has undergone changes over the years, and architectural historians have tried to reconstruct the original east façade with its stairs to the women's galleries. See Vlaardingerbroek (ed.), *The Portuguese Synagogue*, 88–91. However, to my knowledge there is no study of the original enclosure. In some other 17th-century images the east façade is shown without any wall surrounding it; today, the women's galleries are accessed via openings in the north and south façades and the courtyard is enclosed by a party wall with an adjacent building. My conjecture is that de Hooghe's plan and sketch in Castro Tartaz's book (Fig. 3) was a stylized representation meant to emphasize orderliness and resemblance to the Temple. After all, they also inaccurately represent the actual shape of the complex, which was not actually rectangular, and the size and position of the buildings within it. Further study is merited.

many images of it for communal consumption, clearly focusing on the layout. In contrast, another artist, Gerrit Adriaensz Berckheyde, does not seem to have seen the memo. He painted the Esnoga from the south-east, in a 1675 version with a hut obscuring the view in a way that de-emphasizes the relationship between the outbuildings and the synagogue itself; and then some years later in a way that eliminated any enclosure at all on the east side and fabricated an east façade to look like the front of a building, open to the street.[42] The contrast affirms the intentionality of the other depictions.

De Hooghe also produced a commemorative engraving depicting the interior of the grand synagogue filled with people, including Jews in the midst of ritual performance as well as observers. The scene, which might depict the inaugural celebration itself, is topped by a floating image usually read as an allegory for Dutch toleration of Jews (see Fig. 9).[43] It shows two female figures representing Amsterdam and the Dutch Republic, where Amsterdam is directing the Republic to gaze at two Jewish figures on the left. A caption in Latin reads: 'The republic thrives on freedom of conscience.' The intended identities of the Jewish figures are not perfectly clear; one appears to be a priest, with Torah scrolls. The other, holding the tablets of the Ten Commandments, has sometimes been assumed to be Moses, so the pair would be Moses and Aaron. Miriam Bodian points out that the second figure appears to be female and suggests that she represents 'Judea', i.e. its tribulations in exile.[44] To my knowledge, no one has noted the small figure behind these two, somewhat in shadow, holding a framed image of a building that could very well be the Esnoga complex. Perhaps it represents the artist or the architect; perhaps it is a reference to the significance of the edifice.

According to one interpretation, the engraving as a whole faces outward from the Jewish community, speaking to a Dutch viewer using the trope of Jewish witness, the idea that Christians tolerate Jews as bearers of the original revelation. The caption is readily understood as touting the

---

[42] Gerrit Adriaensz Berckheyde, 'View of the Ashkenazi and Portuguese Jewish Synagogues' (1675) and (untitled) view of the Esnoga from the south-east (c.1680–5). These images are reproduced in Vlaardingerbroek (ed.), *The Portuguese Synagogue*, 25 and 91.

[43] Yosef Kaplan examined the viewership of some other images of the synagogue in 'For Whom Did Emanuel de Witte Paint His Three Pictures?'. On de Hooghe's portrayal of Jewish Amsterdam, see Baskind, 'Distinguishing the Distinction', 4, and R. I. Cohen, *Jewish Icons*, 35–8.   [44] See Bodian, 'Portuguese Jews', 323–5.

ILLUSTRATIONS

1599

[handwritten introductory paragraph, largely illegible]

... em 28 de Sebat 5359

[a list of signatures follows in three columns, largely illegible]

FIGURE 1. Signatures ratifying the *Acordos,* 1639.

Stadsarchief Amsterdam, Archief van de Portugees-Israëlietische Gemeente (SA334, 19), fos. 5ᵛ–6

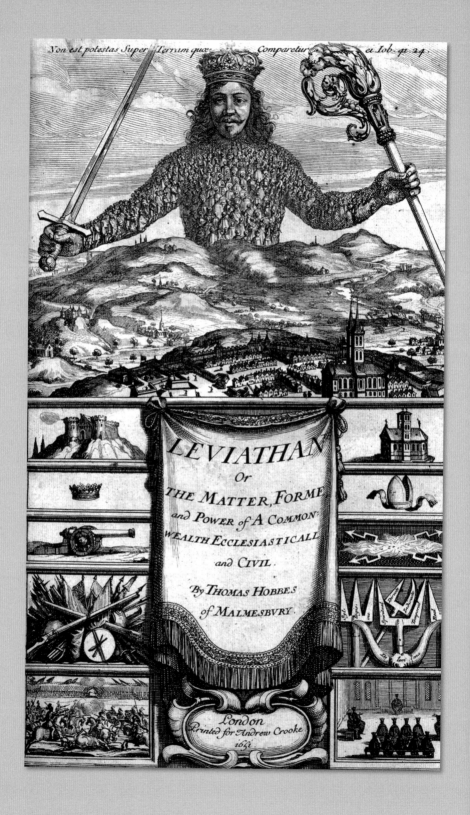

Non est potestas Super Terram quæ Comparetur ei Iob. 41. 24.

LEVIATHAN
Or
THE MATTER, FORME
and Power of A COMMON-
WEALTH ECCLESIASTICALL
and CIVIL.

By THOMAS HOBBES
of MALMESBVRY.

London
Printed for Andrew Crooke
1651.

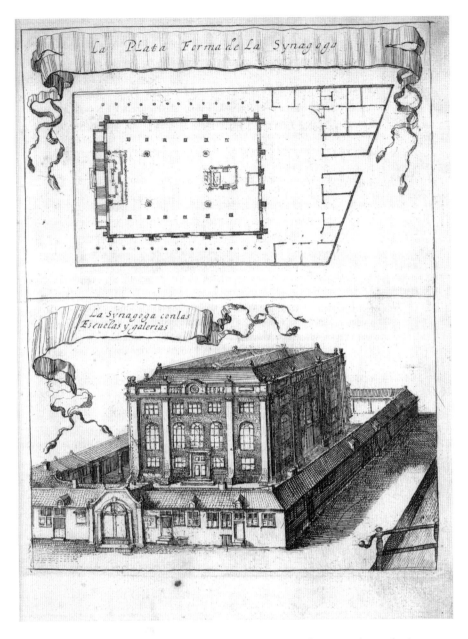

FIGURE 2. (*left*) Frontispiece of Thomas Hobbes, *Leviathan* (London, 1651), engraved by Abraham Bosse.

FIGURE 3. (*above*) Detail of Romeyn de Hooghe's illustration of the Esnoga's exterior and footprint, included in the 1675 commemorative volume *Sermoés que pregarão os doctos ingenios*, ed. David de Castro Tartaz (Amsterdam, 1675).

Allard Pierson, University of Amsterdam, ROG A-757

TEMPEL SALOMONIS.

Afbeeldinge van den grooten ende Heerlijken Tempel

Hoogduijtse JOODE KERCK

FIGURE 5. The 'Grote Sjoel' of the Ashkenazi community, located across the street from the Esnoga. Justus Danckerts, *Hoogduijtse Joode Kerck* (printed gravure etching, 1671).

Collection of the Jewish Historical Museum, Amsterdam. Collection J. van Velzen

FIGURE 4. (*left*) Leon Templo's model of the Temple of Solomon complex with outer wall, as depicted in *Biblia Hebraica*, ed. Joseph Athias (Amsterdam, 1667).

Collection of the Jewish Historical Museum, Amsterdam

FIGURE 6. The interior court of the Esnoga from the east side, with rear service entrance in the foreground and main formal entrance (shown from the interior) in the background. Etching by Romeyn de Hooghe and Pieter Persoy, *De Scholen, Suyverplaatsen etc.*
Collection of the Jewish Historical Museum, Amsterdam. Acquired with the support of the BankGiro Loterij

FIGURE 7. The entrance to the sanctuary building surrounded by courtyard.
Photo: the author

FIGURE 8. The synagogue complex depicted as a part of the bustling Amsterdam streetscape. Etching by Romeyn de Hooghe, *'T Profil van de Kerk.*

Collection of the Jewish Historical Museum, Amsterdam

FIGURE 9. Romeyn de Hooghe's depiction of the synagogue opening, 1675 (*De Portugese Synagoge te Amsterdam tijdens de inwijding*).

Collection of the Jewish Historical Museum, Amsterdam. Acquired with the support of the Prins Bernhard Cultuur Fonds

benefit of Jews as transmitters and interpreters of biblical and legal wisdom, suggesting that both biblical law and also contemporary exilic Jews could be intellectually and religiously useful to the Dutch city and state. It is a message that correlates well with Dutch Calvinist interest in Jewish post-biblical texts and personal tutelage with Amsterdam's Jewish scholars in the seventeenth century.[45] In total, in this reading, the engraving communicates that Dutch civic discourse was informed by Judaism, and Jews were therefore welcome, as transmitters and symbols of divine law and precursors of the Dutch identity as the 'true Israel'. As Bodian has recently discussed, there is also a message of 'mercantilist providentialism' there, as reflected in a poem attached to some versions of the etching.[46]

But the framing of the engraving as a whole requires a secondary reading as well. The synagogue as a public space, as it is presented in the image, does not well reflect the principle of 'freedom of conscience', which bore specifically on individual opinions and private devotional practice,[47] supporting the kind of hidden and enclosed churches described above. In contrast, the main image in de Hooghe's engraving depicts nothing so much as openness, the bustling space of the new synagogue filled with diverse people. (Male people, that is; in the image, the women in the galleries are reduced to barely perceptible silhouettes.) The composition seems to erase the fourth wall of the structure, so that the whole interior can be viewed like a diorama and the crowd can be imagined spilling out into the courtyard. In this arrangement, both in the image of the synagogue floor and in the allegorical figures floating above, it is the non-Jew who serves as a witness to a public spectacle of Jewish society.

Jewish viewers of this image might take pride in the notion that Judaism was intellectually valued by Christians and take comfort in Dutch tolerance—noting the above signification of the caption about the republic —but they might also read it in another, more inwardly focused way, seeing the 'republic' in question as the Jewish commonwealth. After all, the engraving was clearly not intended solely for Dutch viewers: a special edition of it was printed on silk for members of the building committee,[48] and similar images were reproduced within the commemorative volume, which

---

[45] See Katchen, *Christian Hebraists*.   [46] Bodian, 'Portuguese Jews', 325.
[47] See B. Kaplan, 'Fictions of Privacy', 1043–4. Miriam Bodian has explored how Amsterdam's Sephardim treated the notion of 'freedom of conscience': Bodian, '"Liberty of Conscience"', p. CP4.   [48] See Vlaardingerbroek (ed.), *The Portuguese Synagogue*, 130.

was all in Spanish and Portuguese and clearly written with a readership of community members in mind. De Hooghe's image conveys a sense of the Esnoga as a Jewish civic space in several ways. It places the sanctuary within the frameworks first of communal administration and then of the city itself by displaying the names of communal leaders and donors along the left and right sides, literally framing the sanctuary within the lay administrative structures that made it possible—just as Castro Tartaz did textually, framing rabbinic sermons with dedications to lay leaders.

Two inset images at the top corners reinforce the same emphasis on architecture and setting, zooming out to show the sanctuary's outer edges: the one on the left shows the footprint of the whole complex with the sanctuary at the centre, and the one on the right shows a streetscape with the sanctuary peeking out above the protective wall separating it from the plaza outside. The image thus captures both the openness of the space in the sense of being public, a recognized component of the wider body politic, and also its enclosure, in the sense of being a distinct sphere with clear boundaries.

This high visibility, contrasting with the more inconspicuous Jewish architecture of earlier times, was, in a sense, a precursor to a nineteenth-century Jewish movement towards a more prominent presence in the built environment of the European city, as architecturally monumental synagogues began to stake a place for Jews as part of the European public.[49] However, this parallel with the move into the modern public sphere could lead to a misreading of the Esnoga's signification in its own day. The emergence of a 'public sphere'—or a 'private' one, for that matter—central to many accounts of the development of modern politics was far from simple, and even further from complete at this historical stage.[50] While the Esnoga signalled itself as 'public', in the seventeenth-century Dutch context this suggested political separation at least as much as it did integration: if the Jewish community was a public, it was separated from the Dutch public.

[49] The civic excitement, dignitaries, and visual culture of the inauguration of the Oranienburgstrasse synagogue in Berlin (R. I. Cohen, 'Urban Visibility', 744–6), for example, recapitulated the Esnoga's inauguration, including comparison of the synagogue to the Temple of Solomon. See also Snyder, *Building a Public Judaism*.

[50] I refer of course to Habermas, *The Structural Transformation of the Public Sphere*, and its historiographical descendants, including and alongside new interest in domestic and family life in early modern Europe. B. Kaplan provides an important discussion of how it relates to religious toleration in 'Fictions of Privacy'. See also Goodman, 'Public Sphere'.

As a civic sphere, it did not necessarily directly impinge on that of the city, but neither did it push towards a sense of Jewish individuals' integration into the Dutch body politic.

On the contrary, it strongly suggested a polity unto itself, as the enclosure designed for the Esnoga suggested not only separation but also jurisdiction or territory, as in the walls of a city. The walled enclosure was a significant innovation, contrasting not only with most European synagogues of the age,[51] but even with the Ashkenazi building across the street,[52] as well as contemporary public churches. The idea of the 'city' in English today usually suggests conjoined geographical and juridical territory, but early modern thinkers saw two different senses. The French legal theorist Jean Bodin noted that the city as a geographical place was represented by the Latin *urbs* (as in our modern 'urban' and Bodin's French *ville*), whereas the juridical space was represented by the Latin *civitas* (and the French *cité*).[53] The former was defined by a shared location of residence and day-to-day interaction; the latter was defined by political realities. A commonwealth or *civitas* transcended the physical location in which it was situated (just as the polity as a whole transcended the aggregate of its members) to mean something that went beyond those physical, constituent forms.[54] The communal system of the Kahal Kadosh had already treated the community as this kind of civic whole; the evocation of a walled city in the Esnoga complex reflected and instantiated it.

This signification differed from that of Jewish ghettos and quarters throughout Europe,[55] even walled ones, which were primarily residential zones. The Jews of Amsterdam did not live in a physically demarcated quarter or ghetto (though many were indeed concentrated in a particular area). Moreover, the physical enclosure of ghettos was imposed from without, reflecting relegation rather than self-determination, and totally lacked the

---

[51] The two synagogues of nearby Fürth, also built in the 17th century, were surrounded by a semi-private space, made so by the marginal location of the two and an open area surrounding them. According to Stiefel, non-Jews could have freely entered, but they would have had to seek it out. That is a different scenario than that of the enclosed Esnoga. See Stiefel, 'Architectural Origins', at figs. 3 and 4.

[52] There was a fence shielding the front entrance, but not from public view. It did not have a public area to itself, but rather had ancillary buildings tacked on adjacent to it. Stiefel, 'Architectural Origins', at n. 51.   [53] Miglietti, 'Sovereignty', 20.

[54] Brett identified 'a critical early modern tension between the commonwealth as a situated space and as a body that of its essence defies situation'. Brett, *Changes of State*, 7.

[55] See Calabi et al., '"City of Jews"'.

theopolitical order represented by the careful arrangement of the Esnoga within the courtyard and walls. The Venetian ghetto, in the words of one historian, was physically and architecturally 'disharmonious, asymmetrical, unstable, and even dangerous . . . a subversion of Venice's political and social order'.[56] The Esnoga complex turned the signification of the ghetto on its head, imitating and recapitulating Dutch modes of ordering, but in a distinctly Jewish style.

The notion of the Esnoga as embodiment of the Jewish civic sphere, or *civitas*, is also supported by the particular way it used Temple symbolism to combine the sacred with the civic. In recent years historians have recognized that the designs of both the Sephardi and Ashkenazi synagogues in Amsterdam were deeply influenced by other seventeenth-century interpretations of the Temple, both Christian and Jewish. A particular internal layout designed by the Spanish architect Juan Bautista Villalpando to mimic the Temple had been adopted in a number of synagogues in eastern Europe, and also inspired Leon Templo's elucidation of the Temple's architecture in Amsterdam and Haarlem's Nieuwe Kerk.[57] In turn, the architects Bouwman and Stalpaert followed the same concepts in their plans for the Amsterdam synagogues.[58] More generally, Villalpando's work was a more detailed and historicized version of a long tradition in Spanish Catholicism of treating churches like the Temple.[59] And in Protestant churches, self-conscious emulation of the Temple emphasized the church's identity as the true Israel, representing a spiritualized and universalized understanding of the church as the body of its members.[60]

Prior to the seventeenth century, synagogues had often referred to the Temple in their interior furnishings and decor—especially the design of the ark and Hanukah lamps—and dedicatory texts. The idea of the exilic synagogue as a *mikdash me'at*, or 'lesser sanctuary', is well known.[61] However, it was not typical for a synagogue as a whole to echo or copy the Temple

---

[56] Katz, *Jewish Ghetto*, 15.
[57] See Kravtsov, 'Juan Bautista Villalpando'.   [58] Ibid. 324–30.
[59] See Lara, *City, Temple, Stage*, 112–13.
[60] Spicer suggests that it was a polemical move against Catholics whom they saw as wrongly identifying the church as the edifice. *Calvinist Churches*, 2, 158–61, 224–6. Helen Rosenau pointed out the similarity of the Esnoga to the Protestant 'Temple' of Charenton, France, built in 1622 and destroyed in 1686. See Rosenau, 'The Synagogue and Protestant Church Architecture', and Perelis, 'Jewish Sacred Architecture', 232.
[61] See Mann, 'Towards an Iconography'.

so literally.[62] As places for group prayer, study, and communal gathering, synagogues fundamentally contrasted with the historical Temple, a place for elite priestly activity with inner areas forbidden to the Israelite public.[63] This opposition was not easily reconciled without the aid of supersessionism or allegory, as in Christian millenarian thinking. The adoption of Villalpando's Temple-based model in eastern European synagogues has therefore been explained as a reflection of messianic and kabbalistic fervour among the Jewish population there from the beginning of the seventeenth century, and likewise for both of Amsterdam's synagogues constructed in the wake of Sabbatianism, as well as synagogues in the Americas that followed its example.[64]

The messianic context may well be relevant to the Esnoga, too, but its design differed from all of these other examples by setting the sanctuary within a walled enclosure. It bridged the two kinds of Temple reference by combining the inner sanctum dedicated to holy rites with a wider space signifying other forms of communal gathering and lay government. It was, of course, common for Jewish communal spaces to accommodate multiple functions, but the Esnoga with its courtyard and outbuildings did not simply mix them; it separated them into orderly components of a whole. It evoked not the Temple alone but the Temple complex, adding precisely that arena of public assembly and worldly engagement that the former lacked, and thus rhetorically reclaimed the public dimension of the Temple from its symbolic use representing the body of the church. Its arrangement represented an analogy between exilic and biblical communal life, highlighting the fact that both combined politics with religion, combined meaningful self-rule with a sacral purpose. In so doing, it captured the messianic meaning of rebuilding the Temple and inverted it by embedding it within the framework of diaspora lay communal government.[65]

---

[62] Mann's treatment of the issue focuses primarily on decorations, especially the ark and Hanukah lamps, and briefly suggests that the overall rectangular shape of most synagogues intentionally echoed the Temple. Mann, 'Synagogues', 164.

[63] See Krinsky, *Synagogues*; Heller, 'Western Ashkenazi Synagogues', 178–9.

[64] Kravtsov, 'Juan Bautista Villalpando', 323–4, 331; Leibman, 'Sephardic Sacred Space'.

[65] Leibman argued that the Esnoga, as well as the 18th-century synagogue in Newport, Rhode Island, perpetuated a 'neo-Solomonic order' based on Templo's *Retrato* in accordance with Menasseh ben Israel's messianic interpretation of the dispersion of Jews into England and the New World. Since the context of the construction of the Esnoga was removed from Menasseh's outlook, I believe a different interpretation is required whereby the order she describes was translated into a sense of the civic nature of a Jewish community.

Rich European artistic and iconographical traditions symbolically associated enclosed atriums and courtyards like this one not only with the Temple complex but, by extension, with the holy city. As one historian described it, 'the atrium is a spatial filter, a distinct area, another city-within-a-city: the *City of God* realized in this world'.[66] It was common to imagine present-day cities, from Rome to Venice to Bruges, as versions of the heavenly city, whether an Augustinian City of God or a spiritualized Jerusalem.[67] Diverse early modern Christians played with and subverted a distinction between the earthly, temporal, or concrete city on the one hand, and the celestial or transcendent one on the other, often using an image of the biblical Temple synecdochally as a stand-in for Jerusalem.

The notion of the Holy City also evoked eschatological resurrection and restoration,[68] along with conversion and salvation. The atrium or courtyard that had been present in the biblical temples and in early churches served in early modern times as a model for the large church and conversion centres constructed in Mesoamerica to absorb indigenous people into the church.[69] Iberian Jews were privy to this cultural theme, especially considering the widespread perception that native Americans were descendants of lost tribes of biblical Jews, and that their 'rediscovery' had eschatological import. The Jewish public edifice that they built in Amsterdam recapitulated the conversionist move from idolatry into sacred community, now suiting their own adoption of a Jewish sacred community. Especially noticeable in this regard are the colonnaded porticos that were located within the courtyard of the Esnoga (visible at the bottom left of Fig. 3), which echoed the structure used in some Spanish churches, where the porticos were used to shelter catechumens—normally, converts from Judaism and Islam.[70] The visual reference to such structures subtly signalled the Kahal Kadosh members' own identity as returnees to Judaism. More generally, the symbolism of the holy city reinforced the sense of the courtyard as a special kind of gathering place, one where the coming together of individuals into a discrete body held deep significance.

[66] Bonet Correa, 'La Ciudad Hispanoamericana', quoted in Lara, *City, Temple, Stage*, 18.
[67] Lara, *City, Temple, Stage*, 96–7.   [68] Ibid. 42.   [69] Ibid. 18.
[70] See ibid. 24–5. The colonnades were specifically requested by the community and originally ran all along the north and south sides of the courtyard. The side behind the synagogue building was probably bordered by a simple fence rather than a colonnade, in contrast to de Hooghe's depiction in Fig. 3 but as depicted in Fig. 6. See Vlaardingerbroek (ed.), *The Portuguese Synagogue*, 84–5.

As we have seen, the aggregation of individuals in the Kahal Kadosh was not only spiritual but also distinctly political, so that the *civitas* here was also—especially—a civic sphere. And as various members expressed in their inaugural sermons, a strong reading of the building project within the community was as a domain of lay rule. Indeed, territory could be constituted as much by civic structure as land in the seventeenth century, as historians have begun to recognize.[71] In the founding period and first decades of the existence of the Kahal Kadosh, the influential rabbis Saul Levi Morteira and Menasseh ben Israel had commented that Jews did not have a 'republic, land, or government' anywhere. Now, in the Sabbatian period, when many community members saw the Kahal Kadosh as a republic and the Mahamad as its government, the Esnoga fitted the bill for something like territory. It signified a turn to the democratic and the local in place of the monarchical and the messianic, a turn to an existing edifice in place of an expected or imagined one rebuilt far away in Jerusalem. With the value of messianic restoration diminished in light of present political accomplishments, the Esnoga represented a Jewish politics that could counter Sabbatian expectation.

Disruption of Civic Order

Imagine Isaac Vellozino's words spoken aloud in the new building, on the sixth day of the building's use: a new synagogue, courtyard, and outbuildings, grand and public, declaimed as the Mahamad's realm. How was this message received? As Vellozino hinted, the construction had not been easy. It had taken five years to complete this building project, years longer than it took the Ashkenazi community to build its synagogue across the street, albeit smaller and lacking outbuildings. In practical terms, the delay resulted from a combination of a complex and challenging fund-raising environment and plain bad luck. A dispute over a major bequest that would have helped finance the construction held things up for a crucial year or two, and the delay meant that the Mahamad was still pulling things together in 1672, the year of military defeat and political chaos known in Dutch as the

---

[71] Revising a widespread view that the emerging conception of sovereignty in early modern Europe was uniquely focused on land in the 'Westphalian' sense. Annabel Brett argues for this in ch. 7 of *Changes of State*; so does Benton in *A Search for Sovereignty*. Westphalian sovereignty is so called after the 1648 Treaty of Westphalia and has deeply informed modern political thought. One treatment that gets at its impact is Ford, 'Law's Territory'.

rampjaar, or 'year of disaster'. In March, French and British armies invaded the Dutch Republic, conquering several provinces and coming close to taking Holland. Popular anger at the Grand Pensionary Johan de Witt and his government was expressed in public demonstrations throughout the summer, and in August de Witt resigned, only then to be assassinated and publicly mutilated. The Dutch economy suffered badly from war and instability, with a market crash and international trade at a standstill; as a community whose coffers were filled primarily by the contributions of merchants and brokers, the Kahal Kadosh was especially affected.[72] This was hardly an easy time for them to shoulder the extra fiscal burden of a lavish building project. As Jonathan Israel put it: the 'prosperity, independence, and very existence of the Republic' were severely threatened and as a result 'public building ceased'[73] in Holland. To top off their troubles, when the project was finally nearing completion two years later, in August 1674 a historically violent storm damaged the partially constructed synagogue, destroying a number of windows and a section of the women's gallery.[74]

Nevertheless, the leaders of the community persisted, apparently viewing the project as essential, even existential. Castro Tartaz dramatically recounted the dark times of the building project in terms of wider political events, ending in a reawakening of communal pride:

Our illustrious nation was very uncomfortable due to the crowding of the congregation—so much so that the tightness caused strife during prayer, and some commotion . . . The tumult of the war disturbed us with the decline in profits and lack of trade, and the lands were lost . . . It seemed indecent to continue the work in such a calamitous time, [as we were] so astonished by our ruin that we could only see our misfortune . . . All was loss and discomfort, until Divine Providence in the guise of nature helped us in our conflicts, allowing us to adjust our peace with the unbeaten Monarch of Great Britain . . . Here the spirits revived, the state began to open its eyes, and the nation to lift its head.[75]

---

[72] Israel, 'Republic'.   [73] Israel, *The Dutch Republic*, 796.
[74] The storm of 1 August 1674 has been called a hurricane in the historiography of the synagogue, but it has a fascinating history of its own. Called the 'terrible tempest' in Dutch culture, it was immortalized in art and lore, especially in Utrecht, where the damage was worst. Because of its extremely rare intensity and short duration (it passed in minutes but tore roofs off houses, destroyed bridges, and unmoored ships), it was assumed to have been a tornado until recently, when historical meteorologists hypothesized that it was a type of storm called a 'bow arch'. See van der Schrier and Groenland, 'Reconstruction'. On the Esnoga damage, see Fuks and Fuks-Mansfeld, 'Inauguration', 493.   [75] Castro Tartaz, 'Prologo'.

For bringing them through these trials, speakers at the inauguration duly praised the *parnasim* as good stewards. But there was another dimension of the troubles that was also acknowledged in the speeches: internal discord. Even after the Franco-Dutch war ended and political stability returned with the installation of William III of Orange as Stadtholder, the spectre of violent popular intervention in politics still loomed in the minds of the Dutch governing elite, and the emphasis on the active authority of the citizens remained a feature of local Dutch politics. Indications are that the leaders and members of the Kahal Kadosh similarly experienced ongoing competition and mistrust. Indeed, it is likely that the community's governing elite were especially disturbed by de Witt's death, since he had generally been supported by the merchant class of which they were a part.[76]

Some indeed betrayed a sense that their vision of communal harmony might have been more aspirational than descriptive. For example, Eliyahu Lopes commented in his speech, the fifth in the series: 'All peoples value unity and seek it in their politics because necessity—or reason of state—teaches it even when love does not dictate it.'[77] Lopes suggested that the political unity of the Kahal Kadosh was achieved despite real differences and even antipathy—in his words, when 'love does not dictate it'. Harmony and congruity, Lopes reminded his listeners, were not necessarily natural, easy, and loving, but rather could be hard won and needed to be strictly enforced. Vellozino, too, offered a warning, reminding his listeners of that other biblical building project, the tower of Babel, and cautioning that it had been destroyed due to division in its builders' commonwealth.[78]

These remarks were intentionally generalizing, with speakers offering platitudes about disharmony in general, in a setting where they could not reasonably discuss specific circumstances within the Kahal Kadosh. However, they offer some clues to surrounding events. When Lopes emphasized the religious justification of the Mahamad's rule, indicating that a Jewish republic was superior to others because of its reliance on Jewish law, he continued: 'Among the people of God, on the other hand, this is not observed as a dictate of reason, but as a commandment of the law.' The

---

[76] See den Boer and Israel, 'William III'. Their financial and mercantile involvements with governments are widely discussed, as in the following: Swetschinski, *Reluctant Cosmopolitans*, 130–43; Israel, 'An Amsterdam Merchant'; id., 'Manuel López Pereira'; and Swetschinski, 'The Spanish Consul'.

[77] Lopes, 'Sermão Quinto', 96.   [78] Vellozino, 'Sermão Sexto', 124–5.

comment might easily be passed over as an anodyne remark that Judaism teaches unity, but such a claim cries out for clarification. How does Jewish law compel communal unity? The particular way it can be said to do so is by means of the *ḥerem*. His comment was actually a pointed reminder of the power of excommunication, the central tool of unification in the Kahal Kadosh, and also a bitterly disputed power of the Mahamad during the years between 1670 and 1685.

Other sources confirm that the ban—and the Mahamad's governing authority that it supported—was an issue during this time. In his 1666 *Certeza*, Abraham Pereyra copied a passage from a Spanish political work, editing and inserting phrases that tailored it to address issues within his community:

There should be equality in the government, and no individual should be favoured in taxation more than another. In order for the voice of the commonwealth to be in tune, not only is it necessary that everyone pay the same, but also that those who are remiss be punished, because these usurpers break the divine precepts in laws of sanctity. The zealous governor must observe this policy, empowered by the right conceded to him by the divine Law to make laws for the common good and sustenance of the poor. With these weapons in hand, the governor will impose equal justice, and the public will see that transgressors of the divine precepts are punished, and that transgressing a *ḥerem* corrupts the people and disturbs the peace, depriving us of the Lord's grace.[79]

Pereyra referred to a number of the most central elements of communal politics: the *ḥerem*, the underlying reliance on Jewish law, the authority of the lay leaders to tax and to ban. He finished with a discussion of the sin of Akhan in the sack of Jericho, which is a common source for rabbinic discussion of the *ḥerem* and also a key story about rebellion and disobedience.

Five years later, while the synagogue project was under way, he addressed the same topic. In his *Espejo* (1671) he truncated the paraphrase and removed the specific admonitions about taxation and the ban. He now devoted an entire chapter to 'how unity and concord are a fundamental principal of the commonwealth',[80] with a sharper tone and a greater sense

---

[79] This translation is based on Méchoulan's Spanish edition. Méchoulan identifies some of the passage as paraphrased from Diego de Saavedra Fajardo's *Idea de un príncipe político-cristiano representada en cien empresas* (1640); the lines cited here appear to be Pereyra's own interpolations to Saavedra Fajardo's text. Pereyra, *Certeza*, 168–9.

[80] The title of Discurso II, ch. 6 (pp. 162–4).

of urgency as he called for obedience and loyalty and emphasized the mortal danger that division posed to a polity: 'It is well known that a commonwealth is very strong and incontestable if it is unified; and if not, it is very weak . . . If it is divided, it will not be able to withstand troubles or face the enemy.'[81] Note that there was also a slightly different message this time, as he called for 'unity among those who reign over the people and govern the commonwealth'. He wrote that 'judges and ministers' must be 'unanimous in their decisions and the actions they take should be skilful and effective. They should work in silence and deliberate with prudence, so that when their decisions come to light no discord can be seen in them.' The passage seems to acknowledge problems within the Mahamad as well as between the rulers and the people.

Pereyra, Vellozino, and Lopes warned that unity mattered in ways that cut to the heart of Jewish communal existence. To some extent, all of this is an expression of the normal give and take of real-life governance, and for these writers that was part of the point: they took pride in portraying the difficult realities of self-rule precisely because they were proud of self-rule, proud of possessing a real and actual commonwealth. They self-consciously explained it in terms normally reserved for statecraft as a way of posturing as state-builders. 'In concord there is strength' was the motto of the Dutch Republic,[82] and at a moment of shared difficulty, these prominent Jewish community members averred that they shared both the challenges and the remedies of other polities.

At the same time, the discord faced by the Kahal Kadosh was indeed serious. The Mahamad was suffering a series of overt challenges to its authority, and these affairs revolved around a small set of flashpoints: unity, the synagogue, the Mahamad's authority, and the *ḥerem*. Recall that the Mahamad reaffirmed its governmental authority, including the use of the *ḥerem* as part of the wider communal system, in 1670, when community members individually signed to attest their recommitment. The Mahamad also requested—and received—a similar affirmation from the magistrates of Amsterdam: first, in 1670, they confirmed that they could impose the *ḥerem*, and then in 1675 they did the same regarding the specific infractions of not attending synagogue and not paying dues, actions that signalled their insistence on including the entire body of the nation within the Kahal Kadosh.[83]

---

[81] Pereyra, *Espejo*, 162–3.   [82] See Frijhoff and Spies, *Dutch Culture*, 93.
[83] See Y. Kaplan, 'Social Functions', 134, and Swetschinski, *Reluctant Cosmopolitans*, 187, 257.

Individual members who objected to the Mahamad's decisions had few options: they could ignore them, argue with them, take the Mahamad to court, or remove themselves from the community. We find examples of all of these actions between 1670 and 1683.[84] A number of community members—an active donor to communal charity named Joseph Abarbanel Barboza, former *parnas* Isaac Henriques Coutinho, one Isaac Penhamacor and his son, a group of heirs of the wealthy Jacob del Sotto, and others —all bucked the Mahamad's authority not only by disobeying it, but even by openly and argumentatively expressing their disagreement with its decisions. Each of them, in one way or another, tried to circumvent or overturn a ban imposed by the Mahamad. Though these disputes might seem to be mere conflicts of class and clan, driven by social and financial pressures, they all began or ended with explicit questioning of the authority of the Mahamad, rather than being strictly limited to litigation of the details of the original disputes. And all of them became highly visible battles fought in the public forums of the stock exchange, the synagogue, the streets of Amsterdam, and Dutch courts. They were brought to light by other historians before me, but I summarize them here to show how they added up not to a time of petty infighting but of political upheaval.

In 1675, Isaac Penhamacor and his son attacked the Mahamad and the rabbi, ignored a *ḥerem* imposed upon them by continuing to attend synagogue despite it, and turned to Dutch authorities to revoke it. Two letters from the Mahamad to the Amsterdam government regarding the Penhamacor affair emphasize their need to wield the *ḥerem* to enforce payment of communal dues or taxes, in order to provide for their poor—shorthand, in their political language, for unity and authority concentrated in the hands of the Mahamad.[85]

In another rather extended drama, many members of a particular extended family, the del Sottos, refused to settle a deceased family member's estate—a matter of a sizeable fortune—in accordance with the Mahamad's demands. Members of the Mahamad in 1670 claimed that discussions with Jacob del Sotto before his death led them to expect a large

---

[84] My understanding of these complex disputes is based largely on the details already illuminated by Kaplan, Hagoort, and Swetschinski, though in some cases I interpret specific documents slightly differently. See Y. Kaplan, 'Social Functions', 133–9; id., 'Bans' (Heb.); id., 'Deviance and Excommunication'; id., *From Christianity to Judaism*, 193–9; Swetschinski, *Reluctant Cosmopolitans*, 249–59; and especially Hagoort, 'The Del Sottos'.

[85] These letters are reproduced in Y. Kaplan, 'Bans' (Heb.), 534–8.

bequest to support synagogue construction.[86] When del Sotto died, however, his heirs denied the existence of a will leaving such a gift. Mysterious deathbed messengers and furtive searches featured prominently in the cinematic affair that followed, which has been discussed by Yosef Kaplan and Lydia Hagoort. The legal wrangling between the Mahamad and del Sotto's family was carried out through communal announcements, bans, notaries, law enforcement, and multiple levels of appeal in Dutch courts. Some of the del Sottos' particular actions, including setting up a prayer quorum complete with a designated *parnas* (lay leader), attempting to retrieve furnishings of theirs that were currently in use in the synagogue, and purchasing land for a separate cemetery, strongly suggest a conscious intention to secede and found a separate community.[87] Eventually, most of the del Sottos returned to the Kahal Kadosh, but the fallout lasted to the end of the decade and beyond, as the heirs retained for themselves a small section of the cemetery, and arguments about it and other issues are visible in communal records as late as 1679. Abraham del Sotto petitioned to be readmitted to the community only in 1680, and three more heirs requested membership in 1683; a few members of the family never returned.[88]

Further, relations between the Kahal Kadosh and Ashkenazi Jews in Amsterdam were strained as a result of the affair, as the Mahamad asked the German and Polish congregations to ban the heirs in solidarity, but the Germans refused. Around the same time, the Mahamad announced that they would no longer offer any charity to German Jews, and they also expressly prohibited members of the Kahal Kadosh from patronizing German butchers—very likely an act of retribution for refusing to support the Mahamad's case.[89] In fact, the significance of the legislation about meat is deeper than it might seem, as it was also a feature of the Kahal Kadosh as a separate economy (or 'commonwealth'). Likewise, the 1670 proposal to build a new synagogue for the Kahal Kadosh seems to have been in part a competitive response to the parallel Ashkenazi project completed that

---

[86] Such a gift, though technically going into the community's charity coffers, would have considerably lessened the impact of the building project on communal finances. Kaplan discusses this issue in *From Christianity to Judaism*, 196–8. Isaac Orobio de Castro played a central role in this drama, as he testified that del Sotto had spoken to him about the intended loan before his death (p. 197).

[87] Hagoort made this astute observation: Hagoort, 'The Del Sottos', 46–7.

[88] Swetschinski, *Reluctant Cosmopolitans*, 252–8; Hagoort, 'The Del Sottos', 53–4.

[89] Hagoort, 'The Del Sottos', 43.

same year,[90] a project that had marked the Ashkenazi Jews of Amsterdam as financially, culturally, and institutionally separate.[91]

The cutting off of aid, separation of markets, and building of distinct edifices were all part of a new insistence that the communities were administratively, financially, and *politically* separate. The change in Ashkenazi fortunes and their new visibility on the Amsterdam street complicated the self-conception of the Kahal Kadosh. At the time of the *Acordos*, the religious, ethnic, and political cohesiveness had been rolled up together with the geographical, as almost all of the Jews present there were part of the nation; the few Ashkenazim merited only a brief, exceptional mention. The new possibility of transferring to another fully established Jewish community in the same locale undermined the very move to singularity that the *Acordos* had achieved and forced a reckoning with the basis for communal unity, authority, and distinctiveness.

On the part of the del Sotto heirs, defiance of the Mahamad on one particular matter translated into opposition to their rule in general, and perhaps especially to the Esnoga project, with all that it signified. Another set of disputes also revolved around exclusion, membership, and authority, as well as the same material factors—the synagogue, cemetery, and meat market. In 1677 a petition was signed by ninety-seven members of the Kahal Kadosh in opposition to the ban on buying poultry from Ashkenazi butchers.[92] One man, Bueno Aragon, had already been subjected to the *ḥerem* for violating this prohibition, and when another, Joseph Abarbanel Barboza, was now placed under the *ḥerem* merely for protesting against it, Barboza appealed to the city authorities. The magistrates decided in Barboza's favour and told the Mahamad to rescind that *ḥerem*. The Mahamad obeyed, but followed up by declaring that Barboza was no longer a member of the community—now using their authority as heads of the community to eject a member without explicit recourse to the halakhic construct of the *ḥerem* underlying the community's structure and their own authority. It was a move that has been described as a secularization of the *ḥerem*; as such, it stripped exclusion down to its pure social or political element.[93] In doing

[90] Fuks and Fuks-Mansfeld, 'Inauguration', 492.
[91] Kaplan explains the cutting off of charity to and prohibition of meat purchases from the Ashkenazim as a response to a new assessment of their status because of their new synagogue. *From Christianity to Judaism*, 196.
[92] The text of the petition is found in Y. Kaplan, 'Bans' (Heb.), 538–9.
[93] This series of events is detailed in Y. Kaplan, 'Social Functions', esp. pp. 136–9

so, they opened a door for other dissatisfied members to separate community membership from other forms of belonging by abdicating their
official membership without any intention to give up religious practice.
Several swore before Dutch notaries that they were no longer members;
the Mahamad countered that religious services were only available to
members; and thus the old tension between prayer groups and communal
cohesiveness, between the religious and the social or political component
of the Kahal Kadosh, rose again. Barboza reconciled with the community
by 1679, but others were slower to do so.[94] In this affair, both parties—
leaders and subjects, or would-be private citizens—experimented with
translating the community's religio-political structure into a purely political, or a purely religious, one.

Finally, the complaints of Isaac Henriques Coutinho also connect
back to the synagogue-building project and the fundamental authority of
the Mahamad. Coutinho, who had served on the Mahamad at the time
of the initial proposal to build the new synagogue, objected to the seat
he was given when a later Mahamad made new assignments. In a letter
addressed to the lay board in 1680, Coutinho took issue with their governance in terms that echo the speeches at the synagogue's dedication:

> There is no Gentile tribunal in Europe that would offer judgement on a matter
> in which one of the judges held an interest . . . and in your council, as God-
> fearing men, you should behave the same way . . . My lords, I say that you . . . are
> blind since you do not see that authority is not maintained by any flotilla or naval
> Armada, nor by four thousand horses or other great infantry, but rather by recti-
> tude in everything, which is greater than all those weapons. This is what gives
> one authority and respect and brings unity.[95]

Coutinho was barred from the synagogue for his impudence but was also
told he could not pray at home, effectively forcing him to reconcile with
the Kahal Kadosh on the Mahamad's terms if he wanted to observe Jewish
prayer.[96] Coutinho, like others before him, protested the Mahamad's decision to the Amsterdam city magistrates.[97] Practical government and legal
affairs here align with the rhetorical and symbolic discourse of communal
politics.

---

[94] Ibid. 133–9; Y. Kaplan, 'Bans' (Heb.), 522–32; and Swetschinski, *Reluctant Cosmopolitans*,
251–2.   [95] My translation of the Portuguese text published by Kaplan in 'Bans' (Heb.), 539.
[96] Whether Coutinho was trying to pray alone at home or with a quorum is a significant
question; see Ch. 4.   [97] Y. Kaplan, 'Bans' (Heb.), 530–2.

Coutinho's dispute was ongoing in 1680 when Hakham Aboab, the most prominent communally employed rabbi and the sole rabbi remaining of the four installed at the founding, intervened in the controversy in the most public way possible—in print. He published a pamphlet defending the Mahamad's right to use the communal ban and specifically accused unnamed rebels of denying that right in order to undermine the community as a whole.[98] It is difficult to know how Aboab's pamphlet was received but the scandals continued and, faced with the spate of cases disputing the Mahamad's bans, the city magistrates temporarily revoked the community's independent right to excommunicate in 1683, instructing the Mahamad to refrain from imposing any bans without their approval.[99] This ban on bans could not have been more significant, since, as I detailed in Chapter 1, the investment of the Mahamad with the right to use the ḥerem was not an ornament but a keystone in the political structure of the Kahal Kadosh. Its loss—and more generally the fact that some community members were openly disputing it—was a sign of changes to the fundamental understanding of the legitimacy of communal authority. Only a few years passed before the status quo was reinstated with respect to the ḥerem specifically, but in a general sense, the damage was done. After this, the Mahamad imposed bans much less frequently and the council itself appears to have lost some of its primacy in communal organization.[100] This shift came at the time of an overall decline in public political discourse in the Kahal Kadosh, the true end of traditional messianic expectation among Sabbatians, and a wider set of political changes that brought the Dutch 'Golden Age'—and most intense era of European 'crisis'—to an end.

These disturbances, though varied and often apparently petty in their immediate concerns, had deep significance in the culture of the Kahal Kadosh. The lawsuits, petitions, and conflicts in general are productively understood as a kind of political speech. The historian Douglas Catterall observed that in Holland at this time, conflict 'was frequently a medium for conducting everyday and even high politics'. Legal proceedings as well as public disputes and complaints were 'part of the polity in direct and legitimate ways', as a civic society was increasingly understood as the site of affairs that were '"politick" or not of the church'.[101] Affairs within the Kahal

---

[98] See Ch. 4.
[99] Y. Kaplan, 'Social Functions', 134–5; Swetschinski, *Reluctant Cosmopolitans*, 252.
[100] Y. Kaplan, 'Deviance and Excommunication', 150.
[101] Catterall, *Community without Borders*, 186.

Kadosh Talmud Torah beg to be read in the same way, as individuals exercising what means they had to access political agency—both within and, complexly, beyond the boundaries of the Jewish civic sphere.

As political speech or activity, these conflicts articulated objections to fundamental components of communal authority, with four interrelated issues at play: the construction of the Esnoga, the boundaries of the Kahal Kadosh, the *herem* as a political tool, and the extent of the Mahamad's power. The plaintiffs in these cases did not want to leave the Jewish fold but rather to change the politics within it—or else form a new Jewish community. The del Sottos tried to set out on their own, others tried to join the Ashkenazim, and still others wanted to remain religiously connected to the Spanish and Portuguese congregation but not subject to the Mahamad and to the Kahal Kadosh as a commonwealth. They objected to the Mahamad and the particular structures and institutions of the Kahal Kadosh Talmud Torah, not Judaism or Jewish community in its essence, and even their objections to lay authority were not a clear-cut matter of lay versus rabbinic; they did not necessarily obviate the concept of a Jewish commonwealth but rather worked within it to pursue interests that were not accommodated by the current forms of its politics.

The intensity of dissent during this decade and a half is unmatched by anything earlier or later. Discussion and argument centred on an understanding of the community as a religious polity, reflected in the construction and celebration of the Esnoga, whose structures and spaces represented the community as *civitas*, or civic realm. Idealization of unity in multiplicity went hand in hand with a particular image of the ideal place of religion in the Jewish polity as privileged but disempowered. The arguments were visible and serious enough to become a focal point of major public speeches intended to celebrate the community at the moment of its great accomplishment in completing the Esnoga, and in the light of the centrality of the *herem* as the fundamental basis of communal authority, the unassailable authority commanded by the Mahamad, and the insistence on an absolutely unitary community at the heart of the community's politics, it is not hard to see why. The orations, disputes, and other writings reflect broad engagement with ideas about the very nature of a Jewish community as a political body. A carefully constructed vision of secular and sacred roles affirmed the community's proper functioning, unified and harmonious under a Mahamad that enacted divine politics, imitating God and

biblical leaders alike. At the same time, the disputes suggest dissatisfaction
with such a vision on a conceptual level. And like Shakespeare's lady who
'doth protest too much' the cascade of voices declaring that the Jewish
governors had achieved perfect communal harmony inadvertently called
attention to the dissonance that was only thinly covered over.

To what causes can such a breakdown in communal politics be attributed? Certainly, the rise to self-sufficiency of the Ashkenazi community
in Amsterdam, along with the well-known political developments in the
Dutch Republic at the time, were factors. So were more conceptual factors.
In the same year that the Esnoga plans were first announced, Spinoza's
Theological-Political Treatise shocked Europeans with its interpretation of
biblical law supporting his stance against clerical authority in the ideal
republic. The republic that Spinoza had directly in mind was the Dutch
Republic, and from that perspective the scenario he envisioned would do
away with the Mahamad's authority, including the power to ban, since he
clearly declared that no entity other than the sovereign should be able to
excommunicate.[102] In fact, in this way the *Treatise* undermined the basis for
the Kahal Kadosh and invalidated the commonwealth model of Jewish
community altogether. This seems well aligned with the rebellions carried
out here, albeit without explicit ideological bent.

At the same time, as we know, Jewish readers in the Kahal Kadosh read
their community as a 'republic' as well. Just as we read de Hooghe's image
of the Esnoga's interior through their eyes, so may we try to understand
how they would read Spinoza as taking up questions that applied to them
within their Jewish republic. From this internal perspective, the *Treatise*
unequivocally—if surprisingly—supported the Mahamad's wielding of the
ban, as he argued for the aggregation of all temporal powers, including
excommunication, to the lay magistrate. Here, one could see the rebels as
taking an anti-Spinozist stance, rejecting the despised heretic's diminution
of clerical authority and what they saw as lay overreaching. The Mahamad
(and the Jewish commonwealth) was buttressed in a way by Spinoza's insistence that Jewish law was political in nature, given as the law of the biblical
commonwealth. However, that insistence led him to argue that Mosaic law
was obsolete without sovereignty. One way of opposing Spinoza's problematic conclusions about Jewish religion qua law was to de-emphasize the
political or civic element championed by the Mahamad, making the con-

---

[102] See *TPT*, 252, and my more detailed discussion below in Ch. 5.

gregation more like a voluntary religious association. For a community seeing itself as a Jewish *civitas*, the *Treatise* posed an extraordinary paradox. It brought to the fore the inherent contradictions and underlying tensions of the exilic Jewish community, without ever directly addressing exilic Jewish communities per se.

Sabbatianism, too, raised the stakes and heightened the tension over these same concerns—in the big picture, as in the fate of exilic communities, but also in terms specifically of the Esnoga, the *ḥerem*, and lay authority. For example, the 1670 ban on buying Ashkenazi poultry was an aspect of the Mahamad's tightening control of communal affairs; but it also reinstated a prohibition that had been lifted in 1666 in anticipation of messianic redemption. It was one of many such regulations that were all nullified in one act at the height of Sabbatian excitement, a step that has been explained as an effort to avoid creating unnecessary avenues for sin or separation from the community at a time of imminent redemption.[103] An unnoticed dimension of the lifting of the prohibition is that in a time of messianic kingship, *kashrut* would still matter, but communal boundaries would presumably not. In contrast, when the prohibition on kosher meat from outside the Kahal Kadosh was reinstated in 1670, it was a return to a model of the community as a political and economic body unto itself. After all, the records do not indicate that the ritual appropriateness of meat butchered by Ashkenazim was itself suspect; the regulation prohibited purchase, not consumption, as a matter of belonging to the commonwealth.

Sabbatianism, after all, had the potential to drastically disrupt the political order of the Kahal Kadosh. Fundamentally, the prospect of messianic restoration was at odds in almost every way with the locally embedded, discrete, concrete diaspora Jewish commonwealth. Proudly independent and geographically grounded, lay-led and ethnically particular, the Kahal Kadosh was limited to one group of Jews, united in a pact of common allegiance, rather than joining together with Jews universally in a messianic kingdom. In the worldwide Jewish empire imagined by Sabbatian followers at the height of the movement, discrete communities and their leaders were to be obsolete, or at the very least subject to a Jewish imperial authority, as indeed news went out across Europe that Sabbatai was dividing up

[103] The Mahamad listed the regulations for which a *ḥerem* would no longer be a punishment, and someone carefully went back through decades of records to note the repeal on each page where a ban was originally declared—a fascinating commitment to archival accuracy facilitated by the ongoing indexing that had been maintained since the signing of the *Acordos*.

the lands of the diaspora under his own appointed kings. Successful Sabbatianism, at least one version of it, meant Jewish monarchy in diaspora. The counter to such a vision was not merely continued presence in the diaspora but pointed continuation of republican political arrangements.

The Sabbatian context thus also provides a partial explanation for the Mahamad's action in 1670, the same year it began the Esnoga building project and began to feud with the heirs of Jacob del Sotto, of re-establishing the terms and basis of its rule by having members sign to affirm their allegiance and the Amsterdam magistrates reiterate their approval. Whatever immediate impetus there may have been for them, these actions were the beginning of a new phase in which the community's leadership substantively rejected the pragmatic possibility of Sabbatian return, replacing it with a reinvigorated Jewish *civitas*. While a rabbinic reaction to Sabbatian religious antinomianism has long been observed, here we find its counterpart among lay leaders, building a bulwark against Sabbatian threats to communal authority.

The decision to build a grand new civic centre in the same year is partly attributable to the same motivation. Whereas messianic followers envisaged at least some degree of ingathering, bringing the permanence of diaspora institutions into doubt, the Esnoga was a dramatic instantiation of those very institutions. As a brick and mortar installation it countered any thoughts of mass departure to the Holy Land and represented ongoing Jewish presence in a particular locale. Though the synagogue itself might endure in either scenario, the meaning imparted to it in the architecture of the complex as a whole and in the inaugural speeches was specifically and pointedly aimed at embracing the community—with its ethnic particularity and lay rule—as the basis of Jewish political life. The transcendent political longing that might be directed towards a messianic ingathering was redirected towards local political gathering in the form of a *civitas*, with all the symbolism of the Temple and the holy city.

The reason for the building project mentioned in the congregational records, attributed to Aboab in his inspiring sermon that kicked off fundraising and cited in Castro Tartaz's introduction—that a larger space was needed to avoid the many 'disturbances' that took place in synagogue—is usually understood as referring to population growth.[104] Another likely

---

[104] Stiefel, 'Architectural Origins', and Fuks and Fuks-Mansfeld, 'Inauguration'.

source of disruption immediately before 1670 was that community members continued to argue over the status of certain Sabbatian changes to the liturgy. The most controversial of these was the Ninth of Av, a day of fasting and lamentation that Sabbatai had turned into a feast day in honour of his own supposed birthday and the symbolic reversals of the messianic age. Indeed, Gershom Scholem described the abolition of the fast, 'with much pomp and circumstance and amid public enthusiasm', as 'the climax of the movement', and noted that some believers continued to alter the service for the Ninth of Av as late as 1673.[105] The Esnoga was inaugurated on the sabbath following the Ninth of Av (a fact the printer Castro Tartaz emphasized in his title for the volume by noting that it took place on Shabat Nahamu), rhetorically framing the event—and hence the meaning of the new synagogue—in part in connection with the holy day. The recommitment to the local community was contrasted with the mourning of the destruction of the ancient Temple.

Kahal Kadosh members generally avoided explicit mention of Sabbatai Zevi in public discourse and official records. However, one speaker at the synagogue's inaugural celebration referred to it in subtle ways his audience would surely have recognized. Towards the end of his oration on the final night of the week-long series, David Sarphati elaborated on a rabbinic tale of a Roman prince who was born on the Ninth of Av and died during Hanukah, meaning that Jews were expected to join their Roman neighbours in national celebration on a Jewish day of lamentation for national defeat, and then join them in mourning during a joyful holiday commemorating a Jewish political victory. Liturgically, both holy days connect with the fate of the biblical Temple, Hanukah celebrating its liberation and the Ninth of Av lamenting its destruction; Sarphati used the parallel to address the Esnoga as an edifice of Jewish civic and religious pride within a national history of alternating independence and subjection, as part of his extended meditation on the relationship between politics and religion.[106] But in addition, both holy days were also indelibly linked with the Sabbatian drama of the previous decade. I have already mentioned the Sabbatian meaning of

---

[105] Scholem, *Sabbatai Ṣevi*, 658, 893. He discusses changes to this and other fasts and festivals in the Jewish calendar elsewhere as well, including pp. 616–31 and 883–4. See also the letter of Joseph Halevi to Sasportas in February 1667, indicating that Amsterdam's Sephardim were, after the apostasy, continuing the Sabbatian practice of reciting the priestly blessing every sabbath. Halperin, *Sabbatai Zevi*, 118–21.

[106] I discuss Sarphati's use of this tale at length in Ch. 6 below.

the Ninth of Av; Hanukah was also a significant moment in Sabbatianism, as it was during the week of Hanukah at the end of 1665 that Sabbatai rallied believers in his home town of Smyrna; and a year later in Amsterdam, it was close to Hanukah, in early December 1666, that Sabbatai's apostasy was 'definitely confirmed and accepted in Amsterdam as an undeniable fact'.[107] In the dramatic climax of the movement, therefore, believers there had experienced the loss of their messianic king at the same time as they lit candles in celebration of an ancient victory, in a juxtaposition uncannily similar to the ancient one Sarphati described.

Many in Sarphati's audience also knew that the 1675 sermon was an updated version of one he had given two years earlier at Passover. In the earlier version, he had concluded with some triumphalist remarks about ultimate redemption in connection with the holiday, urging the community to persevere in its construction plans despite the disasters taking place around them, and praising the Mahamad for their aggressive efforts to do so. He amplified the dissonance between disaster and pride highlighted in the contrast between Hanukah and the Ninth of Av by noting that the building project, too, had seemed inappropriate in the face of Dutch troubles: 'When the world erupts in wars (says reason of state)', he said, 'there should be a stop to grand building.'[108] Yet construction continued in faithful anticipation of future success. Sarphati thus aligned the completion of the Esnoga with the Passover redemption and messianic expectation.

The timing of the 1673 Passover sermon connected it even more clearly to Sabbatianism, as it coincided with a visible and dramatic renewal of the movement among some members of the Kahal Kadosh. A new messianic announcement had just been received from the movement's prime mover at the time, Abraham Cardoso, calling for the messiah's return and the final unfolding of messianic events to begin on the coming Ninth of Av, approximately six months away. In a dramatic *crise*, the poet Daniel Levi de Barrios began hearing voices and seeing signs on the first day of Passover, believing that he was able to interpret current geopolitical events as leading to Sabbatai's return as king.[109] Barrios may have been eccentric, but at least until this point he was not alone in such hopes; on the contrary, they were

---

[107] On 1665, see Scholem, *Sabbatai Ṣevi*, 374, and on 1666 see ibid. 754.

[108] Sarphati, 'Sermão Septimo', 144. The 1673 version is Sarphati, 'Sermão que pregou', MS EH 48 C 25.

[109] Y. Kaplan, *From Christianity to Judaism*, 228, citing Sasportas, *Tsitsat novel tsevi*, 363ff. (Kaplan's translation).

known and still surprisingly uncontroversial. When Sarphati then reprised the gist of his 1673 speech in 1675, things were different only to a degree, and the personal and political drama of the previous decade had not yet receded in memory.

In a rare public acknowledgement of the presence of Sabbatian themes and questions in communal life, Sarphati thus connected the Esnoga to Sabbatian religious inversions and, critically, to the wider national and political resonance of both. Sarphati's listeners would not have failed to note his meaning, especially as he invited them to read between the lines: 'I say little, but much should be understood; I say much, but it must be in few words.'[110] Sarphati addressed not only Sabbatian expectations but also the experiences of the Kahal Kadosh and the difficult position his co-religionists found themselves in. The resolution he offered, difficult and nuanced, was to embrace the Esnoga and all that it signified as its own sort of national religio-political triumph.

Indeed, the Esnoga complex itself signified something similar. The sanctuary's correlation to the architecture of the Temple was evocative of messianic redemption, but it could only ever be a symbol. The synagogue was, irredeemably, still a place of prayer and not of sacrifice, a site in the diaspora and not in Jerusalem. In contrast, the coming together of a body of Jews as a public or spiritual *civitas*, represented by the walled enclosure, was a dimension of exilic life that came closer to actually realizing political aspirations. It translated messianic hope into a distinctly presentist lay politics, where the coming together of people into a holy assembly had simultaneously religious and political significance.

Others referred, if not to Sabbatianism directly, then at least to the theme of exile in relation to the congregational edifice. Recall that Castro Tartaz wrote in his prologue to the commemorative volume that the week-long festivities 'seemed more like a Passover in a liberated Temple than a festival of captivity in a synagogue'.[111] Eliyahu Lopes, too, whom we observed above noting that reason of state recommends unity, attempted to find commonality among his listeners when he said:

I know there are three things that we all greatly desire: First, the increase of this Holy Congregation with wealth, business, and assuredness in enterprise; second, victory over our enemies and, thus crowned triumphant, to force them into a

---

[110] Sarphati, 'Sermão Septimo', 138.   [111] Castro Tartaz, 'Prologo'.

golden peace; and third, that this house will be the last one of the captivity in which we suffer so the offences and vexations and vituperation of so many, and are battered by all.[112]

Everyone could share a hope for economic prosperity and an end to the wars that were inhibiting it, and Lopes's third wish, seemingly simple, was finely wrought to bridge a gap between Sabbatians and non-Sabbatians, between separatists and champions of the Mahamad. Those who embraced the exile in the form of autonomous communities and those who still looked for its imminent end could agree on the hope that the Esnoga would be the last 'house of the captivity'.

Speakers at the inaugural festival treated the Esnoga as a physical instantiation of the community as a local, bounded, lay polity: a commonwealth, or *civitas*. It symbolized the Mahamad's rule in the midst of a decade of disputes focused on precisely that; and more broadly, it signalled a renewed commitment to lay Jewish political organization in the diaspora —a powerful but controversial stance at this moment of Sabbatian disappointment and Spinozistic challenge. Its construction was one dimension of a campaign of refoundation, wherein the Mahamad and their supporters pushed to solidify and entrench their vision of communal authority against a wave of disruption and uncertainty. The disputes that took place throughout these years are a sign of the pervasiveness of such uncertainty as well as the multiple levels of its resonance. As we shall see, the symbolic renewal of the Jewish commonwealth was accompanied by a new constitutionalism, as well as various explorations of its religio-political implications.

[112] Lopes, 'Sermão Quinto', 91.

FOUR

COVENANT

SOCIAL CONTRACT AND CONSTITUTION IN THE CROSS-HAIRS

WHEN Hakham Isaac Aboab da Fonseca took up his pen to write a treatise on the *ḥerem* in August 1680, the situation as he saw it was dire.[1] More than forty years had passed since the *Acordos* had been ratified, installing him with three others in the position of official rabbis in the newly formed Kahal Kadosh Talmud Torah. Now he was the only one remaining of those peers; the others had long since passed away, and he felt called to defend the fundamental principles of that constitution as the community faced multiple rebellions.

To call Aboab's pamphlet a treatise does not do justice to the passion and urgency he expressed in it.[2] Written in Portuguese for easy perusal by the members of the *nação*, it is both a desperate plea and a learned admonition to avoid the dissolution of the community. According to its own framing, this work, titled *Exortação, paraque os tementes do Senhor na observança dos preceitos de sua Sancta Ley, não cayão em peccado por falta da conviniente inteligencia* (Exhortation to God-fearers who observe the holy law to avoid sin due to lack of proper understanding), responded to some community members who took issue with the Mahamad's control over the ban and, by extension, its control over the community. The rabbi addressed their claims point by point, using rabbinic precedent, his own halakhic

---

[1] Aboab, *Exortação*. The date at the end of the text is actually printed as 4 Elul 5480, but this must be a mistake deriving from correlation with the Gregorian date of 1680. There is no question about the authorship or dating of the pamphlet, as the title page says 'Feito pello docto Senhor Haham Moreno A-Rab R. Yshac Aboab Ab-Bet-Din, & Ros-Yesibá do Kahal Kados de Talmud Torah. Estampado em Amsterdam. Em Caza de DAVID TARTAS ANNO 5440', and a Hebrew approbation on the final page gives the same date of 4 Elul 5440 (29 Aug. 1680). There is only one known extant copy of this text, held at the Ets Haim Library in Amsterdam.

[2] For the context of political pamphleteering, see Reinders, *Printed Pandemonium*.

innovation, and European political concepts to enter the fray, fully sharing in these rebels' mental world as he confronted their arguments against the communal status quo.

Despite the immediacy and severity of the communal crisis to which it attests, Aboab's *Exhortation* has not yet been written into the history of Amsterdam's Spanish and Portuguese Jews.[3] Between the lines of his defence of the communal *ḥerem* it is possible to discern both a pragmatic threat to the unity established by the *Acordos* and an abstract debate about the nature and status of that founding agreement as a constitution and in terms of Jewish law. Aboab did not name his opponents, referring to his offstage interlocutors only as 'them' and 'some', occasionally describing them as 'disturbers' (*perturbores*) or worse, but the issues he treated bore on actions taken to subvert the Mahamad's authority throughout the decade of the 1670s and described above in Chapter 3. In the light of Aboab's treatise, it is possible to arrive at a more nuanced understanding of the debate occasioned by the rebellions of figures like Coutinho, Barboza, and members of the del Sotto family. His discussion connects the dots, showing how the issues they raised in fighting the Mahamad's authority to ban them were ideological as well as practical. Their concerns dovetail with the religio-political implications of treating the community as a civic body, as reflected in various ruminations on the Mahamad and the synagogue treated throughout the present book.

The first lines of the *Exhortation* urge its readers 'to follow the examples of other congregations, in which people fear to hear the word *ḥerem* spoken aloud, and who would rather suffer the greatest and most ignominious insult' than violate one.[4] Over the course of thirty-four quarto pages, Aboab explored how the *ḥerem* was a cornerstone of Jewish communal life against which neither individuals nor factions had recourse. He marshalled rabbinic literature ranging from the Talmud to sixteenth-century responsa in support of the central theme that the *ḥerem* was a manifestation of the authority of the *kahal* (the congregation, or people), unified as a Jewish public or a collective. As such, the *ḥerem* was, in his view, unilateral and

---

[3] This work was nearly unknown until recently. It was mistakenly attributed to Matathia Aboab in Kayserling, *Biblioteca*, on which most subsequent bibliographies of Aboab da Fonseca's work were based. That mistake was corrected in Da Silva Rosa, *Die spanischen und portugiesischeen*, and the book is properly listed in den Boer (ed.), *Spanish and Portuguese Printing*. I treated the work for the first time in Albert, 'The Rabbi and the Rebels'.

[4] Aboab, *Exortação*, 2.

sacrosanct. It must not be corrupted in any way. Exemptions to and dilu-
tions of the *ḥerem* violated the deeper covenant that formed the very basis
of Jewish life and even of Judaism itself.

Along the way, Aboab revealed something of the way his opponents
approached the issue. It comes as no surprise that he portrayed them as
rejecting central principles of the community, but the particular principles
in question are more unexpected. The reputation of the Portuguese former
conversos as having difficulty accepting the religious and institutional
structures of Jewish life might lead us to see them as sceptics or proto-
secularized men who cared little for the rabbinic or spiritual authority represented by excommunication. After all, there were many who exhibited
only partial commitment to communal membership, intermittently or perpetually occupied the margins of the congregation, and struggled indeed
with the strictures of rabbinic Judaism.[5] Although religious communities
were key to the Dutch social fabric, they were, ultimately, voluntary associations, and it was possible to live in Holland without being a part of one.
Spinoza was able to be removed from Jewish life but not convert; and in
fact many others, conversos and former conversos, occupied a similarly
grey area on the 'margins' of this community.[6]

In the cases that disturbed communal affairs in the 1670s, however, the
disputants were far from marginal.[7] And despite some arch rhetoric, Aboab
did not treat the troublemakers as outsiders, ignoramuses, or mere scof-
fers. He referred to their 'doctrine' and reported that they 'said' and 'announced' various things in order to 'dissuade'; in response, Aboab made
and supported his own 'claims'.[8] When he wrote that they 'presume to
know more than they do', called them 'deluded', and accused them of
'prey[ing] on the weakness of those who are ignorant of the truth', he suggested not that they were marginal but that they were wrong, and that they
might be influential enough to persuade others. Though he insulted his
opponents and questioned their motives, such as when he called them
'flatterers [who] cloak themselves in the law to corrupt [or prostitute; lit.,
'sell'] that very same law',[9] or treated them as Machiavels motivated by

---

[5] See Y. Kaplan, 'Portuguese Community', 146, and id., 'Social Functions'.
[6] As Yosef Kaplan showed: see 'Alternative Path', 20, 'Social Functions', 114–15, and 'Wayward New Christians'.   [7] See Y. Kaplan, 'Bans' (Heb.), 528–9.
[8] i.e. *doutrina, dizer, alegar, publicar, desuadir/presuadir, pretender*.
[9] Aboab, *Exortação*, 2. The phrasing has overtones of common anti-Machiavellian tropes.

some 'accursed reason of state', he still ascribed ideas to them—and in these phrases, he subtly acknowledged the political nature of the issues at hand. As the title of his pamphlet reflects, he was concerned that well-meaning God-fearers would be duped into following their lead. He also acknowledged in a softer tone that at least some of the false claims he countered were made with good intentions.

Not only did Aboab acknowledge that his opponents were committed to certain arguments, he also gave a sense of their values and aims. In his portrayal, they appear not to have dismissed the *ḥerem* but to have engaged with it, making serious political and halakhic claims about how and by whom the ban might be used and how it related to Jewish political authority and the constitution of the Kahal Kadosh in particular. This is a crucial point: the rebels, whoever they may have been, appear to have understood the basic religio-political system of the Kahal Kadosh that I have reconstructed through close reading of the *Acordos*. At least to some extent, they accepted its internal logic, as they argued over how the principles underlying the community should be interpreted and enacted to form a new community or a different kind of community. They were not trying to leave Judaism, whether religiously, culturally, or socially; nor did they disparage the *ḥerem* out of a conviction that oral law or rabbinic authority was invalid. Nor did they reject wholesale the idea of lay administration or of organized Jewish community.

What they were doing was trying to secede from the community, rejecting the particular authority of the Kahal Kadosh with its ban wielded by the Mahamad, to form their own congregation or prayer quorum. Nowhere did Aboab narrate the specific divisive events that led him to compose the *Exhortation*, rather seeming to take for granted that his readers were in the know, so today's reader must piece together the context. However, he referred in one place to a comparable situation in sixteenth-century Salonika, where, wrote Aboab, 'the same thing happened among them as among us': the community 'suffered various disturbances' and some members 'separated themselves from the Kahal', whereupon it was 'ordered, among other things, that no one might separate from his *kahal*, nor make a new Synagogue beyond those that they already had in that city of Salonika, and they enforced their decree with all the curses and *ḥerem*s'.[10]

---

[10] Aboab, *Exortação*, 31. He referred to Isaac Adrabi's *Divrei rivot*, published in Venice in the

This rare moment of attention to events rather than ideas affirms what can be surmised from the challenges to the Mahamad's authority that had taken place over the previous decade: namely, that some members had tried not to free themselves of communal attachment altogether but to secede. For example, the rebellions of the del Sottos fit this assessment. They had congregated, in flagrant transgression of communal rules, for a separate Friday prayer service *before* being banned, so their sabbath gathering cannot be understood as a pragmatic response to exclusion. The group's purchase of a separate burial ground followed so closely, just eight days later, that it was likely planned in advance. In 1671 and again in 1675 the Mahamad petitioned Amsterdam's burgomasters to reiterate the basic exclusivity of the community—in 1671 specifically asking them 'put into law that no one may have a separate minyan or much less a separate synagogue'.[11] The twists and turns of the del Sottos' wrestling match with the Mahamad over inheritance, documents, cemetery space, and other issues have obscured the essential point that they had tried to break away as a group.[12]

Aboab's *Exhortation* makes their efforts appear yet more consequential and reveals that such threats to the unity of the Kahal Kadosh had touched off an internal debate that spread beyond the del Sotto clan. After all, others, like Joseph Barboza and Isaac Henriques Coutinho, claimed the right to pray outside of the communal synagogue. Coutinho argued to the burgomasters that the Mahamad's decrees prevented him from practising as a Jew, since they excluded him from the synagogue and forbade him to pray in quorum at home. When the ruling was issued in favour of the Mahamad, supporting the council's right to rule as it saw fit ('as long as he wishes to be a Jew he will have to abide by the regulations of the church'[13]), Coutinho asked a higher court that he be restored to the community or allowed 'to pray at home with eight or nine companions'.[14] Coutinho is the most obvious example in the record book of an individual who had raised such challenges and was not yet reconciled to the community in 1680 at the time of

late 16th century. Note, in his wording, subtle acknowledgement that in Salonika there were not one *kahal* and synagogue but multiple ones.

[11] And 'that the governance of the community should be as it has been'. SA 334, 19, fo. 628.

[12] Swetschinski, *Reluctant Cosmopolitans*, 256. Hagoort also reads the sources to indicate that the del Sottos intended a permanent secession; see 'The Del Sottos', 46–7.

[13] Swetschinski's translation; *Reluctant Cosmopolitans*, 205. See SA 334, 19, fos. 727–8.

[14] Y. Kaplan, 'Bans' (Heb.), 531, and see Swetschinski, *Reluctant Cosmopolitans*, 205–6.

the *Exhortation*, so it is possible to suggest that he stood at or near the centre of Aboab's concerns. But his complaints must be seen as part of a general uproar about the unitary nature of the Kahal Kadosh and the Mahamad as its government.

Aboab did acknowledge the theoretical possibility that an individual might pray at home without political motives. 'I see that they tell me', he wrote, 'that the *ḥerem* only includes praying outside of the synagogue with a minyan, and that they obey, and want to do it in their houses.'[15] The phrase 'in their houses', which could also be translated more loosely as 'privately', suggests an intentional effort by the rebels to avoid the appearance of forming a separate community by both Dutch and Jewish standards. They made use of the Dutch concept of private, domestic worship, which was theoretically unregulated, as opposed to worship in a public, or collective, space like the Esnoga. In response, Aboab offered his only moment of accommodation, allowing that such private prayer was indeed kosher. However, he advised against it, averring that it would be 'to their detriment, since prayer in the congregation has great strength and valour, and solitary prayer poses great risk . . . But the Lord never disapproves of the prayer of the general Congregation.'[16] Here, Aboab the rabbi spoke as a shepherd to stray sheep, with spiritual rather than legalistic or institutional overtones. It is an exception that highlights the rest of the work's fundamental concern with the more political implications of separate group prayer. 'The point of it all', as Aboab summarized his treatise in its conclusion, was to show that since 'the unity of our Holy Kahal [was] constituted with the approval of all and signed by all in the presence of its Hakhamim under pain of *ḥerem*, those who want to separate themselves against the agreement cannot do it, nor can anyone in the world free them from the punishment it incurs.'[17]

As Aboab's concluding statement hints, attempts at secession and the ideas justifying them had wider implications. They overlapped with other debates, especially in terms of constitutionalism, the authority of the people, and the rabbinic role. Aboab laid out eight main points, including:

---

[15] Aboab, *Exortação*, 29–30.

[16] He continued: 'The prayer of a man is only heard in synagogue, meaning that any other [prayer] is in vain.' See BT *Berakhot 6a* and Maimonides, *Mishneh torah*, 'Laws of Prayer', 8: 1. Aboab, *Exortação*, 31.   [17] Aboab, *Exortação*, 33–4.

First, to show the force of the *ḥerem* and its stipulations. . . . Second, the authority of the Kahal is so great that it needs no other addition. Third, the Mahamad has the same authority whether it was elected juridically, that is, elected by the Kahal or by the majority of it when that is the custom; or when the Kahal, possessing the same authority, has given it to the first elected officials, so that they would successively pass it on, electing those they find worthy and not reproved by the generality. Fourth, when there is a Hakham salaried or elected by the Kahal, whether elected by the Kahal or the Mahamad, his participation is required. Fifth, the *ḥerem* has the same value as all those since that of Moshe Rabenu, in which all the generations present and future are obligated, without being able to claim absence or ignorance, because a quality of the subjects does not affect a *ḥerem* or the virtue that the Lord God gave it.

These points obviously transcend the narrow question of whether a second congregation or a prayer quorum was permitted, and they require a great deal of unpacking. Aboab's extended treatment offers a systematic interpretation of the meaning of the ban in the community and in Judaism.

For the purposes of this discussion, Aboab's treatment can be organized into three interrelated areas of concern: the Mahamad's *ḥerem* as a keystone of government, the status of the constitution, and the role of the rabbi. In the first area, he addressed the halakhic logic underlying the *Acordos*, which set up the *ḥerem* as the basis for communal authority, to be wielded by a small group of laymen. He treated the *ḥerem* as a collective oath, a result of the pooling of individuals' political will, and hence an instantiation of the lay Jewish rule that had existed since biblical times. He particularly addressed the relationship between the Mahamad as a representative group and the *kahal* as the collective.

In the second area, Aboab entered into a debate on the ongoing force of the initial pact that bound this particular community (the constitution, or *Acordos*). Ultimately, he suggested that the *Acordos* were as inviolable as Jewish law, interpreting them as something more like a covenant than a constitution in order to emphasize irrevocability. Accordingly, he echoed a Hobbesian stance against the right of revolution. Third, Aboab explained the role of the rabbi with respect to the *ḥerem* and communal enactments in general. He defended lay control over the *ḥerem*, hinging rabbinic excommunicatory power on an appointed communal office rather than any inherent authority deriving from rabbinic credentials or halakhic expertise.

The present chapter will focus on the first two areas, leaving the third—the question of clerical authority—for Chapter 5.[18]

Throughout, Aboab's and his opponents' ideas intersected substantially with Christian thought of the same era about covenant and constitution, excommunication and ecclesiastical power. Aboab leaned in to the state-like understanding of the community, treating its government as having a unique and permanent claim to authority. His opponents, on the other hand, advocated a looser understanding of community and greater freedom to congregate, greater power on the part of members and rabbis, more accountability on the part of the Mahamad, and a more contingent, contractual interpretation of the *Acordos*.

The Mahamad versus the *Kahal*

'This, then, is the crime', wrote Aboab: the rebels 'declare that when some individuals separate themselves from the holy congregation, if they amount to ten, they form a separate congregation and free themselves from the *ḥerem*'.[19] In other words, any quorum of ten men—the number required to legitimize group prayer—constituted in itself a separate body with the inherent right to secede from the Kahal Kadosh and govern itself. 'Against them I say', the rabbi continued, 'if this were true (which it isn't), what would be the value of the *ḥerem*?' His exasperation is tangible, as the rebels' claims simultaneously undermined and made use of the *ḥerem* as a theopolitical construct.

The question Aboab and his flock were addressing was deceptively simple: could a group of individuals remove themselves from the community by forming their own minyan, or prayer quorum? What made it an especially vexed issue was that the communal system set up in 1639 was based on the absolute identification of the political body with the religious one, ultimately understood as such a quorum. As I discussed in Chapter 1, the membership of the Kahal Kadosh, the specific institutionalized community and its government, had to be coterminous with the *kahal*, the congregation of individuals whose collective authority empowered the government.

---

[18] Early modern historians are accustomed to thinking about the *ḥerem* in terms of lay–rabbinic power dynamics, and, partly for this reason, I set this dimension of Aboab's thought aside for the moment. Clearly, it was an issue for Aboab and his congregation, but I suggest that it was actually secondary to the other issues Aboab treated, particularly his characterization of the ban as covenantal and constitutional.   [19] Aboab, *Exortação*, 13.

The community was understood to derive its governing authority—its authority to compel its members—from its being a 'congregation'. In their usage, the idea of a 'congregation' was equivalent to that of a *kahal*, or assembly, essentially a group of at least ten ritually eligible individuals. Following the approach of the medieval Spanish halakhic authority Nahmanides in *Mishpat haḥerem* (The Law of the Ḥerem), they treated such a group as halakhically empowered not only to perform rituals permitted exclusively to a minyan, but also to create a political body or *tsibur* (public) by forming a compact among them of mutual allegiance and obedience. Such a compact Nahmanides described as a collective oath, meaning that a decree enacted by the group became binding on all members as though each one had sworn to it.[20] The collective oath was also understood as the establishment of a *ḥerem*.

The conception of the *ḥerem* as a collective oath that creates a political body differs from its common understanding as an act of exclusion from a religious community. It is a conception based on the biblical use of the term for something devoted or consecrated to God, in the sense that it must be destroyed rather than be used by people or set apart from such destruction to serve a sacred purpose. Possessing multiple senses and having evolved over millennia, usage closer to its present sense as 'excommunication' dates only from the talmudic era, when it could refer to an individual vow to avoid interaction with a person.[21] In geonic times the *ḥerem* came to be associated with formal communal decrees, violation of which would incur imposition of a ban, now meaning more extensive social separation,[22] as a person would be set apart from the body of the community in an inversion of the notion of a consecrated/cursed object. In rabbinic treatments the *ḥerem* retained its association with destruction and desecration as well as legal mandates and oaths, and by the Middle Ages it was possible for Nahmanides to connect it with the ruling authority of a local community as a kind of compact, using biblical examples of collective oaths to justify prioritizing the all over the one.[23]

[20] See Nahmanides, 'Mishpat haḥerem', 295–6; Lorberbaum, *Politics*, 108; Zohar, 'Civil Society'; Finkelstein, *Jewish Self-Government*, 149; and Faur, 'The Status of Communal Oaths'. Menachem Lorberbaum has argued that the views of Nahmanides and some others near his historical milieu facilitated a distinctly political arena within the community. See Lorberbaum, *Politics*. Aboab and his interlocutors clearly followed this tradition, though he was also aware of, and used, a range of other medieval rabbinic views regarding communal authority.
[21] See Benovitz, *Kol Nidre*, 94–9.   [22] Ibid. 106.   [23] Ibid. 107–9.

Aboab's discussion similarly underscores unity, which in his telling must be maintained at all costs. He makes the point through the story of the massacre of the Benjaminites (Judg. 19–21). In this (frankly abhorrent) biblical episode, the rape and murder of the concubine of a Levite travelling in the land of Benjamin prompts the rest of the tribes to vow revenge and mount a campaign of destruction against Benjamin's tribe, leaving it close to total extinction. Relenting after the fact, and distraught at the prospect of losing an entire tribe, the Israelites recognize that they must provide wives for the remaining men of Benjamin in order to preserve the genealogical line. However, they have previously sworn together not to give their daughters to Benjaminites, and this creates a quandary with unity at its heart: should they violate their collective oath, or lose an integral part of the Jewish people? Their solutions involve more violence. First, they slaughter the inhabitants of Jabesh-Gilead, saving only the virgins to become wives to the Benjaminite men; this is justified on the grounds that the men of that place were separatists, having broken with the initial collectivity by refraining from the fight against Benjamin. To make available still more potential wives, they then arrange the kidnapping and forcible marriage of the virgins of Shiloh, since their fathers would thus technically not be violating their oath by giving the women willingly. In Aboab's version the dramatic tale emphasized the inviolability of the Israelites' collective oath, as he concluded: 'even though it meant committing no small violence, they judged that this was a lesser evil than violating the *herem*', and set separatism as a sin deserving death.

The story sets the tone for what Aboab saw as the existential stakes of the constitutional crisis before him. The rabbi assumed that his readers would follow his logic that the collective oaths to destroy the Benjaminites and to keep their daughters from them constituted a *herem* among the swearers—a conclusion based on rabbinic interpretation, and not obvious on the face of the biblical text. He and, apparently, his intended readers shared an understanding that a *herem* was not a specific injunction or act of excommunication, not an individual instance of punishment or even a threat thereof, but rather a pact or blanket agreement of participation on the part of the people. This was the nature of the *herem* that Aboab and his congregants were debating in the pages of the *Exhortation*—and that stood as the keystone of the communal system. It was this kind of *herem* that was established by the *Acordos*, the 1639 constitution, in which the congregation became a political body by dint of its unification, unilaterally obligating its members to follow its rules and obey its leaders. The *ḥerem* representing the will of the unified group gave the community its authority, and the entire body of members signed the *Acordos* to signify their consent and allegiance—an act construed, at least now in 1680, as a collective oath. The agreement empowered the Mahamad to act as the agent of the group and, by extension, to wield its *ḥerem*, since the authority inherent in the assembly of Jews was transferred to the Mahamad as their government proxy.

In this system, separate congregations (even mere prayer quorums) would disrupt the absolute correlation between the body of the congregation (the *kahal*) and that of the population governed by the Mahamad according to the constitution, i.e. Spanish and Portuguese Jews in Amsterdam. Permitting multiple congregations to exist would destroy the unity and political authority of a single constitution for all of the city's members of the *nação*, which delegated the power of *ḥerem* to the Mahamad. In order for everyone to be party to, or subject to, the same *ḥerem*, everyone had to be part of the same *kahal*, and it was the fact that the lay leaders governed a congregation, rather than a collection of congregations, that made the *ḥerem* clearly their prerogative according to this way of thinking. Now, at the time of the *Exhortation*, Aboab's 'disturbers' claimed for themselves what all agreed was the authority of a *kahal* to form a *ḥerem*, but since one already existed, what they claimed was the right to 'form a separate congregation and free themselves from the [existing] *ḥerem*'.

One problem with the rebels' view was that the original *ḥerem*—the original collective oath, in the form of the *Acordos*—had explicitly prohibited precisely this. Referring to the second article of the *Acordos*, Aboab wrote: 'the *ḥerem* includes [*o ḥerem comprende*] that there cannot be any other synagogue in the city of Amsterdam or its environs, and that no one may assemble a quorum for prayer, except under the conditions listed there'.[24] Seen simply as a rule backed up by the threat of excommunication, Article 2 had a key flaw: what was to stop a group from seceding? If some men wanted to remove themselves from the Kahal Kadosh, then

---

[24] Aboab, *Exortação*, 13. The *Acordos* say that no other congregation may be formed; Aboab's gloss of 'congregation' as 'synagogue' affirms that what he battled was full secession and the creation of a rival community, and not merely an attempt to pray at home in a quorum of ten men. It also recalls the centrality of the physical synagogue in the political self-conception of the Kahal Kadosh, and reminds us that the growth of an Ashkenazi community in Amsterdam challenged the basis of the system laid out in the *Acordos*.

excommunication—removing them from the Kahal Kadosh—was hardly a consequence to be avoided.

Many have noted this apparently fatal flaw in excommunication as the highest punishment in premodern Jewish communities, highlighting as it does the ultimately limited nature of Jewish self-rule. Spinoza's reputed nonchalance about—or embrace of?—his expulsion fits it to a tee. But Aboab's question, 'then what would be the value of the *ḥerem*?', was apropos in an internal political sense as well. If authority derived only from unanimity then it could be disrupted all too easily; if it was based on the will of the people, then what would become of it when the will of the people shifted or divided? How was the Kahal Kadosh anything other than a voluntary association? Indeed, was it?

One way of approaching such an impasse was to fall back on external validation of communal authority, as both the Mahamad and secessionists had done throughout the 1670s and would continue to do through the early 1680s. Such litigation regarding the limits of the Mahamad's authority connects these affairs to a broader narrative about communal autonomy and its eventual decline, and it underscores the precarious position of Jewish self-rule, especially in a polity with rapidly changing attitudes towards toleration and church–state relations. Notable, however, is that at least some secessionists did not limit their efforts to forcing the Mahamad's hand from the outside. Nor did the Mahamad limit its response to the arena of the Dutch legal system, but rather used the community's constitution and halakhah to argue their position. The external, sovereign state was not the only political frame that either side dignified with substantive engagement. They also sought to justify their actions within the logic of the community's theopolitical system, treating the ban on new prayer quorums as part of an original agreement and the *ḥerem* as the source of communal authority.

Within such a frame, the rebels' violation of Article 2 (whether proposed or ex post facto) would be a violation not of a regulation but of the original *ḥerem*, which, as Aboab put it, 'included' such a prohibition. As such, it was a violation of their own prior oath—the very type of violation, as Aboab emphasized, that the Israelites had refused to commit when faced with the extinction of the tribe of Benjamin. Aboab, following Nahmanides, expressed the theory clearly: if the inhabitants of a certain place 'set[25]

---

[25] Aboab frequently uses the word *deitar*—to throw, give, or extend—and sometimes uses

a *ḥerem*, their *ḥerem* is valid to obligate the minority to obey them, and such a *ḥerem* is firm and incontrovertible. Therefore, someone from such a city who transgresses it is banned [*enhermado*] as if he transgressed his own oath.'[26]

A significant part of the *Exhortation* revolves around such oaths and whether or how they might be counteracted. Aboab took swipes at a few of the rebels' strategies. One was to argue that an individual oath to defy a decree or *ḥerem* was sufficient to exempt that individual from it[27]—a view that Aboab countered with reference to the responsa of two prominent Salonikan rabbis, Samuel ben Moses de Medina (Rashdam, 1505–89) and Isaac ben Samuel Adrabi (d. *c.*1584). These responsa dealt with similar efforts by individuals or groups to exempt themselves from the community, including members who took oaths not to obey communal decrees.[28] On solid halakhic ground here, Aboab had no trouble showing that an oath to disobey a law (or to renege on a prior oath) was not considered a valid oath.

Another approach the rebels took was to delegitimize the original communal *ḥerem* as it applied to them. In this vein Aboab's responses point to a claim by the rebels that they themselves had never sworn obedience or personally assented to the rule of the Mahamad or the obligation to obey its *ḥerem*. One of Aboab's responses, in which he followed *Mishpat haḥerem*, fronted the quality that made the communal *ḥerem* collective rather than individual, political rather than personal. He explained that, unlike a regular oath, a *ḥerem* required no explicit assent or even knowledge on the part of the swearer: 'The difference between a *ḥerem* and an oath is that if a man adjures another it means nothing unless the [second] party responds by saying "amen"; but in the case of the *ḥerem* of a *beit din* or *kahal*, if it makes an ordinance under pain of *ḥerem*, it is valid whether he responds with "amen" or not.'[29] (Note, as an aside, the equivalence he suggests between a rabbinic court (*beit din*) and an assembly of laypeople (*kahal*).)

---

pôr—to place, put, pose, or set. I translate it here as 'set' as I find a nuanced difference between his terms and 'impose'. Both *deitar* and *pôr* have more a sense of creation or establishment; 'impose' connotes its use as a punishment, as in imposing a *ḥerem on* someone.

[26] Aboab, *Exortação*, 8–9.   [27] See Elon, *Jewish Law*, ii. 713.
[28] Against an assumption that these were necessarily halakhic oaths, the fact that a number of Kahal Kadosh members swore before Dutch notaries that they were no longer members of the community, in a kind of pre-emptive move against excommunication, raises the fascinating possibility that they saw these Dutch civil oaths as operating both beyond and within the sphere of communal and rabbinic law.   [29] Aboab, *Exortação*, 8.

According to Aboab's statement, in the context of communal government every individual member was legally treated as having assented to decrees made according to an empowered body—whether or not the person had in fact been physically present for those decisions, in agreement with them, or even aware of them. Nahmanides justified this claim based on the biblical Nehemiah's imposition of an oath upon his people, emphasizing that the authority wielded by the community was continuous with such biblical political authority.[30] As Aboab paraphrased Nahmanides, individuals did not have to assent to this obligation 'since the Senate [i.e. Sanhedrin] had authority to set a *ḥerem*, as it says in Nehemiah 13: 25, *And I cursed them . . . and adjured them by God*'.[31]

Apart from the reference to biblical times, Aboab's view that the Mahamad's decrees were binding on a population regardless of individuals' consent partook of a widespread understanding of the authority of a polity. A kingdom or republic, even if theorized as deriving its authority from consent or contract, did not require ongoing affirmations of that assent, and a person born into it did not need to formally accept his or her status as a subject in order to be one. It was also consistent with the language of the *Acordos*, which declared that the subject population would automatically include all future local members of the nation, whether they arrived by immigration or by birth. Such perdurance was a feature of a polity or commonwealth in early modern political thought.[32] For Aboab, thinking halakhically, it meant that the Kahal Kadosh persisted as a binding authority irrespective of the personal oaths of its subjects.

The rebels in the Kahal Kadosh, by contrast, were promoting a vision of the community as some other kind of association, where members' relationship to the whole was intentional and individualized. Such a vision did not eliminate collective Jewish authority, as might be implied by the notion of a voluntary association as it is used in Jewish historiography to mean a group without temporal power over its members, following Moses Mendelssohn's objection against the communal *ḥerem* on principle. The rebels, as we know, did not oppose the *ḥerem* or communal rule in general. Instead,

---

[30] The books of Ezra and Nehemiah in general promote an idea that the Second Temple leadership perpetuated Mosaic authority despite their legal innovations. Najman, 'Introduction', 1666. Nahmanides also notes that this kind of *ḥerem* was not part of Mosaic law, but 'is known from tradition'. Nahmanides, 'Mishpat haḥerem', 294, and Lorberbaum, *Politics*, 107.

[31] Aboab, *Exortação*, 8.   [32] For example, in Johannes Althusius; see Ch. 1.

they sought to democratize the community and treated its constitution as directly contractual.

To do so they addressed the collectivity in terms of the halakhah of the *herem* as opposed to the stipulations of the *Acordos*. Some, Aboab reported, denied the Mahamad's right to impose the *herem* because the council consisted of only seven men, and not ten, the minimum to constitute a *kahal* or a *tsibur* and thus a *herem*. He wrote: 'This *herem* is what they claim to be invalid, except in a group of ten, which they call a congregation. They say that, being fewer, they [the members of the Mahamad] have no authority to impose a *herem* on someone, but rather to swear, each one for himself.'[33] The logic of this argument rejects not the formation of a binding compact among the members of a congregation but the transfer to a proxy of the authority such a compact creates. It is safe to say that those making this argument understood well that this was exactly what communal leaders claimed that the *Acordos* did. After all, the lack of any ongoing role in governance for members (apart from holding office), i.e. the lack of congregation-wide elections or referenda, was a feature that set the Kahal Kadosh apart from many Jewish communities of the era.

Furthermore, in Aboab's view, at least, the founding act was irreversible. He wrote that 'no power can annul or invalidate the *herem* that the Kahal Kadosh took upon itself when everyone signed in the presence of the four *hakhamim*'. The *herem* itself—correlated with the creation of a community, a body of people subject to the *herem*—was now established fact. And this particular *herem* included the establishment of the Mahamad as its governors. In terms of its use to excommunicate a person, on the other hand, Aboab grudgingly allowed that recourse to the body of members as a whole was theoretically possible. Referring to a specific ban rather than the collective oath, he wrote:

When someone violates this *herem*, there is no option other than to let him remain banned,[34] aside from the *kahal* itself absolving him, which requires at least as many people as the original signers. Even this, though possible, ought not to be done in my opinion, since it goes against the unity and conservation of the *kahal* and the feeding of the poor.[35]

[33] Aboab, *Exortação*, 9.
[34] In Aboab's wording, someone who violates a *herem* is *enhermado*. The former refers to the original communal agreement and the latter refers to a person's status requiring exclusion.
[35] Aboab, *Exortação*, 3–4.

In other words, reverting to the authority of the people would be destructive of communal government. The words Aboab uses here, 'unity and conservation' and 'feeding of the poor', were stock phrases that referred to the ultimate purpose of the community and its rules.

Aboab's brief reference to a seemingly obscure claim leads outwards to a wider resonance. In addition to the disputes already mentioned, another scandal was playing out in Amsterdam in 1680. A rabbi named Jacob Sasportas arrived that summer from Livorno to take up a position heading the Ets Haim yeshiva in place of the aging Aboab. Sasportas was by all accounts a cantankerous man, particularly focused on rabbinic normativity and opposition to Sabbatianism. Hailing originally from Morocco, he had led a peripatetic life, dwelling in Amsterdam in the 1650s (when he worked and developed a close relationship with Menasseh, and quarrelled with Morteira) and then in various places, including a few years in Livorno.[36] Just before his departure from Livorno Sasportas had engaged in a public argument about the authority of the lay leadership there. In fact, he intended to publish a pamphlet on the subject of the Livorno Mahamad's errors, an act that was only avoided by some diplomacy carried out by the leaders in Livorno and Amsterdam. When the Livorno Mahamad asked their Amsterdam colleagues to quiet the rabbi, the latter responded with a peacemaking attitude, agreeing to keep Sasportas from writing so harshly against communal government, but also advising Livorno's leaders to revise a particular decree regarding adjudication of disputes using mercantile rather than rabbinic law, saying that it showed insufficient respect for halakhah.[37]

In this well-known episode, Sasportas has mainly been interpreted as objecting to the Livorno Mahamad's move to incorporate mercantile law into communally administered justice. The encounter has been seen as part of a pattern of competition between rabbis and lay leaders and erosion of halakhah.[38] But another complaint that Sasportas had voiced was similar to

---

[36] On Sasportas in general, see Dweck, *Dissident Rabbi*; on his relationship to Menasseh ben Israel and Saul Levi Morteira, see there, pp. 44–51 and 62–8 respectively.

[37] On the dispute, see Toaff, 'The Controversy' (Heb.); Tishby, 'Letters' (Heb.); Dweck, *Dissident Rabbi*, 283–6; Walzer et al. (eds.), *The Jewish Political Tradition*, i. 424–9. Toaff includes Hebrew translations of the letters, and some of the sources are published in English in *The Jewish Political Tradition*.

[38] Tishby ('Letters' (Heb.)) interprets this passage as saying that the decision of the *parnasim* went against the wishes of the people. Toaff, 'The Controversy' (Heb.), looks at the Livorno

that of the rebels in Amsterdam, that collective decrees could only be enacted by the people and not by a group of leaders. In an open letter, Sasportas had written that Livorno's Jewish lay leaders' 'agreement [*hascamah*, i.e. regulation], their decree, their bans [*niduim*, a lesser form of excommunication], their *herem*s, and the decree of their judgement [*gezer dinam*] are all invalid both because they were not approved by the public [*nitmanah mehatsibur*] and because they cancelled the first agreement against the wishes of the whole people or the majority thereof, and not only for this outlandish decree'.[39] Sasportas addressed not only how the Mahamad's authority related to rabbinic authority, but also how it related to that of the members, the *kahal*. As opposed to Aboab's admonition that recourse to the whole *kahal* was dangerous and destructive of communal authority, Sasportas emphasized that the Mahamad's decree in this case specifically had to be 'approved by the *tsibur*', that is, ratified directly by the congregation—'the whole people or the majority thereof', phrasing that Aboab echoed verbatim. That the two rabbis both weighed in on the question of how communal government related to the will of its people suggests that it was an issue in both communities at the time.[40]

It would seem that Amsterdam's dissenters were already active before Sasportas arrived, and it is possible that they developed their halakhic arguments independently, citing as they did Nahmanides on the laws of the *herem*. However, there is a strong possibility that they were allied with or even led by Sasportas on his arrival.[41] Aside from significantly raising the stakes of the dispute, the alignment of the dissenters with the views of a figure like Sasportas signals clearly that the fault lines in the Kahal Kadosh did not divide rabbinic from lay or committed from uncommitted

haskamot in addition to the letters, resulting in a slightly different impression. He suggests that the decree in question was not new and was only slightly strengthened in the late 1670s, so Sasportas was objecting to an established system rather than reacting to an innovation. In that case the dynamic would be similar to that of Amsterdam.

[39] Tishby, 'Letters' (Heb.), 157.

[40] In fact, Sasportas may have been summoned to Amsterdam as a response to the uproar there. As Dweck indicates, Sasportas included in his book *Ohel ya'akov* the text of a letter inviting him to Amsterdam that spoke of the need for a restoration of order in the Kahal Kadosh. Perhaps not coincidentally, the same letter posed a halakhic query about inheritance law, related to the legal issues at the heart of the del Sottos' claims. Dweck describes the letter in *Dissident Rabbi*, 283; and see Tishby, 'Letters' (Heb.), 148.

[41] As an aside, Sasportas apparently often touted his own genealogical relationship to Nahmanides. Dweck, *Dissident Rabbi*, 9.

members. From Aboab's perspective, as he made clear, the rebels struck at
the heart of the authority of the Kahal Kadosh: they used its essential justification—that the ability of the collective to enforce regulations derives
from the members themselves—to justify breaking it apart. From the
rebels' perspectives, it seems, the Mahamad or, by extension, the Kahal
Kadosh, was perverting that authority by preventing further rightful exercise of it. The fault line ran through the foundation of the community.

Social Contract

A debate about oaths as part of governing authority was taking place
beyond the Jewish communal setting as well. In their debate, Aboab and the
rebels relied on medieval halakhah but simultaneously participated in a
wider European culture disposed towards such political agreements. Oaths,
whether individual or collective, were part of a deep vein of contractualism in European political history. The English self-image as a 'covenanted
nation',[42] for example, along with medieval examples like the Aragonese
oath of allegiance,[43] speak to the way sworn pacts or covenants ran through
multiple traditions including Roman and common law, as well as canon
law and halakhah. By the second half of the seventeenth century, the new
theorization of the social contract and the rise of constitutionalism were
making such agreements a focal point of the European political landscape,
and they would come to dominate the new politics of the modern West.
As others have convincingly shown, at this pivotal moment Christian contract theories were shaped in part by their proponents' interest in biblical
models, including Jewish interpretations of them. In fact, covenant and
constitutionalism have been framed by historians of both Jewish and European culture as the signal contribution of Judaism to Western politics.[44]
The intracommunal affairs of the Spanish and Portuguese Jews at the peak
of European interest in contract theory suggest that the influence went
both ways, as Aboab and his congregants comfortably mirrored various
stances of Christian contemporaries in facing their own constitutional
crisis.

That a covenantal, contractual, or constitutional understanding of com-

[42] On England as a 'covenanted nation' and the early modern flood of oath-taking understood both as the making of a contract with God as witness and also as constitutive of political
bodies, see Vallance, *Revolutionary England*.   [43] See Giesey, *If Not, Not*.
[44] Elazar, 'Political Theory'; Novak, *Covenantal Rights*; and Elazar, 'Covenant'.

munal authority prevailed in the Kahal Kadosh is evident from Aboab's views, the rebels' objections, and the *Acordos* themselves. The rabbi and his congregants agreed that the community was formed by an agreement of the people to abide as one body by the decisions of the community as a whole; that agreement was reflected in the *Acordos*, with the consent of the people clearly shown by members' signatures. The differences among the parties hinged in large part on their interpretations of this document: Aboab treated it as a constitution, i.e. a document establishing a perpetual, binding commitment governing a population. The rebels treated it as a contract, i.e. a legal agreement among specific persons subject to potential abrogation. Both of their interpretations entailed a certain relationship to Jewish law, conceived as a covenant. Their respective claims about the nature of the pact that bound them substantiated their arguments for and against the right of the people to rebel against or remake the government.

These same issues marked many other early modern constitutional debates,[45] and there is ample reason to view the *Acordos* as a constitution in general terms as 'a set of norms (rules, principles, or values) creating, structuring, and possibly defining the limits of, government power or authority'.[46] This document officially established the new community and built the framework of its government, setting it up as an enduring entity across the generations in perpetuity. Central features of constitutions and constitutionalism include limitations on government power including in the areas of rights, enforcement, and compliance; 'entrenchment', a technical term referring to mechanisms for changes to the constitution by means that differ from ordinary legislation, sometimes requiring special committees or supermajorities; and a distinction between rulers and the state itself, connected with some treatment of the underlying authority of the constitutional state, or location of its sovereignty.[47]

[45] See Lloyd, 'Constitutionalism', 258–60 and 287–97.

[46] Waluchow, 'Constitutionalism'. Similar themes, especially regarding the limitations on government power, are highlighted in Lloyd, 'Constitutionalism'. A 'modern' constitution is, in McIlwain's understanding of it, the 'conscious formulation by a people of its fundamental law' (*Constitutionalism*, 5). Applying such a definition to the *Acordos* foregrounds the inconsistencies at the heart of the lay community.

[47] These themes are adapted from a list in Waluchow, 'Constitutionalism'. Waluchow's list also includes 'writtenness', an important quality even though its universality is debatable. It was certainly a key quality of the *Acordos*, as the document was kept at the front of an elaborate archival system, and the text itself lays out instructions to have the document printed, with a copy going to each member and to each individual who might become a member in the future.

The *Acordos* fit this profile, clearly articulating the basis of government authority (a combination of external validation, Jewish law, and the authority of the *kahal*), the boundaries of the commonwealth (being made up of all Spanish and Portuguese Jews in Amsterdam and its environs), and the obligations of both government and subjects (faithful and dispassionate service and total obedience respectively). The document established the procedure for the government's self-perpetuation, whereby each cohort of the Mahamad would choose its successors, half of the group being replaced semi-annually. Sets of rules or individual decisions made by the Mahamad on its own subsequent to the establishment of the original *Acordos* did not have the same status, reinforcing the sense that the *Acordos* was a fundamental document of establishment, differentiated from ongoing legislation.[48] The *Acordos* also set in place a procedure for making changes to the constitution itself: Article 42 established an auxiliary council or constitutional committee, a group of six officials, two from each original congregation, whose special approval would be required for any changes to the rules laid out in the *Acordos* themselves.

The *Acordos* do not ascribe to themselves the label of 'constitution'. However, the *Exhortation* does contain the term, with Aboab referring to the document as the *constituiçoems do Sancto Kahal*, that is, the 'constitutions [i.e. constitutional articles] of the holy congregation [or *kahal*, i.e. Kahal Kadosh]'.[49] As we saw above, Aboab's view of the Kahal Kadosh as established and immovable contrasted with his opponents' apparent sense that congregations, bound internally by their own mutual commitments, could be established and dissolved at will. The rebels' argumentation was not limited to the halakhah of oaths; they also impugned the Mahamad as illegitimate for specific reasons related to the *Acordos*, and made further-reaching claims about the nature of the founding pact. Particularly at issue were the Mahamad's representative capacity and its compliance with the *Acordos* in a discussion that moved squarely into the arena of constitutionalism, suggesting that Aboab's conception was a widely held one and the secessionists understood it well .

---

[48] The set of agreements created by the first Mahamad soon after their installation has an uneasy relationship to the *Acordos*. In form, it is more like the constitution than like subsequent decisions, and therefore lends itself to interpretation as a revised constitution. However, it was clearly the work of the Mahamad alone and it built upon, rather than emending, the *Acordos* themselves. I view it as being more like a set of fundamental laws.   [49] Aboab, *Exortação*, 15.

One central component of the rebels' thinking hinged on the distinction between the *kahal*, in the sense of the assembly of members, and the Kahal Kadosh, the government arms and offices that made up the community as an institution.[50] This distinction was keyed to an essential divide between the people and the government, or the congregants and the Mahamad—the aggregate versus the whole and its head. For the rebels, the aggregate was the sum of the parts, whereas for Aboab the whole was greater than the sum of its parts, transcending the aggregate and represented by the Mahamad alone, whose decisions must be accepted unconditionally while the members had no independent say, despite being integral to the whole. Aboab took an extreme position privileging the whole—the Kahal Kadosh and its government—as against the people's authority that had created it, writing that the rebels 'want to remove authority from the Mahamad, but it is the same as the *kahal*, and cannot be made or unmade according to the needs of the hour'.[51] This statement can be broken down into two remarkable parts: first, that the Mahamad's authority was 'the same as [that of] the *kahal*'; and, second, that it could never be divested but rather, once established, remained irrevocably with the Mahamad.

The first part insisted that the Mahamad could govern with as much authority as the people would have done if the congregation were a direct democracy with each decision put to a majority vote. Although rabbis from the Middle Ages onwards granted that local leaders rather vaguely referred to as 'good men of the town' (*tovei ha'ir*) could enact decrees,[52] they usually treated the authority of such men as individual, temporary, ad hoc, or contingent on the ongoing participation of community members in some way —a rabbinic perspective that aligned with typical forms of communal organization. A number of medieval decisions granted different degrees of authority to an entire *kahal* acting together, a majority, and a representative body.[53] Aboab, on the other hand, saw no role for the body of community members—for the *kahal* as an aggregate. This was related to his refutation of the rebels' view that the Mahamad could not impose a *ḥerem* because it was a group of only seven, as we saw above. There, he argued that the Mahamad represented the full *congrega* and wielded the *ḥerem* in place of

---

[50] A distinction that correlates to the one between *Gesellschaft* and *Gemeinschaft* as discussed in Ch. 1.

[51] Aboab, *Exortação*, 15.   [52] Walzer et al. (eds.), *The Jewish Political Tradition*, i. 379–429.

[53] See Elon, *Jewish Law*, ii. 715–27.

the collectivity. Here the articulation is slightly different and more expansive: the Mahamad's authority was 'the same as' that of the *kahal*. It was not limited at all by the fact that it was a step removed from the population, as a representative body.

Such a statement was possible because in Aboab's view the underlying authority of the population had been fully transferred to the government, explaining that the Mahamad was a proxy for the *kahal* even though it had been chosen by the immediately preceding Mahamad and not by general election:

> The Mahamad has the same authority whether it was elected juridically, that is, elected by the Kahal or by the majority of it when that is the custom; or when the Kahal, possessing the same authority, has given it to the first elected officials so that they would successively pass it on, electing those they find worthy and not reproved by the generality.[54]

We may infer that the rebels had argued that the Mahamad was only legitimate if elected directly, a claim that would correlate with their other view that the Mahamad was too small a group to create a *ḥerem* on its own. In this context, however, their position also implies a rejection of the constitution itself, as they claimed that the mechanism of government it had established was not halakhically compliant. In contrast with that approach, Aboab described a transfer that had taken place when the people signed the *Acordos*. That act established the Mahamad, turned the members into subjects, and removed the latter's authority; as he wrote, 'the Kahal has given [its authority] to the first elected officials so that they would successively pass it on', adding that the Mahamad's authority could not be 'made or unmade according to the needs of the hour'.[55]

Aboab cited no Jewish authority to support this view, though he did so for other claims in the *Exhortation*. It was, on the other hand, critical to the way the 'right of revolution' and the authority of the people were argued among Christian Europeans. The status of the people's original authority and that of the established government after a transfer in the form of an original social contract were central. Building on traditions that a sovereign's rule was dependent on the consent of the ruled, the upheaval of

---

[54] Aboab, *Exortação*, 32–3. In a little-noted episode, Aboab's former colleague Menasseh ben Israel had publicly expressed opposition to this system in a sermon in 1655. SA 334, 19, fo. 383.

[55] He echoed the rabbinic view that jurisprudence evolves to suit the 'needs of the hour'. In this way Aboab was distinguishing the government of the community from halakhah per se.

Aboab's time brought the rights of the governed and right of rebellion to the forefront of political discourse. Did the people or nobility still possess in some sense or form the original authority that they had wielded in forming a political society? If a government defaulted on the underlying pact by not living up to expectations or betraying the common good, were the people free to make a new one? Was the establishment of the agreement or giving of consent a locatable historical event, and thus a contract subject to legal analysis, or was it a hypothetical or vanishingly distant event, assumed to have taken place in time immemorial?

Aboab addressed the second of these questions directly, arguing that the *Acordos* remained in force even if some of its terms had been violated. He attributed a precise claim to the rebels: 'They say that one of the constitutional articles of the Kahal Kadosh stipulates that six extra people be elected for all the affairs of the Kahal Kadosh, and since this was one of the first constitutional articles, and it is no longer observed, therefore we are free from the rest.'[56] As Aboab explained, this refers to the provision for future amendment to the *Acordos* in Article 42. A perusal of the Mahamad's record book shows that at first, the special six-member constitutional committee was maintained. For at least the first decade after 1639, whenever a member of the six passed away, another man was named in his place. Likewise, throughout this time the committee was regularly consulted regarding decisions of the Mahamad that would touch on the *Acordos* themselves. At some point after 1650 the practice ceased, without comment in the records—a lapse that, in actuality, did represent a breach in compliance. Aboab accused the rebels of using this lapse cynically to undermine communal authority as a whole. Perhaps the rebels were indeed looking to exploit a mere technicality, but on the other hand they may have understood the lack of a valid constitutional committee as a live issue. The Mahamad's records suggest that the committee of six was relevant to some of the most contentious disputes of the 1670s, including a wholesale reassignment of seating in the new synagogue, which raised angry opposition, and disagreement over the place of rabbis in the communal system.[57]

---

[56] Aboab, *Exortação*, 15.

[57] When it came time to assign seats in the new synagogue—the very issue at the heart of Coutinho's initial complaint, and a serious one given the political and hierarchical order of the Esnoga as a civic space—the Mahamad called up an 'adjunct' council of six men to make recommendations. No reason is given in the records for creating this committee, and it is not explicitly related to Article 42, but the structural similarity is striking.

In addition, the *Acordos* appointed rabbis by name, even setting their ranks and salaries, rather than establishing a rabbinic office, so the communal rabbis had a strange constitutional status. Until 1655 the constitutional committee was called up when changes were made to the terms of their employment.[58]

Evidently, the complaint about the constitutional committee was compelling, and Aboab's response was robust, with three prongs. First, he offered a somewhat unconvincing argument that Article 42 had responded to the needs of the moment during the process of unification in 1639, and over time lost its purpose as full unity was achieved.[59] His second response engaged the precise language of the article to argue legalistically that the Kahal Kadosh and its officers could not be held responsible for doing away with the constitutional committee since the six members of the committee itself, and not the Mahamad, had been tasked with its maintenance.[60] Like his first defence, this one is specific and circumstantial. The third prong of Aboab's response is more fundamental: 'In the event that they had done so', i.e. that the Mahamad had violated Article 42, 'and that affairs had not been governed as they should have been (which is not true), bad government cannot remove the value from the *ḥerem*. What else could the disturbers want than that with the breaking of one agreement, all would be broken?'[61] In other words, even if the constitutional committee had been eliminated unlawfully—even if the Mahamad had acted contrary to the *Acordos*—the Mahamad's status would remain literally unimpeachable.

Aboab's characterization of his opponents' view was dismissive, portraying Article 42 as just one of many technical components of an underlying pact, or calling the lapse 'bad government', but his tone belies the fact that this particular article did have special bearing on the Mahamad's authority and on the validity of the constitution. The committee of six was not just any constitutional detail; as an outside authority deriving directly from the original congregations, it was the only check on the established government and the only ongoing connection to the *kahal* as an underlying collective of individuals. In ignoring it the Mahamad could be said to

[58] See details below in Ch. 5.

[59] Aboab: 'When this was instituted, it was to satisfy the three congregations and, unified, subdue them . . . because the Lord must conserve us against the wild winds. When the cause ends, that which is caused has its end; it has already been lost from memory, and there are no longer two from each synagogue' (Aboab, *Exortação*, 15).

[60] 'Since they all died without naming others in their place, the cited *acordo* was undone by its own self' (ibid. 15–16).   [61] Ibid. 16.

have usurped constitutional power. When he was faced with such a claim, Aboab's dismissiveness served his underlying view that the Mahamad's authority to rule, symbolized by the *ḥerem*, was both chronologically and legally prior to actual acts of governance, and hence fundamentally unaffected by its conduct. The constitution established the Mahamad; thereafter, the Mahamad was the government, for good or for ill.

In contrast, the rebels appear to have argued that the Mahamad's failure had invalidated communal rule in the broadest sense. They treated the *Acordos* as an ordinary contract, subject to violation, revision, and/or dissolution by those who were party to it. A violation of the terms of the document they signed would invalidate the contract, and, crucially, individuals could just as easily create a new contract since they were not in a fundamentally different position, theoretically, from the 1639 members of the *kahal*. In other words, they saw the people as continuing actively to possess power even after the creation of such a contract. In contrast, Aboab passionately argued that an established Kahal Kadosh superseded the people of the *kahal*: once empowered, a government could not ever be overturned. In his view, as we already saw, the authority of the *kahal* had been 'given' or transferred to the Mahamad, and the Mahamad's authority was then fully equal to that which the *kahal* once possessed; the people were reduced to subjects. They could no longer assert themselves as a *kahal* to create or alter the decisions or regulations of the Kahal Kadosh.

The essential fissure between Aboab and his interlocutors—could the people rebel against a sovereign government and form a new one?—will be recognized as aligning, in the most basic terms, with the well-known difference between the contractual politics of Thomas Hobbes and John Locke. Hobbes argued that government exists because the people agreed to give up some freedoms in exchange for protection and leadership, putting an end to the war of all against all. In that original agreement, the power previously possessed by every person was subjected to that of the sovereign, who then wielded all political authority. In his view, people bound by a political covenant cannot free themselves to form a new one: 'They that have already Instituted a Commonwealth, being thereby bound by Covenant, to own the Actions, and Judgements of one, cannot lawfully make a new Covenant, amongst themselves, to be obedient to any other, in any thing whatsoever, without his permission.'[62] Hobbes, a royalist who was

---

[62] Hobbes, *Leviathan*, 122.

opposed to the rebellion against the crown in England's Civil War, composed *Leviathan* in large part as an argument for the people's continuing obedience. Even if a king's sovereignty was understood as ultimately derivative of the people's natural rights, as it was widely understood to be, the transfer was not reversible.[63] It is understandable how Aboab could find Hobbes's attitude to be a sympathetic one.

Following out the contrast, the rebels—refracted through Aboab's treatment, as we must keep in mind—seem at first to follow neatly Locke's justification of the people's 'right to revolution'. In his *Second Treatise of Government*, Locke argued that when a government acts unlawfully it breaches the trust that empowered it, and the people 'have a right to resume their original liberty, and, by the establishment of a new legislative, (such as they shall think fit) provide for their own safety and security, which is the end for which they are in society'.[64] Like the rebels, and in opposition to Aboab's recourse to eternal covenant, Locke argued that the underlying right that had empowered the lawmaker is not damaged but rather upheld when the people have recourse to it. The similarity is clear: the rebels saw the people's power to establish a government, i.e. to create a *ḥerem*, as being retained *in potentia*. As Locke wrote:

There remains still *in the people a supreme power to remove or alter the legislative*, when they find the *legislative* act contrary to the trust reposed in them: for all *power given with trust* for the attaining an *end*, being limited by that end, whenever that *end* is manifestly neglected, or opposed, the *trust* must necessarily be *forfeited*, and the power devolve into the hands of those that gave it, who may place it anew where they shall think best for their safety and security. And thus the *community* perpetually retains a *supreme power* of saving themselves from the attempts and designs of any body.[65]

Locke's view depends on an understanding of the pact between people and government as one of mutual benefit, and his argumentation hinges on government violation of that essential purpose, evaluated through its adherence to the law. Whereas in Hobbes the original contract (or covenant) is the only relevant one and particular sovereigns can neither abdicate nor be replaced, for Locke law affects governmental legitimacy. When a government breaks the law, violating the constitution, that government is itself

[63] The death penalty was an exception, a point that was more tied to views of excommunication than it might seem. See Ch. 5.

[64] Locke, *Second Treatise*, 113 (§222).   [65] Ibid. 78 (§149).

'rebelling'. Aboab's opponents make precisely this claim by saying that the Mahamad's violation of the *Acordos* invalidated the constitution and freed the people to set a new one.[66] Aboab saw the threat inherent in this claim, that the people's assertion of their original right would undo the government entirely: 'What more could the rebels want than that with the breaking of one agreement, all would be broken?' As Locke wrote, 'this power of the people can never take place until the government be dissolved'.[67]

Given their general knowledge of European politics, it is indeed likely that Aboab and his congregants knew at least the contours of contemporary arguments for and against the right of revolution and the continuing authority of the people. Twenty-five years after its original publication in English, and over a decade after its appearance in Amsterdam in Dutch and Latin, *Leviathan* was already a fundamental component of European political thought. Moreover, there was a copy of the book in Aboab's library at the time of his death in 1693.[68] As for Locke, while *Two Treatises of Government* did not appear in print for almost another decade (not until 1689), it is likely that he developed the theses it contained, including the justification of the right to revolution, around 1679–81,[69] just when Aboab and the rebels were airing their differences. At this time, Locke was on the Continent, and it is not unlikely that some of his opinions were known among the Amsterdam intelligentsia, not least by Isaac Orobio de Castro, who followed such matters closely.

Locke's articulation of the right to rebellion is similar to the secessionists' position, and his *Two Treatises* are among the best known in seventeenth-century thought, but it is not strictly necessary to turn to him to find sources for this kind of claim. Rebellion and civil instability were pressing concerns of the day in Amsterdam, as much as they were in England. Just as the speakers at the 1675 dedication of the Esnoga evoked the Dutch Republic's motto in their calls for unity, so would some populist-

---

[66] A subtle difference is that, for Locke, if the people replace the faulty government this act does not break the original contract but, rather, restores it.

[67] Locke, *Second Treatise*, 78 (§149).

[68] It appears on a list of his books put up for auction after his death—a fact that surprised the master bibliographer Alexander Marx in 1944 when he first discovered it. Marx, *Studies*, 210–11. Yosef Kaplan surmised that the non-Hebrew list was mistakenly attributed to Aboab (Kaplan, 'Perfil').

[69] Laslett, 'Introduction', in Locke, *Two Treatises*, 35; Armitage, 'John Locke', 605–6; and Milton, 'Dating Locke's Second Treatise'.

minded Kahal Kadosh members have followed the debates that raged in
the young republic, both on the street and in print, calling leaders to task
for failing to defend the common good. This Dutch legacy of resistance to
tyranny and the rights of political subjects was central to its identity, as it
stemmed first from its war for independence from the Spanish monarchy.
Althusius, Grotius, and Cunaeus all contributed to theorizing the interconnected issues of just war, sovereignty, and the people's rights in the first
half of the century[70]—a tradition taken up in turn by British thinkers, who
saw in the Dutch Republic a 'bulwark against royal tyranny'.[71] In the 1670s,
Samuel Pufendorf, a thinker in the tradition of Hobbes and Grotius born
in Germany and active in Leiden in the early 1660s, also defended the
rights of the people to rebel, as his account of the political contract was
based on the idea of delegating to others, but not divesting oneself of, the
natural right of self-preservation.[72] In an approach that intersected with
the Kahal Kadosh's conception of oaths discussed above, Pufendorf wrote
that God's covenant with his creatures did not require people's consent, but
that pacts and promises between people do require it, even though it may
often be silent or tacit.[73]

Althusius, too, had earlier articulated the right of the people to rebel in
a way that anticipated Aboab's rebels, arguing that the commonwealth is
formed by a contract between people and ruler, and if the ruler fails to
uphold it the contract is inherently broken, leaving the people not only
allowed but obligated to form a new polity with a new constitution.[74] Cast-
ing the net even wider, Jean Calvin had argued for a right of resistance,[75]
and one could also look to sixteenth-century Spanish sources like Francisco
Suárez for the origins of the Kahal Kadosh members' view of the polity

[70] Haitsma Mulier, 'Language', 180; Kossmann, 'Development'; and Johnson, *Sovereignty*,
81–100, esp. 83.

[71] Dunthorne, 'Resisting Monarchy', 143.   [72] Johnson, *Sovereignty*, 94–6.

[73] Pufendorf, 'On the Law of Nature and of Nations in Eight Books', in *Political Writings*,
167, 170–2.

[74] '[I]f the supreme magistrate does not keep his pledged word, and fails to administer the
realm according to his promise . . . It is then conceded to the people to change and annul
the earlier form of its polity and commonwealth, and to constitute a new one . . . Because a
proper condition of the agreement and compact is not fulfilled, the contract is dissolved by
right itself . . . Thus Bartolus says that a legitimate magistrate is a living law, and if he is condemned by law he is condemned by his own voice.' Althusius, *Politica*, 134. See Carvajal, 'Teoría'.

[75] McClintock, 'Johannes Althusius' *Politica*'. Johnson traces it from Aquinas to Luther and
these later thinkers in *Sovereignty*, 22–99.

as deriving from the underlying sovereign natural rights of the people.[76]
In the immediate surroundings of Aboab and the rebels in Amsterdam, the
brothers Johan and Pieter de la Court were popular political voices in
Dutch that expressed the continuing rights of citizens to make sure that
the state worked in their interest, though their specific claims were somewhat farther afield from the ones made in the Kahal Kadosh.[77] Even if the
Jewish debaters did not see themselves as political philosophers, like the de
la Courts, they well understood the implications of the ideas they expressed, recognized the sphere they were operating in as a political one, and
—whether consciously or less so—made use of categories and stances that
were active in the political world around them.

Covenant

By far the closest such source to the particular context of Spanish and Portuguese Jewish Amsterdam is Spinoza's *Theological-Political Treatise*. In that
work, published a decade before the present dust-up, Spinoza wrote that
the ancient Hebrews, in a state of nature because of being bound to no person by covenant, transferred their sovereign right to God, agreeing to do
whatever God would tell them. 'This promise, or transference of right to
God', Spinoza says, 'was effected in the same manner as we have conceived
it to have been in ordinary societies, when men agree to divest themselves
of their natural rights. It is, in fact, in virtue of a set covenant, and an oath
(see Exod. xxxiv. 7), that the Jews freely, and not under compulsion or
threats, surrendered their rights and transferred them to God'[78] to form a
theocratic polity. Indeed, he says, they 'surrendered . . . all their natural
right'.[79] This arrangement, though paradigmatic of covenant formation,
was short-lived according to Spinoza, as the Hebrews soon 'abrogated their
former covenant, and absolutely transferred to Moses their right to consult
God and interpret His commands'. Once Moses held this 'sovereign kingship', then, the people 'had plainly forfeited the whole of their right'. Spinoza adds: 'We may here notice, that though the people had elected Moses,
they could not rightfully elect Moses's successor; for having transferred

[76] Suárez and the writers of the 'second scholastic' were precursors of Hobbes and Locke
in their rights-based contractualism. See Brett, *Liberty*, 1–2, and Lloyd, 'Constitutionalism',
292–7.
[77] Haitsma Mulier, 'Language', 188. The question of rights is intertwined with that of religious liberty, or 'freedom of conscience'. See Bodian, 'Portuguese Jews'.
[78] Note the reference to oaths.   [79] *TPT*, 219.

to Moses their right of consulting God . . . [they] were bound to accept as chosen by God anyone proclaimed by Moses as his successor.'[80] Aboab's justification of the ongoing authority of successive Mahamads follows the same logic.

However, in Spinoza's thought the idea of an original social contract (conceived as an oath) that transferred the people's power to a government stands in tension with his insistence on the people's retention of that power in some form.[81] As he titled chapter 17 of the *Treatise*: 'No one can, or need, transfer all his rights to the sovereign power.' Spinoza's view that the Hebrews had been able to 'abrogate their former covenant' with God was a discrepancy that he somewhat lamely explained by saying that theocratic rule 'existed rather in theory than in practice . . . The Hebrews, as a matter of fact, retained absolutely in their own hands the right of sovereignty'[82] during the theocratic period. After the covenant that formed the republic of Moses, too, in Spinoza's view the people retained some agency, and in fact for him the natural rights underlying the state could never be fully renounced by the people. Indeed, the premiss that the citizens of a republic possessed some degree of their natural right was crucial to his theory of the state, and Spinoza himself indicated that he differentiated his political thought from Hobbes's primarily on these grounds.[83]

A useful framework for thinking about Spinoza's intended balance between retention and loss of rights is a distinction between *potestas*, meaning the authority to govern, and *potentia*, people's inherent power.[84] Spinoza suggested that the people gave up the former but retained the latter, meaning that they have no right to contribute to government decisions in a practical sense, but they still have a theoretical or potential power that ultimately gives them agency in the state, meaning that their political activity is carried out by means of it. Spinoza's sense that the people continue to exercise power by means of the commonwealth, rather than totally subjecting themselves to it as a separate actor, reflects his democratic bent, where democracy is understood as an explanation of the source of a republic's authority rather than its structure of government. For him it explains why anyone would reasonably enter into a political covenant: it is possible to accomplish much more in cooperation with others.[85]

[80] *TPT*, 221.
[81] Steinberg, 'Spinoza's Political Philosophy', §3.6.
[82] *TPT*, 220.
[83] Steinberg, 'Spinoza's Political Philosophy', §2.1.
[84] Barbone and Rice, 'Introduction', 16–19. And see Israel, 'How Does Spinoza's "Democracy" Differ?', and Field, *Potentia*.
[85] Garrett, '"Promising" Ideas', 205.

On the surface, Spinoza's defence of the people's natural rights and ongoing agency in an established state—along with his additional view that the people had abrogated the original covenant with God to form a theocracy—aligns roughly with the stance of the rebels, who argued that the same inherent power of the people that had constituted the first *ḥerem* could now make a new one. In their eyes, when the people established a pact or contract to form a civic body they had not lost their *potentia* and they had not renounced their agency. With Spinoza's reputation as the ultimate Jewish rebel, it would be easy to assume that these figures looked to the *Treatise*. Perhaps they did, but for Spinoza himself this stance did not translate into an argument for the right of resistance or rebellion, as it did for Locke and others. On the contrary, Spinoza tended towards strong condemnation of rebellion.[86] If subjects retained some aspect of their power, he believed, they must use it for the support and betterment of the commonwealth, not to undermine it.

Spinoza's specific position need not have directly supported either rebels or rabbi. What is key is that Kahal Kadosh community debaters, Spinoza, and seventeenth-century Christians all participated in a common discourse regarding government authority based on collective agreement. They all shared a set of conceptual tools for thinking about how a republic's authority was constituted—whether it was a biblical, diaspora Jewish, or European Christian republic. Of course, Spinoza would not have agreed that the Kahal Kadosh should be a republic in the first place, since he rather envisaged a Dutch commonwealth without self-ruling religious subcommunities and, ultimately, undermined Judaism as a separate religion. But his conception of the ideal republic shares much with the logic underlying the Kahal Kadosh, constituted by the *Acordos* as a civic entity or polity, a logic that we can now say was apparently widely understood within the community.

Spinoza's treatment was particularly relevant to the debates discussed by Aboab because it brought to the fore questions about how to understand the historicity as opposed to the eternality of such an agreement, with implications for the relationship between Jewish law and historical Jewish polities. Focusing on both the theocracy and the Mosaic republic, his use of biblical narrative was naturalistic, treating the development of the Hebrew commonwealth as typical of any commonwealth. Indeed, he pointedly

---

[86] See Della Rocca, 'Getting His Hands Dirty'.

insisted on the historicity of a political contract: the covenant 'was effected in the same manner as we have conceived it to have been in ordinary societies', he wrote, as he explained that the Hebrews surrendered their natural rights by means of 'a set covenant, and an oath'.[87] His stance supported his view that the biblical relationship between God and the Jewish people was not eternal or supernatural, but rather temporary, political, and expedient. Chosenness, he famously indicated, was a matter of the Hebrew nation coming out on top in the geopolitical affairs of the day,[88] and the particulars of Mosaic law were designed to suit the Hebrew nation in its time and place. The events described in the Bible are thus not taken as establishing any permanent covenant but merely as providing an example of the sort of pact that may be made to establish a polity. (The law of Moses was not intended as an eternal divine law but rather as set of rules for the republic of Moses.) For Spinoza, then, a social or political contract was a pact made within history by known parties. He was far from the only one. John Selden, for example, saw the contract underlying a state to be accessible in historical terms—if extremely distant—and he advocated 'looking to the contract' to resolve disputes.[89]

For both Hobbes and Locke, in contrast, the original social contract was a transfer of authority and establishment of civil government that took place in some time immemorial. Even though it continued to define current relationships for them, these thinkers did not trace the contract to a known event.[90] For Hobbes, the agreement was imbued with a sense of eternality in the past that was matched by a sense of open-ended duration into the future, along with an inaccessibility to adjustment or adjudication. He differentiated covenant from contract on the basis that a covenant features deferred delivery of the contracted thing, so that such an agreement centres on promise and faith in its fulfilment.[91] It is the word 'covenant', in fact, that Hobbes used to refer to the agreement by which a commonwealth could be established, as quoted above. In calling this original agreement a covenant he intertwined the past and future of a politically formative pact and set it on a different level from ordinary contracts that might be negotiated, signed, and verifiably either complied with or defaulted on. A contract, like a written constitution, might be historically grounded and subject to legal discussion; not so the covenant underlying civil society or a

---

[87] *TPT*, 219.   [88] *TPT*, 8, 45–54   [89] Malcolm, *Aspects*, 35.
[90] Ibid. On Locke, see Macpherson, 'Introduction', p. xiii.   [91] Hobbes, *Leviathan*, 94.

long-established polity, which mirrored natural relations between father and child or God and man.

Although Aboab did not adopt precisely the same distinction, it illuminates an aspect of his disagreement with the secessionists in his community, one that also draws us into consideration of how he viewed the relationship between the *Acordos* and Jewish law, treated in terms of the Sinaitic covenant. He opened this part of the *Exhortation* with a response to a specific secessionist claim: 'Let's move on to the disillusionment of another absurdity', he wrote. 'They say that they were not present, nor did they sign such a *herem*, and thus did not approve it, and thus it seems to them that they are not obligated, which is a false doctrine.'[92] As we saw above, some rebels said that they were not subject to the community's authority because they did not sign the *Acordos*, personally consenting to be ruled. Their claim treated the *Acordos* more as a contract than as a constitution—or if a constitution, one that was essentially historical, legal, and manifest within normal social relations, unlike a covenant.

As we have already seen, the *Acordos* did stipulate that they applied to those who would come in the future, pre-empting this objection and, in effect, positioning the document as a constitution. But unlike other points in the *Exhortation*, where Aboab had recourse to specific constitutional articles, here he invoked the irrevocability of the Mahamad's authority in another way, thinking on a greater scale. He responded with a general statement about the *herem* writ large, making it out to be as eternal as the Sinaitic covenant. In fact, he went so far as to call that first covenant a *herem*, to wit: 'We say to them, do you not see that the *herem* of Moses was extended to the last generations?'[93]

Later in the treatise he repeated that 'the [community's] *herem* has the same value as all those since that of Moshe Rabenu, in which all the generations present and future are obligated, without being able to claim absence or ignorance'.[94] There was, in fact, a strong basis in medieval halakhah for the view that communal decrees were binding upon future generations and newcomers, partly justified by the model of the law of Moses.[95] Confirming that Aboab was not going out on a limb, his interlocutors seem not to have objected to the comparison between the *Acordos* and Mosaic law.

---

[92] Aboab, *Exortação*, 16.   [93] Ibid. 16–17.   [94] Ibid. 33.

[95] Solomon ben Abraham Adret and Nahmanides both justify it by comparison with the acceptance of the Torah. See Elon, *Jewish Law*, ii. 731–5.

They accepted, at least for the sake of argument, that the Sinaitic covenant was, like the *Acordos*, a pact or agreement (a political one, as Spinoza portrayed it?), and they agreed that all Jews eternally were party to the Sinaitic pact. But they did not believe that they were to be considered obligated because they had lately arrived and been absorbed into the Jewish people, by birth or conversion. Rather, Aboab wrote, 'they justify their argument with what the sages say, that all souls, embodied or to be embodied in the future, were present [at Sinai]'.[96] The Mosaic covenant was only considered universally binding, they pointed out, because the rabbis understood every Jewish soul from every era to have been present for its acceptance. The resulting standard was that anyone not consenting was not obligated, so, not having been present in 1639, they did not have to accept the *Acordos*.

The secessionists doubled down on the idea—an idea that we can now see was generally recognized within the Kahal Kadosh—that the *Acordos* were indeed a *ḥerem* for which the biblical covenant was a relevant model. They argued within that frame that Jewish traditions positing universal presence at Sinai led to the conclusion that the communal *ḥerem* was more of a contract—an agreement between particular people—than a constitution—an enduring document establishing a polity. Their stance accorded with the view expressed by Spinoza that the Sinaitic covenant was relatable to 'ordinary societies'. Aboab, for his part, batted away the idea of universal Jewish presence at Sinai as merely metaphorical, and instead depicted the law of Moses itself in distinctly constitutional terms: in his words, as 'a document that, in truth, Moses left us, entrusted to the future generations'.[97] While the rebels turned the *Acordos* into a contract, the better to break the former, Aboab turned the Sinaitic covenant into a constitution, to sanctify the latter.

Aboab was especially indignant that the rebels treated the *Acordos* as an ordinary contract to be made or unmade at will, and leaned hard into a sense that this *ḥerem* was just one instantiation of the larger, enduring *ḥerem* that was the covenant between God and his people. In a passage that seems on its face to diverge dramatically from the contractarian and republican view of the Kahal Kadosh, he wrote: 'Since we are directly protected by him [God], he may be called our king, and we his beloved vassals, as Moses the prophetic luminary expressed in Deuteronomy 33: 5, *And he was King in Israel* ('King' referring to the Lord God, of course) *when the heads of the*

---

[96] Aboab, *Exortação*, 16–17.   [97] Ibid. 17.

people assembled, the tribes of Israel were together [unified].'[98] But Aboab did not see God's kingship as opposed to the sanctity of a commonwealth, a civic society or polity created by a mutual pact among a group of individuals.[99] The passage follows a comment that the rebels 'do not consider how much they offend God by dividing the Congregation, the glory and happiness of which consists in unity, with the help of His sovereign grace'. Rather, he saw the contract at the heart of any Jewish polity or society— a *kahal*, congregation, or people—as subsumed within the higher divine covenant, not unlike the way an incorporated city or other civic association made use of the legal system of the state under whose aegis it was formed. The biblical covenant established the essential relationships between people and God and among people, setting fundamental Jewish law. A *ḥerem*, as part of that law, incorporated and sacralized a group of individuals by means of their collective oath or contract, connecting the group and its particular, constitutionally established law into the wider, holy, relational system.

As did Hobbes, Aboab saw the contract at the heart of the polity as an image of the covenant between God and people, parent and child, or lord and vassal: it was universal and, if not actually ahistorical, then at least inherited from a past distant enough and different enough from the present as to operate on a different plane. And he was like Hobbes in treating such a polity, once established, as unbreakable, with the agreement underlying it definitive of all social and political relations. The way Aboab used the *ḥerem* as a placeholder both for a collective pact that constitutes a particular polity and for Mosaic law gave it new weight. The political language of the day transformed a rabbinic justification of communal authority into a political stance with much wider—and more extreme—implications.

Were the rebels, then, adopting a more traditional stance than that of their appointed spiritual leader? Not really. When they argued that the covenant of Moses was binding on them only because their souls had been present at Sinai, they treated even that covenant as essentially a contract between parties: if they had not been there themselves, they suggested, they would not be bound by it now. Likewise, the pact made among Spanish and Portuguese Jewish men in Amsterdam in 1639 was just that. Its

---

[98] Ibid. 11–12.
[99] A seeming contradiction between popular authority and theocracy here may be clarified by Spinoza's insistence on their combination.

signatories were bound to obey its stipulations, but the only contractual obligation that could span generations was that of Jewish law. In this way, Aboab was right that the rebels undermined the status quo: although they did not reject the *herem* per se, they rejected the understanding of the Kahal Kadosh as a commonwealth that the *Acordos* had built using the laws of the *herem*, and more broadly, they undermined an understanding of the binding nature of local decrees that had prevailed among Jews in Europe since the Middle Ages. Instead of seeing the *Acordos* as the constitution of a polity that endured, they saw it as a contractual agreement in compliance with Jewish law. They rejected not the *herem* itself but what the Kahal Kadosh had made of the *herem* in concocting a self-image as a common-wealth. That self-image was indeed new, but in countering it, the rebels also moved in a new direction.

The rebels as they appear in Aboab's *Exhortation* remained committed to Judaism, understood as an obligation to uphold Jewish law, but objected to the political authority claimed by the Jewish community. They were a pro-halakhah, anti-commonwealth contingent the likes of which are other-wise unknown—except, it must be observed, in what we know of Jacob Sasportas. Before coming to Amsterdam, we recall, Sasportas had opposed what he saw as the occlusion of halakhah and rabbinic leadership in favour of mercantile law and lay power in Livorno, and he brought the drama with him. Sasportas's activities are too readily interpreted as a simple matter of competition for power between lay leaders and rabbis in a changing world—one in which rabbinic law was incrementally losing sway over some aspects of Jewish life. The wider disruptions and discussions revealed by Aboab's treatise complicate such a view. Neither Aboab nor the secession-ists could be said to have been insufficiently respectful of halakhah or of rabbis; quite the opposite. Rather, what emerges is a battle over the nature of Jewish community—as a commonwealth or a congregation, governed by a constitution or a contract—where the battle itself was waged simultan-eously within a halakhic and a political frame.

Opposition to the Mahamad's rule during the Sabbatian era can be understood, as it has been before, as a result of social tensions and changing circumstances, stemming from a focus on money, status, exclusivity, and power, even as a result of some degree of early Enlightenment or proto-secularization, and as the start of a shift away from the semi-autonomous community that still stands at the centre of most accounts of the dawn of

Jewish modernity. What is now clear is that there was also another facet of the community's troubles during this time, a political one with both practical and abstract dimensions, hinging on the relationship between religious authority and civic unity. The men who took part in the affairs of the Kahal Kadosh during this era made explicit the political logic inherent in the *Acordos* in order to deconstruct and debate it. They thereby transformed it, as their way of thinking—like all of ours—was shaped by the discourse of their era. Their times were chock-a-block with debates both petty and soaring over who might rule, on what basis, and how. The talk of the town turned not only to contracts and commonwealths but specifically to the Bible, its laws, and its promises, and it was entirely natural for Amsterdam's Spanish and Portuguese Jews to take it up. The indebtedness of seventeenth-century Christian political thought to Jewish influences—as well as the earlier formation of some halakhah within Christian contexts—made it possible for their debate to take place entirely within a traditional framework of rabbinic thought about the *kahal* and at the very same time to echo with great verisimilitude the most crucial issues in contemporary political theory.

FIVE

RABBIS

EXCOMMUNICATION AND POLITICAL AUTHORITY

THE PUBLIC DISAGREEMENT between the senior rabbi Isaac Aboab da Fonseca and dissenters within the Kahal Kadosh was fundamentally about communal authority. One prong of the debate revolved around lay leadership, engaging with the constitution of the community in ways that were deeply entangled with wider considerations of the contractual basis of commonwealths and the rights of the people. But as we know, neither a European commonwealth nor the Kahal Kadosh was perceived as exclusively lay during this era of controversy over church and state. Although the particulars of the relationship between politics and religion were under the microscope, they remained a bonded pair in both ultimate and also quite immediate senses: like all earthly affairs, those of a polity served a higher purpose, and the temporal power of religious institutions and their representatives could be both intertwined with and at odds with the workings of government.

In parallel with Christian politics, in the eyes of Kahal Kadosh members the community was a commonwealth, to be sure, but it was a Jewish one, with its fundamental aim being to support the expression of Judaism in every sense and its fundamental values being identified with Judaism. Such a parallel raised two issues simultaneously: what role should religion, in this case Judaism, play in the commonwealth? And how did the fact that the religion in question was Judaism affect the nature of the commonwealth? The way I approach these questions, the first was internal and pragmatic, even if infused with wider, more abstract ideals. The second question came from a comparative and reflective—sometimes polemical—stance and interrogated Jewish political identity in a Christian world.

The present chapter takes up the first question, looking at how some members of the Kahal Kadosh thought about Jewish religious temporal authority in the communal machine. (Chapter 6 takes up the second.) We have already seen that to some extent the system privileged Jewish law and also its representatives, rabbis. Communal authority was theorized using the laws of the *herem*, giving the Kahal Kadosh a halakhic basis, and the founders who wrote the constitution set up the rabbinic function to operate within the communal system but also transcend it. In a good light, the situation imbued the community with the mystery of revelation, the eternality of covenant, and the weight of Jewish ethics. Thus it appears in the writings of Abraham Pereyra, whose thoughts on the subject appear above in Chapter 2 and below in Chapter 6, and who worked to portray the Kahal Kadosh as a holy polity, infused with the divine will and in harmony with celestial politics. Rabbis, treated as teachers and leaders on a higher plane and perceived as connecting with a long unbroken tradition, lent their authority to the worldly affairs of the community.

From another vantage point it is not surprising that, as bridges between the spiritual and the temporal in communal politics, rabbis also figured in the argument over communal authority that takes shape in the pages of Aboab's *Exhortation*. The rabbinic role was a logical target for any move against the system, and in fact the secessionists set it in their scopes, with Aboab reporting that they complained that the *herem* at the heart of communal politics was not supported by sufficient rabbinic authority. To counter that view and uphold the status quo, he laid out an argument that made explicit an implicit but fundamental fact of the system established in the *Acordos*: that a rabbi's authority to ban came only from his official status in communal government.

Although our knowledge of the rebels' views is limited to what Aboab wrote about them, others wrote about rabbinic authority in ways that flesh out the stakes of the debate and reveal a full complement of views on the matter. Among them was the polemicist, philosopher, and self-styled 'politico' Isaac Orobio de Castro, who addressed it in the course of his extensive discussion of the sceptre of Judah. Whereas Aboab contended that rabbis received authority over communal affairs from the community itself, and hence, ultimately, from the people, Orobio de Castro interpreted rabbis as representatives of an external divine order with its own temporal authority. Ironically, thus, the rabbi defended the lay communal system and the politico elevated the rabbinate.

The contrast between their two perspectives hinges not on how much authority rabbis should have, but on where that authority comes from. It exposes a new dimension of the changes undergone by the role of rabbis in early modern European Jewish culture more broadly. Across diverse contexts in early modern Europe, the rabbinate was increasingly professionalized, with a particular role being institutionalized for rabbis as employees or officials of individual communities.[1] This shift appears to have been widespread but not uncontroversial, as prominent rabbis like Jacob Sasportas in Livorno, Leone Modena in Venice, and Joel Sirkes in Poland objected to lay arrogation of authority that they said belonged to rabbis, though their objections are one-sided and should be read with that in mind.[2] The trend has also been associated with a proto-Enlightenment lowering of religious authority in general, along the lines of the 'European crisis of conscience', as well as disillusionment in the wake of Sabbatianism that eroded whatever simple, unquestioning obedience to rabbis and halakhah the average Jew is imagined to have had before.[3]

It would seem that the deck was stacked against rabbinic authority as Jews moved towards modernity and that rabbis' instrumentalization at the hands of lay leaders was one more predictably bad hand. Complicating that picture is that in Amsterdam's Kahal Kadosh rabbis were professionalized and the communal system was laicized, but the community's spiritual head weighed in to defend that fact rather than to object. His defence—alongside the views of the unnamed rebels, Orobio, Pereyra, and others—tells us that the alignment of priorities and ideologies was not black and white in a world of greying rabbinic authority. A distinction between spiritual and temporal authority, rather than between lay and rabbinically trained leaders, is key to making better sense of how changes to both the rabbinate and the community played out.

Rabbinic Status

In his *Exhortation*, Aboab acknowledged that the secessionists made a sober indictment of communal authority on the basis of insufficient rabbinic involvement. 'They make another bad argument based on similarly false grounds', he wrote, namely, 'that this *ḥerem* has no value because it was not

---

[1] See Teller, 'Laicization', and Bonfil, *Rabbis and Jewish Communities in Renaissance Italy*, introduction and ch. 5.

[2] See references below.   [3] See Ruderman, *Early Modern Jewry*, 57–98, 133–58.

made with the authority of a *ḥakham*'.[4] Although his phrasing allows for a reading of the claim as quite narrow, his fulsome response reveals its wider importance. The issue was not only whether a rabbi needed to approve a ban but, expanding outwards from there, whether communal government was legitimate when its officers were exclusively lay. If the *ḥerem* was the source of communal authority and it was invalidated by lack of rabbinic approval, then so were the decrees of the Mahamad.

Aboab's treatment of this central issue is the longest and the most involved of any in the *Exhortation*, and it is also the area in which he most explicitly innovates. His first approach is to emphasize that the *ḥerem* had not been established without the authority of a *ḥakham*: 'I deny this, because four *ḥakhamim* were involved in the agreement in question, and also signed.'[5] Here it becomes clearer that 'this *ḥerem*' refers to the *Acordos*, or possibly the article of the *Acordos* that established the communal *ḥerem*, since the *Acordos* were signed by the rabbis. His wording seems careful, since the rabbis did not sign *qua* rabbis, as far as evidence from the document shows, but only as fellow members of the *kahal*. That the rabbis 'were involved in the agreement' is vague, probably intentionally so. It seems that the rabbis who were then serving individual congregations, or were to be appointed as communal rabbis, were consulted in the drafting of the document. This makes sense because the communal system did indeed rely on halakhic conceptions of *kahal* and *ḥerem*. Alternatively, Aboab could mean that the *Acordos* themselves included rabbinic appointments, but this is a less natural reading of his remark. Either way, his message in defence of the communal *ḥerem* shifts its basis in rabbinic authority all the way back to the moment of founding. It underlines his belief that the government itself was established with rabbinic authority and thenceforth operated legitimately without it, including in wielding the ban.

His second response was a little more unexpected. He wrote that 'if this argument were true' and the Mahamad's will was indeed insufficient to authorize a *ḥerem*, 'it would mean that the *kahal* does not have enough authority to create a *ḥerem* on its own, which would invest the *ḥakham* with unchecked authority',[6] a scenario that he saw as obviously absurd—and,

---

[4] Aboab, *Exortação*, 14. 'This *ḥerem*' refers to the immediately preceding discussion, which is about the *ḥerem* that 'includes' the prohibition of additional congregations—so it could be read as being either the *Acordos* in general or the particular article, Article 2, that stipulated the prohibition.   [5] Aboab, *Exortação*, 14–15.   [6] Ibid. 15.

possibly, intended to be particularly alarming for his independent- and democratic-minded congregants. With this, Aboab switched gears to argue that no rabbi was actually needed, implying that the aforementioned rabbinic 'involvement' in the establishment of the communal *ḥerem* was supererogatory. According to this view the *ḥerem* did not require a rabbi, since the authority to rule (enforced and represented by the *ḥerem*) arose from the *kahal* (i.e. its people) alone. The rabbinic role was limited to advising on the community's structure in halakhic terms.

Aboab's view was continuous with the logic that underlay the Kahal Kadosh in the *Acordos*, granting the full authority of the *kahal* to the Mahamad, but nevertheless reads as quite extreme since conventional wisdom holds that excommunication was always a rabbinic prerogative among premodern Jews, with an indelible legal and emotional connection to the rabbinate.[7] Although the Kahal Kadosh gives the lie to that universal rule, Aboab does seem aware that his move to divest the *ḥerem* of any need for rabbinic authorization was outside of the mainstream. In order to support it, he delved deeply into legal nuance and precedent concerning the *adam ḥashuv*, that 'important man' (expressed in Aboab's Portuguese as *homem estimado*) whose approval is needed to validate a communal ordinance according to the Babylonian Talmud and subsequent rabbinic interpretation.[8]

Two central questions drive most halakhic attention to this rule: which decrees require the approval of such a person, and what qualifications, if any, must he possess? It is the latter issue of who qualifies as an *adam ḥashuv* that preoccupied Aboab, as his argument went against the typical view that he must be a particularly learned or wise man. Most sources that served as precedents for Aboab assumed that this was the meaning of the phrase, with debate centring on what specific credentials indicated the requisite learning or wisdom.[9]

---

[7] Albert, 'The Rabbi and the Rebels', 173–6.

[8] BT *Bava batra* 9a: 'Certain butchers made a mutual agreement that anyone who slaughters on another's day will have his hide [i.e. that of the slaughtered animal] ripped. One of them went ahead and slaughtered on another's day, and they ripped his hide. The case came before Rava, and he ordered them to repay him. Against this, Rav Yemar b. Shelemiah cited: "And they may enforce their decree". Rava offered no reply. Said Rav Papa: He appropriately offered no reply. That applies only where there is no prominent person [*adam ḥashuv*]; where there is a prominent person, they cannot unilaterally make decrees.' Translation from Walzer et al. (eds.), *The Jewish Political Tradition*, i. 389–90.

[9] Elon concludes that 'the great majority of halakhic authorities agreed . . . in requiring that

Aboab interpreted *adam ḥashuv* differently, saying that such a man need not be a rabbi or scholar, but rather someone who was 'particularly well respected by the inhabitants of the city, such that he is elected by them and charged with the affairs of his city and *kahal*'.[10] In other words: the *adam ḥashuv* is credentialled by his communal government, by the lay members of the *kahal*. Aboab moved carefully in supporting this claim. He cited several sources that supported components of his argument,[11] but ultimately, he had to confront the venerated *Shulḥan arukh*:

The only thing that can be brought against [my view] is the authority of Hakham Ribi Joseph Karo, whom we follow in everything. He says in his *Shulḥan arukh* ... [that a *kahal* has the authority to create ordinances] in a city where there is no *ḥakham*, but if there is one, [they] will be null unless made with his approval.[12] This seems to contradict what we maintain, suggesting that even the *kahal* requires the authority of a *ḥakham*. With all due respect, he is mistaken, as is anyone who thinks that the name *homem estimado* can only mean *ḥakham*.[13]

Aboab's hesitation to go against such an authority is palpable, but he found it necessary in order to defend his crucial claim, repeated at the end of the treatise for emphasis, that 'the authority of the *kahal* is so great that it needs no other addition' in the form of rabbinic authority.[14] It would be 'absurd', in his words, for the presence or absence of a single man to trump the political will of the whole. Aboab's stance is a stunning repudiation of the alignment of the *ḥerem* with rabbis and an inversion of claims that lay leaders overstepped their authority. In his view, halakhah dictates that the

---

the "distinguished person" be '"a distinguished scholar (*ḥakham* . . .)"'. Elon, *Jewish Law*, 751–9. Bonfil assumes that an *adam ḥashuv* must be a rabbi but perceives that confusion over the precise meaning of the term contributed to the establishment of the official community-appointed rabbi in Italian contexts. Bonfil, *Rabbis and Jewish Communities in Renaissance Italy*, 114.

[10] Aboab, *Exortação*, 23.

[11] Aboab cited a number of sources that support parts of his argument, including several medieval Sephardi rabbis: Nahmanides (Moses ben Nahman/Ramban, 1194–1270), Solomon ben Abraham Adret (Rashba, 1235–1310), Nissim ben Reuben Gerondi (Ran, 1320–76), Jacob ben Asher (Ba'al Haturim, *c.*1270–1340), Joseph Habiba (14th–15th c.), and Asher ben Yehiel (Rosh, *c.*1250–1327). Lorberbaum pointed out that several of these figures emphasized the public role of the *adam ḥashuv* as part of their general move towards a view of *kahal* politics as taking place outside of the narrow purview of halakhah. Lorberbaum, *Politics*, 104, 184–5 nn. 30–2.

[12] Following Maimonides, *Mishneh torah*, 'Laws of Sales', 14: 9–11. See Walzer et al. (eds.), *The Jewish Political Tradition*, 418–19, and Lorberbaum, *Politics*, 105.

[13] Aboab, *Exortação*, 22–3.　　　　　　　　　　　　　　　　　　　　[14] Ibid. 32.

ban is a power of the people, and it would be a rabbinic overstep to demand personal authority over it.

Still, he did not erase rabbis from the government of the Kahal Kadosh. Ultimately, he arrived at a statement that he presented as his original insight. 'I offer a distinction to resolve all this: namely, that if the *ḥakham* is [s]elected by the *kahal*, then the Mahamad requires his participation.'[15] This is put even more clearly in the treatise's conclusion: 'When there is a *ḥakham* salaried or designated by the *kahal*, whether chosen by the *kahal* or the Mahamad, his participation is required.'[16] In the case that there was a rabbi (like himself) who had an official position as part of the government of a community, then and only then did the rabbi's authority contribute to the community's political authority.

Such an arrangement was ideal according to Aboab: while he was adamant that a *kahal*'s rule did not fundamentally require a rabbi, he allowed that the government of a *kahal* would certainly be bolstered by the inclusion of a *ḥakham* among its officers.[17] Such a situation was the best of both worlds. However, the Mahamad was legitimate even without it, and a rabbi who was not 'salaried or designated by the *kahal*' had zero impact on the *kahal*'s *ḥerem*. Aboab's commitment to the politics of the Kahal Kadosh was deep indeed. As important as he considered rabbis to be, he saw their temporal power as entirely contingent on the government and constitution that a *kahal* set up. A rabbi could impose his judgement at the communal level, he suggested, *only* through the status conferred on him by the *kahal*. His own authority was thus, in his eyes, embedded within the framework of the by-laws and the government based on them.

The rabbi's extended reflection on the issue gives new depth to our understanding of this dynamic beyond Amsterdam as well. An example from the time of the founding of the Kahal Kadosh, revealed by historian David Malkiel in his exploration of Venetian Jewish self-government in the first half of the seventeenth century, is instructive. As he explains, the Venetian Jewish lay governing council, called the 'Small Assembly', enacted some decrees limiting the excommunicatory authority of rabbis in the city and affecting who could receive a credential as a communal rabbi. They specified that 'none of the distinguished rabbis can get involved in any of

[15] Lit., 'company'. This language echoes that of the Mahamad's record book, which indicates the presence of the *ḥakhamim* at gatherings for certain decisions. Aboab, *Exortação*, 25.
[16] Ibid. 33.   [17] Ibid. 23.

the community's affairs, neither to order nor to command, but only to teach the laws of the Forbidden and Permitted, and to issue excommunications on the basis of the mandates of the authorities'.[18] Rabbis, in other words, were to teach and oversee ritual, but not to 'order or command': there could hardly be any more pointed way of saying that rabbis did not have temporal authority.

Some rabbis, including the well-known Leone Modena, responded angrily that the lay leaders were disrespecting learning and halakhah. Modena even produced dramatic poetry lamenting the contemporary abandonment of the scholarly ideal,[19] couching the development in the way that it is often received in modern historiography, as part of a long-term shift away from rabbinic authority and halakhically ordered Jewish life. But as Malkiel pointed out, the Small Assembly's moves were not intended to impinge on rabbinic authority in general. The statute differentiated between rabbis who served the communal government and those who did not, reserving certain powers to the three rabbis who served the Assembly and giving them an official place within the government hierarchy.[20] Modena's objection to the statutes probably had as much to do with the fact that he was excluded from that hierarchy as it did with a substantive assessment of the policy.[21] A rabbi who was employed by the community, Samuel Judah Katzenellenbogen, supported the Small Assembly's decrees.

Aboab's parallel defence of the Kahal Kadosh status quo four decades later reflects the debt that his own community owed to this move in Venice, as the Kahal Kadosh had cited 'the style of Venice' in its constitutional definition of the ban as a lay power.[22] After all, tension over this feature of communal government had been visible at the start, with Menasseh ben Israel's open defiance of the Mahamad's right to impose a ban on him in 1640. Although it seems to have died down over the intervening decades, it had not disappeared completely. The year before he left on his fateful mission to England (which was also the year before Spinoza was excommunicated), Menasseh preached that members of the Mahamad should be selected in a different way: specifically, that they should be elected by the congregation and not appointed by outgoing members of the council. In an entry dated 18 Adar II, 5415 (spring 1655), just a few weeks before the upcoming

[18] Malkiel, *A Separate Republic*, 175–8.
[19] Ibid. 165–8; see M. R. Cohen (trans. and ed.), *Autobiography*, 34, 152.
[20] Malkiel, *A Separate Republic*, 172.   [21] Ibid. 168–74.   [22] See above, Ch. 1.

selection of new officers, the Mahamad recorded Menasseh's offence in this sermon and its resulting intervention. The council warned the rabbi that he must not preach anything directly or indirectly contradicting the constitution or regulations.[23] If he did so, the matter would be put to the 'six deputies of the unification of the nation'[24] for the appropriate punishment. That is, they would turn to the constitutional committee.

Two aspects of this incident, to my knowledge previously unnoticed by historians, are significant. First, this was a constitutional crisis. It was a clear case where a communal rabbi was pressing up against what was permitted to him as an employee and as a rabbi. He took direct issue with the community's system of government—in a sermon in the synagogue, no less, rivalled in its public provocatory nature only by Aboab's printed pamphlet twenty-five years later. Unlike the first time Menasseh opposed the Mahamad's rule, this time the council threatened recourse to the constitutional committee, which stood as an independent bridge back to the people's authority at the foundation of the Kahal Kadosh, as well as a bridge between the lay and the rabbinic sectors of the leadership. As an aside, this later incident suggests that Menasseh's oft-noted difficult relationship with the Mahamad ran deeper than his frustration at professional marginalization, to involve differences of principle. In both cases he explicitly went against the very foundations of communal government.

Second, this is the last place I have found in the record book where the original constitutional committee is referenced. Recall that the *Acordos* appointed *ḥakhamim* by name, even setting their ranks and salaries, rather than establishing a rabbinic office, giving them an awkward status dependent directly on the constitution rather than on the looser system of subsequent lay governance, even while they were hierarchically lower than the Mahamad. As I laid out above (see Ch. 4), for about the first decade and a half, the constitutional committee was actively maintained in continuity with the original six members, and the six 'deputies of the unification' were called in when changes were made to the employment status of the *ḥakhamim*. That lasted right up to the moment in 1654 when Morteira retired, having served for forty years, and gave over his preaching responsibilities to Aboab, who had just returned from Brazil.[25]

---

[23] SA 334, 19, fo. 383. 'Contradicting the constitution and regulations' = *contra os acordos da nação e escamots de K.K.*

[24] 'Six deputies of the unification of the nation' = *os seis diputados da união da nazão.*

[25] For example in SA 334, 19, fos. 232, 251 (5408); 347 (5413); 358, 363, 372 (5414).

However, by the time three of the four original *ḥakhamim* had passed away at the end of the decade, the practice was no longer current, as several rapid-fire changes to the rabbis' status were then recorded without any reference to the committee.[26] At that point Aboab alone had a clear constitutional appointment as *ḥakham*, since later rabbis were hired without formally amending the *Acordos*. At least, it seems clear that the Mahamad saw Aboab's status that way, as they clarified in their minutes in 1660 that only Aboab could issue a marriage contract, a power limited to what they called 'salaried *ḥakhamim*', and as late as 1673 they made a distinction between his title, *ḥakham*, and that of other salaried rabbinic scholars, calling the others *rubissim*.[27] (Aboab's employment, too, could be questioned, since changes had been made to it without recourse to the external committee.)

While the 1655 incident of Menasseh's controversial sermon is the last reference to the constitutional committee of 'six deputies' in connection with rabbinic appointments, it is not the last appearance of such a committee in the record book. Memory of the group of six and its purpose had apparently not been lost even a decade later because in 1665, when the Mahamad decided to repeal a large number of prohibitions from the communal regulations, they convened just such an external group—though now not calling them the 'six deputies of the unification of the nation', but rather 'adjunct gentlemen called to discuss the reform of the *hascamot*'.[28] Further, when they reassigned seats in the Esnoga and adjusted the taxation of members in 1675, connected with the rollout of the new synagogue, they convened a similar group of six 'adjuncts' to sort it out.[29]

---

[26] The next entries with bearing on the employment of the rabbis are the ones that touch on Menasseh's departure for England the following year and the reassignment of some of his duties to Aboab; and after that, the salaries of *ḥakhamim*. SA 334, 19, fos. 397–8, 399, 402. A year after that, in 1656/7 (5417; fo. 417), the death of David Pardo, one of the original *ḥakhamim*, is mentioned in passing as the Mahamad took up a request to employ his son as a cantor.

[27] In 1658 the Mahamad decreed that the only person who could issue a marriage contract was a salaried *ḥakham* of the *kahal*. SA 334, 19, fo. 433 (15 Sivan 5418). Underneath that entry, a note dated 5420 (1660) clarified that with the subsequent passing of Saul Levi Morteira, the sole remaining *ḥakham* authorized to issue a *ketubah* was Aboab. On 14 Nisan 5433 (31 Mar. 1673) they imposed a reduction in the salaries of communal employees because of their fiscal crisis, and in the Mahamad's note Aboab is the only one listed as a '*ḥakham*'; Aguilar, Jacob Judah Leão, and others are listed with 'R' before their names. SA 334, 19, fo. 676.

[28] SA 334, 19, fo. 551 (10 and 25 Av 5425), calling the extra panel *senhores adjuntos chamados para se tratar de reformar as Ascamot*. They note that they addressed all decrees punishable by ban, beginning with the unification and proceeding through all additional *ḥerems*.

[29] This process is most likely the reason for the creation of a manuscript now in the Ets

Throughout this period the same men were called up to help deal with these and other actions that touched on essential questions of authority, as they specified that the process conformed to 'the *Haskamot* [Agreements] and Constitution of this Kahal Kadosh'.[30] But they do not appear in entries regarding rabbis. One example is particularly instructive: in 5428 (1668) the Mahamad moved to prohibit public opposition to the communal rabbi's views, declaring a prohibition, on pain of *ḥerem*, of writing or even speaking ill of him. They framed this decision as expanding *Haskamah* 43 (that is, one of the initial community by-laws produced by the first Mahamad), which prohibited pamphlets and 'defamatory papers' that went against the Mahamad's decisions. In order to apply this regulation to the case of opposition to the rabbi, they slotted Aboab into the category of community representative rather than of independent spiritual leader.[31]

In 1680, when the Mahamad decided to hire two new rabbis, they called in the same committee, having not done so for an issue relating to the communal rabbinate since the mid-1650s.[32] By then, of course, one of the secessionists' claims against communal government touched on the fact that the status of the communal *ḥakham* was in question since the constitutional committee had lapsed. Aboab presented himself in the *Exhortation* as fully ensconced within the communal system, as bearing communal authority by virtue of his legitimate status within an established government. His opponents, on the other hand, undermined the premiss that his status was inherently superior to that of other rabbis who might be employed by the congregation. They questioned his legitimacy because of these issues of constitutional continuity, and they also cast doubt on the notion that such privileged rabbinic status should exist at all, as they indicated that the authority to ban belonged to rabbis as rabbis, independent of communal status, and indeed, that a rabbi, and not merely any official, was necessary to validate a community's ban.

Haim Library that contains a list of the adult men in the congregation in 1675, along with an accounting of costs related to synagogue construction and the communal regulations regarding *imposta*. See Zagache (ed.), *Libro*, MS EH 48 D43.

[30] *Escamot and constituisoins deste KK.* See SA 334, 19, fo. 827 (23 Shevat 5440), and see there fo. 832 (11 Adar II 5440).

[31] SA 334, 19, fo. 597 (5428): 'A paper shall be posted at the gates of the synagogue that, increasing *haskamah* 43, anyone speaking ill of *ḥakhamim* orally or in writing will be put in *ḥerem*, *nidui*, and *shamta*, with all the curses of the holy law.'

[32] SA 334, 19, fo. 833 (26 Adar II 5440).

The parallel with Modena's complaint so many years earlier in Venice, then, highlights competition not between lay leaders and rabbis but within the rabbinic field, between those with communal office and without it or with lower status. Jacob Sasportas once again comes to mind, as we already saw that he favoured a more direct role for halakhah in governance as opposed to communal law, and he was not a neutral force in relation to the uproar Aboab was trying to quell. Sasportas was employed as the head of the Ets Haim yeshiva—a salaried position, to be sure, but not the equivalent of being named a *ḥakham* of the Kahal Kadosh; in other words, not a position that authorized him to excommunicate according to the understanding that Aboab shared with the Mahamad. The possibility that Aboab's 'disturbers' were allied or at least ideologically aligned with Sasportas, suggested above with respect to the validity of the lay government, meshes well with the notion that the *Exhortation* was written in part as a rebuttal of a rabbinic competitor. After all, it drew on many of the same medieval Iberian and early modern Ottoman responsa that defined Sasportas's rabbinic world-view to sharply oppose the newcomer's philosophy of Jewish government.[33] More generally, Sasportas consistently saw independent rabbinic authority as a central component of the respect for Torah and Oral Law that he thought was missing especially among the Spanish and Portuguese Jews.[34] Sasportas even expressed an intention to impose a *ḥerem* of his own on the lay leaders of Livorno, in parallel with the behaviour of his former friend and employer Menasseh ben Israel decades earlier.[35]

These issues went beyond the Sephardi diaspora as well. In a penetrating discussion of similar debates in early modern Ashkenaz, Jay Berkovitz examined the opposition between the rabbis Joel Sirkes, who insisted on rabbinic approval for communal enactments, and Ya'ir Hayim Bacharach, who saw communal law as independent of sacral or rabbinic law and formed for a different purpose. Berkovitz describes Bacharach's attitudes as being similar to evolving conceptions of the makeup of any political body, particularly those of Jean Bodin and Samuel Pufendorf, to the effect that 'the legitimacy of the communal establishment [was based on] its elected

[33] For example, Aboab used Rashdam (Samuel ben Moses de Medina) and Adarbi instead of Rashi, who made a similar argument that an oath not to obey a communal decree is a 'vain oath'. See Rashi, responsum 247, translated and discussed in Walzer et al. (eds.), *The Jewish Political Tradition*, i. 397.   [34] Dweck, *Dissident Rabbi*, 13–23.
[35] Tishby, 'Letters' (Heb.), 148 n. 1; Dweck, *Dissident Rabbi*, 283.

status, its representative capacity, and the legitimacy of law founded on principles of equity and justice'.[36] Bacharach's thinking, like Aboab's, made space for politics at the heart of the community and took contemporary theory to heart, though drawing on a somewhat different set of political ideas.

Sirkes, on the other hand, specifically opposed the use of the *ḥerem* by the lay-led Council of Four Lands, and Adam Teller has cited Sirkes's indignation at a lay *ḥerem* as evidence of the marginalization of the rabbinate from that body: 'Who gave you permission', Sirkes asked, 'to issue a general *ḥerem* without the agreement of the great wise men [i.e. the leading rabbis]? Even though you are elected delegates from all the communities in the Kingdom, your *ḥerem* may be quite worthless.'[37] Note that the 'general *ḥerem*' here evidently refers to a decree backed by the threat of a ban on a transgressor. Teller shows that, contrary to the assumptions of earlier scholarship, the Council did not have rabbinic members approving or justifying its bans.[38] In the Council, too, the disagreement was resolved with the incorporation of rabbis into the political administration in a fixed, low place. Around 1670 rabbis began to have a consistent, institutionalized presence alongside the Council,[39] and Teller suggests several contexts for this change: reorganization after mid-century wars, the Council's efforts to strengthen its social authority, and a reaction to Sabbatianism. The permanent rabbinic body attached to the Council served primarily as a court and governed censorship, whereas the lay council continued to be the primary issuer of administrative decrees, including those involving the *ḥerem*, an arrangement that was quite similar to that of the Kahal Kadosh Talmud Torah.

A few general observations arise from Aboab's *Exhortation* and what it reveals about the politics of the Kahal Kadosh in relation to these other contexts. For Sirkes as for Aboab's rebels, the ban was the flashpoint for

---

[36] Berkovitz, 'Crisis', 193–4. On the related but distinct question (which Sasportas later pressed in Livorno) of whether communal decrees had to conform to Jewish law, Berkovitz writes: 'In his [Bacharach's] view, the *qahal* was empowered to act according to its own understanding, without concern for consistency with Jewish law. Communal legislation was justified by the fact that it was intended for the "preservation of the collective body" while also designed to serve as a barrier against corruption and immorality' (p. 193). See also Berkovitz, 'Rabbinic Leadership'.   [37] Teller, 'Rabbis without a Function', 383.

[38] Similarly, a 1672 decree against Sabbatian followers (referring back to 'the great and terrible *ḥerem* . . . which was imposed during the Lublin fair of 1670') was signed only by the four lay elders. Teller, 'Rabbis without a Function', 384.   [39] Ibid. 376–7.

arguments over rabbinic authority with respect to communal legislation; this much has already been acknowledged by historians. Less visible across contexts has been the debate these thinkers shared about the nature and extent of the authority of lay leaders understood as representatives or elected delegates.

Second, Aboab's perspective also highlights the extent to which rabbinic subordination did not necessarily mean marginalization or disrespect, even (or especially) in the eyes of some rabbis. Like Katzenellenbogen in Venice and Bacharach in Germany, Aboab embraced an idea of communal authority that was essentially political and *of which rabbis were an essential part*, even if rabbis did not serve as issuers of communal rules. The perspectives of rabbis like Sirkes, Modena, and Sasportas must also be read in the light of that distinction. Their rhetoric lamented the lowering of rabbinic status, but how such perceived diminishment was manifested seems more complex than first meets the eye. While we may agree that all of this constitutes some kind of 'crisis of rabbinic authority', this crisis did not necessarily feature the erosion of authority but rather a reconceptualization and repositioning of it.[40]

Jewish Erastianism

Within the microcosm of this tumultuous decade or two in the life of a single congregation, elements of large-scale trends and changes in European Jewish life appear with more complexity than has been imagined. An intensification of lay authority is visible here, to be sure, but we also see a multidimensional reaction to that authority, not merely on the part of rabbis competing (or allied) with them for power, but also on the part of shrewd community members. Their objections, though perhaps 'traditional' in the sense of respecting and relying upon halakhah and centuries of custom regarding communal governance, were far from conservative. They were, by contrast, entirely *au courant* with European politics and they followed the most galvanizing ideas of their time—as did the rabbi himself.

Yosef Kaplan called the legal battles over the Mahamad's right to the ban, which formed the background of the *Exhortation*, a process of 'secularization of the *ḥerem*', whereby the revocation of community membership without a formal ban (a way of getting around the Amsterdam magistrates'

---

[40] See Ruderman, *Early Modern Jewry*, 133–58.

temporary injunction against the Mahamad's use of the *ḥerem*) stripped excommunication of its sacral dimension.[41] This Kaplan views as symptomatic of a wider tendency towards seeing Judaism as a way of life rather than a religion, by which I understand him to mean increasingly enacting Jewish observance and communal affairs for cultural or social reasons rather than out of belief in the halakhic and liturgical system as spiritually compelling or literally commanded. Kaplan writes that these events were 'cracks . . . in the walls of [communal] autonomy . . . [that] heralded the developments that would characterise Jewish life throughout Europe in the age of Emancipation'.[42]

This latter comment is, I think, borne out by the new evidence of Aboab's *Exhortation*, but perhaps in an unexpected way. Both rabbi and rebels technically upheld the notion of communal authority over its members. The *ḥerem* was evidently still deeply embedded in a system that assumed the interconnection of the sacral with the secular—or rather, of the sacral with the temporal. The whole extended affair reflects an intensification of the political dimension of the ban, acknowledging that the 'political' touched both sacred and worldly or civic elements.

For as we know, separating these elements entirely to create a secular sphere was not yet an aim of European thinkers. In the seventeenth century, their precise relationship to one another was a central concern—if not *the* central concern—in the public square, with almost everyone in agreement that religion and politics, sacred and temporal, ought to cohere. Questions about the extent to which religious authorities should have temporal power or authority, and what its relationship to the state should be, were part of that century's fundamental realignment of church and state. In a dynamic that looks very much like the one that took place among Jews, clergy lost such privileges as control over heresy trials, self-taxation, and participation in government bodies. A view gained ground that any polity was necessarily both civil and ecclesiastical at the same time, leaving no room for a church to have its own separate temporal authority. This view was commonly referred to as Erastianism and as one historian wrote, 'if there was a revolution in the mid seventeenth century, it was Erastian . . . in nature. That is to say, it was a revolution which subordinated the clergy to the laity and the church to the state.'[43]

---

[41] Y. Kaplan, 'Social Functions', 136–8.
[42] Ibid. 139.   [43] Sommerville, 'Hobbes', 162–3.

The relationship between the Jewish and Christian realignments was not a simple matter of the minority tagging along on the majority's journey to modernity. As they did in many areas of early modern political thought, Christians made use of Jewish history and sources to find models and rationales for their political ideals, and Aboab's *Exhortation* makes it clear that Jews, too, made use of such interpretations of their own history. In this arena, biblical history and halakhah were made to serve Erastian views and opposing ones alike.[44] Thomas Erastus himself, a physician and lay follower of Zwingli for whom Erastianism is named, argued that the ancient Sanhedrin or judges had ruled on religious as well as civil matters, and therefore that present-day civil authorities also should decide on matters of religious law.[45]

Indeed, it was a commonly voiced opinion that Jews had never distinguished between civil and religious jurisdiction, but rather had one single Sanhedrin that heard cases of all kinds. Hebraists like Hobbes, the English constitutional scholar and social contract theorist John Selden, and the Dutch Hebraist and political thinker Hugo Grotius argued that Israelite priests had had no special juridical power, and that in the time of the Sanhedrin, no distinction had been made between civil and ecclesiastical power. Grotius wrote that the Jews themselves saw the Sanhedrin and subsequent rulers as equivalent to and descended from the royal line, that is, as essentially civil.[46] Spinoza, too, in accordance with his argument against the political authority of clerics,[47] stated flatly that 'in the Hebrew state the civil and religious authority . . . were one and the same'.[48] The state combined both elements and thus clerics were firmly ensconced within (and subordinated to) it. As Selden put it: 'There's no such thing as spiritual jurisdiction; all is civil; the Church's is the same as the Lord Mayor's.'[49] Opponents of this arrangement saw it differently, but were also able to find support in the Bible, claiming, for example, that the biblical high priest, who could depose kings, was the forerunner of the Pope; or that the state

---

[44] See Nelson, *Hebrew Republic*, which treats this issue throughout, and Prior, 'Hebraism'.

[45] See Gunnoe, 'Evolution'; Prior, 'Hebraism'; and Nelson, *Hebrew Republic*, 92–4.

[46] Sommerville, 'Hobbes', on Selden's view in particular. Nelson, *Hebrew Republic*, 101–4.

[47] Steinberg, 'Spinoza's Political Philosophy', §3.

[48] *TPT*, 219. And again: 'In fact, between civil and religious law and right there was no distinction whatever' (*TPT*, 220).

[49] Selden, *Table-Talk*, 73. See Rosenblatt, *Renaissance*, 244.

and the church were formally distinct among the Israelites as the administration of civil and religious affairs was separated.[50]

The ban, or 'excommunication' in Christian terms, figured centrally
in these debates.[51] For Christian Erastians, this meant that the temporal
power of excommunication should be in the hands of state authorities, on
the understanding that the ultimate aim and justification of the state was
the divine will. To be clear, excommunication in this context was something
very different from the ban in Amsterdam's Kahal Kadosh: it primarily
meant that the excommunicate would not be allowed to receive the holy
sacrament, a symbolic or spiritual act of exclusion of the individual from the
body of the church. It could also lead to corporal, even capital, punishment
(as the English Archbishop William Laud was particularly known for advocating) or fiscal consequences, since release from excommunication could
be bought. It was not primarily a social punishment in the sense of shun-
ning or banishment, as in Jewish communities, though there were informal
social consequences to being deemed a heretic. Nevertheless, it similarly
represented temporal power derived from sacred authority. Clericalists
claimed that the church rightfully decided what beliefs and actions were
to be deemed incommensurate with religion, meaning that clergy should
decide on dogma and impose corporal punishment, independent of the
state. Selden and others (including Spinoza), conversely, saw not only corporal punishment but even oversight over right belief as the purview of the
state alone, wherein clergy might advise and guide but never rule.

Erastus's treatise laying out his views on civil and religious jurisdiction, a sixteenth-century work that continued to be republished, was
specifically about excommunication,[52] drawing on the New Testament, the
Hebrew Bible, and Josephus to analyse ancient religious discipline.[53] He
saw the Sanhedrin as the same as a synagogue, as a 'gathering of Jewish
magistrates'.[54] In his more detailed and extremely learned work, Selden
also brought the history of the *herem* to bear, asking whether (ancient) Jewish excommunication could be understood as civil or only spiritual, as a

---

[50] Sommerville, 'Hobbes', 169.

[51] Sommerville shows that the authority to excommunicate was specifically at issue several
times in English politics in the 1640s and 1650s. Jason Rosenblatt called excommunication 'the
flash point in the debates over clerical and secular power'. Rosenblatt, *Renaissance*, 244.

[52] Erastus, *Explicatio gravissimae quaestionis utrum excommunicatio . . .* (London, 1589). It was
published again in Amsterdam in 1649 and in English translation in 1682.

[53] See Nelson, *Hebrew Republic*, 92–4.   [54] Prior, 'Hebraism', 48.

proxy for the same question as applied to Christendom. His view was that it was profoundly civil—as, for example, Jewish excommunicates were banned from participation in society but not prohibited from performing sacred rituals.[55] Excommunication in this view was a civil punishment for civil crimes in a situation where—crucially—civil law and civil courts were indistinguishable from God's law and courts. The same, he believed, should be the case in England; other important political thinkers followed suit.

As far as biblical history was concerned, the Hebraic model worked nicely for such thinkers' efforts to show that church and state were one and the same in general. But the critical question of excommunication posed additional challenges since its interpretation and significance were altered in rabbinic thought after the end of the Second Temple period. Selden and Grotius were interested not only in biblical-era Jewish traditions but also in what the rabbis had said about excommunication, and even in what Jews practised up to their own day. In explicating the view of 'the Hebrew masters' (post-exilic Jewish sources) on excommunication, Grotius specifies that its highest degree was 'applied to someone who would have been condemned to death by Mosaic law, but could not be killed since the authority of imposing capital judgment had been taken away; his company and touch were shunned by everyone'.[56] According to him, exilic Jewish life was derived from the authority of the biblical commonwealth, but in exile, without such a commonwealth, it had lost its ultimate authority, significantly, represented by the authority to impose the penalty of death.

Selden and Grotius began with the assumption that exilic Judaism still seamlessly integrated civic with religious authority just as the republic of Moses had done, even if it was now more limited. The difference between the Jewish politics of the biblical past and those of the exilic present, as they understood it, was that after the end of the Hebrew state, rabbis stood in for biblical judges, transforming the former sovereign political authority into rabbinic law. That is, whereas in biblical times sovereign temporal and divine government were one and the same, in their view, in exile, where Jewish self-government was not sovereign, it still had the character of being a combination of civic and religious, where rabbinic law and rabbinic courts were the government. However, as we know, this was an inadequate account of Jewish communal life in early modern Europe, which was increasingly systematized with a lay orientation. In reality, at least within

---

[55] Sommerville, 'Hobbes'.   [56] Grotius, *De imperio*, 395; see Nelson, *Hebrew Republic*, 102.

the Kahal Kadosh after 1639, there was what could accurately be called an ideal Erastian relationship between clergy and commonwealth. The rabbi was an employee of the congregation, and the lay leadership controlled everything including the ban.

Aboab himself winds up looking quite Erastian. He, too, was able to look to the biblical polity for the same inspiration—and his similar conclusions about the proper make-up of his present-day commonwealth were most likely mediated by early modern Christian interpretations, even while they were well in line with Jewish sources. Aboab related the authority of the ban to the ancient Jewish state no fewer than four times in the *Exhortation*, repeating that a congregation possesses the full authority of the ban just like the king or the 'Great Senate'—citing Nahmanides, but using Cunaeus's term for the Sanhedrin, and deploying the claim for purposes more like Grotius's than Maimonides'.[57] Aboab's sense, supported by Jewish tradition and helped along by Christian Erastians, was that divine law had always supported—and in his own day continued to support—the rule of laymen. In other words, he saw the Jewish community the way Christians of his day saw their polities, and pointedly not the way Christians saw Jewish communities.

It is possible to imagine a different Jewish Erastian stance: that the synagogue was equivalent to a minority church in a system—not incidentally, like that of Holland—where such churches were voluntary associations ideally without independent temporal power. Spinoza's *Theological-Political Treatise* looks like an (albeit somewhat far-fetched) attempt at this model, as he proposed a state religion reduced to a very basic set of principles that could accommodate a version of Judaism if—and only if—it was denuded of any claim to temporal authority.[58] Indeed, he is clear that no entity aside from the sovereign should have the power to excommunicate,

---

[57] 'It is known that all Congregations have full authority over their *yehidim* [congregants], to order them in their city as did the Great Senate of Israel' (citing Nahmanides); Aboab, *Exortação*, 19; and 'The same will also be true if he does not accept said *herem*, or if he is not present, as will be stated below, since the Senate had authority to set a *herem* as it says in Nehemiah 13: 25, *And I cursed them . . . and made them swear by God*'; Aboab, *Exortação*, 8.

[58] Although he indicated that Jewish law is not divine law, he sought universal religious principles in Scripture and implied that Jews shared them and could participate in the republic if only they gave up their attachment to chosenness, difference, and self-rule. On the vision that Spinoza shared with Hobbes of a civil religion and the uniqueness to the Dutch setting of the possibility that Jews might be able to share in a civil religion, see Bodian, 'Portuguese Jews', 1, and the commentary she cites there.

a lesson he draws from the successes of the ancient Hebrew common-wealth.[59] Those who see the *Treatise* as a reworking of an original, now lost, treatise that Spinoza composed in response to his excommunication have read this rebuke of the temporal power of religious sects as a rejection of the legitimacy of the Kahal Kadosh's ban altogether,[60] since a Jewish ban would compete with that of the state.

As is clear from the way Spinoza applied the question of the ban to ancient Hebrews and present-day commonwealths, any discussion of the *ḥerem* entailed consideration of the status of Jewish law and independent self-rule after the loss of the Temple and ancient Jewish sovereignty. For Aboab, Jewish law in its eternality and divinity sanctified and validated lay Jewish self-rule, even lay excommunication. For Christians like Grotius, who imagined that Jewish communities vested all authority in rabbis, and hence in Jewish law, the relationship between past and present was easy to reconcile: Jewish excommunication in exile had been spiritualized under essentially religious leadership. For Spinoza, knowing full well how the Kahal Kadosh was lay-dominated even with respect to the ban, the rela-tionship between biblical and exilic Jewish law was not as simple. Rather than conveniently assuming that the law, which was originally political, had been transformed into something spiritual among contemporary Jews, for him it was necessary to limit the relevance of Jewish law to that original political context.

The Ultimate Punishment

Another prominent member of the Kahal Kadosh wrote briefly about the ban not long before the time of Aboab's writing, and his comments suggest a fourth view distinct from those represented by Aboab, Spinoza, and Christians like Grotius. Isaac Orobio de Castro is known primarily as a polemicist and secondarily as a philosopher or theologian.[61] As a midlife immigrant to the Jewish community, Orobio had already enjoyed social and professional contacts with influential members of the Spanish and French nobility. He portrayed himself as a political and intellectual adviser, a kind

[59] 'He who strives to deprive the sovereign power of such authority, is aiming (as we have said) at gaining dominion for himself', etc. *TPT*, 252.
[60] Feuer, *Spinoza*, 24.
[61] On Orobio, see the brief biographical introduction above in Ch. 2, and the bibliography cited there.

of royal counsellor or 'favourite', and after his arrival in Amsterdam in 1662 this vocation was folded into his strong sense of Jewish particularity, as he took an equivalent position within the elite of his new community. Among other roles, he served on the Mahamad in 1669–70, that fateful time witnessing the renewed ban on meat from non-Sephardi butchers, the decision to raise money for a new synagogue, the beginning of the dispute with the del Sotto family, and the new articulation of the Mahamad's powers, with repercussions in communal conflict for over a decade.

Orobio referred to the *ḥerem* in the course of a detailed discussion of the fate of the famed 'sceptre of Judah', predicted by the biblical patriarch Jacob to be retained by the descendants of his son Judah.[62] The lines of Genesis about possession of the *shevet* stood at the heart of many polemical exchanges regarding the meaning of Jewish exile, as Christians interpreted it as predicting the end of Jewish kingship (sovereignty) with the coming of the messiah. Orobio's treatment, appropriately, focused on the nature of Jewish self-rule from the biblical era to the present.[63] Having explained that the sceptre represents a more general kind of 'rule' (*mando*), and not specifically kingship, Orobio indicated that rabbis still possessed that rule in exilic communities, and hence the sceptre was still in Jewish hands.

As Orobio explained, in the benediction that Jacob delivered to Judah,

Jacob said that ... even if the rule, meaning the power of the king or lord to punish subjects, would be removed from Judah, his tribe would retain control over the legal office, which would keep the people in the holy laws by explaining them and spiritually punishing transgressors, as in excommunication and separation from the congregation, which is a civic death.[64]

In this initial statement, Orobio seems at first to make a distinction between spiritual and temporal power like Grotius's, with exilic rabbis ruling spiritually as opposed to the actual rule that represented the 'power of the king or lord to punish'. He portrays their power to excommunicate as analogous to the death penalty, calling excommunication a civic death, but at the same time appears to limit their role by describing their purview

---

[62] Gen. 49: 10: 'The sceptre will not depart from Judah, nor a lawgiver from beneath his feet, until Shiloh comes.' See Ch. 7 below for other possible translations and interpretations of this critical verse.

[63] I return to Orobio's interpretation of Jewish political history through the lens of the sceptre of Judah in Ch. 7.

[64] Orobio, *Prevenciones*, MS Ros. 631, pp. 73–4. See Albert, 'A Civil Death'.

as 'spiritually' punishing transgressors and explaining the law. Likewise, he later calls them 'masters who . . . teach the most exact observance of the sacred precepts',[65] emphasizing their religious as opposed to governmental function.

Thus far his position was extremely close to that of Grotius, conveying that rabbinic law was a spiritual echo of the political authority of pre-exilic Judaism. But Orobio proceeded to make assertions about rabbis' authority that carried his argument in a different direction. He wrote that 'they have so much authority over the people, conceded by God himself in the law . . . that it is not lawful for anyone to repudiate their decrees'.[66] Such a description of their decrees and their authority over the people counter-balances his emphasis on the spiritual and lends a more governmental tone to what follows: that no one may 'invent or maintain any understanding of the divine law other than that which the ancient sages pronounced and the present ones teach'. The rabbis as interpreters of law made *decrees*—and, as Orobio proceeded to say, also sat in judgement: 'these same doctors . . . are absolute judges of the people throughout the world, not only in what pertains to ceremonial rules and legal precepts, but also in all civil and criminal law'.[67]

The last sentence did crucial work for Orobio, indicating that rabbis judged not only in religious affairs ('ceremonial rules and legal precepts'), but just as much in the stuff of government—'civil and criminal law'—and they did so 'absolutely'. In their sacred function, the rabbis were not lower than lay government, but higher; not limited to one mode of life or one community, they operated universally. The image Orobio created is one of a halakhic polity run by rabbis, where religious law, halakhah, is the every-day law of the commonwealth. This view is the opposite extreme from Aboab's lay-centric understanding of communal politics, and one that could be well suited to Christian Hebraist views—except for one crucial polemical shift: where Christians saw a break, Orobio saw continuity; and where they saw a shadow of biblical sovereignty, he saw fullness.

Grotius had explained that the ban was the replacement for the death penalty, which Jews could not impose without sovereignty. In a passage that Orobio almost certainly would have paid attention to since it also addressed the forms of excommunication among Jews, Grotius had

[65] Orobio, *Prevenciones*, p. 75.   [66] Ibid.   [67] Ibid.

also called criminal jurisdiction 'the sword'[68] and included banishment within this category. He specified that the Romans gave the Sanhedrin the right to banish as well as to impose some forms of corporal punishment, but that since 'the authority of imposing capital judgment had been taken away', Jews were obliged to replace the death penalty with the highest form of ban.[69] Orobio turned the idea on its head to argue that the ban, in fact, perpetuated that ultimate authority, merely in a different form.

What is most striking about Orobio's claim about the rabbis' role is its combination of ultimacy and temporality: their rule, in his depiction, is both absolute and real. In fact, his comments seem designed specifically to counter a view that Jews lacked such authority, as they come in response to the following polemical challenge: 'Christian doctors generally allege that our scribes or legal judges do not possess rule [*mando*] or jurisdiction anywhere because they cannot punish with corporal punishment'[70]—an allegation like Grotius's that Jews had not retained this power after the loss of their independence. Orobio retorted that they did indeed rule, possessing *mando*, since the prerogative to impose the *ḥerem* was, like the death penalty, an ultimate punishment. It constituted real temporal power, even sovereignty, as he explained that by *mando* he meant the 'power of a king or lord to punish his subjects',[71] and elsewhere parsed it as 'dominion, sovereignty, and independence'.[72] Emphasizing that *mando* did not mean some secondary or limited form of administration, he wrote that one could not be considered to rule if one was subject to another king, since 'it is not the same to command as to be commanded, to obey as to be obeyed, to dominate as to be dominated, the one being a blessing and the opposite a curse, like God put on Eve, that she would be subjected to the man'.[73]

The relation of excommunication to the death penalty did not come from thin air, and in order to perceive the full contours of Orobio's move, some attention to how the death penalty stood in for ultimate political authority in both Jewish and European political traditions is helpful. To begin with, Jewish rituals of excommunication that were practised at least in some communities were quite morbid, involving the snuffing of (black) candles, the expulsion of air from a leather bag, and other similar symbols of death.[74] The association was more substantive as well. In the

---

[68] Grotius, *De imperio*, 395.
[69] Ibid. 395.   [70] Orobio, *Prevenciones*, MS Ros. 631, p. 73.   [71] Ibid., p. 74.
[72] 'Dominio, soberania, o independencia'; ibid., p. 76.
[73] Ibid., p. 68.   [74] Malkiel, 'The Ghetto Republic', 136–7.

Hebrew Bible the *ḥ-r-m* root has the senses of consecration to God, that is, being irrevocably set aside, and of utter destruction.[75] One instance of that usage is in Joshua 6: 17–21, where the root appears to have the senses of consecrating, proscribing, and exterminating, in different places. In addition, a talmudic passage offers a derivation for *shamta*, another form of the ban, from the words *sham* and *mata* to mean 'there is death'.[76] One modern edition translates it as 'a designation of death', following the statement of Abraham ben David (*c.*1125–98) that *shamta* is a special form of the ban whereby a mortal curse is pronounced on the excommunicate.[77] Grotius's mention of the ban as death penalty designated this as the difference between *shamta* and *ḥerem* or *nidui*.[78]

As Beth Berkowitz has argued, the death penalty was an important part of the construction of rabbinic authority in general, so it is not surprising that elements of it carried over, translated into different terms, by later thinkers interested in political authority in biblical and rabbinic contexts.[79] We already saw that reference to the Sanhedrin's right to impose capital punishment was part of the medieval justification for the authority of exilic leaders by means of the *ḥerem*. Nahmanides mentioned *shamta* in particular in this connection, and Isaac Abravanel also wrote in his commentary on Deuteronomy 17 that violation of the rulings of the Sanhedrin was punishable by death.[80] Maimonides wrote that 'whoever rebels against a king of Israel, the king is permitted to kill him. Even if someone of the people is ordered to go someplace and he did not go, or ordered to stay in his house and he left it, he faces the death sentence [*ḥayav mitah*].'[81]

---

[75] For example in Num. 21: 2.   [76] BT *Mo'ed katan* 17*a*.

[77] BT *Mo'ed katan* 16*a*, n. 23. *Talmud Bavli: The Schottenstein Edition*, xxi: *Tractate Moed Katan*.

[78] Grotius, *De imperio*, 395. Grotius does not use the phrase 'civic death'. Greenberg and Cohn, 'Herem', translate *sham mitah* as 'civil death', suggesting that it might share a common source with Orobio.

[79] Beth Berkowitz's treatment of capital punishment in early rabbinic discourse does not make a connection to the ban; nor does it appear from her thorough discussion of the relevant scholarly literature of the past century that such a connection was an important part of modern Jewish ideas about the death penalty. It is likely that the deep connection between excommunication and the death penalty is post-talmudic and pre-modern. Berkowitz, *Execution*, 25–64.

[80] See Netanyahu, *Don Isaac Abravanel*, 165.

[81] Maimonides, *Mishneh torah*, 'Laws of Kings', 3: 8, 10. Compare this to the wording of the article of the *haskamot* granting the Mahamad the authority to impose house arrest, enforced by the *ḥerem* (SA 334, 19, fo. 21). See Funkenstein's discussion of this passage in *Perceptions*, 159–60, and Blidstein, 'On Political Structures'.

Aboab also related that a violation of the *ḥerem* (as collective oath or injunction) was punishable by death in biblical tales. He cited, for example, King Saul's condemnation to death of 'his son Jonathan for transgressing the *ḥerem* that he decreed'.[82] His extended, impassioned account of the extermination of the inhabitants of Jabesh-Gilead, an atrocity carried out in order to avoid violating a *ḥerem*, also underscored its absolute nature; and he cited Joshua 7: 13 (again following Nahmanides), saying that Joshua 'had the right to condemn the rebel Akhan to death for committing a sacrilege', and he spoke of 'Joshua's decree that is mentioned in the text of the *ḥerem*', referring to Joshua 6: 26, where the spoils of Jericho are banned. The text of Spinoza's ban, in fact, which is recorded in Portuguese in the Mahamad's minute book, includes the words 'cursing him with the *ḥerem* with which Joshua banned Jericho'.[83] Finally, Aboab summarized his view at the end of the *Exhortation* with a reminder that the *ḥerem* stands in for the death penalty, which could only be imposed by a sovereign Jewish government: 'Thus, we enlighten those who do not know the force of the *ḥerem*, which, as we have said, is so great that in the time of our happiness, and when we possess the kingdom, he who has transgressed it will deserve death—whether it has been put by the King, or the great Senate of Israel.'[84] Aboab echoed Abravanel and Maimonides—as well as Grotius— but instead of looking back to biblical times, he looked ahead to a time of messianic sovereignty in which, he allowed, either a king or a senate might govern.

Orobio wrote before Aboab, so if he knew of these rich Jewish traditions, he did not learn of them from the *Exhortation*. Other likely sources were translations of key Jewish legal texts and compilations like Menasseh's *Conciliador*, accessible to former conversos like Orobio, who would not master Hebrew and rabbinic sources on his own. Even more likely were the Latin and vernacular texts written by medieval and early modern Christians that he knew well and cited extensively in the *Prevenciones*. More generally, Orobio's Spanish education would have instilled in him a basic knowledge that capital punishment was an element of sovereign power—a component of early modern culture that has received much

[82] Aboab, *Exortação*. He cites 1 Sam. 14: 26: 'When the troops came to the beehives and found the flow of honey there, no one put his hand to his mouth, for the troops feared the oath.' The passage does not use the word '*ḥerem*'. The actual condemnation is in 1 Sam. 14: 44.

[83] A translation has been published in Kasher and Biderman, 'Why Was Baruch de Spinoza Excommunicated?', 98–9.   [84] Aboab, *Exortação*, 32.

attention from theorists and historians, not least Foucault and Derrida, who both interpreted the spectacle of public execution as a performance of state sovereignty in this era.[85]

One common early modern view of the death penalty followed a tradition inherited from Thomas Aquinas, who wrote that it was justified along the lines of amputation of a diseased limb that threatens the body as a whole,[86] in alignment with the common deployment of medical models for politics in medieval and early modern thought. Hobbes, for example, described disorders and diseases of the commonwealth in medical terms as part of his notion of the commonwealth as a body politic. In a passage cited above, Abraham Pereyra followed this tradition and compared excommunication to the amputation of a diseased limb. A counterpart in Jewish sources is the talmudic statement that a *ḥerem* penetrates all of the limbs of the banned person, connected with the association of *shamta* with death and lesser forms of corporal punishment.[87] Nahmanides echoed this source, and Aboab referred to it in the *Exhortation*, saying that the limbs of anyone who transgressed a *ḥerem* by interacting with a banned person were themselves thoroughly penetrated by it.[88]

The authority to take the lives of subjects was also associated in early modern political philosophy with the authority to wage war, itself a frequently cited criterion of sovereignty.[89] Some of the same justifications apply to the use of arms and force against subjects who make themselves enemies of the common good or violate the essential pact.[90] Althusius wrote: 'If the people does not manifest obedience, and fails to fulfil the service and obligations promised in the election and inauguration in the

---

[85] Foucault, *Discipline*, 48; Derrida, *Death Penalty*, i. 3 and *passim*. Although the historicity of some of their observations can be disputed, the essential point stands that capital punishment, with its ultimacy, was important in the development of modern conceptions of sovereignty. See Friedland, *Seeing Justice*, esp. 11–13, and the bibliography discussed there.

[86] Megivern, *Death Penalty*, 116.

[87] BT *Mo'ed katan* 17a.

[88] 'Therefore someone from such a city who transgresses it is banned as if he transgressed his own oath, which will penetrate all of his limbs and, as the Prophet Zechariah says in 5: 4, *it shall consume them to the last timber and stone*.' Aboab, *Exortação*, 9.

[89] Here again, there is a basis in the Hebrew Bible, as Deut 20: 17 employs the *ḥ-r-m* root to prescribe a war of extermination against foreign nations.

[90] Johnson explains: 'For medieval writers and Luther alike [i.e. in a tradition that Johnson shows also extended to 17th-century political thinkers], *bellum* meant the prince's use of force against both the external and the internal enemies of the order, justice, and peace of the political community.' *Sovereignty*, 64.

constituting of the supreme magistrate, then he is the punisher, even by arms and war, of this perfidy and violation of trust, indeed, of this contumacy, rebellion, and sedition.'[91] Spinoza, too, indicated that sovereignty consisted of the ability to compel subjects by force, including the death penalty: 'The sovereign right over all men belongs to him who has sovereign power, wherewith he can compel men by force, or restrain them by threats of the universally feared punishment of death.'[92] Bossuet similarly took the death penalty—which he called equivalent to banishment—as a sign of sovereignty, using God's expulsion of Adam ('He banished him; he told him that he had incurred the penalty of death') as proof that God 'has visibly exercised a personal empire and authority over men'.[93]

As Locke summed it up:

Political Power then I take to be a *Right* of making Laws with Penalties of Death, and consequently all less Penalties, for the Regulating and Preserving of Property, and of employing the force of the Community, in the Execution of such Laws, and in the defence of the Common-wealth from Foreign Injury, and all this only for the Publick Good.[94]

Locke's point in this passage was to distinguish what he named political power, the power of 'a magistrate over his subject', from other forms of power, such as those between father and child or master and slave. Political power, he said, is what is possessed by 'a ruler of a commonwealth'—in other words, a sovereign operating in the sphere of a state.[95] So this ultimate power was being conceptualized specifically as a sign of political *mando*.

Aboab and Orobio had this complex of traditions about excommunication, Jewish law, capital punishment, and sovereignty in mind as they sorted out who had power or authority in Jewish communities, and why. The death penalty, even among Christians, was inseparable from religious narratives about the fate of Jewish law in exile, and for the Jews of the Kahal Kadosh it bore on a wider understanding of what a Jewish community was and why it existed. Orobio's position differed from Aboab's in that Aboab

---

[91] Althusius, *Politica*, 134.   [92] *TPT*, 204–5.   [93] Bossuet, *Politics*, 40.
[94] Locke, *Two Treatises*, 268. Derrida cited Locke prominently in the first session of his seminar on the death penalty, commenting that 'the sovereignty of the state is first of all the right of death, the right to exercise the death penalty'. Derrida, *Death Penalty*, i. 14.
[95] For Pufendorf the right to punish did not exist until there was a civil society to possess it; otherwise, only a victim had any right to harm or kill an offender. Saastamoinen, 'Hobbes', 198.

realistically deferred the full power of the death penalty to a time of Jewish return to sovereignty, whereas Orobio went as far as he could, within reason, to suggest that a form of sovereignty was available to them right there in the present day.

They also differed in that Orobio named the ban as a power of rabbis whereas Aboab claimed it for the community. Committed though he was to locating a form of Jewish *mando* in exile, he recognized that such a claim about Jewish communal authority was problematic from a Christian perspective as well as from a Dutch one.[96] It was untenable to say that a Jewish community was sovereign on the basis of its lay government. As a commonwealth formed by the common agreement of its members, it had legitimate, but not ultimate, authority: it was subject to a higher, sovereign polity.[97] Instead, to argue for some sort of exilic Jewish self-rule that could be understood as a manifestation of the ultimate power represented by the sceptre of Judah, Orobio took a page from anti-Erastian thinkers in arguing that religious leaders were representatives of a separate, eternal, divine authority. Rabbis, as representatives of the law of Moses, inherited and transmitted that authority, apart from and beyond any civic or political organization, right up to the present day.

In fact, Orobio saw Jewish ultimate power as independent of communal organization or boundaries. He described it as transcending communal boundaries ('throughout the world', above), and his emphasis on the absolute superiority of rabbis emphasized that their authority, deriving from divine commandment, preceded and superseded that of lay leaders with their contractual collectivities and ad hoc decrees, obviously authorized by humans rather than God. In this, his thinking had something in

[96] Philipp van Limborch, Orobio's interlocutor in the famous polemical 'friendly conversation', had already in 1662 flagged the problem of Jewish excommunication impinging on Dutch sovereignty. Part of Limborch's letter is found in Meinsma, *Spinoza*, as noted in Y. Kaplan, *From Christianity to Judaism*, 276. I cannot claim that he knew this directly from Limborch. Kaplan indicates that *Prevenciones* was completed around 1679–80, but Limborch and Orobio apparently only met in 1682. Possibly one of those dates is inaccurate; more likely, further study will reveal that other Calvinist preachers and theologians made similar claims before Limborch. Limborch began preaching to the Remonstrants in Amsterdam in 1667, just a few years after Orobio arrived there, and soon after the arrest and conversion of Sabatai Zevi. But he had already been interested in the Sephardi community for a long time. On his relationship with Orobio, see Y. Kaplan, *From Christianity to Judaism*, 270–85, and van Leeuwen, 'Philippus'.

[97] Sovereignty defined in terms of territory and the use of force was more clearly unavailable to Jews than if it were defined by, say, law or kingship.

common with that of Aboab's rebels. The rebels' argument that a *ḥakham*
was required for the legitimization of any communal *takanot* could imply
that a *ḥakham*—understood now not merely as a learned person but as a
bearer of the authority of the divine law—possessed an authority stemming
from a different source than that of the *kahal*. They seem to have seen rabbis as temporal agents of the divine law and lay leaders as agents of a different, lesser, and more contingent kind of authority, even if—especially
because—that authority was validated and legislated by some rabbis. The
same contrast applies to Orobio's difference from Grotius: for Grotius, the
Sanhedrin's jurisdiction over bans proved that civil authorities had reigned
supreme. For Orobio it supported a view of ecclesiastical—that is, rabbinic—independence.[98]

With a reputation as an early enlightener, and having been a politically minded lay leader himself, Orobio might have been expected to lean
towards a view of Jewish life less infused with veneration of rabbinic law.
On the other hand, he served on the Mahamad only once, quite early in
his time in Amsterdam. Moreover, throughout his work, Orobio was preoccupied with the meaning, validity, and ongoing relevance of Jewish law.
He was also preoccupied with refuting Spinoza, who treated Jewish law as
essentially political—and who was aligned with the Erastian position that
the state should govern both civil and religious affairs. Orobio articulated
a position that was just as rationalist in orientation as Spinoza's, but that
justified the ongoing relevance of both Jewish law and Jewish self-rule.
Ironically, his view, like Spinoza's, could devalue Jewish communal autonomy, at least the version of it that existed in the Kahal Kadosh.

The *ḥerem* has long been recognized as a critical feature of early modern
Jewish communities, as well as a flash point in evolving and contested relations between rabbis and lay leaders, between rabbinic and other forms of
authority, and between the religious and the social dimensions of Jewish
communal life. The complex views discussed here—views of how and why
a community, as opposed to a rabbi, could be vested with the power to
excommunicate, and of the basis on which any exilic Jewish entity could

---

[98] See also Grotius on the Jewish right to exclude people from the synagogue on doctrinal
grounds: *De imperio*, 419–21.

wield such power—point to the particularly political understanding of the *ḥerem* that was important to Jewish and Jewish-adjacent political thinking towards the end of the Dutch Golden Age.

Aboab's treatise thickens the connections between Spinoza's thought and Jewish discourse of the time, revealing how both were embedded within the church–state battles of their day. The way members of the Kahal Kadosh treated the *ḥerem* was the product of interaction between intellectually open, connected Jews and Christian thinkers interested in how Hebraic traditions and Jewish sources supported their views of the relationship between religion and politics. It is widely recognized in early modern historiography that Christian political ideas, and especially those regarding church–state relations and the status of religion in a republic, were developed with close attention to the idea of an ancient Jewish republic. Visible now is that Christian interpretations of the Hebraic tradition had an impact, in turn, on Jewish ideas, indeed on Jewish ideas about the meaning of their self-government and their status in exile—ideas at the very heart of Jewish identity.

SIX

POLITICS
EXILE AND THE JEWISH
REASON OF STATE

IN A SERMON delivered on the final night of the Esnoga's inaugural celebration in 1675, a young intellectual named David Sarphati[1] remarked to
the gathered congregation:

This is how the Mahamad has navigated the winds of late: by sometimes celebrating politics and leaving religion aside, and other times elevating religion and
dropping politics. . . . Reason of state is absurd in the abstract, and religion is
dishonoured by independence. What can be done? The wind changes, and we
would go straight.[2]

Sarphati's words are, on their face, extraordinary. In a forum dedicated to
the opening of a new place of worship, this lay intellectual praised the
communal leadership's willingness to 'leave religion aside' when necessary.
Moreover, he called such strategic acts justifiable by 'reason of state', laying out an initial opposition between the communal government—understood as inherently political—and religion. In the context of the strife that
bubbled and brewed in the Kahal Kadosh during the years just before and
after the completion of the grand edifice, Sarphati's words also ring as an
acknowledgement of the inherent difficulty of keeping a community whole,
an essential problem of Jewish politics in exile.

Sarphati, the son-in-law and protégé of Isaac Orobio de Castro, was
praising the Mahamad in terms drawn from general European discourse
about ethics and piety in statecraft. As many in the audience would most
likely have recognized, his comment recalled the words of the Flemish

[1] Sarphati was also known as David de Pina or David Sarfati de Pina. Like Orobio, Sarphati
was both a physician (he completed his studies at Leiden and also received training from
Orobio himself) and an intellectual, preaching in the community as head of the Magen David
yeshiva. See Y. Kaplan, *From Christianity to Judaism*, esp. 207, and Swetschinski, *Reluctant
Cosmopolitans*, 196 n. 96.   [2] Sarphati, 'Sermão Septimo', 144–5.

writer Justus Lipsius that 'it is a greater problem than the inexperienced suppose to preserve a straight course on that turbulent sea',[3] a line from the beginning of his *Six Books of Politics or Political Instruction*, one of the most widely read political works of the seventeenth century.[4] Sarphati's words also evoked Machiavelli's notion that a ruler must 'be prepared to vary his conduct as the winds of fortune and changing circumstances constrain him', and sometimes 'disregard the precepts of religion', as human affairs are buffeted by unpredictable *fortuna*.[5]

Along with his winking reference to Machiavelli and Lipsius, Sarphati's open use of the phrase 'reason of state' called to mind a broad debate about religion in politics, one with a history as long as it was rancorous. Essentially meaning 'statecraft', the phrase could be a neutral way of referring to the activities and strategies of a governor or government, along the lines of an art or science: Giovanni Botero described it in his influential late sixteenth-century *The Reason of State* as 'the knowledge of the means by which [a state] may be founded, preserved, [and] extended'.[6] But more often the phrase specifically connoted the absence of religion in those activities, and the rich reception history of Machiavelli brought to the expression a connection with pragmatism at the expense of (religious) idealism.[7] Botero's ostensibly neutral characterization in fact waged war against a Machiavellian distinction between the demands of statecraft and conventional moral or religious standards. Along with a swathe of European—especially Catholic—thinkers, Botero saw it as impossible for true, well-crafted, and effective 'reason of state' to run counter to religion, and conservatively suggested that founding, preserving, and extending a state are all activities best performed in accordance with Christian ethics and dogma. The interests of a Christian state, in his view, fundamentally could not be served by

---

[3] Lipsius, *Politica*, 227.

[4] Lipsius's works were read in both the Dutch Republic and Iberia, and were more widely translated than most (Baldwin, 'Translation'). A Spanish edition of *Six Books* was published in 1604, and 1675 saw the fourth edition of his complete works in Latin; see Lipsius, *Politica*.

[5] Machiavelli, *Prince*, 62. The reception of Machiavelli by the second half of the 17th century across Europe, including in the Dutch Republic, centred on the role of religion and morality in politics and the state. See Haitsma Mulier, 'Controversial Republican'.

[6] Botero, *Reason of State*, 3. On reason of state and governance, see Curtis and Jones, 'Reason of State', which introduces a special issue on the subject; Viroli, *From Politics*; and Zarka (ed.), *Raison*.

[7] Lazzeri, 'Gouvernement'; Méchoulan, 'La Raison d'état', esp. 256; and Senellart, 'Raison d'état'.

un-Christian behaviour, so there was no theoretical difference between religion and reason of state.

Sarphati's blatant and public praise for the Mahamad's strategic irreligion was thus all the more striking. He made no bones about aligning himself with the Machiavellian view. Despite wading into potential controversy, taking a position on questions about church power that were active in Dutch politics, and coming perilously close to the supposed heresy of Spinoza's recently published *Theological-Political Treatise*, Sarphati's oration shows no sign of hesitation or dissimulation. He claimed without any compunction that Jewish communal life was, indeed, political. In fact, the sermon's central theme homes in on the question of how to understand Jewish politics.

His sermon complicates an image of the Kahal Kadosh Talmud Torah as a community preoccupied by fear of association with Spinozistic thinking or Dutch Christian moral judgement. It also belies any sense that Amsterdam's Spanish and Portuguese Jews were constrained by intellectual moorings in the Catholic world. For it was not only Sarphati himself thinking this way, and his comments did not come as a surprise on that Friday in August. On the contrary, the organizers knew the gist of his talk in advance, since it was an expanded version of a sermon he had already delivered two and a half years earlier, during Passover in 1673, as discussed above.[8]

Like the revised version that was published in a fancy book along with the other inaugural orations, the original sermon (preserved in manuscript) was a meditation on the religio-political dilemma of the Jewish community in exile, discussed through the lens of several examples of real or apparent conflict between 'religion' and 'politics'. There was an important difference, however: the original was delivered at a moment when the completion of the synagogue building project was endangered by war, natural disaster, and fiscal woes, and so served as a call to action rather than a valediction. This theme must have resonated enough to merit the sermon's repetition in commemoration of the synagogue's completion, now with its ending dramatically revised to reflect the project's unlikely success.

Other members of the Kahal Kadosh wrote of the community's 'reason of state' and referred to Machiavelli too, at various times, though not in the same way as Sarphati. Aboab, for example, wrote in his biblical paraphrase

---

[8] See Ch. 3. A manuscript copy of this earlier sermon indicates that it was delivered at the Abi Yetomim yeshiva. Sarphati, 'Sermão que pregou', MS EH 48 C 25.

that Korach's revolt against Moses was motivated by 'the harmful politics of the reason of state', as the rebels were looking out for their worldly interests rather than bowing to divine authority.[9] He also commented that politics without deference to religion led Pharaoh to mistreat the Jews because 'the reason of state reigns among Princes, even to the point of tyranny'.[10] The phrase was in common usage, always with reference to this troubled relationship between religion and politics. Isaac Orobio de Castro also used the phrase around this time, as I explain below; the rabbi Saul Levi Morteira had used it earlier in the century, but not with regard to Jewish communal affairs.[11]

Abraham Pereyra, who was probably in the room when Sarphati delivered the updated version of the sermon, must have especially objected to Sarphati's theme. He had published two books within the previous decade in which he advocated the integration of religion and politics and adapted fierce anti-Machiavellian writings into the Jewish communal context. In his 1671 book *Espejo de la vanidad del mundo*, Pereyra raged against the 'politico' who pretends to promote 'reason of state' while advocating practices that go against its real interests, goals like justice, harmony, and sanctity. Echoing Giovanni Botero and others, Pereyra scoffed at the notion that the 'reason of state' is opposed to the promotion of religion, 'as if there were some reason of state other than that which the divine Law teaches, which preserves the state [*estado*] of his people, and which God, in his grace, gave us for our improvement and conservation. And these politicos (better called the impious) separate the reason of state from the Sacred law.'[12] Ideally, Pereyra wrote, governors (i.e. the Mahamad) should prioritize religious edicts, ethical considerations, rabbinic authority, and the people's religious observance. In long sections devoted to what he called 'divine politics' (*política divina*), Pereyra dished out pious advice to leaders and citizens alike, in order to form a more perfectly religious Jewish polity.

[9] Aboab, *Parafrasis*, 182.

[10] Ibid. 451. Pharaoh's politics were discussed by Christian thinkers as well, including in discussions of whether it was right to expel Jews from Spain.

[11] See A. Melamed, *Wisdom's Little Sister*, 355–70.

[12] Pereyra, *Espejo*, 396. See similar wording in Pereyra, *Certeza*, 163, and compare to 'The politicos use the mask and sweet name of reason of state . . . to set reason of state apart from the law of God, as if the Christian religion and the state were mutually exclusive', in Ribadeneira, *Tratado*, 452; translation in Braun, 'Bible', 552–3. See Méchoulan, *Hispanidad*, 165, on Ribadeneira as an important anti-Machiavellian writer. Throughout his edition of *Certeza*, Méchoulan indicates passages where Pereyra followed earlier Spanish writers particularly closely.

There is no question that Pereyra's and Sarphati's interpretations of the true reason of state differ from one another. By Pereyra's standards, Sarphati appears to be a Machiavel indeed; and in the light of Sarphati's praise of lay communal governance, Pereyra's account of a commonwealth guided by divine law appears conservative and idealistic. Their two ways of thinking about communal government reflect deeply divergent perspectives on the nature of a Jewish community, but they begin with a shared assumption that the community is profitably understood in political terms. From that starting point, both also approach more essential questions about how communal politics relate to Jewish politics writ large and what, if anything, differentiates Jewish politics from those of other peoples. Pereyra and Sarphati thus attended to the very idea of Jewish politicality. As they took up the understanding of politics as a universal mode of human activity that was by then common among European thinkers, the exilic condition became the basis for a new problematic of Jewish particularity to accompany more practical theopolitical questions about good government, divine will, exile, and power.

Pereyra's Divine Politics

Although government affairs were not Pereyra's primary concern, they form a thread running throughout his two books as he brought general early modern thought to bear on the Jewish context. Each of Pereyra's books contains a significant section devoted to proper government of the Jewish polity, meaning the community—the *república*, the Jewish commonwealth. He prescribed roles and standards for the behaviour of its people and its leaders, both office-holders and also soft leaders such as elders and teachers. His focus was not limited to leaders' own personal benefit or their duty to others, but rather an overall sense of the community as a site of politics.

The fourth section of *Certeza* is devoted in its entirety to politics. Its first chapter is titled 'Política divina que deven seguir los buenos gobernadores' ('The Divine Politics that Good Governors Must Follow'), and subsequent chapters follow the same theme, describing and justifying the need for justice, clemency, prudence, generosity, and piety in government. In *Espejo*, the parallel section on politics is much longer, making up about a quarter of the book as a whole, and it elaborates more fully on the concept of *política divina*.[13] Pereyra did not originate this phrase, but he made it a focal point of this second book, and it provided the title for the central chapter in this section.[14] His expanded treatment devotes more space to the ideal qualities of the people as opposed to the governors alone, exhorting 'subjects' of the commonwealth to act in accordance with religious dictates since their behaviour constitutes the religious quality of the commonwealth itself. *Espejo* also contains more of a pointed message about harmony in communal affairs, probably reflecting the fractious events that had erupted within the Kahal Kadosh after 1666, including open dissent and disobedience of the Mahamad. Pereyra's political ruminations were intended for the ears of community members and leaders, as he emphasized that a governor is 'the peace of his republic'[15] and wrote: 'This is not only speculative, but also very practical, especially for those in power.'[16]

The person of the governor was crucial to Pereyra's vision of the divine polity, since both the temporal success and the spiritual state of the entire polity depended on him. In one typical example, he repeated a classic claim that one who cannot govern himself cannot govern others,[17] interpreting it to mean that a sinful person cannot encourage piety in others, and thus advising leaders to 'first rein in your vices and reduce your sins, and then try to rule others'.[18] In another example, Pereyra invoked aphorisms from Plato, Aristotle, and the Bible regarding the necessity of prudence in a ruler, and then characterized prudence as a religious virtue, acquired through piety. He compared communal leaders to biblical Jewish political leaders, declaring that 'the most important thing for ruling and commanding is prudence. . . . The best way to achieve prudence is to pray to God, the fount of all virtues . . . as did David, Solomon, Jehosaphat, and the other God-fearing kings.'[19]

Pereyra also advocated a close and even deferential relationship between lay leaders and rabbis. In fact, the subtitle of the chapter called

---

[13] Pereyra, *Espejo*, 118–251.

[14] Francisco de Quevedo (1580–1645) referred frequently to 'divine politics', and Pereyra used his work. See Robles Carcedo, 'Abraham Pereyra', 328. See also Vellozino, 'Sermão Sexto', 104–5, discussed above in Ch. 3. The idea of 'divine politics' might also be fruitfully compared to the 'angelic politics' described by Antonio Enríquez Gómez, a Spanish converso and, by some accounts, a crypto-Jew, in his 1647 *Política angélica*. See Révah, 'Un Pamphlet', where part of this work is reprinted.   [15] Pereyra, *Espejo*, 150.   [16] Ibid. 156.

[17] Ibid. 136 and elsewhere. Pereyra could have had this common remark from many sources, but Barrios notes in *Triumpho* that 'Solon advises: "If it is your ambition to govern, first learn to be governed, because he who does not govern himself thus cannot govern others well."' Barrios, *Triumpho*, 6.   [18] Pereyra, *Espejo*, 150.   [19] Ibid. 135.

'Política divina' in *Espejo* is: 'On how governors should rule with the advice of the professors of the Law, and zealously obey them'.[20] It repeats a theme that had been introduced in *Certeza*, that lay leaders must act with personal piety and also incorporate rabbinic concerns into their governance: 'The governors, therefore, in order to justify their government, avoid censure, and take a path of certainty, must subject their dictates to the Law, eschew human considerations in favour of its observance, and resolve affairs with the advice of the professors.'[21] These comments were carefully composed. In the commonwealth Pereyra described, government was formally in the hands of lay decision-takers, just as it was in his community, but the religious behaviour of the governors made the government divine. 'These are the politics [or, perhaps, 'policies'] that the zealous governor must keep and observe in his government, with divine assistance.'[22]

Pereyra set divine law on a pedestal, but his model differed from Orobio's seen above, in which rabbinic authority was disconnected from the workings of communal administration. Although Pereyra acknowledged that divine law and communal law were not identical, he saw them as working in tandem, as he advised governors to 'keep the law of God, and those of the government, and you will deserve the title of good governor'.[23] He addressed the way the two types of law intersected when he mentioned in *Espejo* the halakhic underpinnings of the *Acordos*, writing that the lay leaders' powers of 'taxation are strengthened by the fact that the government was established by the right conceded in the divine Law to make laws to sustain the population and the poor'.[24] In another passage, he suggested that excommunication was a shared power of the 'professors and governors', i.e. rabbis and Mahamad, calling them 'the heart of the republic' and explaining the necessity of cutting off diseased limbs from the body politic.

Indeed, Pereyra addressed violators of the law with anti-Machiavellian fervour.[25] In *Certeza*, Pereyra followed in the footsteps of the sixteenth-century Spanish writers Ribadeneira and Marquez in attacking the followers of Machiavelli, who 'go along with the infernal politics of the times', writing that such politicos believed 'that one must accommodate the public good instead of the Law (as if God's commandments would pervert it)'.[26] Méchoulan, Pereyra's primary modern expositor to date, says

[20] Pereyra, *Espejo*, 152.   [21] Pereyra, *Certeza*, 165.   [22] Ibid. 168–9.
[23] Pereyra, *Espejo*, 150.   [24] Pereyra, *Certeza*, 168–9.
[25] On Pereyra and anti-Machiavellianism see also A. Melamed, *Wisdom's Little Sister*, 355–65.   [26] Pereyra, *Certeza*, 165.

that the merchant-turned-pietist reacted 'with the energy of a Spaniard' to impieties ranging from atheism to paying insufficient attention in synagogue, suggesting that he had absorbed the obsessive interest in heresy that was characteristic of the Inquisition.[27] Pereyra founded his Amsterdam yeshiva in the very year Spinoza was excommunicated, and he sat on the Mahamad at the time of the ban against Juan de Prado.[28] Pereyra also made playful reference to Spinoza by punning on his name,[29] as did other Amsterdam Sephardi sources in the commonwealth years.[30] In Méchoulan's account, it was Pereyra's battle against heterodoxy that underlay his anti-Machiavellian politics.

Pereyra may have used Machiavelli as a stand-in for Spinoza, as Méchoulan suggested, but his interest went beyond heresy, and far beyond Iberian cultural attachment, to engage with politics for their own sake. He took aim not only at those who contaminated their religion with politics but, especially, at those who failed to govern religiously enough. In 1670s Amsterdam, where Spinoza had just published his *Theological-Political Treatise*, and the de la Court brothers, popular leaders and political thinkers, were 'enamoured' of Machiavellian ideas, Pereyra would have found plenty of fodder for outrage.[31] He wrote, in *Espejo*:

This minister of Satan [Machiavelli] first disseminated his perverse doctrine in Italy, where he was named the Italian secretary (or sectarian). These are the founts from which the politicos are fed; these are the precepts with which they guide themselves (or blind themselves); this is the Judaism that they observe,

[27] Méchoulan wrote that Pereyra shared 'with the officials of the Holy Office a preoccupation with matters of orthodoxy, good behaviour, desire for the honour of God', asking: 'why does there arise, in the middle of a work of piety and instruction, a critique of Machiavelli very similar to those of the Spanish political thinkers of the golden age?' (Méchoulan, *Hispanidad*, 78–9).   [28] Ibid. 51.

[29] Kaplan and Méchoulan both pointed out Pereyra's pun in *Certeza*; Méchoulan, 'La Pensée d'Abraham Pereyra', 72, and Kaplan, *From Christianity to Judaism*, 323; but Méchoulan says that it originated in a work of Fray Luis de Granada, which Pereyra playfully adapted to refer to Spinoza and Juan de Prado; Méchoulan, 'The Importance of Hispanicity', 369. Pereyra also made many more references to *espinas* in *Espejo*, 76, 166, 293, and 350, for example, which might suggest an intensification of his attention to Spinoza at the time of the publication of the *TPT*.

[30] Barrios makes the same reference in *Triumpho* and in *Corona de la ley*. See Méchoulan, 'La Pensée d'Abraham Pereyra', 73, and Israel, *Radical Enlightenment*, 171. The pretended silence regarding Spinoza may be seen as analogous to the early modern Spanish avoidance of Machiavelli's name, maintaining the fiction that no one read his works, even though everyone responded to him. (I thank Antonio Feros for this observation.)

[31] Haitsma Mulier, 'Controversial Republican', 250ff.

those who read his contagious doctrine. Clothed in sheepskin, they . . . kill and cripple the treasure of the Lord like wolves, teaching them to govern as though God had no providence with them.[32]

He also personalized the message, confessing:

It pains me terribly to consider the superficial religion that some put forward, with the mantle of law, even when they carry out atrocities. They only take the name of Jews for reason of state, being imitators of that early generation whose sinful ignorance obligated the divine justice to decree the flood and drown all of creation because of their wickedness.[33]

Like Christian anti-Machiavellians, Pereyra was deeply alarmed by the possibility of government divorced from religion in his own community. Pereyra's political programme, while intensely religious, was much farther-reaching than ferreting out heretics. He was concerned with the difficult relationship between worldly affairs and religious obligations—specifically, for Jews in a Jewish political context.

Reason of State

Sarphati, by contrast, treated religion and politics as contrapuntal rather than simply harmonious. He queried the relationship rather than taking it as axiomatic. He announced hyperbolically that 'the dogmas of politics and the dictates of religion are so contrary that they cannot stand except in opposition: he who embraces one in search of truth looks down on the other as scandalous lies; he who infallibly decides by politics is absurdly crass in religion'.[34] Soon afterwards, however, he exposed this opposition as unstable and turned the assertion on its head: 'Religion must be a form of politics, since politics are a subject adorned with religion. The form of one proves the necessity of the other; religion is so necessarily predicated on politics, that politics are therefore predicated on religion.'[35] His wordplay obscures it somewhat, but the message is that religion plays out in a real world, a world necessarily conditioned by politics. Anything approaching religious purity would be only hypothetical; it would not be actualized. Likewise, politics inherently carry religious meaning as they constitute the world of human activity.

---

[32] Pereyra, *Espejo*, 396. He also accuses politicos of being only superficially religious (p. 296).
[33] Pereyra, *Espejo*, 296.   [34] Sarphati, 'Sermão Septimo', 139.   [35] Ibid. 146.

This theme then runs throughout the sermon: that politics and religion are equal and opposite, mutually necessary and intertwined. Sarphati was no enlightener, no maskil: he did not advocate the removal of religion from political life or the removal of temporal authority from religious groups. Instead, in early modern fashion, he took up the knotty question of how the two distinct spheres relate to each other. He suggested that the sphere of politics is lower, more terrestrial, than that of religion, yet vitally important to it. Politics needs religion to give it meaning; religion needs politics, too, and not only in the mercenary sense that political activity promotes or defends religion. In a more essential sense, religion is not fully realized if it is kept elevated above worldly affairs. As Sarphati put it: 'Who would make political judgements without the [religious] devotion that distinguishes his discourse from atheism? Who would speak of devotion without the politics that prevent observance from appearing to be mere superstition? *Raison d'état* is absurd in the abstract, and religion is dishonoured in independence.'[36] Sarphati discusses a number of stories from the ancient world to elaborate on this very point. Two in particular are illustrative: Caleb calming an Israelite rebellion, and competition between biblical kings.

Numbers 13–16 tells of several attempts of the biblical Israelites to rebel against Moses' leadership, the most famous of which is Korach's rebellion. With various disputes on the Mahamad's authority raging within the Kahal Kadosh Talmud Torah, these stories must have had an added degree of piquancy. In Sarphati's sermon, he addressed not Korach, whose claim against Moses along with other members of the house of Levi was essentially religious ('All the community are holy . . . and the Lord is in their midst'; Num. 16: 3), but rather an earlier rebellion of all the people, questioning the directive to invade the land of Canaan. In a complaint that might stand in for that of returned conversos dissatisfied with the Mahamad's heavy-handed leadership, the Israelites complained that they would have preferred to stay in Egypt than to die or be captured in battle following Moses' foolish orders. The invasion of Canaan richly echoed the Mahamad's insistence on constructing the Esnoga; as a metaphor it played on the opposition between ingathering and dispersion, between wandering and rootedness, congregation and edifice.

In the midst of this outcry, Sarphati explained, Caleb 'hushed the people before Moses' (Num. 13: 30) and stood up to defend the plan. Sarphati

[36] Ibid. 145.

followed a midrashic account of this interaction, in which Joshua had been
the first to try to calm the rebels but was silenced by the mob. Caleb succeeded where Joshua had failed by first pretending to be sympathetic to the
rebellion. Only after captivating the crowd through his false and evil words
did he begin to persuade them to return to loyalty.[37] Sarphati interpreted
Caleb's actions as enacting effective reason of state, sighing: 'Ah, divine
Caleb, who cannot be a good Politician without being founded in Religion,
who cannot be Religious without being founded on Politics'. With his typical wordplay Sarphati waxed on, describing to his listeners how Caleb

quieted them with reason of state and persuaded them with devotion, and could
not persuade them with devotion without using reason of state to quiet them.
Thus politically Religious, he seemed to speak evilly, and thus religiously Political, he surely spoke well, and nothing will end well without using both, with such
certainty that they would seem to be one.[38]

'Seem to be one': religion and politics were not the same, but in the actual
workings of human communities they were unavoidably interdependent.
Sarphati's audience would have agreed that the ultimate end of entering
Canaan was laudable, but might also have sympathy for the Israelites who
reacted with despair and resentment against the leaders who ordered them
to make sacrifices for that end. Sarphati's Machiavellian interpretation of
the midrash powerfully suggests that even the rabbis of the Talmud knew
that without the deception and dirt of politics, religion fails. Thus, he
argued, politicos like him might seem debased, but ultimately acted for the
religious good.

In fact, Sarphati suggested, even God engages in Machiavellian politics
when it comes to earthly affairs. 'God is . . . accustomed to our reasons of
state, and . . . attentive to the points of our religion . . . He protects us from
harm, condemning us with some damage: not enough to exterminate us,
but only to correct us.'[39] Even God cannot sail straight amidst changing

---

[37] BT *Sotah* 35a: 'And Caleb stilled the people concerning Moses—Rabbah said, [It means]
that he won them over with words. When Joshua began to address them, they said to him,
"Would this person with the lopped-off head speak to us!" [Caleb] said [to himself], "If I
address them [in the same strain as Joshua], they will answer me in like manner and silence
me"; so he said to them, "Is it this alone that Amram's son has done to us!" They thought that
he was speaking to censure Moses, so they were silent. Then he said to them, "He brought us
out of Egypt, divided the Red Sea for us and fed us with manna. If he were to tell us, Prepare
ladders and ascend to heaven, should we not obey him! Let us go up at once and possess it
etc.".'   [38] Sarphati, 'Sermão Septimo', 147–8.   [39] Ibid. 152.

political winds: God, like earth-bound politicians, dissimulates, and might set pure idealism aside when existentially necessary. The comment is a play on the traditional notions that the tribulations of exile are punishments intended to help Israel atone for its sins, and that God accommodated the language of humans in his divine law. In contrast to Pereyra's use of the expression *política divina*, in which the ruler must show deference to religion, Sarphati suggested that God defers to the reason of state at times.

As it turns out, Sarphati was not alone in this view. His mentor Isaac Orobio de Castro similarly suggested that God dissimulated for political reasons, withholding the punishment Israel deserved in order to send a message to the nation.[40] It was to Orobio that Sarphati dedicated the printed version of the sermon, with elaborate praises that clearly situate the physician and intellectual as a politician: 'What else for the one who gave such prudent advice and such politic counsel? Being such a politico, you were named professor and adviser to the king at the most illustrious university in France.'[41] As much as Pereyra's identity was pious, Sarphati's was political, and where Pereyra distrusted the politico, Sarphati wore the label with pride. Further, in Sarphati's dedication he praised Orobio for giving up his high status in the Christian world in order to join the Jewish community, 'voluntarily giving up the conveniences of the great cities, the praises of the academies, and the great rewards of your office in order to serve God here, so freely without fear, and publicly without worry'.[42] The move was an example of religion winning out over politics in the sense of embracing Judaism over worldly hierarchies, as well as in the sense that it was a move away from the dissimulation of converso life. Because of the widespread cultural perception of conversos as deceptive, they were sometimes associated with the idea of a politico.[43] Orobio was able to remain a politico, but now a Jewish one—lowered with respect to Christians, but with new internal harmony between religion and politics.

---

[40] 'Israel well deserved this definitive death sentence . . . to be removed from the memory of men, for all the sins that their republic committed . . . But the divine reason of state refused to execute this justice because, the Lord said: "Many times I have given to nations the strongest signs of my greatness, divinity and omnipotence, protecting and conserving Israel against human power."' Orobio also referred to the 'reason of state' in the workings of the ancient republic of Judah; *Prevenciones*, MS Ros. 631, pp. 66 and 77.

[41] Sarphati, 'Sermão Septimo', 133.   [42] Ibid.

[43] See Magnier, *Pedro de Valencia*, 354. According to Maravall, *político* referred to someone who read Tacitus, Lipsius, and Arias Montano in a Machiavellian way. See Magnier, *Pedro*, 349–52.

By contrast, in 1672, Pereyra's close associate Moses Raphael d'Aguilar wrote a response to a question about the ethics of dissimulation for the greater good. The question, sent from Venice but prefaced by an introduction penned by a member of the del Sotto family, which was then in the midst of their dispute with the Mahamad, asks whether Jewish law permits lying or dissimulation, and part of the discussion deals with biblical examples of God's apparently false speech to men. Aguilar responded that these are examples of divine accommodation to human understanding—an argument that avoids the view that God might intentionally deceive for a higher purpose.[44] The exchange highlights attention to the same issues addressed by Sarphati in other communal contexts in the early 1670s.

Pereyra did acknowledge that rulers—unlike God—must sometimes set aside honesty, equanimity, or justice in order to preserve the spiritual benefit of the group. An unethical, unfair, or ungenerous act can be read as ultimately pious because of its service to the common good. He treated rulers' secrecy or unfairness less as a necessary evil than as a part of the mysterium of a harmonious republic, as long as they were attentive to spiritual standards in general, which included paternalistically supporting the people's obedience and individuals' piety. Governors might sometimes have to dissimulate,[45] working behind the scenes like the gears of a clock, playing the republic like a harp, plucking the right strings at the right time. These comments are in the vein of Botero's remark (copied by Pereyra) that good governors are in tune with the 'inclinations' of their subjects in order to use or manipulate them, and not, in fact, atypical of seventeenth-century anti-Machiavellian thought.[46] Such behind-the-scenes political machinations, however, were of a different order than working against religious law or piety.

It is difficult to avoid the conclusion that Sarphati, Orobio, and their like were among the politicos that Pereyra so reviled, and that he understood them as promoting a kind of godless governance within the Jewish

[44] Aguilar, *Preguntas*, MS EH 48 A 11, §6, 50ff. (dated 12 Nisan 5432).

[45] Pereyra, *Espejo*, 167. He refers to the example of Saul pretending not to hear his detractors (1 Sam. 10: 27).

[46] Ibid. 150: a governor 'must be acquainted with the natural inclinations of his subjects, in order to know how to deal with each one as he deserves, since in this consists the fine skill of governance'. Barrios follows Pereyra (or Botero) on the same point; Isaac Cardoso also cites Botero's reason of state in *Excelencias*, 235. See Lazzeri, 'Gouvernement', 104, 116*; Schaub, *Portugal*, 49; Condren, 'Reason of State', 18; and Braun, 'Bible'.

context. Pereyra's politicos dissimulated, but not as conversos; they were Jewish political counsellors who cloaked themselves in a false veneer of religion—Jewish religion. He called them 'infernal politicos, wise counsellors by profession, with the mask and name of reason of state (which is generally called conservation and improvement by Princes and Governors)'.[47]

Sarphati's Politic Religiosity

The political for Sarphati was low but necessary, the matter that gives shape and reality to formless religion.[48] Politics represented the hard necessities of actual governance, and more broadly, they related to external, practical, or worldly concerns, as opposed to the spiritual, pious, or divine. Sarphati's discussion of a second ancient tale shows how he justified the Mahamad's governance. In a playfully provocative reversal, he associated the lay leaders not with the universally extolled King David but with Jeroboam, traditionally seen as a wicked king.

He began by suggesting, with his typical symmetry, that both kings had erred in their single-mindedness:

David could hardly publish the praises of his devotion without breaking the laws of state with disorderly leaps,[49] and Jeroboam could hardly uphold the politics of his state without the absurdity of idolatry with his idols. One undid all of politics to show his religiosity, and the other undid all of religion and revealed himself as political.[50]

Here David is religious and Jeroboam is political. David's intense religiosity is portrayed as being out of sync with the normal affairs of the world, even to the point of danger, illegality, and self-destruction: David made himself ridiculous. Jeroboam's politics, on the other hand, compromised essential principles in order to maintain the state.

The opposition between the two also calls to mind the wide range of meanings *política* had in early modern Spanish, ranging from 'policy' to 'politesse'. Indeed, it is not always obvious how to read it. There are some examples that lean towards an interpretation somewhat removed from statecraft, such as the sense of *política* as akin to the modern 'polite', reflecting the communal elite's preoccupation with social graces, or 'politic' as an

---

[47] Pereyra, *Espejo*, 395. [48] Sarphati, 'Sermão Septimo', 145–6.
[49] See 2 Sam. 6: 14–23: 'And David danced before the Lord with all his might.'
[50] Sarphati, 'Sermão Septimo', 139.

adjective in the sense of tactful and strategic. 'Genteel' might even suit in that context, a possibility that also emphasizes the degree to which it was politic to blend in with Gentile society. This range of meanings is also apparent in the real efforts within the Kahal Kadosh to maintain manners and civility, which were identified as a form of political self-awareness among its members and leaders. For example, a regulation banning excessive noise-making on Purim was part of an effort to regulate appearances and represent the Spanish and Portuguese in a way that would be appealing to the wider society, contrasting the ideal comportment of a *gente política* with the rough and loud activity of *bárbaros*, barbarians.[51] In fact, a number of regulations cite concern about how Christians would perceive the community, including some in the 1670s that prohibited betting on the outcomes of Dutch military battles.[52]

One may interpret such regulations as 'politic', primarily concerned with appearances, reputation, or good breeding, but Sarphati made clear that these qualities were also 'political' in the governmental sense. Many of the prohibited activities could also be read in such a light; the Mahamad's choice of wording may indicate not only a concern about politesse, but also a politic desire to curb public displays of national-religious pride and violent aggression towards the Gentile world. Sabbatian messianic expectation would be such a display. On Purim, blotting out Haman's name is a ritual enactment of the victory of Jews over a persecutor.[53] Likewise, betting on military campaigns would raise concerns about Jews' lack of loyalty to the Dutch state, or at least create a spectre of political separateness. In fact Sarphati opened this sermon with the remark that 'When the world erupts in wars (says reason of state), when the victories of the enemy are enduring, there should be an end to building with grandiosity and solemnizing its dedication with festivities!'[54]—highlighting how inappropriate the Esnoga's opening festival seemed in the light of con-

---

[51] Y. Kaplan, '*Gente Política*'; he translates *gente política* as 'people of good breeding'.

[52] Ibid. 38. Calling it a form of the 'civilizing process' posited by Norbert Elias or early modern social disciplining, Kaplan suggests that the leaders' concerns were not necessarily shared by the population (p. 29). Likewise, when Kaplan discussed the 'political concepts' of members of the Kahal Kadosh he primarily focused on their valuation of noble lineage as a dimension of 'the problem of exclusion and the boundaries of self-identity'. Y. Kaplan, 'Political Concepts', 45–50.

[53] As Elliott Horowitz showed, Purim was long associated with carnivalesque reversals of the powerless condition of Jews and even with sanctioned violence. Horowitz, *Reckless Rites*.

[54] Sarphati, 'Sermão Septimo', 144.

temporaneous Dutch disasters. Religious freedom meant enacting essential principles, but such success could only be attained in accordance with hierarchical demands and worldly expectations. A polity whose government behaved like David could lower itself, even 'break the laws of state'.

The need for politics to temper religion is essential in this view, with the full spectrum of meanings of politics coming into play. The Mahamad, said Sarphati, was right to behave politically, smoothing things over so as to make the building project possible. He turned the contrast around to suggest that the people, insisting on religious enthusiasm, were behaving more like David with his disorderly leaps, while the Mahamad stuck to protocol, saving them from the unintended effects of their foolhardy passion. (Here again, David could stand in for Sabbatians, whose continued passion after 1666 was tamped down by a realistic and increasingly diaspora-minded Mahamad.) Sarphati's words were a call for measured diplomacy over jingoism and zealotry, just as much as a reminder of the need for good manners.

On Jeroboam's part, on the other hand, according to Sarphati the mistake was too much politics and, more importantly, politics of the wrong sort. Long traditions among both Jews and Christians heaped scorn on Jeroboam, who was reviled for having broken up the Israelite kingdom by setting himself up as king of the ten northern tribes and for having built alternative temples there featuring golden calves. In Pedro de Valencia's words: 'Jeroboam, first king of Israel, is the foremost example of faithless and unjust kings, who practise *raison d'état*, and follow the path of ill-omened perversity.'[55] This king was typically seen as idolatrous, tyrannical, and sinful.

But as with David, Sarphati's presentation of Jeroboam's fault diverged from tradition. Sarphati condemned Jeroboam not for faithlessness but for superficiality and pride. His Jeroboam was overly concerned with status and external displays of respect. Sarphati explained that if Jeroboam were to go to the Jerusalem Temple, where only the king of the southern kingdom could sit, his rank there would be lower than that of Rehoboam. Sarphati imagined Jeroboam's reasoning, having the bad king exclaim:

In the holy court there are only seats for the Kings of Judah; Rehoboam will sit on the throne like a king, and he would put me at his foot like a vassal? O scandal

---

[55] Pedro de Valencia, *Tratado*, 93–4, quoted in Magnier, *Pedro de Valencia*, 363.

of all politics! The Kings of Judah have an obligation to publicly read the laws of kingship; Rehoboam will read them like a king, and he would have me hear them like a vassal? O dishonour of all reason of state![56]

In Sarphati's telling, Jeroboam had the chance to sit in the Temple but rejected it because he would only be second-best there. Sarphati put a sharp point on his assessment of the king's mistake, saying that Jeroboam 'considered [heavenly] glory on one hand, and dignity on the other, and chose to lose the glory by reason of state rather than lose his state by reason of glory'.[57] One risks losing everything for the sake of worldly honour.

We may read in these comments, perhaps, a condemnation of those community members who objected to the new seating assignments in the Esnoga. We may also read here implicit reference to the tension between the community as a political domain with its own 'temple' and the idea of a messianic Jewish political regime. The Mahamad would be Jeroboam in that scenario, having rejected a chance at the messianic Temple because it would lower their own diasporic status. On the other hand, the tale also implicitly indicts those who sought messianic sovereignty rather than exilic semi-autonomy, for seeking absolute primacy ('like a king') where they ought to be satisfied with a lower, but still recognized, exilic status ('like a vassal'). Sarphati exhibited a politic ability to leave interpretations open while building a multi-layered and richly allusive discourse.

In the religious realm, he suggested, such superficial political hierarchies ought to disappear. Sarphati related another rabbinic account in which God offers to forgive Jeroboam for his sin of idolatry: if the king will repent, he will then be granted eternal glory along with the Davidic kings. But Jeroboam carries his petty concerns over into the afterlife. He rejects the offer because he wants not only to sit with the kings in the world to come, but to have the highest rank among them.[58] He loses out because he

---

[56] Sarphati, 'Sermão Septimo', 141. See BT *Sanhedrin* 101*b*. 'He reasoned thus: it is a tradition that none but the kings of the house of Judah may sit in the Temple Court. Now, when they [the people] see Rehoboam sitting and me standing, they will say, The former is the king and the latter his subject; whilst if I sit too, I am guilty of treason, and they will slay me, and follow him.'   [57] Sarphati, 'Sermão Septimo', 141.

[58] BT *Sanhedrin* 102*a*: 'After this thing Jeroboam turned not from his evil way. [1 Kgs 13: 33] What is meant by, after this thing?—R. Abba said: After the Holy One, blessed be He, had seized Jeroboam by his garment and urged him, "Repent; then I, thou, and the son of Jesse [i.e. David] will walk in the Garden of Eden". "And who shall be at the head?" inquired he. "The son of Jesse shall be at the head." "If so", [he replied] "I do not desire [it]."'

is unable to differentiate properly between the political and the religious; as Sarphati explained, 'reason of state does not permit public displays of preeminence—as though such matters existed in heaven, the house of God, with separate doors for the simultaneous entrance of different ambassadors, or with semi-circular seating so as not to suggest superiority of one over another'.[59] In Sarphati's sarcastic description Jeroboam sees heaven as a kind of celestial royal court where considerations of 'reason of state' cause jealous visitors to vie for formal status, and Sarphati's imaginative language conveys the ridiculousness of an afterlife paradise in which diplomatic niceties must be observed. Jeroboam was wrong, said Sarphati, to think that the superficial rivalries of political status would be reinforced eternally —not because they are unnecessary in life but, on the contrary, because they are particular to this life.

Sarphati's treatment of the relationship between religion and politics was subtle, reflecting an evolved perception of the ways both categories operate—whether in the ancient Israelite community, the Kahal Kadosh, Holland, or exile writ large. Sarphati assumed that the relationship was fraught, and that it was not always obvious which actions ultimately best served religious aims. This is quite a different mindset from that of Pereyra, who seems very certain not only about the religious path but also about its superiority to politics.

Still, both of them saw religion and politics as bound tightly together. They shared a view that politics were inherently lower than religion but at the same time necessary for the promotion of religion. They, like many of their compatriots in the Kahal Kadosh, embraced the communal system in which temporal authority was vested in lay leaders with religion in a critical supporting role. They expressed a commonly held view that religious precepts had to operate by means of communal actions and institutions if religion was to have true relevance, and likewise the political world was meaningless—atheistic and Machiavellian—if it lacked the ultimacy, morality, and authority provided by religion.

New Concepts of 'Religion'

Pereyra and Sarphati represent different ways of applying a newly developing language of religion and politics to Jewish life. They used early modern

[59] Sarphati, 'Sermão Septimo', 140.

European political terms of art to reflect on Jewish communal affairs in the vernacular. Both men deployed a sense of politics as related to governance or statecraft ('reason of state'), in discussing the politics of the Jewish commonwealth. They actively claimed the category of politics for themselves, as Jews, and in the present day.

Such a claim was possible for them because they treated politics and political ideas as a sphere of human activity that not only crossed national and religious lines but also transcended different forms of polity to apply naturally to the community with its state-like form. The sense of politics as a universal sphere or category accords with an increasing abstraction of political theory among Christian Europeans, a change that Quentin Skinner identified with the formation of modern political thought as we know it. Skinner traced how political discourse evolved from advice directed to individual rulers, first city leaders and then monarchs in the 'mirrors for princes' genre, into a 'civil science', in the words of Thomas Hobbes.[60] In this literature the polity, the 'commonwealth', or the state emerged as a non-specific referent for the arena in which political activity, or statecraft, occurred. As discussed above in Chapters 1 and 2, members of the Kahal Kadosh established and conceived of their community in ways that made it easy to consider it as a commonwealth, and thus to apply this discourse to it.

The way members of the Kahal Kadosh used the word 'religion' in a Jewish setting was enabled by a parallel conceptual advance. The abstract idea of 'religion' as a universal sphere emerged in the same period, in a connected process: just as politics came to be seen as a mode of activity that crossed political boundaries, religion could be seen as existing across particular religious contexts. A marker of the new usage is said to be found in the use of the term 'religion' to describe the traditions of others as readily as one's own. The ancient and medieval *religio*, in contrast, was generally not applied to rites other than the speaker's, nor is there an equivalent term to the post-Enlightenment 'religion' in the ancient Latin-speaking West or most non-Latin cultures. Historiographers of the term 'religion' have pointed out that today's usage, marked by universality, supposed neutrality, and mental distance, is unique to modernity, traceable to the pressing interconfessional conflicts of the early modern period. Brent Nongbri has emphasized that the modern idea of religion emerged within (and thus was

[60] See Skinner, *Foundations*, vol. i, esp. pp. ix–x, 33–5, 113–28, and id., 'Hobbes's Changing Conception'.

permanently inflected by) the Christian political thought of the late six-teenth and early seventeenth century.[61]

Pereyra and Sarphati had evidently absorbed this innovation. For them, religion and politics were conceptually distinguishable. However, they were still intimately connected in practice, and thereby fell short of an-other marker of the modern: 'the idea of religion as a sphere of life separate from politics, economics, and science'[62]—the expectation that politics and religion were activities that would take place apart from one another. In Pereyra's writing, religion seems universal and identifiable, but not isolable. It is crucial to everything, but receives little sustained attention on its own. Religion is fully imbricated within a web of morals, institutions, commit-ments, and practices, and the polemical message of his sections on 'divine politics' is precisely that neither politics nor religion can stand alone.

Pereyra used the word *religión* similarly to the way he used other terms taken from the Christian political context: universalizing and leaning towards a political view of the community while maintaining realism. For example, he explained that the furtherance of religion was a crucial respon-sibility of the Mahamad, who must faithfully 'execute justice, conserve *religión* with all vigour, maintain the peace without disturbance, banish those who disturb it, teach the fear of God with meditation on the divine Law, favour its teachers, and listen to their discourses, because if one does not follow this path, one eventually loses like Jeroboam and his cohort'.[63] The reader was to understand that Jewish government must be infused from top to bottom with 'religion', a general term. What he meant by 'reli-gion' here seems to be 'the careful fulfilment of what God has comman-ded'—an action-oriented concept that was the primary sense of the Latin *religio* in Christian writings of the sixteenth century and before.[64] Yet it

---

[61] The classic is W. C. Smith, *The Meaning and End of Religion*, and a great deal of more recent scholarship has focused more directly on the early modern period. See Despland, *La Religion en Occident*, which deals with the period up to the late 18th century, as well as Despland and Vallée (eds.), *Religion in History*; Bernand and Gruzinski, *De l'idolatrie*; Harrison, '*Religion*'; and Nongbri, *Before Religion*. See also J. Z. Smith, 'Religion, Religions, Religious'.

[62] Nongbri, *Before Religion*, 7; but note that I take this quote out of context to make a differ-ent point here.

[63] Pereyra, *Certeza*, 172. He refers to BT *Berakhot* 55a: 'Rab Judah also said: Three things shorten a man's days and years: To be given a scroll of the Law to read from and to refuse, to be given a cup of benediction to say grace over and to refuse, and to assume airs of authority.'

[64] Feil, 'From the Classical *Religio* to the Modern *Religion*'.

is abundantly clear that Pereyra meant Jewish religion: the entire passage is couched in terms of what Judaism has to teach the governor.

Did Pereyra, then, use 'religion' in the modern sense? On one hand, he did treat it as a universal. The meaning of the phrase 'promote religion with all vigour' is different from that of 'promote Judaism with all vigour'. Pereyra chose not to insert 'Judaism' there, but rather left the generic term in place. He conveyed that the governors were to promote *religion* as opposed to politics, *faithfulness* as opposed to faithlessness—without specifying Judaism or the law of Moses or any other such term. The choice also lent his words universality and emphasized that Jewish leaders were engaged in the same activity as Christian ones. Mirroring a wider European process, Pereyra's transposition of terms led him to treat Jewish government as an example of government in general, and Jewish religion as an example of religion in general.

On the other hand, however, religion was still not operating in a neutral way; rather, the 'religion' mentioned here is assumed to be the religion of the author, and he assumes the reader agrees that it is the one 'true' religion. Indeed, he emphasizes the superiority of Jewish law to other systems of religious precepts. Among the Spanish Late Scholastics and their contemporaries the term was still used in the old way, such that political writers like Bodin, Lipsius, Althusius, and others were at a loss for how to square religious difference with their use of religion to justify a common political order.[65] In Pereyra's *Espejo*, composed two or three generations later than those works but relying heavily on them, the same conflict is apparent.

Sarphati took a less one-sided approach to the question of which should predominate in the community, and a less sanguine approach to their coherence, but likewise treated religion and politics as two sides of a coin. Religion and politics were not separate 'spheres of life', but rather mutually distinguishable modalities or practices. They were modes or standards of thought or behaviour that could be adopted or neglected alternately and at will with regard to the same institutions, practices, and settings.

Pereyra's and Sarphati's inconsistent and complex treatments of 'religion' in a political context were not unusual. The modern (Protestant) understanding of religion with which Jews contended in the eighteenth and

---

[65] Feil, 'From the Classical *Religio* to the Modern *Religion*', 36–7.

nineteenth centuries was, in the time of Spinoza, only beginning its ascendancy; the seventeenth century was marked by messiness, ambiguity, and intentional disruption surrounding the category of religion. The explorations of the relationship between religion and politics that we find in the works of Pererya and Sarphati were a precursor to the later intellectual innovations that took Jewish communal life in quite a different direction from the one our seventeenth-century Jewish writers pursued.

According to conventional wisdom, the Jewish categorization of Judaism as a 'religion' per se did not develop until well into the modern period, and Jews' adoption of the term reflected a shift in Jewish communities to more closely mirror Christian churches of the time, isolating the 'religious' (ritual and dogmatic) components from others, such as the social or political. Leora Batnitzky's *How Judaism Became a Religion* revealed this innovation, showing how the categorization of Judaism as a religion was a disputed and complex move in the eighteenth century and beyond, and one that altered the course of Jewish culture. Defining Jewish modernity as beginning with the acquisition of citizenship, she emphasizes that 'it was simply not possible in a premodern context to conceive of Jewish religion, nationality, and what we now call culture as distinct from one another'.[66] These three components were inextricably combined as Jewish life was experienced through the community, which combined multiple functions.

Batnitzky's observation is borne out among members of the Kahal Kadosh in the 1670s, with one caveat: they added politics to the triad of religion, nationality, and culture as interconnected elements of community. The writers we have discussed did not classify Judaism as a religion to the exclusion of its other dimensions, but rather recognized Judaism to be both 'religious' and 'political' in a generic sense.[67] This, I argue, was a significant innovation, as these writers fitted their own reflections into wider—and from a certain perspective, alien—categories. Their sense of Judaism as a religion still sat alongside their ethnic and social conceptions of it, but in the 1670s, as we have seen, it began to do so somewhat more uneasily in the light of new political thought.

[66] Batnitzky, *How Judaism Became a Religion*, 4.

[67] Yosef Kaplan argued that certain developments in the use of the ban precisely in this period indicated an emerging perception among Amsterdam's Sephardim of Judaism as a religion rather than as a 'way of life'; 'Alternative Path', 16–17.

Divine Law and Exilic Politics

Pereyra's and Sarphati's discussions reveal the intellectually fruitful tension inherent in making Jewish life 'political' in the European language of the day. In one sense Pereyra's view was straightforward: that Jewish politics are truly divine, as opposed to the false religiosity that in his view defined both Christian politics and Machiavellianism. He embraced the idea that there is a special relationship between Judaism and politics, helped along by the fact that many of his preferred Christian political thinkers also turned to Jewish sources and biblical history out of a belief that the divinely established Mosaic state constituted the ideal relationship between religion and politics.[68] As opposed to the classical sources that animated the political debates of the Renaissance humanists, in the seventeenth century biblical and rabbinic sources seemed to offer a politics that was divinely revealed: *política divina*. Pereyra even commented that, 'as all the other nations admit', divine politics are 'properly attributed to the Israelites'.[69]

Pereyra thus knew that Christians privileged Jewish politics. Along with the generic concept of politics, he was Judaizing a particular narrative posited by Christians, that Judaism and politics had begun as inextricable one from the other, but later became disjointed with exile. Therein lies the seed of the challenge that the new theopolitics posed for Jews. One of the hallmarks of the novelty of their treating Jewish life as political is that the politics they grappled with as a perceived universal were actually particular to the early modern Christian context. The problem is not merely that a one-size-fits-all concept might not suit the particular Jewish case but, more deeply, that Christian politics of the time were imbued with values and assumptions that were inimical to various elements of Jewish corporate affairs seen as political.

Above we saw that Aboab, Orobio, Spinoza, Grotius, and others addressed the present status of Jewish law within the framework of its being originally the law of a religious polity. We saw how the limitations on Jewish self-rule in exile gave rise to a variety of views on what kind of authority rabbis and lay leaders possessed. Pereyra, too, grappled with this issue. He particularly celebrated *Ley*, or *ley divina*, often repeating that the polity was run according to divine law. There are two distinct ways to understand

[68] See Méchoulan, *Hispanidad*, 40–4, on how the Spanish 'appropriation' of Hebrew texts created an avenue of approach for Pereyra.   [69] Pereyra, *Espejo*, 395.

this: on the one hand, it can simply mean that the community is governed in a pious manner, with an effort to follow divine will and act in accordance with the dictates of Judaism. This is continuous with his sense that the Mahamad promoted 'religion'.

On the other hand, it can also mean that divine law is literally the law of the polity. This is a meaning that is special to Judaism, conceived as a religion of law, and one that echoes the terms according to which Christians privileged the biblical polity. It also echoes the common conception that within Christendom Jews were permitted to live apart in separate communities, 'according to their own law'—a construction that was used by Daniel Levi de Barrios and Isaac Cardoso in emphasizing the independence of Jewish communities around the world and throughout history.[70] Such a conception was problematic, not only because of the reality of limited juridical independence in Jewish communities, but even more because the communities known to Pereyra, Barrios, and Cardoso were lay-led. The offices, procedures, and hierarchies elaborated in the communal constitution had little to do with Jewish law and more to do with the typical composition of associations and communities in early modern Europe. Rather than taking a distinct position, Pereyra made as much as he could out of the elasticity of the idea of law, which could simply mean religion in seventeenth-century Spanish, but on the other hand also had a semantic relationship to government.

In the wider intellectual culture of which the Amsterdam Sephardim were a part, Jewish politics were seen as a special case of integration with religion. But that vision was based on biblical Jewish politics where Mosaic law was the law of the land. Applying the same characterization of Jewish theopolitics to the exilic community required either turning a blind eye to real life affairs or finding some other model of what Jewish politics were. Pereyra's approach was more or less the first, glossing over the difference between Jewish communal politics and the superior divine politics that 'the nations admit' that Jews possessed.

Sarphati, in contrast, trained his eye directly on the exilic condition. In precisely the way that politics were the lower, debased side of the religio-political coin, so was exile the necessary, worldly, compromised status of a religio-political people. Since all politics were, in his view, marked by a

---

[70] Barrios, *Triumpho*, 31. He cites Cardoso as his source; see Cardoso, *Excelencias*, 17.

nearly irresolvable conflict between real and ideal, between status-seeking and religious passion, the Jewish exilic experience constituted, in fact, a political experience par excellence. Politics, in his eyes, were tied to the earthly realm and also, in the Jewish case, to the non-Jewish world: participation in that world represented a fundamental compromise but also enabled Jewish life to continue. Associated with outward appearances and low but necessary work, *política*—in its full range of meanings from gentility to statecraft—smoothed the way for Judaism in the Gentile world.

The dedication of the new synagogue proved an especially appropriate context in which to reflect on this relationship. Several of the sermons called for unity, harmony, and obedience, reflecting a sense of the Esnoga complex as a political space and thus as a symbol of the interconnection of the sacred and the governmental in the commonwealth, for good or for ill. Despite various crises and obstacles, the Mahamad had persevered. Sarphati connected with this context through a leitmotif of opposition between celebration and mourning, making gains and suffering losses. As quoted above ('when the world erupts in wars . . .'), he commented that the grand building and its dedication were incongruous at a time of general difficulty. The incongruity was a matter of the community's own troubles, but even more a sign of misalignment between the Jewish community and the surrounding society. Although in one sense the Kahal Kadosh suffered in parallel with Holland (since the enemy of the Dutch was also the enemy of the Dutch Jews), the successful completion of the new synagogue complex represented a victory for the community's own distinct interests over and against the Dutch troubles.

Through elaboration on this theme Sarphati highlighted such misalignment as a core characteristic of the Jewish political condition. Good politics (i.e. reason of state) would dictate projecting solidarity with their hosts instead of ostentatiously displaying their own separate success, whereas religion dictated the pursuit of a new synagogue despite any superficial issues of hierarchy or crass self-interest. On the other hand, it was only by means of effective politics that the religious goal was achieved ('this is how the Mahamad has navigated the winds of late'). Sarphati also shared the sense with Castro Tartaz and others (see Chapter 3) that the Esnoga was a site of Jewish politics, as he explained that politics are the matter that gives shape to the insubstantial form of religion. They give it reality, even if in so doing, they also inherently corrupt it.[71] Religion—any religion—is only ever embodied, and in its embodiment it becomes particular and political. Political life, therefore, is that constant compromise, and Jewish politics are especially compromised as a Jewish leader must navigate Jewish and Christian waters simultaneously.

Sarphati explored similar issues through another midrashic tale, this one taking place in a period of domination of the Jews by the Roman empire and thus emphasizing the heightened politicality of exilic life. In this story, a Roman prince was born on the Ninth of Av, a day of Jewish fasting and lamentation, and died during the joyful festival of Hanukah. Jews were thus required to mourn at a time of Roman national celebration and celebrate at a time of Roman national mourning. The Ninth of Av and Hanukah are, significantly, not merely religious celebrations in a general sense, but commemorations with national and political meaning. Hanukah marks the victory of the Maccabeans in retaking Judaea, and the Ninth of Av laments the loss of the Temple, commemorating the start of exile. When Jews kindled lights at Hanukah, they asserted a politics distinct from that of the host state and expressed the continuity of their own national political history, which involved temporary subjection but eventual restoration. Doing so at a time of military defeat among Christians thus not only reflected political distinctiveness, but also might be perceived as threatening or disrespectful, and hence dangerous or detrimental to Jewish interests.

Nevertheless, according to the versions of this midrash in *Lamentations Rabbah* and in the Jerusalem Talmud, the rabbis concluded that Hanukah celebrations must go on: in Sarphati's words, they declared that they would 'embrace the demands of religion, even when politics hinders them'.[72] The story ends disastrously, with a rigorous persecution of the Jews for their disloyalty.[73] In the 1675 version of Sarphati's sermon, celebrating

---

[71] He compares it to colour, which only exists as a theoretical quality unless applied to an object. Sarphati, 'Sermão Septimo', 145–6. [72] Ibid. 143–4.

[73] See *Lamentations Rabbah* 4: 22; also 1: 45 and 3: 2–4. One scholar (Applebaum, *Jews and Greeks*, 264), citing a variation on this tale, translated the name of the emperor (טרכינוס) as 'Troginus' (the wicked). Others translate it as Trajan; see *Midrash Rabbah*, trans. Freedman and Simon, vii. 231. Sarphati called him Tarquino, or Tarquinius. For Sarphati's listeners, Tarquinius was not just any emperor, but a tyrant whose rape of Lucretia was a foundation myth for the Roman Republic, a story that was very much a part of Spanish and Dutch literary and popular culture, on which see Pipkin, *Rape*.

the successful completion of the synagogue, Sarphati exclaimed that the Mahamad had actually done better at politics than the ancient rabbis, since the Kahal Kadosh leaders achieved their religious goals without provoking a backlash. Some initial hesitation on the part of the Mahamad, said Sarphati with hindsight, was not a cynical bow to political concerns, but rather a politic reluctance to offend and overtax a troubled community: 'to avoid the beginning of this building was not politics infused with evil, but was reason of state infused with virtue'.[74] The Mahamad had not ignored the demands of politics, as the rabbis did, so much as navigate them, as expressed in the lines quoted at the start of this chapter, to the effect that the Mahamad achieved their aims by 'sometimes celebrating politics and leaving religion aside . . . leaving one to the side when a disgrace arises, then burying a disgrace when an honour is revived and, altogether, not taking a direct path'.[75]

The key point for Sarphati was that the same conundrum was present in all politics. The Jewish republic was like all republics in facing an eternal conflict between religion and politics within its own internal affairs. The universal conundrum was heightened for Jews by the fact that the Jewish polity also faced a version of the same conflict facing outwards, with respect to non-Jewish authorities. Thus, the Jewish political condition was political twice over; it was the prime exemplar of the human political condition.

Reason of State and Sabbatianism

Sarphati's treatment of Jewish politics says something important about the way he understood exile: unlike those who later concluded that *galut* precluded real politics, he saw the exilic Jewish community as a meaningful site of just such activity. Subjugation to a foreign political regime was not anomalous and did not nullify the internal politics of the subjugated body; domination, subdivision, and compromise were normal political conditions of the real world. Through this lens we can understand how he addressed the challenge of Sabbatianism in his community, and make better sense of Pereyra's known Sabbatian enthusiasm as well.

As mentioned above, Sarphati indicated that King Jeroboam had

[74] And farther on, 'the hesitancy at the beginning is not to be censured, because it was the result of mixing reason of state with concepts of religion. The final end is greatly applauded, because it is religion founded on the dictates of politics.' Sarphati, 'Sermão Septimo', 148–9.

[75] Ibid. 144–5.

chosen poorly in seeking superficial status over eternal glory, but the Amsterdam politico still sympathetically described the wicked king's discomfort at being relegated to second class. Surprisingly, the way Sarphati worked with this story, Jeroboam represented on one level the problem posed by the desire to live as a Jew in a Christian world, where such a choice was seen as an act of separation, rebellion, and faithlessness. His portrayal of David, then, who exceeded the bounds of politic behaviour with his zealous religious observance, could be read as an indictment of indecorous celebration of Jewish worship and rites. Having first dealt with Jeroboam's tragic flaw, Sarphati returned to that king's question, posed to God: '*Mi ba-rosh?* Who should go first?', he asked. 'My religionless politics, or David's religion devoid of politics?' To this ironic quandary, treating King David as 'devoid of politics', Sarphati responded: '*Ben ishai ba-rosh* [the son of Jesse at the head]. The path of David goes first.' Sarphati chose religion, despite its impolitic nature, while alluding to messianic kingship. He continued:

We follow in David's footsteps, since the scandal of not attaining the crown is preferable to the infamy of not acquiring eternity . . . So contrary to politics is religion that one cannot be a good politician without dropping religion, as Jeroboam did in preventing the people from going to Jerusalem . . . O infamous conceits of politics! to give up eternal glory for a temporary crown![76]

Standing in for Sabbatianism here might be either David's 'disorderly leaps' or Jeroboam's idolatry and separatism. He might be imputing to Sabbatians impolitic religious enthusiasm or irreligious (antinomian?) enthusiasm for a worldly crown. In fact, Sarphati's message is in the duality. Did the Mahamad, like Jeroboam, wrongly 'prevent the people from going to Jerusalem'? Or did it keep the people in the true faith like David, preventing a rebellion that sought quick political success at the expense of true faith—'giving up eternal glory for a temporary crown'?

His ambiguity on this point was wise, given the divisions that existed among his listeners, who would have easily recognized the references to the Ninth of Av and the Davidic crown as connected to Sabbatianism. His audience would also have recalled the period around Passover two years earlier, when Sarphati had first delivered the sermon in the midst of a small renewal of Sabbatian expectation. Sarphati suggested that the politicos and the Sabbatians were all seeking the same elusive balance. To us, it

[76] Ibid. 143.

highlights that Sabbatians and anti-Sabbatians shared a perception of Sab-batianism and community as existing along the same spectrum of Jewish religio-political activity. Jewish messianism and kingship were subject to the same universal rules of religion and politics as the Jewish common-wealth, the Christian commonwealth or kingdom, or the biblical polity. Participation in a messianic movement was itself both realistic and ideal-istic, political and religious.

The same combination of idealism and realism is evident in Pereyra's political thought, and in fact, it resolves a small mystery about the man. Pereyra published *Certeza* when he was heading off to meet the messiah, and he wrote *Espejo* in a time of disappointment—as he acknowledged at the start of the book.[77] As a result, the accepted view has been that *Certeza* reflected Pereyra's messianic enthusiasm, composed in order to inculcate the piety that would ensure his co-religionists' personal redemption; where-as by the time he wrote *Espejo* he had moved on to a general ethical stance that left messianism behind. But this view does not account for the fact that Pereyra had not actually moved on by 1671, but rather continued to vocally and actively maintain hope for Sabbatai's return.[78]

More importantly, it does not account for how Pereyra's ideas in these two books related to his messianism in the first place. The two books do not significantly differ from each other in the values or aims they advocate. Neither book reads as a dramatic avowal of belief in imminent world change; neither speaks of Sabbatai himself or of Jewish kingship; neither is mystical. These Iberian-oriented, pietistic, and anti-heretical works seem totally disconnected from Sabbatianism as it is conventionally regarded. On the one hand Pereyra was a conservative thinker, well accepted by the rabbis and leaders of the Kahal Kadosh; on the other he continued to nurse messianic hopes after those same leaders had declared an end to the move-ment. How do these two sides of him cohere? If he was a 'believer' or an

[77] He wrote: 'There is no ill that is not for the good, as Abraham Pereyra experienced in 1666, when travelling with the old desire to rest in the shade of the tree that by God's grace he was able to plant in Hebron.' Pereyra, *Espejo*, 437. Kaplan interprets the 'ill' (*mal*) as Pereyra's former belief in Sabbatianism: Y. Kaplan, *From Christianity to Judaism*, 221 n. 43.

[78] Scholem, *Sabbatai Ṣevi*, 755, 893. See also Yaari, 'Pereyra Yeshivot' (Heb.). The approba-tions and approvals granted to *Espejo* by Aboab and other leaders have been seen as a sign that Pereyra had left Sabbatianism behind before its publication (see Y. Kaplan, *From Christianity to Judaism*, 221–2), but it might merely signal that the contents of the book were not specific to Sabbatianism.

'enthusiast', where is the antinomianism, where is the cult of personality associated with Sabbatianism? If his peers knew about it, where are the fierce efforts to root out and expose hidden Sabbatians, with which we are now familiar from the decades that followed? It contradicts widespread assumptions about Sabbatian messianism to think that Pereyra could have supported it at the same time as he was writing these apparently unrelated, mainstream works, especially after the apostasy.

What his ethical and spiritual advice, his reaction to Spinoza and Machiavellianism, and his Sabbatianism all shared was a desire for Jewish religion to infuse Jewish politics. *Certeza*'s urgent recommendations to both leaders and members of the community served Pereyra's interest in ensuring the clean state of Jewish souls, but they also stand on their own as an articulation of Jewish theopolitics—just as applicable to an exilic Jewish commonwealth as to a Jewish kingdom. The literal messianic vision would, after all, look quite a bit like the Catholic monarchical context that informed the sources he used. In that way, his book could be a guide for governing the coming kingdom just as well as a guide for leading a religious Jewish commonwealth into a political condition that merited redemption. The same is equally true of his *Espejo*.

Having now investigated what Pereyra was after in terms of Jewish politics, his thinking about the community seems entirely continuous with his expectation for Jewish political restoration. Either a messianically restored empire and an exilic commonwealth could be envisaged as a holy polity that operated according to universal political principles and promoted individual and collective salvation through divine law. The continuity in Pereyra's work shows that Sabbatian expectation can be understood as fitting together with a wider sense of Jewish politicality. For Sarphati, the essence of Jewish politicality was defined by the exilic condition and marked by an interplay between ideal and practical, between effort and manifestation, between self-preservation and self-realization, between fitting in and marking difference. Sabbatianism might have been religiously idealistic, but it overshot in the political domain to the point that it became absurd; it might have been politically real, but in its failure it ultimately harmed Jewish status.

The reason of state is not one of the seventeenth-century obsessions that one immediately associates with Sabbatianism. But what we see here is that Pereyra's and Sarphati's interrogation of Jewish politics—including the politics of Jewish particularism, messianism, and exile—was deeply connected to the problematic created by the importation of generic concepts of politics and religion into thinking about exilic Jewish life. Multiple, often warring, parties in the Kahal Kadosh Talmud Torah asked how their politics enacted God's law and intention for the Jewish people. Pereyra's passionate denunciations of the 'politicos' had a mark in Sarphati, Orobio, and their like, even though they were clearly favoured by the Mahamad, at least by the time of Sarphati's prominent speech. Meanwhile, the Mahamad faced rebellion from part of the community, who objected to the Mahamad's aggressive fund-raising for the synagogue project, and who used political concepts to argue against the lay leaders in favour of a more democratic and rabbinically oriented community. It was not only the so-called politicos, but also rabbis, lay leaders, merchants, printers, butchers, teachers, and others who shared in the sense that the realm of Jewish communal affairs was a political one.

A New Jewish 'Politics'

Both Pereyra and Sarphati approached internal communal affairs by applying general categories to the Jewish case, and that very act entailed addressing the larger question of Jewish uniqueness. As they queried what was and was not applicable to Jews, and particularly to exilic Jews, both men suggested that there was something special about Jewish politics as a subcategory of universal human politics. In contrasting ways, both of them argued that exilic Jewish politicality was heightened, rising above that of Gentiles: in their view, Jews in their day were more, and not less, essentially political than other peoples.

For Sarphati the essence of human political existence was the constant play between virtue and pragmatism, and exilic limited self-rule was the epitome of the right setting for that kind of play. For Pereyra politics were above all the workings of divine intention in human society, and a Jewish polity working in accordance with Jewish law was therefore the only divine political society, even to the extent that the Jewish commonwealth was a critical component of messianic salvation. For both, Jews were not uniquely apolitical, but rather hyperpolitical. Jews' political condition and activity was, in their eyes, a crucial aspect of Jewish life and a crucial component of Jewish identity.

Perhaps paradoxically, Sarphati and Pereyra—like many others in the Kahal Kadosh Talmud Torah—reached these conclusions about exceptionalism by translating terms and ideas from the Christian discourse, that is, by embracing and examining aspects of commonality. Pereyra's and Sarphati's perspectives occasioned a wider look at the impact of an increasingly abstract and universal conception of both religion and politics in early modern Europe. Pereyra's work of adaptation was an example of early modern cultural translation, and Sarphati's message about Jewish politics was expressed through Baroque wordplay. Both used what they saw as universal ideas, genres, and standards to address the particular case of Judaism. We saw that the widespread perception of the Kahal Kadosh as a commonwealth facilitated an internal debate over Machiavellianism as a Jewish concern. In essence, the Spanish and Portuguese Jews of Amsterdam adapted the concepts of reason of state and divine politics to the particular problems and preoccupations of a community that bridged various uncertain and tumultuous gaps. Discrete and independent but not sovereign, governed religiously but not halakhically, the Kahal Kadosh was a theopolitical Petri dish for the new discourse of commonwealths.

From one perspective, the substrate for such ideas had always been in place, or at least as long as the self-governed *kehilah* had been the primary form of Jewish collective in Christian Europe. Only with the introduction of viral new ideas did there arise among men like Pereyra and Sarphati a robust exploration, explicit and self-aware, of Jewish politics per se. And as we have seen, such a community-wide exploration was both messy and productive. J. G. A. Pocock observed that the integration of humanist and Machiavellian ideas transformed local Christian discourse in a disruptive, but also creative, process. If, as Pocock wrote, civic humanism was hard to reconcile with 'a society made up of several institutionalized agencies exercising different kinds of power: post-Tudor England, with its king, its law, its parliament, and its church',[79] how much more so did the categories of religion and politics, which were not native to Jewish thought, wreak havoc with the ad hoc balance that had long obtained in Jewish law and communal practices.

In fact, it may well be that the discussions marked here represent the first time that Jews treated internal Jewish affairs as 'political' as the term is used in the modern Western tradition. Quentin Skinner showed that

[79] Pocock, *The Machiavellian Moment*, 329.

political thought in the modern sense coalesced out of earlier traditions of government, theology, and philosophy when the generic notion of the political, and the generic idea of the state as the site of its enactment, entered the European imagination. Writing in Spanish, Portuguese, and Latin as Jewish languages, and using the shared terms of a Latin-centric European discourse, Spinoza's contemporaries in Amsterdam treated their own activities as part of a universal by bringing the new political theory to bear on Jewish institutions and practices. It was a linguistic innovation that signalled a wider moment of cultural translation and innovation.

The concept of the political, and systems of ideas around it, were not new to Jewish tradition; they had already been present in various forms from the ancient world through the early modern. Jewish history is saturated with exposure to non-Jewish political regimes and punctuated by moments of particularly fruitful intellectual engagement with non-Jewish political systems, ideologies, or ideas—including those inherent in Roman law, Islamic jurisprudence, medieval Arabic philosophy, and Renaissance humanism. In addition, as historians of Jewish political traditions have shown, Jewish sources from all eras abound with topics and claims that are self-evidently at the centre of what is now considered to be 'political', even where the word itself is not present: Jews took up questions pertaining to authority, belonging, law, nationhood, and more. Calling such Jewish traditions 'political', using the term etically as a universal, correctly recognizes the tunnel vision of historiography that would limit politics to contexts sharing a conceptual framework with the modern state. Otherwise, earlier traditions and non-European ideas and practices are made to seem irrelevant. A less parochial perspective recognizes engagement with questions of power, punishment, or contract (to name a few examples) as political even if it appears disconnected from modern Western political theory.[80] From this perspective of quasi-scientific objectivity, Jews can easily be seen as having practised politics and thought politically throughout their history.

But we may still distinguish between such diverse thinking and that which partook of a particular set of shared concepts that would form the basis for modern states and politics, and did so self-consciously. With this distinction in mind, what Pereyra, Sarphati, and others were doing in

[80] Neguin Yavari and Regula Forster ask: 'Can premodern traditions of political thought be compared with each other fruitfully? Is global only modern?' See their 'Introduction', 1.

the Kahal Kadosh seems quite new. Our figures engaged in considerations or activities they themselves categorized as 'political' by name. They took up the most urgent questions within Western politics. Significantly, they queried the category of politics itself in relation to Judaism. The innovation I point to here is thus not a Jewish discovery of politics or the political, if politics is understood, from a comparative or phenomenological perspective, as a basic and shared human activity across eras and cultures. Rather, visible in the foment of the Kahal Kadosh is the first point of contact between internal Jewish thought and the emerging modern western European idea of the polity and politics, in all their cultural specificity.

The point is easily missed because that very culturally specific idea of politics purported to be universal, and indeed, it shares an intellectual genealogy with the later 'political science', with its veneer of cultural neutrality. But in reality, the concept of *política* (like the *república*) with which the Jews of Amsterdam reckoned was a unique and particular product of Christian, classical, humanist, and European common-law ideas and practices. In fact, it was embedded in a discourse that was itself attentive to the relationship between Jewish and Gentile, or even Jewish and universal, politics. (It is no accident that the current political turn in Jewish studies was initially connected intellectually with attention to early modern Christian political interest in Jewish sources.) Such attention saturated Jews' own efforts to understand 'politics' in Jewish terms and vice versa. Under these conditions, in this cultural biosphere, hatched the notion that Jewish exilic politics constituted a peculiar paradox. From here emerged the notion of Jewish politicality as problematic in some way, as a question worthy of special consideration.

SEVEN

HISTORY

NARRATIVES OF JEWISH DEMOCRACY AND MONARCHY

T HE early seventeenth-century English exegete Andrew Willet is hardly a household name. But he captured something of the Christian polemics of his era when he wrote that the sceptre of Judah (*shevet yehudah*) must represent 'a reall and visible principalitic in Iudah'.[1] The famous benediction in Genesis 49: 10 that 'The sceptre will not depart from Judah, nor a lawgiver from between his feet, until Shiloh comes'[2] was a core text in debates between Jews and Christians, especially concerning exile, messianism, and Jewish political status, since 'Shiloh' was most often interpreted as a messianic figure.[3] Christians had long argued that the passage predicted that Jews would retain sovereign kingship until Jesus inherited it around the time of the destruction of the Temple and dawn of the exile. In supersessionist polemics, the verse was read as a prophecy of Christianity's rise and Judaism's fall, described in simultaneously religious and political terms.

Jewish thinkers over the centuries developed their own accounts of the sceptre's fate, treating past events, present circumstances, and scriptural meaning in practical and theopolitical terms. The most straightforward rebuttal to the Christian claim was to acknowledge the loss of the sceptre but deny that it had been passed to Christendom. Some, on the other hand, indicated that Shiloh had not yet come, arguing that a semi-autonomous 'lawgiver' stood in place of the sceptre while in exile, or even that the sceptre was in some sense still with Judah, contrary to appearances.

[1] Willet, *Hexapla*, 450.

[2] The JPS translation is not literal: 'The scepter shall not depart from Judah, / Nor the ruler's staff from between his feet; / So that tribute shall come to him / And the homage of peoples be his.'

[3] The passage continues to have symbolic power in Jewish historiography regarding power and politics in the diaspora. See e.g. Mittleman, *Scepter*, 19–35, and Hacker and Harel (eds.), *Sceptre* (Heb.).

Willet's 'reall and visible principalitic in Iudah' resisted the latter approach by insisting that Genesis 49: 10 could not refer to some kind of hidden dynasty or rabbinic court in the diaspora, as some Jewish commentators would have had it. It had to be an actual sovereign principality in the Holy Land. He brought the matter down to brass tacks and forced the hand of his (likely theoretical) Jewish opponents, who could not realistically say they possessed either prince or territory. Indeed, the few medieval and early modern Jewish sources that had claimed some exilic retention of the sceptre acknowledged its diminished form. They cast it as little more than a shadow, remnant, or symbol held by Torah scholars or descendants of Judah down through the generations. Among Jews, the sense of loss ran deep.

In contrast, as we have seen, beginning in the 1660s many members of the Kahal Kadosh Talmud Torah began to reconsider the narrative. They did not claim to have a principality in Judah, but they did see, in their community, a 'reall and visible' polity. They saw such a polity as significant in both mundane and theological terms. But the existence of a Jewish commonwealth in exile did not sit easily alongside a narrative of political establishment, loss, and eventual (messianic) restoration that was embedded at a molecular level in Jewish thought and religion—and that was, in its broadest outlines, shared with Christians as a universal world-historical story. How, then, did Jews in the age of Spinoza and Sabbatianism fit their Jewish exilic polity into the story of exile and redemption? They assimilated the new republican or commonwealth discourse into an older narrative conceived in monarchical terms, and adjusted their views of Jewish history. They situated the present state of Jewish politics within a long-term account of Jewish biblical, and especially post-biblical, affairs. Just as Christians commonly did in their political histories, these Jewish thinkers traced the paths of Jewish polities through the past in order to legitimize them, showing how they were recognized by humans and supported by divine will.

The new generic sense of the term 'republic', with all its capaciousness, had already opened a space for the Kahal Kadosh to be seen as a polity in the broadest sense. The preceding chapters have explored various dimensions of such politicality. Here, however, I turn to the specific sense of 'republic' as a form of government distinct from monarchy, to look at the historical imaginary of Jewish kingship as opposed to other forms of self-rule. In particular, I focus on conceptions of the Jewish polity as being ruled by the people. The new early modern attention to the republic of Moses had facilitated a look at non-monarchical rule in biblical times, but it was up to these Jewish thinkers to pursue the implications for other Jewish political settings, past and present. The men treated in this chapter thought in new ways about the biblical period as well. For both Isaac Orobio de Castro and Daniel Levi de Barrios—a polemicist and a poet, a politico and a Sabbatian—the distinction between kingship and popular rule was crucial to finding meaning in Jewish history.

República de por sí: Isaac Cardoso on the Sceptre

The stage will be set with a short digression into the ideas of another figure, one somewhat removed from the dynamics of the Kahal Kadosh Talmud Torah itself but similarly connected to the intellectual traditions of the converso diaspora. Isaac Cardoso (1603/4–83) was a physician with wide-ranging intellectual interests who had risen to a high rank in Spanish society before shedding his Catholic life in favour of his ancestral Judaism. He settled in Verona, Italy, where he composed his great work of apologetics *Las excelencias de los Hebreos*, which was published in Amsterdam in 1679 by David de Castro Tartaz, the same printer who published the synagogue sermons discussed above.[4]

Among his many reflections on the exemplary qualities of Jewish people, Cardoso included a short explanation of Jewish self-rule in exile, in relation to Genesis 49: 10:

The prophecy of Jacob, that the sceptre of Judah will not be removed, nor the scribe [*escrivano*] from between his feet, until Shiloh (Messiah) comes is miraculously explained thus: it means that the staff of dominion will not be taken away from the Jews until the coming of the Messiah: they will always maintain rule [*mando*], and be self-governed by their sages in their rites, ceremonies, weddings, burials, festivals, and traditions, all in conformity with the law with which God entrusted us.

The verse does not say crown, but rather staff, which indicates some dominion, and the word scribe refers to the sages who decree and sentence accord-

---

[4] On Cardoso, the essential work is still Yerushalmi, *From Spanish Court to Italian Ghetto*. See also Yosef Kaplan's introduction, 'Isaac Fernando Cardoso', appended to his Hebrew translation of Cardoso's *Excelencias*, and Kaplan, 'On the Relation'. See also Silvera, 'Contribution'.

ing to Scripture. Thus also in the Babylonian captivity they had their Judges, although subject to the Kings of Persia and Assyria, and even after the liberation in the Holy Land they had their judges, and sages subject either to Persians or to Romans; the same is true today among the nations, that they have their own governors and deputies as if they were a separate republic [*república separada*], with the concession and privilege of the princes who let them govern themselves according to their own laws and customs.[5]

The carefully worded passage raises a host of questions about Jewish political status in history and in Cardoso's day. His proud description of the Jewish community as a republic was aligned with the outlook of many members of the Kahal Kadosh in the two decades after 1666. Cardoso adopted a subtly different tone from that of the slightly earlier Jewish apologists like Menasseh ben Israel, Simone Luzzatto, and Leone Modena, who emphasized Jews' loyalty and lack of any threat or competition to Christian rulers.[6] Although Cardoso did write about the contributions Jews offered in Christian society, he avoided any sense that they were submissive or lowered, emphasizing instead their distinct positive characteristics and their legitimate separateness as a self-governing group.[7]

In that way, Cardoso's stance on the sceptre of Judah connected with attitudes then current in the Kahal Kadosh, but it differed from that of his recent predecessors in the Sephardi diaspora. In the long and intense history of Jewish–Christian polemics based on the verse, large-scale claims hinged on picayune details of translation and exegesis.[8] *Shevet* can be translated as 'sceptre', as it often is, but it can also mean 'staff' or 'rod'. Though both can be symbols of rule, they resonate differently, with only 'sceptre' specifically representing royalty. Likewise, the words translated as 'law-giver' (*meḥokek*) and 'until Shiloh comes' (*ad yavo shiloh*) in the King James Version quoted above permit a range of interpretations. *Meḥokek* could be rendered as scribe, scholar, or lawyer—all terms with different positions along the spectrum between government rule and legal or religious knowledge, and different potential manifestations within Jewish society. *Shiloh*, for its part, occurs nowhere else in the Hebrew Bible and could be a person

---

[5] Cardoso, *Excelencias*, 22.

[6] See Ravid, 'How Profitable'; Veltri, *Renaissance Philosophy*, 195–225; Septimus, 'Biblical Religion', 402.   [7] See Yerushalmi, *From Spanish Court to Italian Ghetto*, 468.

[8] A number of relevant commentaries are cited in Chazan, 'Genesis 49: 10'; Funkenstein, 'Basic Types'; Posnanski, *Schiloh*; and Menasseh ben Israel, *Conciliador*, 119–25.

('until Shiloh comes') or place ('until he comes to Shiloh'), or it could be a complex verb form meaning 'the one who will be sent' or 'him to whom the people will congregate'. Various exegetes over the ages also quibbled over 'depart', 'Judah', 'nor', 'between', 'feet', 'until', and 'comes', as they tried to parse the precise way the prediction had played out in historical events.

In Cardoso's telling, judges during the first exile, the Sanhedrin, and the lay rulers of the exilic diaspora all possessed what Jacob promised to Judah, keeping it in the hands of his descendants. Jewish sources offered much precedent for such a view, beginning with a passage of the Babylonian Talmud, where the *shevet* is said to denote the exilarch (who had power to enforce laws) and the *meḥokek* is said to refer to the *nasi* (who taught the laws and was descended from Hillel).[9] That passage treats the exilarch, who 'ruled', as the higher authority. In the Middle Ages, Rashi commented that the exilarchs received authority from the kingdom (*malkhut*), whereas scholars in his own day (*talmidim*), who were descendants of Hillel, embodied the *meḥokek*.[10]

In the twelfth century, according to Amos Funkenstein, there developed a new emphasis on subjugation as an essential feature of Jewish status in exile, with Jews and Christians alike beginning to interpret social and political circumstances as a sign of divine favour, and the sceptre of Judah provided a locus for such arguments.[11] Nahmanides wrote in his Torah commentary that the *meḥokek* was a Jewish judge empowered by non-Jewish authorities; he also argued, in his account of the famous Barcelona disputation, that the *shevet* indicated royal rule, only temporarily vacated from Judah.[12] Abraham Ibn Ezra wrote that 'Shiloh' was actually King David, disconnecting the loss of the sceptre chronologically from the rise of Christianity and limiting its significance to Judah's tribe alone.[13] Isaac Abravanel explained that Judah's particular heirs had some kind of leadership position in every generation, from the great exilarchs to latter-

---

[9] BT *Sanhedrin* 5a: '"The sceptre shall not depart from Judah"—these are the exilarchs in Babylon who rule over Israel with a sceptre. "Nor the ruler's staff from between his feet"—these are the sons of Hillel, who teach Torah in the public domain.' See also *Targums*, 151–2, 331.   [10] *Mikraot gedolot*, ii. 176.   [11] See Baer, *Galut*, 40; Funkenstein, 'Basic Types'.   [12] 'Judah did not have a sceptre before David . . . A sceptre only belongs to a king and ruler [*melekh* and *moshel*].' Nahmanides, *Perushei hatorah*, 267–70 (on Gen. 49: 10); 'Vikuaḥ haramban', 304–6 (paras. 11–18); and the English translation in Caputo and Clarke, *Debating Truth*, 925; and in Nahmanides, *Writings*, ii. 660–4. Chazan, 'Genesis 49: 10', lays out the debate and its stakes.   [13] *Mikraot gedolot*, ii. 176. See Chazan, 'Genesis 49: 10', 96.

day scholars, though in exile they made do with a lesser form of rule.[14] Such was the variety and creativity of Jewish interpretations.

After their own early modern expulsion, Spanish and Portuguese Jews had turned in a different direction and saw the scriptural passage in terms of exile, wandering, subjugation, and spiritual suffering. Beginning with Solomon Ibn Verga's *Shevet yehudah* (*c.*1520), a number of commentators treated the Spanish expulsion as an extreme example of the trials of *galut* in general. Ibn Verga explained the title of his work as a play on the term *shevet*, taking 'rod' or 'staff' to mean a tool of punishment:[15] Judah, who had once ruled, now suffered for his sins, flogged by the Almighty with his divine staff. This interpretation granted suffering a central place in exilic life, and it turned a beloved symbol of Jewish chosenness into one of punishment and loss. Samuel Usque put a similar emphasis on Jewish suffering in his *Consolação as tribulaçoens de Israel* (1553), as he explained the trials of exile as fulfilling biblical predictions and looked forward to their end in the time of messianic redemption.[16]

A few generations after Usque and Ibn Verga, another lachrymose interpretation of Genesis 49: 10 was offered by Elijah Montalto (d. 1616), though his was defined more by the experience of post-expulsion converso existence than by the expulsion itself. A converso who attended the court of Louis XIII after leaving Portugal, Montalto agreed that the *shevet* was a rod of punishment, and added that *meḥokek* predicted the laws, statutes, and tribunals (such as those of the Inquisition) that would be instituted to persecute Jews.[17] The same view was passed down by Saul Levi Morteira, who had first come to Amsterdam when he accompanied the body of the deceased Montalto out of France for burial. He later wrote that Genesis 49: 10 'shows us the punishment, whipping, and bloodshed that [Judah's] heirs would have to bear until the coming of that Prince of Peace'.[18]

[14] Abravanel, *Perush hatorah*, i. 766–70. Menasseh ben Israel had published a Spanish summary of Abravanel's interpretation alongside others in *Conciliador*, 124–5, most likely a source for Orobio.

[15] Ibn Verga, *Vara de yehudah*, 21. Ibn Verga published his work in Hebrew about 1520; Spanish (1640) and Latin (1651) translations were published in Amsterdam. On the book and the man, see J. Cohen, *A Historian in Exile*.

[16] Usque, *Samuel Usque's Consolation*, suggested that exilic suffering was redemptive, though he did not refer specifically to the *shevet* in this context.

[17] Montalto, *Libro*, MS Ros. 76, fos. 43ᵛ–45ᵛ. He also emphasized that this was only temporary, explaining that when *shevet* is read as 'sceptre', the verse promises that the monarchy will return to King David's line in messianic days. Montalto, *Libro*, MS Ros. 76, fos. 47ᵛ–48ᵛ.

[18] Morteira, *Obstaculos*, MS EH 48 D3, fos. 76–8.

Morteira's student Menasseh ben Israel marched to the beat of a different drum as usual, emphasizing the hope for restoration promised in Genesis 49: 10, linking the passage with Usque's suggestion that dispersion was key to Jewish survival through the time of exile, up to the messianic age.[19] He recast the image of the *shevet* as a stick or rod, calling it a walking stick that supported the Jews through their wandering. It represented progress rather than injustice, comfort rather than suffering.[20] Menasseh's take was well suited to his intercessionary activities seeking the official admission of Jews to England, a prospect that he hoped would appeal to Christian millenarians as well.[21]

These references to Genesis 49: 10 are examples of the way the culture of the Iberian Jewish diaspora centred exile and loss, with strong expressions of trouble and nostalgia.[22] But they should also be read for the way they stripped the *shevet* of positive politicality, keeping it as a marker of Jewish victimhood and powerlessness rather than self-rule, past or present. Conversos exerted a marked influence on the politics and culture of the Spanish crown in the fifteenth, sixteenth, and seventeenth centuries, both as powerful individuals and, as scholars have increasingly recognized, as a group.[23] Some of them carved for themselves a distinct theopolitical place in the Catholic monarchy, one that was related to the tradition of Jewish self-identification as intimate with kings. The converso awareness of their politicality as conversos, however, directly contrasts with the sense of what was possible as Jews. As conversos, they might be part of a body politic, albeit in problematic ways; as Jews, on the other hand, at least in their perception, they were cut off from any such participation. The Jews of Spain and Portugal had had a taste of what it meant to be a full subject of a sovereign, but after the expulsion, they saw membership in a polity as precisely what Jewishness precluded.

[19] Menasseh ben Israel, '*Even yeqarah*, 72–3. Usque did not connect this 'consolation' with Genesis 49: 10; Usque, *Consolation*, 227.

[20] A similar attitude to exile is present in Menasseh ben Israel, *Hope of Israel*, with the expectation that the lost tribes were awaiting discovery in the New World.

[21] Katz, *Philo-semitism*; Popkin, 'Christian Jews'; Popkin and Goldish (eds.), *Millenarianism*.

[22] See Wacks, *Double Diaspora*; Swetschinski, 'Un refus de mémoire'; and den Boer, 'Exile'; as well as Yerushalmi, 'Exile', and Baer, *Galut*.

[23] See Stuczynski, 'Toward a Repolitization', and the other essays included in the same special issue of the *Journal of Levantine Studies*, especially Yisraeli, 'Were God's People', and Cohen Skalli, 'Don Isaac Abravanel'; as well as other work by Stuczynski, especially 'From Polemics' and 'Pro-Converso Apologetics'; along with Rosenstock, *New Men*.

In a sharp divergence from the above interpretive tradition, Cardoso's interpretation of the sceptre of Judah recognized the existence of Jewish self-governments as settings in which Jews could be full participants, where Jews constituted a body politic. Whereas earlier commentary had accounted for types of individual Jewish leaders, whether rabbinic or lay, that could count as perpetuating Jacob's promise, Cardoso made room for a republic as the manifestation of Judah's *mando*. Strikingly, whereas earlier sources had set non-monarchical rule apart as an explicitly lower form, identifying it with the *meḥokek* (lawgiver) in order to see the prophecy fulfilled through an era without a sceptre, Cardoso emphasized that collective self-rule represented the *shevet* itself even without sovereignty. (He shared with Orobio the rhetorical and linguistic move of insisting that *shevet* need not mean sceptre, but rather 'rule', as the reader may recall from Chapter 5, but the two men used it to different purposes. I shall return to Orobio below.) In calling individual communities 'republics'—a community was a *república de por sí*, a republic unto itself—Cardoso made full use of the new politics of the later seventeenth century to make a proud statement of status, seeing Jewish communities as politically real and legitimate sites of power, or rule (*mando*). He ascribed to them enough significance that they—not rabbis or exilarchs—could stand in for the sceptre in this central theological narrative of Jewish history.

Politics and Jewish Historiography

Ibn Verga and Usque's books belong to a set of historically oriented writings from the sixteenth century. Along with works by Immanuel Aboab, Joseph Hakohen, Elijah Capsali, Azariah de' Rossi, and others, they make up a flurry of chronological and documentary narratives written by Jews in the wake of the Spanish expulsion. Much has been made of this turn to history among early modern Jews, the first of their co-religionists for many centuries to embrace the topic of world events or the genre of the chronicle, apparently prompted by their authors' search for continuity and consolation in the wake of cultural disruption.[24] Yosef Hayim Yerushalmi most

[24] See J. Cohen, *A Historian in Exile*, 1–2 and 6–8. Examples include Baron, 'Azariah'; Ben-Sasson, 'Generation'; Yerushalmi, 'Exile'; and Gutwirth, 'Expulsion'. Scholem's characterization of Lurianic kabbalah, with a narrative 'myth' (as opposed to history) as a response to the same 'crisis', is related. Other treatments of early modern Jewish historiography include Jacobs, 'Joseph ha-Kohen'.

famously celebrated the sixteenth-century flowering of Jewish historiography, which, he said, signalled a shift in perceptions of the Jewish place
in the world. However, he noted, the effort was stunted. Jewish interest in
chronicling post-biblical affairs was not sustained, as Jews turned instead
to messianic or mystical interpretations of the meaning of world events
and the passage of time. This Yerushalmi explained as the inevitable result
of the fact that a fundamental attitude towards historiography in Jewish
culture remained unchanged: the perception of history as extraneous to
Jewish thought, no more than a 'diversion', and certainly not a central
pathway to 'ultimate truths, to spiritual felicity, and to self-knowledge'.[25]

Yerushalmi discussed only briefly the reason why history did not take
hold as a Jewish art or science before modernity. He wrote that the early
modern Jewish thinkers' ultimate rejection of historiography was not a
mere accident of religious evolution, but rather a sign of their fundamental
alienation from the typical stuff of the genre. History told of 'kings and
their wars', both of which Jews lacked, so they could only be bystanders to
history. Ibn Verga, for example, fell back on discussing Christian kings even
though his ultimate interest lay in the Jewish experience under their rule;
and he acknowledged apologetically that 'chronicles of kings' were a Christian occupation.

Robert Bonfil and Amos Funkenstein expanded on similar themes.
Bonfil denied that the works of sixteenth-century Jews could truly be called
Jewish historiography at all because of 'the essential incompatibility of the
subject matter of history, as conceived in those days, and the destiny of
their people the world over'; without 'political and military' activity, Jews
'appeared not to have a history at all, and this was one of the many expressions of the difference between the Jewish and non-Jewish conditions'.[26]
Therefore, premodern Jews could either write about themselves or write
'history', but never do both fully and authentically at the same time. Within
a framework where historiography entails politics, exilic Jews' lack of full
self-determination as a collective makes it impossible to treat the collective
as a historical agent and make the Jewish people the protagonist of its own
tale.

In such a view there is an unexamined identification of politics with
sovereignty and an unspoken assumption that the possession of sovereignty

[25] Yerushalmi, 'Clio', 615.   [26] Bonfil, 'How Golden', 95.

is existentially distinct from other ways of acting and being in the world. Funkenstein, in dialogue with Yerushalmi and Bonfil, took up a more expansive definition of historiography, one that would include most discussions of the Jewish past, including polemical and theological interpretations of Jewish political status rather than only chronicles.[27] In that case, works that acknowledged or even emphasized Jewish subjugation would be counted among premodern Jewish historiographical works. As he wrote, after all, many Jewish writers did see the Jewish people in exile as 'political objects rather than subjects'.[28] They felt themselves to have a unique and significant history, in a universal sense of change over time, even though medieval conventions of historiography as a genre focused on the very thing whose absence made Jewish history unique: a king. In fact, as Yerushalmi would agree, the relationship to kings and kingship was a central component of medieval Jewish collective memory and the new sixteenth-century historiography.

Indeed, the significance of kingship, in both positive and negative senses, to perceptions of Jewish uniqueness cannot be overstated, especially as regards the Sephardi diaspora. After all, before Morteira's rephrasing and the wider realignments of the seventeenth century, what distinguished Jews from other populations in medieval parlance was not the lack of 'sovereignty' or a 'state', since those are both distinctly modern concepts. Rather, they lacked a 'king' or 'kingdom'. What would become modern state sovereignty belonged for the most part, in the Middle Ages, to a human sovereign, and within such a world-view a Jewish community of the sort that had developed in medieval Europe was of a totally different order than a royal realm.

The condition of exile was defined by the lack of a king, especially after the decline of the closest thing to that, the exilarchate. Many remarked on the miraculous continuity of Jews as a nation without territory or sovereign defender. However, the lack did not make them value kingship any less. Even apart from their most intimate connection to the biblical and messianic kings, medieval Jews tended to see monarchy as the highest, or

[27] Funkenstein, 'Basic Types'.
[28] Funkenstein: European historiography was 'first and foremost political historiography; it focused on the clear bearers of political power, on rulers and their actions'. Therefore, 'the communities of Israel, in the Diaspora and in Israel "in Arabian chains", saw themselves as political objects rather than subjects'; *Perceptions*, 16.

indeed the only proper, form of government,[29] and often prized special relationships to the princes and kings of the nations. From status as *servi camerae*, or serfs of the (king's) chamber, to their presence as advisers, physicians, and *négociants* alongside monarchs and nobles, to their activities as intercessors, where individuals advocated for the interests of whole populations, Jewish relationships with the highest rulers often superseded those with local collectives or populations.[30]

A tripartite relationship to monarchy—lacking their own, but cosy with others', and expecting a restoration—was thus a central component of Jewish difference from other nations. The Spanish expulsion, which was described by some Jewish witnesses as a betrayal of the long-standing close alliance between Jews and the crown, forced new notice of that relationship as an inherent source of instability and tension.[31] The early modern chronicles that seem so uncomfortably to focus on Christian affairs were first attempts to consider the era of non-sovereign diaspora as an era in which Jewishly significant events—events that meant something theologically, or perhaps that forged new collective memory, in Yerushalmi's terms—took place.[32] If medieval thinkers could say typologically that exile was an era of kinglessness, the sixteenth-century historiographers turned to the world around them in distinctly early modern fashion to recount, document, and analyse the realities of kinglessness and Jewish adjacency to kingship.

Against that backdrop, Cardoso's valuation of the Jewish republic, specifically as an entity that was self-governed rather than governed by a monarch, stands as a notable shift, and one that aligned with the self-image of members of the Kahal Kadosh. The political language of the day served well to facilitate an understanding of *mando* that fulfilled the Jewish political destiny even though it was not fully independent, as commonwealth discourse made space for a more flexible, contingent, and contract-based association—a Jewish republic—to be a polity, and not only that, but one with historical significance. Still, however, Cardoso did not fully erase the distinction between exilic self-rule and the fuller rule of a sovereign, as he acknowledged that Jews had once been kings and someday would reign again. Like his predecessors, he still treated exilic Jewish political status as

---

[29] Walzer et al. (eds.), *The Jewish Political Tradition*, i. 113, 122–6, 147–65; A. Melamed, 'Attitude', 173–4.   [30] See Yerushalmi, *Servants*, and id., *Lisbon Massacre*.

[31] Yerushalmi, *Lisbon Massacre*; id., *Servants*; Netanyahu, *Don Isaac Abravanel*, 173–80.

[32] Yerushalmi, 'Clio', 616.

inferior, emphasizing its limited and dependent status. He specifically contrasted Jewish republics with kings. He described communities as being self-ruled 'with the concession and privilege of the princes who let them govern themselves according to their own laws and customs'—just as, in the past, judges had been 'subject to the Kings of Persia and Assyria, and even after the liberation in the Holy Land they had their judges, and sages subject either to Persians or to Romans'.[33]

For Cardoso, the distinction between dependent and sovereign was couched, consciously or not, as that between republic and monarchy—between leaders he called 'judges', 'sages', 'governors', and 'deputies' in the Jewish republic, on the one hand, and 'kings and princes' on the other. He celebrated the Jewish republic for what it was, and at the same time perpetuated in substantial ways a traditional way of framing the Jewish relationship to monarchs. In Cardoso's extensive discussion of Jewish greatness, his account of the self-governing republic quoted here was only an aside. He devoted more space in the famous apologetic work to enumerating the lessons that Judaism had to offer to kings, in a politicized version of traditional justification of exile as a chance to serve as a light to the nations.[34] While Jews lacked their own king, they were called to advise the kings of the nations, teaching them the divine politics that their tradition contained, while at the same time proudly maintaining a separate and lower republic of their own.

Cardoso's account also limited Jewish self-rule in exile in another way, as he characterized it as pertaining to Jewish 'laws and customs': their 'rites and ceremonies, weddings, burials, festivals, [and] traditions'.[35] His portrayal of Jewish self-rule as political but simultaneously as limited to religion was an awkward product of this stage of Jewish explorations of the relationship between religion and politics, or Jewish law and temporal authority. Like Abraham Pereyra's treatment of the community as an arena of divine law, Cardoso's portrayal seems, in one light, to move in the direction of later reformers who would limit community to the religious (in the eighteenth century understood specifically as *lacking* political or temporal rule).

[33] He also quoted the ancient Greek historian Strabo: in Alexandria 'the Hebrews had designated streets where they lived according to their law with governors from their own nation, with absolute power, as a republic of their own [*república de por sí*]'; Cardoso, *Excelencias*, 17a. Barrios used the same passage: *Triumpho*, 31.

[34] Baer attributed the origin of this notion to Judah Halevi in *Galut*.

[35] Cardoso, *Excelencias*, 22.

But, also like Pereyra, Cardoso insisted on the political nature of such a religious collective: it constituted *mando*, or self-'rule'; it existed in political
relationship to other rulers; and it was relevant to the broadest and more
important narratives of Jewish political history.

In the light of the problematic established by modern historians like
Yerushalmi, Cardoso's historical account of Jewish political status is significant in that it bridges a perceived gap between communal affairs and
geopolitics, between exilic limitations and 'real' history. Further, Cardoso
seems to identify in the diaspora republic a 'reall and visible' republic, in a
way that anticipates the attention that other modern historians, such as
Baron, Dinur, and Dubnow, lavished on the semi-autonomous community.

Within the Kahal Kadosh in Amsterdam, much more extensive thinking was taking place about how to make the two kinds of Jewish politics
—exilic and sovereign, republican and monarchical—work together in a
master-narrative. Isaac Orobio de Castro and Daniel Levi de Barrios are
two who explored how Jews had ruled in different ways at different times,
offering innovative accounts of Jewish political history that also included
their own community. Each produced a large oeuvre, much of which was
polemical, philosophical, poetic, or eulogistic, and broadly participated in
the cultural modes of their era. In life, the two men clashed. Orobio was
philosophical and polemical, while Barrios was literary and universalizing.
In the 1670s, Orobio tried to counter the ideas of Sabbatian speculators,
having rejected the movement within a year or two of the apostasy.[36]
Barrios, on the other hand, hung on every notice from Sabbatai Zevi and
the interpretations of Abraham Miguel Cardoso, whose Sabbatian beliefs
did not meet the approval of his brother, the aforementioned Isaac.[37]
Orobio and Barrios differed in many respects, but both set their minds to
the relationship between republic and monarchy in the Jewish context,
and in doing so both drew on traditions that emphasized self-rule or the
rule of the people. Orobio located a model for such a republic in the self-
governing biblical tribe of Judah. For Barrios, it was the lay-led diaspora
community and its apotheosis, the Kahal Kadosh.

[36] Y. Kaplan, *From Christianity to Judaism*, 209–34.
[37] Scholem, *Sabbatai Ṣevi*, 894. In the middle of the decade the two fought over a publication
of Barrios's that Orobio saw as both philosophically erroneous and, paradoxically, also plagia-
rized from his own work. See Y. Kaplan, *From Christianity to Judaism*, 229–34, on this 'quarrel'.
Kaplan indicates that they were reconciled by 1677, even though Barrios had not fully
renounced Sabbatianism.

Orobio on the Republic of Judah

In one long section of his polemical opus, *Prevenciones divinas contra la vana idolatria de las gentes*, Orobio addressed Jewish rule through the lens of Genesis 49: 10. Over the course of a long and arcane discussion, Orobio offered several seemingly incompatible interpretative paraphrases of the prophecy regarding the fate of Judah's sceptre. On scrutiny, Orobio's apparent self-contradictions resolve into a consistent overarching scheme of Jewish history. The readings cohere in a chronological account of the vicissitudes of Jewish self-rule, with Orobio imparting different meanings to the passage for different periods of history.

One such reading—discussed above in connection with Hakham Aboab's treatment of rabbinic authority—insisted that, in Orobio's own time, it was rabbis who wielded the ultimate temporal authority represented by the sceptre. He wrote that the *shevet* is best translated as *vara*, or 'staff', and 'not sceptre [*ce[p]tro*], or kingdom [*reino*], as Christians necessarily want to understand it'.[38] The distinction, of course, was that 'staff' denoted any kind of 'rule', what Orobio called *mando*, and not necessarily kingship. In this he agreed, of course, with Cardoso's remark that 'the verse does not say crown, but rather staff, which indicates some dominion, and the word scribe refers to the sages who decree and sentence according to Scripture'. Different, however, was that Orobio saw rabbinic authority in general, meta-communal terms, describing rabbis as judges who ruled over all Jews everywhere, quite apart from communal lay leadership, whereas Cardoso's admittedly vague description rather gives the impression that Jewish self-governing authority was local and mixed, comprising both 'governors' and 'sages'.

Orobio and Cardoso shared similar backgrounds as converso physicians, and they both wrote to a great extent with Christians and Christianity in mind. But where Cardoso was an apologist, Orobio was a polemicist: Cardoso sought to elevate Christian opinion of Jews and Judaism, while Orobio sought theological and exegetical victory. *Prevenciones* showcases Orobio's extraordinary knowledge of Christian sources,[39] and Christian scholars of Hebrew representing a range of perspectives are named in his text. Significantly, many appear as expert expositors—trusted scholarly

---

[38] Orobio, *Prevenciones*, MS Ros. 631, p. 76.

sources—and not only as argumentative foils. The text also shows Orobio's awareness of many earlier Jewish interpretations, though he usually did not name them and seems not to have used Hebrew sources. Rather, he relied on the numerous translations, compendia, and commentaries that were produced in sixteenth- and seventeenth-century Europe. Taking inspiration from this vast store of commentary, Orobio struck out on his own with a complex argument that suited his polemical aims, cleverly accounted for a wide range of textual possibilities, and centred on the key observation that the sceptre need not represent kingship in order to represent rule.

The core of his approach was to say that Judah was promised a republic of his own, for his tribe alone, distinct from the other tribes and entirely independent. Orobio explicitly favoured this reading above others, as the one that was literally and historically correct.[40] It emphasized that the biblical Jacob and his son Judah were real men relating to each other and to the political and cultural circumstances of the patriarchal era, locating the entire drama of the *shevet* within that setting. Orobio expressed the promise from father to son as follows:

As long as the people would live in freedom, [beginning] from the exit from Egypt and entrance into the Holy Land, they [Judah's tribe] would not lack . . . a particular pre-eminence and independent rule, set apart from the rest of the tribes and constituting a different house from all of Israel, as a republic unto itself [*república de por sí*].[41]

Orobio followed Ibn Ezra's interpretation in some important respects, including the idea that Judah's tribe was pre-eminent among the tribes, but only until the rise of King David, identified as Shiloh. At that time the tribe lost its independence as it joined the others as part of a higher kingdom. Orobio described the transition in terms of political theory, explaining that Judah's tribe lost its *mando* by definition when it was incorporated into a larger kingdom:

[39] Orobio's use of Christian sources supports Kaplan's view of him as deeply connected to the intellectual trends of his day in Spain, France, and the Dutch Republic. See Y. Kaplan, *From Christianity to Judaism*, 167–78 and 235–9. In his Gen 49: 10 discussion alone, Orobio mentions, cites, relies on, or responds to Nicholas of Lyra, John Calvin, Juan de Pineda, Immanuel Tremellius (1510–80), Franciscus Junius the Elder (1545–1602), Giovanni Diodati (1576–1649), Arias Montanus (1527–98), Sanctus Pagninus (1470–1536), Grotius, Cocceius, Spinoza, and many more.
[40] Since 'the most fitting explanation of any text of the holy Scripture is that which is deduced from its own context'; Orobio, *Prevenciones*, MS Ros. 631, p. 75.   [41] Ibid., p. 76.

The staff, or particular rule [*mando*], of a republic independent of the eleven [other] tribes would not depart from Judah . . . until Shiloh, his son the King David, would come . . . because all the peoples or tribes of Israel would set themselves under his monarchical government, and then the former rule or republican government . . . would cease and depart from Judah.[42]

Polemically, this served Orobio in denying that the end of Judah's rule, represented by possession of the *shevet*, was chronologically close to the time of Jesus. It also allowed him to deny that Judah's loss of the *shevet* was indicative of a loss of Jewish status, either earthly or spiritual. On the contrary, with the rise of David the Jewish people as a whole gained a kingdom; it was only the Judites who lost their sovereignty as a distinct people. As a blessing from a father to only one of his sons, Orobio pointed out, the prophecy focused on what Judah would have that his brothers would not.[43] The departure of the *shevet* from Judah stood not for Jewish disenfranchisement but for Jewish national political glory to the detriment of Judah's particular tribe.[44]

Orobio's priorities went beyond pinpointing the historical context of the sceptre to focus on characteristics of the Judite republic itself. In positing the true original meaning of the verse as promising a Judite republic, rather than a Jewish kingdom, Orobio reversed the chronological order that was typical of Genesis 49: 10 exegesis among Jews and Christians alike. Instead of being a sceptre that was lost, or that had devolved into some lesser form of rule over time in exile, for Orobio the *shevet* was a staff representing republican self-rule from the start. Relegating monarchy to the time of Judah's loss of status, Orobio implicitly suggested that Judah's republican, pre-Davidic regime was prized in itself and preferable to the monarchy, at least for Judah and his kinsmen.

In addressing not Moses' republic but Judah's, Orobio expanded on contemporaneous interest in the biblical Jewish republic. Abravanel had

---

[42] Orobio, *Prevenciones*, 81.

[43] Nahmanides also made this point in his commentary on the passage.

[44] Orobio may also have been inspired to dissociate Judah's sceptre from the political fate of the entire Jewish people by the efforts he witnessed among Christians in order to connect them. After all, it was only later, during the Second Temple period, that the whole kingdom was called Judah. See Cunaeus's remark that 'Jacob's prophecy about the scepter of Judah refers only to that time when the state began to be named after the Jews' (*Hebrew Republic*, 38). In Orobio's view, why not simplify things and say that the prophecy referred to Judah's own state?

already written that the republic was the ideal form of Jewish polity,[45] but
he focused on the Mosaic republic, as did most exegetes. It was, after all,
only Moses who established a polity governed by divine law, inherently of
interest to Christians exploring church–state relations. Orobio, however,
seems to have been interested in the republic of Judah as a different sort of
example: he was especially focused on Judah's total independence and self-
rule rather than its relationship to divine law. Orobio wrote that, under
David's empire (*imperio*), 'the peoples or tribes [*pueblos o tribus*] of Israel
would be united in a monarchical government; and then Judah would lack
that republican or autocratic [*dispostico*] government, becoming subject to
the monarchy along with the rest of the peoples of Israel'.[46] Note well that
in this passage Orobio treats each tribe as a separate 'people', rather than
seeing all Hebrews (or Jews) as one.

For Orobio's seventeenth-century readers, the scenario he described
was familiar. In the Dutch Republic, independence—in Orobio's terms,
status as a 'republic'—had been shaped by the quest for release from
Spanish imperial rule. Anti-monarchist discourse in Holland made use
of a 'foundation myth' of the biblical Jewish commonwealth, placing such
self-rule in opposition to monarchical subjugation.[47] Stark rhetorical
dichotomies between republican and monarchical rule notwithstanding,
however, in Orobio's time European monarchies and burgeoning colonial
empires were often composite entities, bringing together diverse peoples
into some kind of mixed whole. The relationship between sub-units and
the monarchy that reigned over all was both pragmatically and theoretically complex. It was certainly possible to understand some groups within
an empire as republics unto themselves. Semi-independent city commonwealths—and the Kahal Kadosh—are examples. In another sense, ethnic
and religious minorities were also sometimes referred to as 'republics'
within a wider imperial state.[48]

Orobio himself gave a sense of this scenario through two biblical examples: the tribe of Simeon, who, Orobio said, lived like a foreign nation
within the territory and republic of Judah;[49] and the tribe of Judah after its

---

[45] He contradicted Maimonides' ruling—and the common perception—that kingship was
the preferred form of government for the Jewish people. See Kimelman, 'Abravanel'.

[46] Orobio, *Prevenciones*, MS Ros. 631, p. 76.

[47] Boralevi, 'Classical Foundation Myths'.   [48] See Deardorff, 'Republics'.

[49] Simeon 'did not have his own lot in the land of Israel, but rather always stayed dispersed
in Judah, and had his possessions in the same lot as Judah, remaining thus incorporated into

incorporation into David's kingdom, when it continued to be a 'distinct realm' (*reino differente*) with semi-separate status.[50] One might analogize Simeon among the Judites to Jews in Christendom, or perhaps to a merchant colony in a port city; likewise, Orobio seems to have imagined Judah's status under King David to that of Portugal under Philip II of Spain. Meanwhile, Grotius and Spinoza had both written, along the same lines, that in the era of the Mosaic republic the separate tribes were not fully incorporated into a single polity but, rather, existed as separate polities loosely unified. As Spinoza described it: 'the different tribes should be considered rather in the light of confederated states than of bodies of fellow-citizens. ... They were, in fact, in much the same position (if one excepts the Temple common to all) as the United States of the Netherlands.'[51]

Although a 'republic' could be semi-autonomous, that was not how Orobio meant the reader to conceive of Judah's prophesied republic. In Orobio's telling, the tribe of Judah was sovereign—the only tribe that was so.[52] As he wrote, he intended to prove not that Judah's tribe 'had some separation or independence from the other tribes, but that it would *rule itself*'.[53] As discussed above in Chapter 5, Orobio emphasized that Judah's *mando*, or 'rule', denoted ultimate authority—sovereignty. As he put it, 'it is not the same to rule as to be ruled, to obey as to be obeyed, to dominate as to be dominated'.[54] Judah's descendants' later status as subjects of a monarch was precisely the opposite of what Judah was promised in Genesis 49: 10. Until David's reign, Judah's kinsmen were, in Orobio's eyes, fully their own masters in a self-ruled republic. Orobio's view was a creative con-

---

it. Even though it was a different tribe according to ancestry, it was the same as Judah by habitation. ... This tribe being possessed among the cities and places of Judah, in the political government as in military expeditions, it would follow the government and dispositions of Judah. ... Together they made up a single province, and, not being invaded by enemies, enjoyed a single peace and tranquillity': Orobio, *Prevenciones*, MS Ros. 631, pp. 78–9.

[50] Ibid., p. 81.

[51] *TPT*, 224. Grotius had at first envisaged the new republic as a sovereign union, where the provinces as a group would have a common ruling council—a scenario that he compared to the Hebrew republic when ruled by judges. Later, in *De republica emendada*, he abandoned this view and treated the separate provinces as having their own seats of rule. Tuck, *Philosophy and Government*, 163–4. See also van Gelderen, 'Machiavellian Moment', 217.

[52] Orobio drew on Ibn Ezra's comment that the *shevet* was a sign of Judah's status as a leader among the tribes, noting that when the tribes went out together (to battle), Judah's flag was always in the front, and the *shevet* was a 'staff of greatness' (*shevet gedulah*). Orobio, *Prevenciones*, MS Ros. 631, p. 77; Menasseh ben Israel, *Conciliador*, 122; see Num. 10: 14.

[53] Orobio, *Prevenciones*, MS Ros. 631, p. 77.   [54] Ibid., p. 68.

tribution to contemporary biblical chronology and political biblicism, in
addition to the polemics about the sceptre.

In his insistence on pre-Davidic Judite sovereignty Orobio may have
been influenced by Petrus Cunaeus, who scoffed in *The Hebrew Republic* at
those who might think the sceptre of Judah could mean anything other
than fully realized sovereignty. Arguing against the idea that some lesser
form of rule might still count as retention of the *shevet*, Cunaeus emphasized that 'the sceptre about which the prophecy spoke can only be the
Jewish republic, i.e. that priestly kingdom whose rites and practices were
not, Heaven forbid, some mere afterthought or prop with which to shore it
up, but its very soul and spirit'.[55] In fact, the entire first book of Cunaeus's
famous work can be read as a polemic regarding the sceptre of Judah,[56]
aiming to prove that the Jewish biblical republic's existence depended on
the combination of its own laws and its own land[57]—two criteria for sovereignty—and that without those 'the state was to be annihilated and the sovereignty that had once been given to the sacred nation taken away from
it'.[58] Orobio agreed with Cunaeus that the *shevet* did not indicate royalty;
as Cunaeus put it, 'some very foolish people paint themselves into a corner
by claiming that the honour of being called "sovereign" belongs only to
kings; in fact, any people that has its own state and lives under its own laws
can quite properly take pride in its authority and its sovereignty'.[59] But
Orobio also agreed that the *shevet* did indicate sovereignty, and he set about
to show that Judah had it.

In fact, he followed Cunaeus's method of using details of Scripture to
examine Judah's republic as a realistic state, with military, diplomatic, legislative, executive, and judicial dimensions. Of these he paid particular attention to the military and the legal/judicial dimensions. Regarding the

---

[55] This particular comment regarded the rabbinic court in Babylonia. Cunaeus, *Hebrew Republic*, 35.

[56] He does not mention the passage until chapter 8, but in chapter 9 he explains the genesis of the entire project in a conversation with a colleague about the sceptre of Judah: that 'there was no prophecy in the Holy Book that scholars had sweated over more and yet understood less . . . I therefore believe, with his support, that it is completely right and proper, given the large number of conjectures about this illustrious prophecy, that I too should publish my own' (Cunaeus, *Hebrew Republic*, 38). He also frames the book as an exposition largely of Mai-monides (p. 15), and the monarchy/republic distinction is the main point on which he contra-dicts him (p. 35).

[57] Agrarian law and the sabbatical/jubilee system were especially admired by Cunaeus, who thought that commerce was the seed of republican collapse in the Dutch Republic. See Tuck, *Philosophy and Government*, 167–8.   [58] Cunaeus, *Hebrew Republic*, 32.   [59] Ibid. 40.

former, he explained that Judah was independent 'in military expeditions, mustering of soldiers, [and] resolutions of state',[60] specifically noting that Judites

did not go along as a part of Israel in military expeditions, but rather that Judah was independent, and only joined with the rest when his reason of state obliged him to, or when it was convenient for him. . . . Judah, being independent and separate in the form of a republic from the rest of the Tribes, was not obligated to go out to battle with them.[61]

Military action was, like capital punishment, a widely recognized sign of sovereignty. To name just two examples, Machiavelli wrote that control of the military constituted independence, and Grotius named the ability to defend territory as a key to sovereignty.[62] In the Dutch Republic, the unification of the separate provinces had in the first place coalesced around a joint war effort.[63] For Orobio it was straightforward to recognize Judah's military independence as evidence of the tribe's 'reall and visible principalitic'—comparable to a seventeenth-century sovereign state.

Legal independence, on the other hand, was a more complicated issue since Orobio had to contend with how Judah's independent republic related to the authority of the judges and the law of Moses. He wrote that Judah's tribe had 'a giver and executor of laws different from the rest, which is to have a staff or rule, and scribe between his feet'[64]—meaning, apparently, that the Judite tribe had its own executive and legislative apparatus, setting its own rules that did not contradict biblical law but were separate from it. Strikingly, the relationship between Judah's governors and Mosaic law depicted there is parallel to the one that existed in Orobio's community, between the governors of the Kahal Kadosh and rabbinic law.

In another passage, Orobio wrote that Judah had 'his own judges'[65] and 'an independent judiciary' that constituted its 'rule, [i.e. its] status as a republic'. Orobio threaded a very fine needle in suggesting here that the

[60] Orobio, *Prevenciones*, MS Ros. 631, p. 76.

[61] Ibid., pp. 77–8, citing Deborah and Barak's victory song (Judg. 5: 2–31), which does not mention Judah.

[62] An overarching treatment of the emergence of Westphalian sovereignty and Grotius on the just war is found in Johnson, *Sovereignty*, especially ch. 4, pp. 81–100. Miglietti, 'Sovereignty', argues that Bodin was much more influential in this area than has previously been recognized.

[63] Grotius had seen military endeavours as critical to its unity. Tuck, *Philosophy and Government*, 162.   [64] Orobio, *Prevenciones*, MS Ros. 631, p. 77.   [65] Ibid., p. 76.

judges in Judah decided law in compliance with the law of Moses but were still absolutely independent because they served the Judite government alone. Thus, Judah had 'a judiciary or tribunal of justice with his own private ministers . . . between his feet, which means under obedience to him'.[66] In this view, in order to count towards fulfilling Jacob's promise of a 'scribe between [Judah's] feet until Shiloh comes', Judah's judges did not need to be descended from Judah (as Abravanel had indicated) but rather to 'exercise this office in service of the Tribe of Judah'.[67] This was, Orobio explained, just what 'occurs now in the political Kingdoms of Europe', where a judge's personal nation of origin was irrelevant to the question of whether his court was under a particular king's dominion.[68]

Orobio did account for Mosaic law superseding Judah's jurisdiction, in a way. He admitted that the tribe's 'own judiciary and rule' did not replace 'that universal divine judgement that the Lord instituted in the priesthood and Sanhedrin—that which would be, in terms of appeals, like an ecclesiastical tribunal superior to all others'. Indeed, it was that very authority that was passed on to rabbis in exile, in accordance with his alternative reading of Genesis 49: 10, to wit: 'the holy Patriarch [Jacob] says that Israel will never lack these scribes until the messiah comes, even if it lacks the sceptre [*ceptro*] and kingdom'.[69] The religious authority of the judges, the Sanhedrin, and the rabbis was thus differentiated from the government of a polity in Orobio's complex treatment.[70] The republic of Judah was evidently sovereign because of its executive, legal, judicial, military, and territorial self-rule. It was the picture of a 'reall and visible principalitie'. But Orobio went against the conventional wisdom of the day when he suggested that, among biblical Jews, there was separation between divine law and the republic, or church and state.

Such separation was related to Orobio's conception of the Judite republic's sovereignty as located in the people of the tribe. Here again, he was likely spurred to think this way by Cunaeus. In his polemical biblical Jewish political history, the Christian had glossed over various changes

---

[66] Orobio, *Prevenciones*, MS Ros. 631, pp. 80–1.

[67] Abravanel, *Perush hatorah*, i. 766–70.   [68] Orobio, *Prevenciones*, MS Ros. 631, pp. 71–2.

[69] Saying that the verse can be read as a promise that Judah would retain *either* the sceptre *or* the scribe, meaning the kingship or the rabbinic judge. Orobio, *Prevenciones*, MS Ros. 631, p. 73.

[70] Elsewhere, addressing anti-Jewish attitudes, he wrote that 'Israel is abominated the world over, because nowhere do they enjoy the authority that comes with self-government'. Quoted in translation in Y. Kaplan, *From Christianity to Judaism*, 367.

in Jewish political systems, claiming simply that the sceptre remained with the Jewish people whether they had a king or not:[71] 'this sovereign authority remained in the hands of the Jews from the moment they first acquired it, even though the conditions of the state changed from time to time, and supreme power rested sometimes in the hands of aristocrats and priests, and sometimes in the hands of kings and princes'.[72] Orobio, by contrast, took seriously the change in location of sovereignty when a king was set up. David's empire annihilated Judah's republic by taking away its self-determination and moving the source of sovereignty from the people of Judah to a divinely ordained king. Perhaps Orobio was influenced here by Spinoza's discussion of the original biblical democracy and its fate. I return to this point below.

Divine-Right Monarchy and the Fate of the Sceptre

So much for the period of history during which Judah's tribe had a sovereign republic. We have seen that Orobio was committed to a literal historical reading of Genesis 49: 10 in which the prediction had been completely fulfilled by the time of David. We have also seen that he offered a longer-term, universalist interpretation in which the *mando* promised to Judah's descendants was later retained by Jews, specifically by rabbis, represented by the word 'scribe' or 'lawgiver' (*meḥokek*) in the passage.[73]

Combining the two readings chronologically, and taking into account my discussion of excommunication above in Chapter 5, a picture emerges of a two-part scheme of Jewish history, wherein biblical (republican) sovereignty had its counterpart in the exilic rabbinic authority to excommunicate.[74] In its rough outline the scheme is traditional, with rabbinic law coming to take the place of the lost biblical state, even though Orobio's version creatively recast both components. Still, such a scheme in Jewish

---

[71] Cunaeus defined sovereignty from Roman law sources to the effect that 'a stickler for the strict letter of the law would have to say that sovereignty belonged to the people'. Cunaeus, *Hebrew Republic*, 40–1.   [72] Ibid. 40.

[73] Orobio's clear-cut distinction between alternative readings was mild dissimulation, and his frequent outright statements of correctness regarding one or another clash with their apparent mutual exclusivity, inviting the reader to compound them rather than contrasting them. Van Dam's description of Grotius in 'Introduction', 5, is perhaps true of Orobio, too: that he is *homo retoricus*, one who pleads: he 'makes points rather than holds views'.

[74] Although Orobio's favoured interpretations contradict each other semantically, i.e. they require the words of Genesis 49: 10 to signify different things, they do not contradict each other historically. Put together into a narrative of Jewish history, they fit.

thought calls out for a third part: a restoration. This we find in Orobio as well, in his engagement with the idea of divine-right monarchy. In a third set of comments, Orobio considered the fate of the Davidic monarchy itself, arguing that it had been not overturned but rather interrupted, such that the period of exile was a long interregnum in which David's descendants were legally entitled to the throne and tyrannically prevented from obtaining it.

Orobio began with a technical question of political history: whether the biblical monarchy had been disrupted legitimately or not.[75] On the basis of the principle that rule acquired by force was tyrannical (i.e. illegitimate), Orobio argued that the transfer of sovereignty from the people of Judah to their new king had been voluntary (hence legitimate). In contrast, later transfers of authority had been made unwillingly and by force. The succession of the Davidic line to the Levites and then to the Hasmoneans, the Romans, etc., were therefore illegitimate, and possession of the throne still belonged by right to David's descendants.

Orobio wrote that he was inspired on this point by a Christian claim that the Levites had stolen the kingship from Judah's line in the Second Temple period, meaning that Judah still had it 'by right' (*en derecho*) when Herod came to power.[76] This allowed such Christian expositors to date Judah's true loss of the sceptre to approximately the time of Jesus.[77] But Orobio called out the inconsistency in the Christian claim, objecting: 'anyone moderately versed in the sacred letters will recognize the falsity of this response. First they profess that the priests tyrannized the kingdom, [and] Judah could never lose the right by means of tyranny or force, and then they affirm that he [Judah] lost it by renouncing it to Herod, who was the greatest tyrant that the centuries have known.'[78] Orobio concluded that if the priestly kings were illegitimate tyrants, so were Herod and all of the Christian inheritors of the Roman empire up to the present day, leaving the rightful kingship in the hands of Judah. 'Just as he retained it without

[75] He acknowledged a rich cohort of earlier commentators who raised the issue. Three that he did not acknowledge are Hobbes, who said that the high priests retained the 'Right of Governing' even after losing power (*Leviathan*, 328 (§253)); Spinoza, who wrote that the high priests 'usurped' civil power (*TPT*, 236); and Nahmanides (reported by Pablo Christiani) in *Pugio fidei* (Chazan, 'Genesis 49: 10', 99–101).   [76] Orobio, *Prevenciones*, MS Ros. 631, p. 66.
[77] That is, even though Judah's line did not actually rule during the Second Temple period, it 'never lacked the kingdom by right [*en derecho*] because the Levites held it tyrannically all this time, and by tyranny a right cannot be transferred to the one who holds it' (ibid.).   [78] Ibid.

possession then, he retains it now, [and will retain it] until the Lord delivers him the possession that he awaits.'[79] The rightful Jewish king awaited return to the throne. The interruption was not decreed by God, as many Jewish and Christian interpretations of exile would have it, but rather imposed illegitimately by tyrannical Roman and then Christian rulers.

Orobio did not leave it at that; he offered another, even stronger, articulation of continued Davidic possession of the throne: as a divinely ordained monarchy, Orobio pointed out, it was unalterable by men. David's heirs could not even 'renounce the right to the kingdom' if they wanted to, 'because it was not a human right, but absolutely divine'.[80] Judah's rule had been predicted by his father Jacob, on the basis of Judah's strong leadership qualities; ultimately, those were human matters, relations between men. In contrast, it was God who 'chose David from all Israel, and commanded him to be anointed, and crowned him King of Israel, and promised to perpetuate his rule [*imperio*] through his descendants, without the kingdom belonging to either him or them by any human right or right of the nations, but rather by simple divine decree.'[81] David could not choose to accept or reject the kingship, nor could his descendants. No matter what transpired among men, ending David's dynasty would have required a divine decree.

Proponents of divine-right monarchism in Orobio's day were using such ideas to support actual political regimes, as he knew well. Jacques-Bénigne Bossuet wrote his major works on the divine right of kings between 1670 and 1681, exactly the period when Orobio was composing his *Prevenciones divinas*. In 1662, during Orobio's final year at the French court before leaving for Amsterdam, Bossuet preached his famous sermon 'On the Duties of Kings' in the presence of Louis XIV. Orobio's social and professional circles had also overlapped with Bossuet's in France during the years prior.[82]

One particular anecdote shows how the Christian debates of the day informed Orobio's thinking. A French humanist named Pierre-Daniel Huet was in the midst of a two-decades-long quest to prove that the prophecies of the Hebrew Bible were fulfilled in Christianity—a quest that was the precise inverse of Orobio's effort in *Prevenciones* to show how the Bible

---

[79] Ibid., pp. 66–7.   [80] Ibid., p. 67.   [81] Ibid.
[82] Orobio was immersed in the circle of intellectuals surrounding the Prince of Condé while living in Toulouse around the years 1658–62, among whom Bossuet apparently mingled. Y. Kaplan, *From Christianity to Judaism*, 104.

predicted and counteracted the false claims that Christians would later make. Both Huet and Orobio were influenced by Menasseh's *Conciliador*, a multi-volume tour de force of rabbinic scholarship that compiled and tried to reconcile contradictory interpretations of scriptural passages. Orobio's *Prevenciones* can be seen as an updated and polemicized version of Menasseh's effort, and Huet's *Demonstratio* in parallel terms; they most likely knew of each other. Huet, in fact, had embarked on his project after an encounter with Menasseh had left Huet longing to fully refute the Amsterdam rabbi's scriptural interpretations.[83]

Huet's discussion of the sceptre makes the argument that Orobio said inspired his own: that Judah retained it 'by right' during the Second Temple period. Huet compared it to the English Civil War, saying that the Stuarts had lost the throne but not the right to it, and then had it restored with Charles II.[84] The remark, however, had caused some trouble for Huet, as the estimable Bossuet objected, and he was in a position to censor Huet's work. Bossuet's issue with Huet's reading was not ideological—after all, they agreed on the legal and political correctness of divine-right monarchy. Rather, Bossuet reprimanded Huet for giving a polemically disastrous opening to Jews to argue—precisely as Orobio did—that the *shevet* was not passed to Christians at all, but rather retained by Jews.[85]

It is not a surprise that Orobio had his finger on the pulse of Christian thinking about Scripture, politics, and polemics—we have already seen that he knew Cunaeus, Grotius, Hobbes, and Spinoza, and his debate with the Calvinist Phillip van Limborch is well known.[86] Orobio's discussion of the republic of Judah was a sophisticated response to much Protestant political thought that tended to treat the Jewish republic as an archetype of a polity where civil and religious authority were identical. His scheme also tidily countered Spinoza's relegation of Jewish politics to biblical times and the wider Christian denial of legitimate Jewish politics after the Second

[83] Shelford, *Transforming the Republic of Letters*, 36 and 153.

[84] Shelford, 'Of Sceptres and Censors'.

[85] Shelford describes the extended incident in 'Of Sceptres and Censors', and mentions this particular reprimand at p. 171. According to Shelford, Bossuet also took issue with Huet's reliance on Tommaso de Vio Cajetan (1469–1534), a 16th-century Catholic accused of crypto-Protestantism partly because of his use of Jewish sources but also because of his ideas about the distinction between church and civil government. Orobio repeated one of Cajetan's exegetical points, though he cited Buxtorf as the source (Orobio, *Prevenciones*, MS Ros. 631, p. 73).

[86] See van Rooden and Wesselius, 'The Early Enlightenment', and Y. Kaplan, *From Christianity to Judaism*, 273–85.

Temple. He also responded, it turns out, to largely Catholic, monarchist ways of thinking that persisted during the same era. In fact, despite his reputation as a darling of the early, radical Enlightenment,[87] Orobio posited an enduring ecclesiastical authority that ran through Judah's republic and contemporary Jewish communities alike. His scheme envisaged religious authority as both transcending and undergirding the power of kings—and also of commonwealths.

As many Christian politically minded exegetes did, Orobio found a basis for present-day religion and politics in Scripture and in biblical and post-biblical Jewish history. Orobio's approach was not to compare communal leadership to the republic of Moses, or even to suggest that lay leaders were the political heirs of Judah. (He decided, contra several Jewish commentators, that such leaders—even the storied exilarchs—could not be understood as having retained Judah's sceptre.) Sovereignty as a republic—as a political body governed by its own people—was a fact of early biblical history but now obsolete. The continuity that mattered theopolitically was that of the divinely ordained Davidic monarchy (now possessed by right, even if not in fact) and the ongoing religious authority of rabbis.

Judah's republic nevertheless mattered to Orobio the historian and the Jew. In Judah, Orobio found a parallel, rather than a source, of contemporary lay Jewish authority: sovereignty aside, Judah's tribal self-rule was an apt model for the kind of polities Jews administered. After all, the Kahal Kadosh was—like Orobio's republic of Judah—local, discrete, bounded, self-ruled, ethnically distinct, and host to judges representing a broader religious legal system. Judah's tribal government was a political entity in which Jewishness was a given but Jewish law was only a constituent piece. The polity was not defined by Jewish law or divine rule, though it did leave an important space for their ultimate authority. Even during the biblical era, Orobio suggested, the real republic was on the tribal level: Orobio accorded *mando* to the tribe of Judah, not to Moses and his successors.

Similarly, the Jewish commonwealths of Orobio's time had not been divinely ordained, but rather drew authority from the people in the form of a congregation's authority to impose a *ḥerem*, as the *Acordos* and Aboab's *Exhortation* show. Judah's power was gained through human affairs: he achieved pre-eminence not as a prophet or a priest, but as a leader, favoured by his father, served by his kinsmen. Similarly, Orobio could see the lay leaders in the Kahal Kadosh as having established their position within the realm of human affairs. Lastly, not all Jews could belong to either polity. Orobio's portayal of Judah's tribal republic matches the Kahal Kadosh in that, unlike the republic of Moses, they were both restricted to a particular family of Jews, whether the descendants of Judah or Jews of the Portuguese nation. The local popularly ruled republic was a sphere of differentiation and concrete self-realization. The divine monarchy, in contrast, was universalizing and composite, a melting-pot; and, at least in Orobio's day, not real or visible.

Like Abraham Pereyra, Orobio expected that lay leaders would act with deference to rabbinic teachers and judges. Both men seem a trifle old-fashioned in the Amsterdam of Spinoza's age, harking back as they did to sixteenth-century thinkers and Catholic justifications for clerical rule and orthodoxy. On the other hand, Orobio's vision also gave much space to a sphere that could be described as secular. The 'republic' was a place where the ecclesiastical courts were marginal. The community, as commonwealth, was not the domain of the rabbis: rabbinic authority, given by God, was by its very essence divorced from the authority of a republican government, which derived from the people. Orobio offered a sense of the republic that privileged the worldly, the pragmatic, the corporeal, the genealogical. By refusing to suggest that lay rulers of exilic communities possessed what Judah was promised, he created a model for a Jewish world of lay governance that could stand on its own. Since it owed little to biblical sovereignty or divine chosenness, this commonwealth was also undiminished by its loss. Critical to this innovation was his careful attention to the different roles that monarchy and republicanism had played, and could play, in Jewish history.

Barrios's Scheme of Jewish Historical Progress

As a poet, military officer, and messianic enthusiast, Daniel Levi de Barrios (1623–1701) was unaccustomed to modesty, and it shows in his description of his home Jewish community. In works that radiate with pride, he treated exile not as a stopover but as an era of Jewish political activity with its own inherent and unique value, and placed Jewish diaspora communities on a par with the great political regimes of history. Whereas Orobio treated exilic communities as set apart from the universal divine narrative, Barrios accorded them a central role. Barrios focused on the Jewish people as the source of authority in what he called glorious 'democracies', and explored the Kahal Kadosh as a full, complex polity.[88]

Barrios's panegyric treatment of the community was published in various combinations and editions of discrete essays under the titular essay *Triumpho del govierno popular y de la antiguedad Holandesa*, beginning in 1683.[89] Although these are idiosyncratic and genre-bending pieces, it would be a mistake to dismiss them as mere eccentricities. Many of them are chronicles of prominent institutions and individuals, and overall there is a clear historiographical perspective. Dedicated to the successive members of the Mahamad for several years, they were evidently designed to flatter the governing elite and thus should be seen as offering an idealized reflection of its political self-image, and not only an expression of Barrios's personal views.

Barrios situated the exilic community, as a type, in a global history of Jewish governments, told in terms of universal political concepts. The grand narrative, culminating in Amsterdam's Kahal Kadosh Talmud Torah, justifies and glorifies the government of his community. Barrios showcases the community's antiquity, its conformity with divine will, its legitimacy in terms of political history, its suitability in terms of political philosophy, its excellence in actuality, and its significance in terms of Jewish theopolitics. The arc of his Jewish political story goes from original theocracy through ancient monarchy and aristocracy to present-day democracy, and eventually to messianically restored theocracy. Thus, the classical tripartite classification of polities becomes a chronological schema with a final, transcendent era that will circle back to its origins.

Barrios laid out this schema at the very start of 'Triumpho del govierno popular', the titular essay that leads off the book of the same name, in a dedicatory poem that operates on multiple levels:

> [1] *Democracy* means popular
> dominion in Greek; *monarchy*
> government of one; and *aristocracy*
> designates that of the noble betters.

---

[88] See my discussion in Ch. 2 above; see there also for relevant bibliography.

[89] The content and order vary from edition to edition, but this treatise always serves as an introduction. The other sections include histories of literary academies and charitable associations, descriptions of the community's administration and the building of the synagogue, funerary orations and encomia, and other miscellanea. See Pieterse, *Daniel Levi de Barrios*.

2   The politics of the last are strict,
    those of imperial sovereignty are severe.
    Democracy is gentler,
    and better to the high patron.

3   He chooses the Judge whose rule is wise,
    who teaches with example and just proof,
    more than with words.

4   He who governs this way improves and elevates,
    because the voice of the people is a divine voice,
    and fortunate is the judge who knows to take it up.

5   God created the universe in six days,

6   and divided it into three worlds: the first
    monarchy with high hierarchies;
    the second noble with celestial privilege.
    The third reveals itself as elements in mixed
    and proportional groups.
    A propitious bond now holds all in the *six*,*   *parnasim*
    With unity, with nobility, and with judgement.

7   On the seventh day, God rested;
    his people did well to rest with Joseph.*   *Gabbai
    From the six *Parnasim*, justice comes
    piously to Joseph, who is the seventh:
    these are the seven Judaizing marvels
    ever represented by the tree of the law.

Beginning with a description of three classical forms of government—
monarchy, aristocracy, and democracy—Barrios named democracy as the
divinely favoured form, 'gentler and better to the high patron', because 'the
voice of the people is a divine voice'. He extended the three classes of polity
into an analogy with three celestial realms, where the terrestrial is identified with democracy. Finally, he suggested that the Mahamad of Amsterdam, as a group of seven members, mystically recapitulated the seven days
of creation, tying together the human and the divine into a complete interconnected whole with their 'unity, nobility, and judgement'.

Barrios's highly idiosyncratic praise for his dedicatees offers a key to
his overall intention. He summarized poetically here what he would go on
to argue historically and analytically, that the government of the Kahal
Kadosh represented the culmination of a divine plan in which Jewish poli-

tics would become increasingly democratic until the complete mystical identification of the people's and God's political will would restore theocracy. The marginal numbers that appear above are also in Barrios's printed text, emphasizing the numerology at play in the poem and also serving as a table of contents of sorts: the seven members of the Mahamad correspond not only to the days of Creation but also to the seven sections of the ensuing essay.

As a whole, the Mahamad is like a tree of life, comparable to the seven lower circles of a kabbalistic diagram, or *ilan* (tree). As a unit, the government—like divine revelation, the 'tree of the law'—holds everything together. The correlations are summarized in the title of section 6, on 'the three worlds, angelic, spherical, and elemental, created in six days, which the six illustrious *Parnasim* represent'.[90] The seventh member of the Mahamad, like the sabbath, represents rest and completion of labour.

Barrios's elaboration of this scheme in the body of the text drew on Spinozistic and Sabbatian notions of democracy and exile, along with much else, and requires some elucidation. He began with a simple description of Jewish history as progress from monarchy to democracy. 'Political peoples in general can be divided into three main categories', he wrote, and he laid out how those divisions played out in chronological order in Jewish history:

The first is monarchy, or government of one, like that of Moses, Saul, David and Solomon. The second is aristocratic, or noble, like that of Joshua, the holy Judges, and the Maccabeans. The third is democratic, or popular, like that of the Israelites in Egypt, Babylonia, and everywhere they are found in the Mosaic Law, ever since the Assyrians dispersed those of Israel, and the Romans those of Jerusalem'.[91]

In this brief account of Jewish politics, a few things are of note. First, Barrios included Moses among the monarchs—a categorization that countered more typical contemporary views of the lawgiver's polity as a 'republic'. Instead, it followed Spinoza, who indicated that the people had transferred their innate governing authority to Moses as their monarch. Second, Barrios saw subsequent forms of sovereign Jewish rule as 'noble', emphasizing that pre-exilic Jewish leaders were not representatives of the people, but rather individuals who ruled the populace on the basis of power inherited or

---

[90] Barrios, *Triumpho*, 50–1, but note that there are multiple, inconsistent, pagination systems within this edition. The numbers listed here are the ones given as part of the printed page, and not the ones marked in by hand, on the copy I consulted.   [91] Ibid. 2.

granted to them by some other authority. And third, Barrios identified as 'democratic' all Jewish communities in exile.

Each of the three stages had three parts. Barrios wrote at length about the three true (i.e. in his framing, godly) monarchies,[92] which led up to the 'most perfect' monarchy, that of Moses.[93] From there, Jewish politics apparently transitioned through three stages of the 'Jerusalem aristocracy'. After that, he wrote, since 'the Israelite monarchy did not long endure due to division; and the Jerusalem aristocracy did not last due to discord',[94] 'popular governments were established . . . in the places to which they were expelled'.[95] In other words, the sovereign biblical governments that Jews had possessed were not ideal: they were unstable and prone to dissolution, spelling their demise.

Exilic 'popular, or lower Israelite governments', too, were threefold. Among those, Barrios portrayed the latest as the most glorious. Whereas the first two were localized, first in Egypt and then in Babylonia, the third was the current exile, that of the 'sustainers, or *parnasim*' who spread across the globe, 'shining outward I In various temples among various nations, I Lights of God within them'.[96] Democratic self-government of those he called 'Israelites or Jews' would now endure, said Barrios, 'giving clear light of the eternal divinity among the nations'.[97]

Explaining that each community was a 'republic unto itself',[98] Barrios emphasized, like Cardoso, that Jews had governed themselves in each time and place: 'all the Israelites who were dispersed among the rest of the nations governed themselves in the Mosaic Law'.[99] He cited many Jewish and non-Jewish witnesses and textual authorities about 'Israelite republics in many different places in the world',[100] including Moscow (described by Benjamin of Tudela) and Persia (with 'cities and castles in the mountains . . . [that] aren't under the yoke of other peoples, but rather have a prince'[101]). For Barrios, the significance of these republics was not primarily that they possessed some kind of self-government, or that they enacted Jewish law—

[92] Barrios, *Triumpho*, 8.

[93] Ibid. 19. He described how the monarchical form had become closer to God as it progressed, for example in 'Historia de la monarchia y origen de Ioctan', in *Triumpho*, 9–18.

[94] Ibid. 22. Also: 'The Hebrews irritated the Infinite Emperor in their aristocracy and monarchy'; ibid. 28.   [95] Ibid. 28.   [96] Ibid. 28–9.   [97] Ibid. 31–2.   [98] Ibid. 31.

[99] He cites Menasseh ben Israel here, probably referring to his *Conciliador*, which is mentioned by name a few pages earlier.

[100] He cites Puente's *Conveniencia de las monarchias*, book 2, ch. 15. Barrios, *Triumpho*, 35–6.
[101] Ibid.

though those elements did appear in his account. At least with respect to his historical scheme, the significance of the exilic republics was that they were moving ever closer to democracy, to being ruled by the people themselves.

Community as Democracy

But what exactly could Barrios mean by calling such communities 'democracies'? On its face, it seems like an absurd way to characterize the Kahal Kadosh Talmud Torah, since it was governed by a self-perpetuating council with absolute authority. How can Barrios have expected the members of the Mahamad to appreciate such a portrayal, when they were jealously controlling of their exclusive authority? The members of the congregation themselves—much to the chagrin of some dissidents, as we have seen—had no direct role in setting policy or even selecting leaders. The answer, of course, is that Barrios referred not to the governmental system but to the underlying source of authority, which was understood to lie with the congregation, the people of the community.

He directly addressed the reasons why democracy was the highest form of polity, writing: 'A government of the people is more suitable than a noble or royal one, because there can be no nobles without the plebeians, nor a king without a people. On the other hand, there can be a plebe without nobility or king, electing judges to administer and govern the republic.'[102] The people, in other words, formed the ultimate basis for political authority because they were the only essential component of a polity, even if it had a king.

In his zealous apology for democracy Barrios drew on a wide swathe of ideas prevalent in seventeenth-century political philosophy, which in turn had classical sources, many of which he cited.[103] Barrios's specific attention to the popular origin of state or royal sovereignty had a basis in early modern political theory. Jean Bodin, for example, known as an apologist for absolute monarchy, still turned to the people in seeking a well-reasoned ultimate source of the monarch's authority. The populace, he wrote, must have 'renounced and alienated its sovereign power in order to invest [the

---

[102] Ibid. 7.
[103] Lee, *Popular Sovereignty*, 10; see Straumann, *Crisis*, 278–86. Other precursors can also be found in the Spanish context with which the conversos were familiar. On that context see Brett, *Liberty*.

monarch] with it . . . and thereby transfer[red] to him all its powers, authority, and sovereign rights'.[104] Barrios relied on the same model, whereby the
authority of the people of the Kahal Kadosh had been transferred to
the Mahamad; in fact, as I explored above in Chapter 4, this very matter
had been the subject of much debate and even open revolt within Amsterdam's Kahal Kadosh during the decade leading up to the publication of
his *Triumpho*.

Although halakhah regarding the self-government of communities
clearly underlay the system of the Kahal Kadosh and these latter interpretations of it, there was no clear Jewish precedent for the concept of a
community as a democracy. Some modern scholars have called medieval
communities democratic,[105] and the traditions of government practice and
rabbinic thought that developed in medieval Europe underlay those of
Amsterdam's Kahal Kadosh, making the political culture of the latter all
the richer. However, such explicit attention to democracy or the rule of the
people was absent from the earlier contexts.[106] Likewise, in the realm of
philosophy, monarchy was the primary form of government acknowledged
by medieval Jewish thinkers.[107] The historian Abraham Melamed concluded that those who discussed democracy, including Al-Farabi, Averroes,
and Ibn Tibbon, emphasized that democracy was for the *am ha'arets*, the
uncivilized mob.[108] Even Abravanel did not think in terms of democracy
and popular sovereignty, being ultimately interested in divine rule.[109]

In contrast, Barrios found that the Jewish people possessed a worldwide
network of democracies in exile. His scheme aligned with Jewish traditions
by having democracy take hold only when biblical divine-right leadership
ended, and by imbuing democracy with divine approval by describing the
people's rule as part of God's plan. Still, his text shows awareness that he
might have been rowing against the current with such a view:

With this example as my sword, I vanquish those who claim that royal power is
better for the conservation of peoples than noble or popular power. It is rare to
find a king who puts the well-being of his vassals before his own; and rare to find

---

[104] Bodin, *Six Books*, 26 (ch. 8, book 1).

[105] Daniel Elazar, in 'Communal Democracy', argued that medieval communities were in
essence liberal democracies, and before him Irving Agus, in 'Democracy', studied the 'democratic' dimensions of such communities without Elazar's programmatic bent.

[106] On the contrary, in terms of government structure, 'the various Jewish polities that
existed over the centuries were generally very aristocratic'; A. Melamed, 'Attitude', 173.

[107] Ibid. 173–4.   [108] Ibid. 177–80.   [109] Ibid. 188.

vassals who serve God before the king . . . Thus, I say, monarchy that lacks Moses' fear of God deserves the name of tyranny.[110]

Here he made use of tropes typical of Dutch anti-Spanish discussions of monarchy as tyranny,[111] with explicit reference to Isaac Abravanel as well as various classical authorities including Solon, Pliny, Aristotle, and Plato.

But especially important is the way he interpreted the so-called kingship of Moses. As he explained (citing 'Aristotle, on the authority of Homer'), a monarch puts the good of his subjects before his own and a tyrant does the opposite. An example of the perfect monarch, Moses attended to the 'common utility' and offered to give his life for his sinful subjects.[112] He was the last such ruler because the only way a monarch can be as good as Moses is if he has a relationship to God equivalent to that of Moses. Absent the alignment with the divine will that accompanied prophetic status, individual leaders—even those appointed by God—were doomed to corruption.

Democracy, on the other hand, had the potential to hold all of the people's self-interest together and embody universal justice of a different order. Barrios might have absorbed from Spinoza this considerable valuation of popular authority. Spinoza described an original democratic biblical polity where 'all were equally bound by the covenant, and . . . all had an equal right to consult the Deity, to accept and to interpret His laws, so that all had an exactly equal share in the government'.[113] Spinoza's interest in democracy was in no way limited to the biblical period,[114] but he did not imagine a return to its pure biblical form any more than he imagined a reprise of the unmediated access to God's instructions that biblical Hebrews had before they accepted Moses as their ruler. In the words of Nancy Levene, he valorized 'the struggle to bring about a political order that is truly democratic and truly just, an order that he thinks would be truly and rightly extraordinary',[115] but he also wrote with the realities of the Dutch Republic in mind.

[110] Barrios, *Triumpho*, 2–4.
[111] The de la Courts' anti-monarchical thinking focused on condemning the disastrous properties of monarchy and calling for an undivided sovereign polity. Velema, '"That a Republic Is Better than a Monarchy"'.
[112] Barrios, *Triumpho*, 2–3. (Nimrod serves as the contrasting example of a biblical tyrant.)
[113] *TPT*, 220.
[114] See S. B. Smith, 'Spinoza's Democratic Turn'; Levene, *Spinoza's Revelation*; Israel, 'How Does Spinoza's "Democracy" Differ?'; *TPT*, 205, 301 (*PT*). On the other hand, Barrios seems uninterested in the themes of individual liberty, rights, and justice that occupy Spinoza in this area. See Prokhovnik, *Spinoza*, esp. ch. 7 (pp. 200–36).   [115] Levene, *Spinoza's Revelation*, 9.

Democratic Messianism

Barrios translated such a vision of true religious democracy, the embodiment of justice and divine will, into a messianic culmination of the progression of Jewish political history. Yes, messianic: although he saw the diaspora
as a site of Jewish political fulsomeness and not deprivation, that did not
prevent him from expecting a final transformation. With three monarchies,
three aristocracies, and three exilic democracies, Barrios set up a kabbalistic
scheme of nine parts that become a complete, interconnected whole when
united with a tenth. That tenth, of course, was the anticipated messianic
restoration, which he believed would witness a return to the level of divine
connection that Moses had possessed as the only true (non-tyrannical)
king. Likewise, the seven stanzas of the dedicatory poem suggested a complete 'week' of creation, with God resting at its end.[116]

While democracies were the 'lowest' form of polity in the sense of
nobility, in Barrios's mystical paradox they were also the highest in the
sense of connection between God and the Jewish people. The present
day approaching closer and closer to perfection was a sign of the ever-
increasing presence of God in the Jewish people's midst. Barrios wrote in
'Govierno popular judayco' that 'those who govern the Israelite republics
are like those who, with Moses in chapter 24 of Exodus, *saw the God of Israel:
and there was under his feet as it were a paved work of a sapphire stone, and as
it were the body of heaven in his clearness*'.[117] In the dedicatory poem quoted
above, Barrios identified the Mahamad with 'the voice of the people' and
simultaneously with the created world, the world of earthly things beneath
the divine and celestial realms.

The imagery above conforms loosely with a kabbalistic understanding
of the sefirotic map. At the top, the most noble, exalted, and inaccessible
aspects of divinity have their parallel in political regimes with similar qualities. Barrios correlated the gradual increase of popular rule with a growing
proximity to the divine, such that the wills of the people and of God would
be unified in the lowest sphere, *shekhinah*, or indwelling. As rule became

[116] Barrios's vision owes something to that of Abraham bar Hiyya, whom Yitzhak Baer identified as the first to suggest that all of history corresponds to the six days of Creation, ending in
the redemption of the sabbath day. But for bar Hiyya, according to Baer, the time of exile itself
is relatively unimportant, since 'the inner progress of history really ended with the revelation
on Sinai—all later events are merely steps upon the path that God had laid out from the beginning'; Baer, *Galut*, 28.

[117] Barrios, 'Govierno popular judayco', in *Triumpho*, 46. See Exod. 24: 10.

popular, the plebe was elevated to the level of prophetic politics that Moses had exemplified, replicating the moment at which the entire Jewish people had shared in acceptance of the covenant. The absolute completion of the process of increasing identification between the Jewish people and God's political will was synonymous with the messianic age. Its completion would be a return to an original, pure state—the total democracy of the assembly at Sinai—as well as a climax of a cosmic tale that could only play out through earthly history.

In its messianism *Triumpho* shared some aspects of the Sabbatianism Barrios had embraced earlier, even though it jettisoned imminent messianic kingship in favour of messianic democracy. Sabbatai, the would-be leader of the Ottoman empire, had distributed rulership of the kingdoms of the world in advance to various disciples[118] who, he said, had 'sparks' of the biblical monarchy within them. The act expressed belief in a kind of spiritual-political nobility, with restoration of the monarchy synonymous with *tikun* in the Lurianic sense of reparation of the universe through the return of sparks of divinity to their cosmic place. In the early 1670s, Barrios (with others) had experienced a period of intense Sabbatian expectation, during which he spoke to the rabbi Jacob Sasportas about the expected return of Sabbatai amid a swirl of conversions of European leaders to Judaism, individual leaders aligning with biblical ones.[119]

After this stage, and especially after the death of Sabbatai himself in 1676, Sabbatianism took new directions, and Barrios continued to follow.[120] The kabbalist and Sabbatian Abraham Miguel Cardoso developed an interpretation of messianism as delving into lower realms in order to elevate them. (Abraham was the brother of Isaac Cardoso, whose treatment of the sceptre is discussed above; the two men did not see eye to eye on matters of messianism and mysticism.) In Abraham Cardoso's kabbalistic vision the drama of Sabbatian redemption occurred by means of the unification of the *sefirah* of kingship, Malkhut, with the *sefirah* of Yesod, foundation.[121] His

---

[118] Scholem, *Sabbatai Ṣevi*, 424–31.

[119] In Scholem's words, 'all the Christians (and especially the ruler of Holland, Prince William of Orange) would become Jews . . . the king of France was Nebuchadnezzar . . . and the king of Spain was Hiram, the king of Tyre and such like'; Scholem, *Sabbatai Ṣevi*, 894. See Sasportas, *Tsitsat novel tsevi*, 364.

[120] Barrios used Cardoso's writings in a sonnet in his *Respuesta panegirica* (1677). Y. Kaplan, *From Christianity to Judaism*, 233.

[121] In Cardoso's scheme he placed himself in the role of Messiah ben Ephraim, associated

conception of Yesod was markedly populist, as Cardoso identified it with
his own role. He positioned himself, in the words of Bruce Rosenstock, 'as
an "anti-elitist" Messiah who will share the secrets of Israel's redemption-
bearing knowledge with the whole Jewish people'.[122]

For Cardoso as for others at this stage of the evolution of Sabbatian
thought, messianic politics became symbolic rather than literal,[123] but it is
not obvious that the same was true for Barrios. The shift from monarchy to
democracy recounted by the Amsterdam poet was parallel to Cardoso's
account of a shift from a single powerful messianic actor to distributed
action among all the Jews of the world. Cardoso saw this sharing of mystical knowledge as giving Moses' level of prophecy to all Jews; Barrios interpreted the sharing of Jewish political authority as giving Moses' degree of
political power to all Jews. Both models exemplify *tikun* carried out by individuals whose mystical work collectively restores some original order.[124]

Barrios's account of Jewish history in the *Triumpho* was a radically democratic messianic-political vision, deeply influenced by Sabbatianism but
no longer focused on the figure of Sabbatai himself as individual saviour.
1683, the year Barrios began publishing portions of the *Triumpho*, was also
the year that Abraham Cardoso's expectations shifted.[125] The messianic
scheme Barrios offered was an elegant, and rather different, response to
accepting that Sabbatai himself would not return and become king. The
redemption that Barrios envisaged was not a reversal of exilic bad fortune
but the rightful fulfilment of a process carried out over the centuries
through deep engagement with the circumstances of the diaspora, including political ones.[126] Indeed, *galut* was where the action happened in
Barrios's story; the politics of diaspora were not accommodation to the
politics of the nations, but the fulfilment of Jewish political destiny. In this,
Barrios's vision fitted well, if idiosyncratically, with the mentality of his
fellow Jews in the Kahal Kadosh, as they turned their gaze to their own
politics and granted legitimacy to Jewish emplacement within the world,
by thinking through what Jewish politics looked like without monarchy.

with Yesod, to unite with Sabbatai Zevi, associated with Malkhut. See Rosenstock, 'Abraham
Miguel Cardoso's Messianism'.

[122] Ibid. 68.   [123] Liebes, 'Sabbatean Messianism'.   [124] See Scholem, 'Isaac Luria'.
[125] Rosenstock, 'Abraham Miguel Cardoso's Messianism', 68.
[126] On this dimension of *Triumpho* in relation to Scholem's discussion of the Jewish messianic idea, see Albert, 'On the Possibility of Jewish Politics in Our Time'.

Political Histories

Barrios's treatment of the community was political and messianic, but it was also historiographical, embracing the history of the diaspora in a way that was quite new in Jewish thought. In the essays 'Triumpho del govierno popular' and 'Historia universal judaico', he gave a detailed account of the spread of Jewish people into various European lands in antiquity, connecting biblical names and places with ones that figure in the ancient history and geography of Europe. Included is a complex argument based on a creative etymological analysis that Jews reached both Spain and Holland during the ancient dispersion, creating a myth of antiquity to ground the commonwealth locally as well as in terms of global Jewish history.[127]

Remarks in a similar spirit appear in his 'Govierno politico judayco', 'Govierno popular judayco', and 'Triumpho del govierno popular en la casa de Iacob', each with a slightly different focus in relation to the project of Jewish historiography as a whole. Overall, Barrios tried to prove the antiquity and continuity of Jewish communities throughout the world by piecing together one universal history from the biblical Enoch up to the Mahamad of Amsterdam. In 'Historia universal judaico' Barrios created the impression—through an association between the name of Moses and the Meuse (or Maas) River, among many others—that the dispersion of Jewish 'republics' throughout western Europe in antiquity, and their subsequent expulsion from most of those lands, culminated in the establishment of the Amsterdam community.

While Barrios's efforts might seem outlandish,[128] his Jewish historiography was actually similar to forms of universal history that were common in the era.[129] He understood and reacted to the important conflicts and

[127] For example: 'The second Popular Government began with the Israelites dispersed by the Assyrians and continued with the captives of Judah in Babylonia: the first went as far as *Zarphat*, or *Francia* with the *Chananeos*, and the second spread all the way to Zepharad, now Spain, with the Phoenicians, Babylonians, and the kings of Dara and Fez, which then made up Barbary, which is hidden in the anagram of *Zepharad* which is *Dara Fez*.' Barrios, *Triumpho*, 28; such analysis continues to p. 49.

[128] Harm den Boer called him a 'mixed-up spirit', and the *Triumpho* an 'extremely obscure and confused effort to reconcile religions, countries at war . . . and peoples'; den Boer, 'Exile', 196–7. Gutwirth's comment about Joseph Penso, that his style has stood in the way of sensitive assessment of his work, applies to Barrios. See Gutwirth, 'Penso's Roots', 270–1.

[129] 'The same "method" was used by many contemporaries' and was generally a part of an effort to flatter and show the nobility of a person or a people.' Díaz Esteban, 'Fanciful Biblical Etymologies', 3 and 12.

debates of his day in a way that was culturally appropriate,[130] and his writings were, in turn, perceived favourably by serious people, Jewish and Christian. Such writings were well received because they flattered the recipients, framing their endeavours in ways that highlighted their broader significance—whether that meant praising the leaders of a literary academy for helping divine truth to flower, or praising a king for carrying out God's will in geopolitics. He framed the Mahamad and the heads of various sub-communal organizations as collectively constituting a significant political regime in multiple senses.

More than merely flattering his potential patrons, Barrios's writings on the Kahal Kadosh Talmud Torah are properly compared to other historical works written to justify the authority of existing regimes, participating in a rich early modern culture of official and state histories.[131] *Triumpho* echoes works like Jacques-Bénigne Bossuet's *Discourse on Universal History*, which appeared in 1681, Pedro Mexia's *Historia imperial y cesarea*, and Juan de la Puente's *De la conveniencia de las dos monarquias Catolicas*.[132]

Barrios mentioned more than once the massive tome that was well known among members of the Kahal Kadosh, *Monarchía ecclesiástica, o historia universal do mundo* (1588), by the Spanish Franciscan Juan de Pineda (1558–1637).[133] Pineda's universal history began with Creation and followed the transmission of authority up through his own day to prove that the church, headed by the pope, was the rightful inheritor of the biblical monarchy. Pineda used biblical, classical, and mythical history, as well as religious and political philosophy, to argue that politics were a natural purview of the church, asserting robustly that the Christian spiritual kingdom was also a temporal one.

In *Triumpho* Barrios composed a democratic, Jewish, lay-oriented analogue to those monarchical, Catholic, church-focused works. He showed that Jews, too, could play at the game of tracing the political fortunes of

[130] Barrios argued in *Trompeta* against the temporal authority of popes, in favour of the lay elites of Spain and Austria. Wilke, 'La *Trompette du jugement*', 515–16. See also den Boer, 'Literature', 104–11, and den Boer and Israel, 'William III', on Barrios's reaction to the Glorious Revolution.   [131] See Kagan, *Clio*.

[132] Mexia's was among the books most commonly cited by members of the Kahal Kadosh. Swetschinski, 'Portuguese Jews'. Méchoulan points out that Barrios imitated Puente's style in 'The Importance of Hispanicity', 356.

[133] Pineda was cited by Pereyra, Orobio, Morteira, Isaac Naar, and Aguilar, among others, and is listed by Swetschinski (in 'Portuguese Jews') as commonly cited. Immanuel Aboab also cited Pineda in his *Nomologia*, an influential earlier work in the Sephardi tradition.

one nation back through a cacophony of migrations and conquests. His discussion might even lead the reader to wonder why the Roman empire, from which the Spanish monarchy derived its institutional continuity according to Spanish historians, had any more inherent connection to the Iberian peninsula than Jews did. Both were there in antiquity, and neither was native. That there were Israelites so early on in various European lands (including what would become France, England, Scotland, and Holland) hinted that the Jewish nation belonged as much to those lands as any other nation did.

There were Protestant republican universal histories to answer, too. Grotius's *De antiquitate reipublicae Batavicae* (1610) argued for political continuity between ancient Batavia and the United Provinces by showing that it had been ruled by native aristocrats (*primores*) all along, as against kings who would have countered Batavian liberty.[134] James Ussher's *Annals of the World* (1650)[135] is another example, one among many, in which ancient Jewish history was accorded a central role at the start of a universal sacred and political history. In those works, however, the Jewish polity soon disappeared from view as the chronicle moved towards Christian claims of church and state legitimacy. Barrios's narrative flipped that script, writing universal political history as a fundamentally Jewish story, and carrying Jewish political history up to the present by giving full historical legitimacy to Jewish life after the fall of the Temple, whether ancient or contemporary.

Politics in/of Jewish History

If Orobio's response to Christians centring the Mosaic republic was to replace it with the Judite republic, Barrios's was to replace it with the diaspora democracy. By envisaging Jewish republics past and present and querying their relationship to the monarchies of biblical and messianic times, both men formed appealing counter-narratives to the conventional notion that the Jewish lack of a king signified subjugation, divine rejection, and the failure of a promise of redemption.

The implications of popular Jewish self-rule at various times in history were central to both men's overarching aims. As a theologian, exegete, and apologist for Judaism, Orobio defended Jewish religious legitimacy against

---

[134] See Tuck, *Philosophy and Government*, 164–5.   [135] Prior, 'Hebraism', 48.

Christian claims by means of a new account of Judah's sceptre. As a by-product of that effort, his historical analysis of Judah's tribal self-rule brought to light a biblical Jewish polity more analogous to the Kahal Kadosh than to that of Moses, in terms of the relationship between religious law and lay government. For Barrios, the poet, encomiast and one-time Sabbatian enthusiast, to explain the ultimate meaning of the diaspora community according to God's plan was to reveal the glory of the Jewish people as a political people. Barrios's narrative swirled all nations into the galaxy of Jewish history, as it was the Jewish people who began—and would end—in unification with the divine will, even while the intermediate processes played out in the wide world and according to general principles of human politics.

Barrios's and Orobio's visions of the messianic future were as different as their accounts of Jewish history: Orobio treated the future restoration of a rightful Jewish king as neither imminent nor mystical, and certainly not democratic.[136] But both considered the matter according to what 'occurs now in the political Kingdoms of Europe', as Orobio wrote. Barrios glorified the exilic interregnum while Orobio merely explained it theoretically, but for both of them it supported a perception of their own political condition as normal and positive rather than exceptionally tragic. Seventeenth-century political thought offered new possibilities for understanding exilic Jewish political structures as more than mere stand-ins for the 'real' authority of a dynastic line, as the commonwealth—though not sovereign—was nevertheless 'real and visible'. The binary between kingship and subjugation, between political self-realization and exile, was exploded in the light of communal legitimacy founded upon the consent and participation of the population.

In turn, possibilities opened up for reordering the most essential narratives of Jewish history. Turning to the people rather than to the dream of a king or to the echo of Moses' law meant that exile could be a site of Jewish political agency. Bonfil called early modern Jewish attempts at historiography 'sad' in that they were fundamentally unable to treat the subject matter of history (i.e. politics) and of Jewish experience at one and the same time.

---

[136] According to Yosef Kaplan, Orobio tried to 'expose the fallacy of the active and radical messianic self-orientation which was still prevalent amongst some members of the Amsterdam community to which he belonged'—among them Daniel Levi de Barrios himself. Kaplan, *From Christianity to Judaism*, 376.

Barrios and Orobio can be said to have succeeded in doing this, writing about the history of Jewish polities and politics.

Of course, the Spanish and Portuguese Jews of Amsterdam were far from the first or only Jewish thinkers to perceive communal leaders or communities as powerful, to theorize exilic Jewish authority, to reflect on how exilic Jewish political status related to chosenness and restoration, or to conceive messianic restoration as a worldly affair.[137] What set their perspective apart was a new evaluation of the relationship between Jewish and non-Jewish politics that reflected their absorption of the new seventeenth-century way of thinking about 'politics' per se. Their self-awareness of doing something universal changed the way they approached Jewish history. Not only Orobio and Barrios, but also other writers in seventeenth-century Amsterdam, saw the compromised political condition of Jews in exile not as exclusion from the world-historical stage but rather as a quality that Jews shared with all 'political peoples', to use Barrios's phrase. All of the Jewish writers featured here reckoned—not unreasonably, given the interests of the hegemonic Christians of their age—that particularistic Jewish political history was universally meaningful. In the minds of the thinkers of the Kahal Kadosh, Jews served historiographically as exemplars and as agents.

Yerushalmi suggested that particularistic or spiritual interpretations of Jewish history remained at odds with historiography in the modern age. Beginning with the *Wissenschaft des Judentums*, modern Jewish thinkers embraced scholarly modes of understanding the Jewish past, building a 'vast edifice of historical research',[138] but their activities were still unconducive to 'ultimate meaning' or 'spiritual felicity'. They did not reconcile historiography with collective memory. Funkenstein thought somewhat differently about *Wissenschaft*, pointing out the extent to which nineteenth-century scholarship was itself a meaningful form of Jewish self-expression, even if paradoxically so. In his words: 'for the generations of gradually emancipated and secularized Jews, the uniqueness of Israel came to mean its *universality*'.[139] The problematic of premodern political difference was twisted, with modernization, into a problematic of political sameness that

---

[137] On agency and authority see, for two examples among many, Biale, *Power and Powerlessness*, and Lorberbaum, *Politics*. On chosenness and the messianic age one need only think of Spinoza and Maimonides.

[138] Yerushalmi, 'Clio', 638.   [139] Funkenstein, *Perceptions*, 20.

did not square with the long-memorialized difference. The historiography of Barrios and Orobio sheds some new light on that process.

Yerushalmi situated himself uncomfortably as the mediator between two modes of relating to the Jewish past.[140] Indeed, he presumed not only an opposition between the two but also a 'decisive break' in historical terms, arguing that modern Jewish historiography was not a continuation of early modern efforts but a wholly new enterprise.[141] The historiographical activities of Cardoso, Orobio, and Barrios constitute a halfway point or even a third way. The thinkers of the seventeenth century were not yet burdened by Yerushalmi's 'vast edifice' or by the demand that historiography be neutral or universal only in the scientific sense; they did not experience the disjunction that later made history into 'the faith of fallen Jews'.[142] They enjoyed an understanding of Jewish political history where Jews were the subjects. Their history was both particular, in the sense of making Jewish meaning, and universal in the sense that they understood it to be the story of all creation. It was of their age and also political, exilic, grounded, and authentic.

[140] Yerushalmi juxtaposes the modern Jewish historian with his 16th-century counterpart: 'Whether contemporary Jewry, having lived through its own unparalleled cataclysm, looks to history for its meaning, or awaits a new myth, will also bear discussion. These and other queries arise, unsummoned, "when sleep wanders", even though one knows that the work will continue in the morning' (Yerushalmi, 'Clio', 638). The phrase 'when sleep wanders' recalls Yerushalmi's earlier quotation of Joseph Hakohen to the effect that historiography is a mere distraction from topics of deeper import to Jews. But the scenario is inverted: for Hakohen, history provides amusement in unoccupied hours, while for Yerushalmi, history is the daily work and memory a source of idle musing. Yerushalmi here plays with the chronological flattening that he attributes to premodern Jewish collective memory.

[141] 'There is no continuum between sixteenth-century Jewish historiography and Jewish historical scholarship as we know it and practice it in modern times' (Yerushalmi, 'Clio', 636–7); and see Yerushalmi, Zakhor, 81.

[142] See Myers and Kaye (eds.), The Faith of Fallen Jews. For Yerushalmi on the difference between modern and premodern historiography, see 'Clio', 626.

CONCLUSION

$\mathbb{B}$EGINNING with the unification of the Kahal Kadosh Talmud Torah in 1639, and ending with the 1683 composition of Daniel Levi de Barrios's triumphal history of the community, this study has traced a previously unrecognized Jewish engagement with early modern Christian political thought. In light of the general ideas of politics and the state that emerged in the era of Hobbes and Spinoza, the Spanish and Portuguese Jews of Amsterdam developed a political conception of the Jewish community that was to inform Jewish thought for centuries. They treated the community as a republic or commonwealth, using the new politics to question and interpret communal affairs along with Jewish theology, polemics, and identity. Their perspective spurred new considerations of Jewish status, history, and values in the shadow of Sabbatian messianism and social change.

In the 1630s, the founders of Amsterdam's Jewish community designed it in the form of a corporate society by both internal Jewish and external Dutch standards. The community was constituted with a system in which governing authority originated in the collective agreement of individual members and then was vested in a group of lay officers. A body politic like this one, more administrative than judicial in orientation, was naturally reinterpreted in alignment with the model of a political commonwealth three decades later, when Amsterdam was abuzz with the ideas of Hobbes and related theorists. At that same time, the Sabbatian messianic movement inflamed Jewish political ambitions and shone a spotlight on the complex position of Jews in exile. Amsterdam Jewish thinkers engaged in public, contentious political speech that centred their particular understanding of community. An early modern European Jewish political discourse was born.

If the mid-1660s saw the start of a period of feverish political thinking, by the mid-1680s the temperature had dropped. The discourse thinned. References to politics and the republic became more metaphorical and less concerned with communal affairs. A series of events exemplifies the shift. In 1683, the Sabbatian interpreter Abraham Cardoso gave up expecting the messiah's personal return as king, and the Amsterdam government forbade (albeit temporarily) the Mahamad to make free use of the *ḥerem*, disturbing the keystone of communal authority. Spinoza and Sabbatai themselves had both died. Over the following years, Sabbatianism gradually went underground, the Mahamad never fully recovered the authority it had once wielded, and Aboab died, aged 88, in 1693, finally leaving room for the differently minded Sasportas to briefly serve as communal rabbi for the last years of his own life. Barrios updated the *Triumpho* for a few years—but he left off elaborating on his grand vision to focus instead on commemorating individuals and small groups within the community. For much of the previous two decades a competition had taken place between centralization and democracy, between a civic and a religious understanding of the Kahal Kadosh. In the end, the latter won out.

The political preoccupations of the Kahal Kadosh have allowed us to see early modern politics in Jewish terms.[1] Early conceptions of the state depended on a combination of civic and Christian principles, but the religious character of European political thought did not preclude its application to Jewish self-government. On the contrary, since the Jewish community was also legible as a religious polity, and especially since Jewish texts and concepts were thoroughly imbricated within seventeenth-century Christian politics, our thinkers found much in their own affairs that was analogous to those of the majority. Further, when Jews subjected their own affairs to the kind of political analysis that was increasingly seen as universal, they formed new questions. They queried the relationship between religion and politics in Jewish contexts, and wondered about politics as an enduring component of Jewish life and history. These observations complement the revelation of Eric Nelson's *The Hebrew Republic*, that Christians' close attention to the Hebrew Bible and its Jewish interpreters was key to the evolution of liberal democracy.[2]

The present study also admits the insights of J. G. A. Pocock, Quentin Skinner, and their intellectual heirs into Jewish thought. I have argued that, as a new form of Jewish republicanism, the discourse of the Kahal Kadosh was more continuous with the ideas that forged the modern state in and around the Atlantic than with late medieval or Renaissance Jewish interest in the ideal form of the republic. The earlier Jewish republicanism was

---

[1] I am grateful to Alexander Kaye for this turn of phrase, expressed in a panel at the 2018 Annual Meeting of the Association for Jewish Studies.

[2] Nelson, *Hebrew Republic*; Hazony, 'Biblical Century'.

classical in orientation and focused on biblical contexts. The Amsterdam
Jewish republicanism was, in contrast, explicitly 'political', focused on polities or commonwealths, and concerned about issues such as sovereignty,
constitutionalism, the rights of the people, and corporate unity, refracted
through Spanish, French, Dutch, and English ideas. The figures discussed
in detail throughout this book addressed communal affairs as affairs of state,
largely mirroring the interests and distinctions that dominated Christian
political thought.

The story told here also intervenes in the historiography of the Kahal
Kadosh Talmud Torah. It suggests a higher degree of adaptation to the
Anglo-Dutch setting than has been recognized among a population that so
clearly maintained its strong Iberian identity. It also reinterprets a period of
internal strife in the 1670s and 1680s, revealing ideological and intellectual elements of what had been seen as conflicts of class, clan, or court. In
the preceding chapters I have read the erection and celebration of the new
synagogue complex in 1675 as one dimension of a wider consolidation of
lay communal authority against competing urges like Sabbatian messianism, democratization, secession, and clericalism. Likewise, I argued that a
dust-up over the ban that came to a head in 1680 was as much about the idea
of the community as a political body as it was about the role of rabbinic or
lay authority within it. Along the way, the book has revealed new points of
commonality between Spinoza and his community of origin and offered
a new perspective on the early aftermath of the Sabbatian movement in
Amsterdam.

Below, I offer some overarching historiographical comments on central
themes in the Jewish politics of Spinoza's Amsterdam, revisit some of the
book's central arguments, and discuss two main innovations that were carried forward from there. First, I suggest that the familiar notion of a Jewish community as state-like, with all of its intellectual paraphernalia, was
formed in this context. Encompassing other types of organization such
as a court, congregation, or tax base, the community per se became the
focus in the Kahal Kadosh. It stood in a totalizing relationship to individual members even if its authority was not total in the sense of being fully
autonomous, or sovereign. It was meaningful in itself, as some centred
community—not law, covenant, nation, or belief, but local *community*—as
a source of continuity and sanctuary to a dispersed people. Although its
particulars were specific to Amsterdam, such a perspective was emblematic

of changes taking place across early modern Jewish communities, where a new model was cropping up that featured stronger lay leadership, bureaucratic practices, and other elements of formal, institutionalized government. The Kahal Kadosh's particular concept of the corporate community, so fully developed and comprehensible in modern political language, was later taken to stand in for a more general premodern tradition.

The other lasting result of Amsterdam's Jewish commonwealth discourse was the development of a paradoxical understanding of Jewish politics as both normal and exceptional. The later chapters of this book show how the category of 'politics'—newly conceived in generic terms in early modern European thought—posed a quandary of universalism and particularism for Jews. Jewish thinkers understood themselves to practise politics as any group of people did, but also to have special politics particularly as Jews, as the people at the heart of biblical and eschatological narratives. The view that Jews had politics like everyone else set up powerful new expectations for the roles that Jews could or must play in the world of states, together or as individuals. Those expectations were at odds with the role played by Jewish history and texts in Christian political thought, as they were with internal Jewish interpretations of exile.

A (Godly) Republic Apart

The demise of Jewish separateness is generally taken as a bellwether of modernity. Sometimes understood in terms of cultural or religious distinctiveness, the loss is more often seen as a matter of social or political organization. Jewish communities ceased to exercise temporal power over their members, and Jews gained full membership in sovereign states without special status or the intervening presence of Jewish collectives. For that reason, Spinoza's recurring criticism of Judaism for its self-separation seems quite modern. He wrote in the *Theological-Political Treatise* that a commonwealth like that of the ancient Hebrews would only suit those who 'live apart from the rest of the world; it would be useless to men who must have dealings with other nations'.[3] Mosaic law, he wrote, led the Hebrews to care only about their fellow citizens, those who participated in their separate compact.[4] In his mind, Jews in his own day should participate in the general compact of the sovereign republic along with everyone else.

[3] *TPT*, 237.
[4] That Jews were closed off to outsiders was a trope of anti-Judaism that Spinoza channelled

But for all that he was forward-looking, Spinoza was also widely seen in his own time as a heretic, a fool, and a threat to society. Orobio, Barrios, Pereyra, Sarphati, Aboab, and the rest of the figures who appeared in this book were, in comparison, on the straight path. They surely felt a surging potential in the new age of European commonwealths, which promised to be a golden age of particularistic Jewish politics. After all, the Jewish community could appear as a Hobbesian polity in microcosm, within the Dutch polity. It was a civic body, formed of and by a population sharing geographical, ethnic, and religious identity. Leaders attended closely to its internal cohesion and policed its boundaries. It possessed collective assets and a physical space encompassing sacred and lay functions. During the years studied here, leaders and prominent members of the Kahal Kadosh strengthened the walls of the semi-autonomous community intellectually, practically, physically, and symbolically. For a time, the political understanding of the Kahal Kadosh served as a bulwark against increasing uniformity across general political society. Such a vision pressed back against the emerging trends toward civic parity that would eventually normalize Jews in north-west Europe as citizens of the city or state rather than as members of a separate or even quasi-separate society.[5]

Perhaps the Amsterdam Jewish leaders turned to a political conception of separation to replace other long-standing barriers that were beginning to weaken as well. Previously dependable social and religious distinctions were blurring, not only between Jews and Christians, but also within the Jewish world. Early modern Jews experienced a vast increase in mobility and interaction across geographical and ethno-religious boundaries. Habits and identity-markers in areas from commerce and family to language and halakhah were creating multidimensional cross-cultural encounter and change, destabilizing individual and group differentiation. Among former conversos, fluidity of religion and region was especially strong. A clearly defined and strictly governed local community was a refuge from such a morass. With other markers of Jewish identity in flux, the Kahal Kadosh sought a solid grounding in its political dimension, focusing on the

elsewhere as well: 'As to their continuance so long after dispersion and the loss of empire, there is nothing marvellous in it, for they so separated themselves from every other nation as to draw down upon themselves universal hate, not only by their outward rites, rites conflicting with those of other nations, but also by the sign of circumcision which they most scrupulously observe'; *TPT*, 55.

[5] Sorkin, 'Beyond the East–West Divide'; id., *Jewish Emancipation*.

institution of the community in and of itself.[6] The idea of a local society, intentionally fashioned by means of a binding mutual pact, provided an effective counter to the discomfiting erosion of boundaries that had once seemed set in stone.

The urge to strengthen communal walls was not unique to the Kahal Kadosh Talmud Torah. It is widely accepted that the seventeenth century brought with it an intensification, resurgence, or recasting of Jewish communal organization in Europe, through internal reorganization or through new efforts at rationalization or separation on the part of Christian governments.[7] This flurry of activity took place even as changes were already in motion that would eventually sharply limit the profile and powers of communities, at least in western Europe. It is an irony of Jewish history that community institutions were so strengthened on the eve of their dismantling or transformation. (It is worth pointing out that the narrative of communal breakdown has a profound bias towards the social and intellectual context of the West. For the present discussion, however, that is the immediately relevant context.)

Within the wider tableau of seventeenth-century communal strengthening, Amsterdam's Spanish and Portuguese Jews seem unusual in having reflected on these trends in explicitly political terms. In their arguing and theorizing, they showed how they understood the community as a political body. They asked, and answered, why the community's purview was not limited to religious affairs or Jewish law but rather, like a state, encompassed the whole lives of its members in a system of lay rule. They served as intermediaries between Jewish communal and political traditions and the new politics of the West.

The mix of Spinoza's challenge, Sabbatianism, and European political ideas entailed a re-evaluation of the Jewish politics of exile on a grand scale. Closer up, as the detailed discussions in this study have shown, this shift in perspective among Amsterdam's Spanish and Portuguese Jews played out within the community and in the currency of its government. The ideas

---

[6] See Ruderman, *Early Modern Jewry*, 23–55; Bregoli, 'Your Father's Interests'; Trivellato, *Familiarity*; Roitman, *Same*; Oliel-Grausz, 'Résolution'.

[7] Jonathan Israel observed a 'high point' in Jewish institutions; see Israel, *European Jewry*. On record-keeping and other aspects of communal administration, see Ch. 1 n. 53. See also Carlebach, 'The Early Modern Jewish Community'; Siegmund, *The Medici State*; Malkiel, *A Separate Republic*; and Ruderman, *Early Modern Jewry*, 57–98, and the works cited there. On toleration see my discussion and notes in Ch. 1.

and arguments we have seen throughout this book were thoroughly enmeshed in the specific rules and affairs of the Kahal Kadosh on a granular
level. In large part, this was possible because the community had been
shaped in the first place along the lines of a corporate association—though
without explicitly naming or theorizing it as political, and without the
wider theopolitical resonances that such a body would later take on. The
Acordos show how the community was simultaneously political, religious,
economic, and ethnic. Collectively—sometimes through the voices of dissent—members' writings show how the Kahal Kadosh as an entity held
those aspects together. Its various religious and political elements were
continuous with the halakhah and traditions of European Jewish congregations, but it was reinterpreted and transformed into a European 'godly
republic'.

The formation of the Kahal Kadosh along the lines of a body politic can
be compared to the effort, in the same period, of some Christians to establish 'presbyteries', or local elected church governing boards, and with
parallel Calvinist efforts to shape churches along the lines of republics.[8]
Similarly, the constitutions of New England colonies suggest that their
founders saw them as equally religious and political. Fitting though such a
model might have been for the Kahal Kadosh, it was not uncontroversial;
nor was it to last, among either Jews or Christians. As Michael Winship
showed, by the end of the century, many Puritans were concerned that
those 'godly republics' were becoming more republican than godly. We
saw above that Pereyra was already complaining in 1671 about the 'politicos' in the Jewish commonwealth who removed religion from government,
and in 1680 some sought to rebalance communal government in favour of
more rabbinic judgement. Such positions parallel the lament of the increasing 'preference of mens politicks before Christ's Institutes' expressed by
the Massachusetts Puritan Joshua Scottow in 1691.[9] Eventually, godly
republics, as both religious and civic bodies, would all be forced to become
one or the other. The Kahal Kadosh, like churches in Calvinist Holland,
would take one path (towards 'religion'), while Massachusetts became a
'free state'.

The Hobbesian model of political discreteness was a Trojan horse that
delivered the forces of openness and political integration into the heart of
the Jewish civic sphere. Strong communal authority became unsustainable

---

[8] Winship, *Godly Republicanism*, 39–66.   [9] Ibid. 2.

once halakhic justifications of Jewish self-government were translated into a political vernacular shared with Christian Europeans. When the Jewish communal system became a commonwealth in its members' eyes, it began to rely on the very theories that would weaken it. A by-product of naming the community a commonwealth and treating it as a polity was the recognition of a fault-line between politics and religion, between the *kahal* and the *kadosh*. That fault-line became a rupture with the onset of modernity, and figured prominently in modern Jewish thought, especially in historiography. This book has suggested a new way of understanding its origin.

Spinoza and Sabbatianism

I have highlighted direct connections to Spinoza and Sabbatai Zevi in various events and ideas, showing how those explosive figures were refracted through communal life. But I have not offered a comprehensive account of factions or movements. With only a little conjecture, there are certain alignments that can be noted. We know that the Mahamad and Aboab turned definitively against Sabbatian expectation soon after the apostasy was confirmed at the end of 1666. They put a stop to the celebration of Sabbatai as rising king in formal ritual settings and in terms of any official acts or communications on the part of the Kahal Kadosh. However, they did not stop members from privately speculating about Sabbatai's possible return. Pereyra and Barrios, for example, were Sabbatian believers, in Pereyra's case up to the early 1670s and in Barrios's probably longer.

Against that backdrop, in 1669–70 the Mahamad initiated a massive building project, which I have suggested was aimed in part at counteracting some aspects of messianic excitement by reinforcing the status quo of civic institutions. There were objections. The ongoing fights over the wealthy Jacob del Sotto's legacy for the synagogue and his heirs' participation in the community were not a direct response to Sabbatianism, but still represent its ripple effects as they involved the same bid for renewed authority on the part of the Mahamad. By the end of the decade, additional community members like Barboza and Coutinho also disputed some of the Mahamad's decrees. We cannot know whether they did so out of self-interest or due to specific policy objections, or because they believed on principle—as Menasseh ben Israel once had —that the communal system of Amsterdam's Kahal Kadosh devalued rabbinic authority and/or impinged on the rights of the people. But we do know that such principled claims were made by some of the secessionists who eventually prompted Aboab to respond in print—and in that work it is possible to trace reception of Spinozistic ideas about covenant, constitution, and rebellion. Ironically, those who rebelled against the anti-Sabbatian lay leaders were supported by Sasportas, the great anti-Sabbatian; and Aboab's strong defence of the politics of the Kahal Kadosh had something in common with Spinoza's politics.

Pereyra's simultaneous Sabbatianism and commitment to normative, quotidian Jewish law belies a common assumption that the two were inherently opposed. Similarly, stances on the balance of lay and rabbinic authority aligned in unexpected ways. Aboab championed a view of lay communal authority that had been established by his senior rabbinic colleague Morteira, while Aboab's rival Sasportas took a similar position on rabbinic authority to Menasseh ben Israel, whom Sasportas had befriended in the 1650s. Among the community's intellectuals, those of the older generation, Orobio and Pereyra, shared a fairly conservative attachment to religious authority and an anti-Spinozist political pietism that contrasted with Sarphati's almost libertine outlook. Orobio valued a strong lay government, but envisaged its authority as primarily worldly whereas rabbinic law was divine and eternal. Sarphati adopted a Machiavellian stance on lay communal government but still saw it as definitive of particularly Jewish, divinely ordained politics. Pereyra's *Espejo* contained a warning lest the Jewish politicos lose their way, as he called them to maintain the essential religious mission of the community. Barrios leaned hard towards democracy, as did various members of the opposition against the Mahamad, but did so in such a way as to glorify the Mahamad and treat communal authority as God's will.

These connections expose the way Spinozistic and Sabbatian ideas ran deeply through the community's political discourse and practical affairs. Yet they also show that intracommunal divisions by no means cleanly followed lines of Sabbatian or anti-Sabbatian, Spinozistic, rabbinic, or lay factions. There was not one way to process the Sabbatian messianic potential or its abandonment; nor was there a sole driving force in disputes or religious developments. The same is true about the political theory of the day and especially Spinoza's arguments. The two decades beginning with the climax of Sabbatai's movement were a time of uncertainty and possibility. Changes were balanced, and then exacerbated, by energetic entrenchment and then outraged objection; the time was marked by fervent but often contradictory efforts to do the right thing.

In the 1930s Paul Hazard published a book on the 'crisis of the European mind', in which he posited that democratic ideologies replaced fealty to clergy and royalty around 1680, leading directly to the revolutions of the Enlightenment.[10] As against the wide variety of accounts of the seventeenth-century crisis, Hazard's is remarkably apt, both chronologically and conceptually, when it comes to Spanish and Portuguese Jews in Amsterdam. During the same decade that Hazard was writing, Gershom Scholem developed his omnibus theory of Jewish myth, messianism, and modernity, in which the idea of crisis also figured centrally. He treated Sabbatianism as the crisis par excellence. His well-known narrative described a newly acute awareness of exile developed in kabbalistic circles following the Spanish expulsion. A century later, according to Scholem, Sabbatianism's disenchanting confrontation between the mystical ideal and realistic political expectation forced a deeper crisis that split Jewish experience permanently.[11]

It is difficult to imagine that Scholem was not familiar with the influential thesis of Paul Hazard. But whereas the Frenchman featured Spinoza centrally as a radical rationalist whose rereading of Scripture undermined its reception as revelation, the German Jew virtually never mentioned the so-called 'first modern Jew', instead describing an entirely complementary Jewish crisis of modernity that broke down Jews' relationship to religious authority in another way.[12] For Scholem, as for Hazard, Jews arrived at a fork in the road right around 1680. But for Scholem the widening separation between modern paths was not a reaction to Spinoza or rationalism. Rather, it centred on political (realistic) versus spiritual interpretations of messianic redemption.

On the other hand, the power of mass movements and alienation from traditional authority were underlying problematics in Scholem's work, as in Hazard's. His theory entailed the forces of democratization and the

[10] Hazard, *Crise*; see the recent English edition, Hazard, *Crisis*.

[11] This narrative is laid out with more nuance and complexity in a series of important essays including 'Isaac Luria', 'Sabbatianism', 'Crisis of Tradition', and 'Redemption through Sin'.

[12] As he wrote, explaining the lack of authentic mysticism in the 20th century: 'We do not [any longer] believe in Torah from heaven in the specific sense of a fixed body of revelation having infinite significance. And without this basic assumption one cannot move': Scholem, 'On the Possibility of Jewish Mysticism in Our Time', 15. See Lazier, *God*, 162–4.

loss of reverence for rabbis and lay leaders. But the history through which he approached them seemed far indeed from the world of early modern Christian exegetes and political theorists. Scholem's *longue durée* framing has contributed to a general historiographical impression that modernity constituted a radical disruption of traditional Jewish culture, the roots of which are found in the late seventeenth century. But the relationship of the Jewish crisis to the 'general' one has not been clear. Indeed, David Ruderman noted the 'genuine difficulty in finding coherence in these variegated aspects of Jewish and Christian society'.[13]

The politics of the Kahal Kadosh offer a zone in which these aspects can be reconciled. Reuniting Spinoza and Sabbatianism as a pair of elements that disrupted the Jewish culture of Amsterdam at the same time, a different view of crisis emerges that has more in common with Hazard's observations about political change than with Scholem's about spiritual authority. Sabbatianism fomented ideas about diaspora and exilic institutions, stimulating expectation and disappointment about Jewish political glory, creating new divisions within the community, and raising both doubt and pride in the Kahal Kadosh as a political form that could remain relevant. Spinozistic ideas offered a way of tying immediate and practical disputes to essential questions about God's political intentions for the Jewish people, stimulating discussions about the place of religion in Jewish worldly affairs.

Politics and Law

Taking seriously the political thought of the Kahal Kadosh allows for the reconciliation of another disjunction that has existed in scholarship. Spinoza is usually imagined as having been quite removed from the Jewish culture of the period when he was most intellectually active. This despite the fact that his Jewish background is understood as an important factor in his thought, and he possesses an almost unparalleled status as a symbol of Jewish modernity. The political discourse of his former community reveals that he and they were mutual participants in a shared universe of thought, to a much greater extent than has previously been recognized.[14]

---

[13] Ruderman, *Early Modern Jewry*, 136.

[14] On Spinoza's connection to Jewish sources and traditions, there is much to consult: a selection includes Pines, 'Spinoza's *Tractatus*'; Ravven and Goodman (eds.), *Jewish Themes*; Lasker, 'Reflections'; Harvey, 'Spinoza on Ibn Ezra'. On his relationship to the Jewish future,

Did members of the Kahal Kadosh read Spinoza's *Theological-Political Treatise* and react to it? Or does Spinoza's *Treatise* reflect his knowledge of the political discourse that was growing among his former co-religionists? Probably, both are true, to some extent. We may also ask how much Spinoza knew about Sabbatianism when he composed his famous remarks on the possibility of Jewish political restoration.[15] Because of this comment, Spinoza was later hailed as a proto-Zionist, or, more soberly, as having a precocious vision of Jewish geopolitical success. But his words reveal less interest in actual events than in the question of whether Jews were capable of attaining full political self-realization *qua* Jews. In this, one of only a few moments in which he directly and explicitly addressed contemporary Jewish culture, Spinoza's subject was not Jewish religion or scriptural interpretation or even the rabbinic role, but the political qualities of Judaism and Jews—what I have called in this book their 'politicality'.

One way or another, Spinoza and the members of the Kahal Kadosh were all pursuing the normalization of Jewish politics. Even messianism, in seeking a Jewish king, envisaged a full-fledged Jewish politics; here is the crux of the anachronistic connection with Zionism. Spinoza and the Spanish and Portuguese Jews of Amsterdam laboured to accommodate the ideas that dominated the political and philosophical discourse of their age, in order to evaluate the Jewish political condition. To do so was natural or even necessary, since the political philosophy of the day entailed an essential theological-political challenge to Judaism.[16] Spinoza articulated that challenge and his response to it from a non-Jewish, and yet Jewishly coloured, perspective. His counterparts within Jewish confessional bounds offered Jewish responses to the same challenge, as I have shown. Simultaneously, the prospect of messianic restoration demanded further consideration of how various forms of Jewish political authority related to chosenness and to the long arc of exile and redemption that was ordained for Jews.

In short, members of the Kahal Kadosh engaged in a short-lived

see D. Schwartz (ed.), *Spinoza's Challenge*. See sources cited above in the Introduction to the present volume on studies of Spinoza's relationship to Jewish thought and Jewish identity.

[15] Quoted above in the Introduction, and see references there.

[16] I am grateful to Professor Menachem Lorberbaum for first articulating to me this sense that the 17th century was a moment of theological-political implication for Jews. See the Introduction and Chapter 2 above for discussion.

discourse of political theology.[17] The questions that Amsterdam's Spanish and Portuguese Jews asked themselves were not limited to the place of Jews and Jewish politics in the wider world, such as how Jews ought to be treated, how to understand their status, or even how and to what extent Jewish politics were universal. Writers like Sarphati, Barrios, and Orobio included such outward-facing questions among the issues they took up, as they were occupied by the paradoxical combination of marginalization and centrality with which Judaism was situated in their Christian world. But, in the context of their pursuits, such reflection was secondary to an intrinsic Jewish effort to understand the relationship between the divine and the political.

For these figures, existing within systems that compromised or complicated Jewish authority was not a sign of their exclusion from the world-historical stage but rather a quality that was shared with 'all political peoples', to use Barrios's phrase. Sarphati examined the eternally difficult relationship between religion and politics, describing all politics as only problematically or contingently enacting religious truths, and all divine intention as muddied by the realities of human enactment. Jews' conflict between the competing goods of polity (peace and survival) and piety (the perpetuation of Judaism as a religion, and moral action) was in his view only an extreme version of the same conflict felt by all people—an essential condition of humans whose power is limited by their separation from the divine.

The way some thinkers in the Kahal Kadosh and its orbit wrestled with the theology of Jewish politics and the politics of Jewish theology anticipated what would come in the nineteenth century to be called 'the Jewish question'—the question of Jewish political sameness and differentiation, of their civic and national participation and separation. The new categories of religion and politics that organized the thinking of Jews in Spinoza's Amsterdam turned the community into a site of theopolitical debate. Later on, through the Enlightenment and beyond, Judaism as a religion was disjoined from the drive for Jewish political parity. For the Kahal Kadosh thinkers, however, such parity still involved separation and parallel self-

<hr>

[17] Graham Hammill and Julia Reinhard Lupton write that early modern 'political theology reflects and feeds on a crisis in religion, whether that crisis is understood historically (as Reformation) or existentially (as doubt, skepticism, or boredom)'; Hammill and Lupton, 'Introduction', 1.

government rather than integration. They saw analogy or comparability rather than equivalence or equality, and they sought it as a collective rather than as individuals.

Talya Fishman wrote that 'Jewish culture failed to complete an "authentic" process of secularization akin to that which transformed the dominant culture, that is, a process wherein Jews confronted and revalued concepts indigenous to their own tradition'. Instead, the nineteenth-century process of modernization was fundamentally a redefinition of Jewish life according to Christian patterns, and 'indigenous concepts and thought patterns that might have been modernized were neglected and ultimately abandoned'. But, she says, 'certain texts produced in the early modern period can stand as mementos of the internally impelled modernization of Jewish thought that was never completed'.[18] For Fishman, Spinoza's *Treatise* is one of those texts; I suggest that the texts adduced in the present study belong to the same category. This book includes several examples of such modernization of 'indigenous concepts and thought patterns', including the way the *Acordos* became a constitution, the congregation became a civic sphere, the role of the rabbi in excommunication became a matter of lay authority, and communal organization became 'political'.

Another example that I addressed only in passing, but about which there is much more to be said, is the reconceptualization of Jewish law. The Kahal Kadosh was not an anti-halakhic or a-halakhic sphere; on the contrary, its system was based on a halakhic understanding of the authority deriving from a quorum of men. However, the community had its own constitution and laws that were of a very different nature from the stuff of rabbinic decisions; neither rabbis nor halakhah 'ruled' in the Jewish commonwealth, not even by means of the *ḥerem*. This was not necessarily a new condition, as Jews across medieval Europe had often been led by laymen on their own terms, as scholars are increasingly recognizing. But lay rule became theoretically problematic when the rationale for Jewish separation began to be questioned, against the backdrop of Christian debates over clericalism and toleration. The formation of the Kahal Kadosh as a fundamentally political body, rather than a judicial or legal entity, made it difficult to correlate with the long-standing notion that Jewish self-government allowed Jews to live according to 'their own law'.

[18] Fishman, *Shaking the Pillars of Exile*, 64–5.

CONCLUSION   311

The combination of halakhic and lay forms of rule also complicated certain efforts to apply contemporary political thought to the community as a polity. Any facile equivalence that might be drawn between the biblical Hebrew commonwealth and the exilic Jewish commonwealth fell apart. The appeal of the biblical model for most political thinkers was its supposedly ideal identification of divine law with government law: the laws of the Jewish state were the same laws that Moses received from God. For a Christian, who already believed that the Christian spiritual kingdom had replaced the letter of Mosaic law, it was relatively straightforward to conceptualize a structural analogy between the contemporary Christian commonwealth and the Mosaic republic without worrying about the governmental laws of the commonwealth not being biblical in origin. But for Jews who were steeped in such Christian thought but also operated within a frame of reference where rabbinic law was a perpetuation of Mosaic law, i.e. where that same ancient law was still in play, a question arose about the relationship of biblical/rabbinic law to Jewish government. In the writings of Aboab and the secessionists, as well as of Pereyra and Orobio, there was an evident struggle to satisfactorily characterize the place of rabbinic law in a lay-led commonwealth. Their images of the ideal polity were conditioned by a Christian conception of the Mosaic republic that was not suited to a latter-day Jewish political context.

The profile of Jewish law within the community and its ongoing legitimacy were also part of the aftermath of Sabbatianism, though not as simply as the well-known Sabbatian 'antinomianism' would lead one to expect. Far from suggesting that messianism would overturn or invert Jewish legal norms, Pereyra and Barrios, for example, glorified Jewish law in the context of a holy Jewish republic as *part of* their Sabbatian-inflected messianic enthusiasm. After all, messianism presupposes that divine will is enacted through political activity. Rather than apostasy or transgression, they embraced a different mode of Jewish politics: the Jewish commonwealth. They amplified a conservative sense of divine law as a defining feature of Jewish communal politics, but glossed over the marginalization of halakhah in day-to-day worldly affairs and disputes as the community was actually governed. Others, such as those who sought to secede from the Kahal Kadosh, took a maximalist position on rabbinic authority as opposed to lay administration. In another surprising twist, in pushing for greater rabbinic authority, their actions militated against obedience to the existing official rabbi, who saw his own authority as legitimated by the established (lay) community.

In the light of that cluster of issues, Spinoza's argument that the laws of the biblical polity were purely political in nature, and therefore not valid in exile, was a turn of the knife. The same intuition that underlay the self-image as a commonwealth—the intuition that Jews were political like other peoples—was used by Spinoza to undermine the Jewish commonwealth. The Jewish thinkers of the Kahal Kadosh did not have any trouble rejecting Spinoza's conclusions with regard to the validity of rabbinic authority in terms of a post-biblical law that set standards of personal ritual and moral behaviour. But Spinoza's account of Jewish law as political law was more difficult. It demanded a coherent explanation of how exilic Jewish social life related to halakhah and how each related to biblical politics. Fundamentally, it asked whether or how Judaism was still political in nature. It pressed and interrogated Jewish politicality, identified with legalism.

The answer that some members of the Kahal Kadosh settled on was to see a religiously significant politics in the community rather than in law. That way, they did not have to give up politicality or law. As we have seen above, they connected law with 'religion', a sphere of activity that was deeply interconnected with the political but still conceptually distinct from it. The community, on the other hand, became the sphere that correlated structurally to the biblical kingdom or republic, a political sphere even without the ancient sovereignty, and independent of the use of divine law in its workings. We saw this especially in Orobio, who accorded a separate sovereignty to rabbinic law. He saw the long arm of Jewish law as reaching into the realm of communal affairs but not fundamentally constituting them. He saw the possibility of a Jewish polity with an altogether different basis: the rule of its own people.

The image of the Jewish polity that Orobio and his colleagues developed aligned well with the reality of the Kahal Kadosh Talmud Torah, which respected and gave space to Jewish law but was not concerned first and foremost with the administration of rabbinic justice. The image and the reality contradict a common assumption that premodern Jewish self-government prioritized halakhah: in other words, that Jewish self-rule was established wherever and to whatever extent possible in order to enact Jewish law. The assumption ultimately derives from a pervasive idea that Jewish separateness writ large centres on the possession and practice of a distinct law, and from the related narrative myth of the Jewish legal system as a replacement for an earlier, now lost, sovereign government. That myth is a product of the early rabbis' own polemic, and the legal nature of what they constructed can be seen as a product of the Roman system that made space for minority law.[19] The different approach of the Kahal Kadosh reminds us that law is not the only form such a replacement could theoretically take. The Spanish and Portuguese Jews chose instead an administrative polity.

The idea of a national *nomos* or a minority law was well attuned not only to the Roman context but also to the post-Roman world of the European Middle Ages, and various Islamic contexts that centred law in conceptions of religious and political difference. In golden age Amsterdam, however, at the dawn of modern politics, there were new notions of 'rule'. No longer were courts (and kings) the primary shape of government. Now, the polity or the state included judges and monarchs, but was also made up of constitutions and bureaucracies. The republic or commonwealth was an aggregate of individuals with a common allegiance, common interests, and common rights, in an administrative system. The model that members of the Kahal Kadosh pursued was a logical way of understanding Jewish semi-autonomy in the new era.

Afterlives: Community

In what follows, I offer a preliminary sketch of the way in which seventeenth-century innovations in Jewish political thought were received and transmitted through modern Jewish intellectual history. In short, I suggest that contact between Jewish traditions of self-government and the ideas that would make modernity set off a big bang whose effects are still felt today in Jewish thought. Diaspora community and statehood are still locked in a relationship that features some of the same problematics of exile and restoration, religious authority and social contract, politicality and alienation, that were first explored among Spinoza's peers. The state-like image of exilic communities endured because it aptly used modern political language to describe something seen as traditional.

Uses and interpretations of excommunication are a case in point. Mem-

---

[19] I am grateful to Natalie Dohrmann for this observation and others that informed my thinking about the category of law in Jewish history.

bers of the Kahal Kadosh fought bitterly over the ban, all within a frame of reference that assumed it to be a crucial locus of temporal, i.e. political, rule. Their interpretations were indebted to Christian views of excommunication as a temporal power granted to religious authorities. Christians apparently understood Jewish excommunication in this way, too, and, at least from the start of the seventeenth century, expressed doubts about the *herem* in relation to Christian hegemony. As discussed above, Grotius recommended limiting the Jewish power to excommunicate; the Venetian government investigated whether excommunication violated the sovereignty of the republic; and Amsterdam officials both repeatedly affirmed and eventually revoked the Mahamad's right to impose the ban. The key to recognizing this early concern about the Jewish 'state within a state' is that excommunication was understood to be not solely spiritual but also a temporal power that had the potential to undermine a Christian government under which a Jewish one was established, just as its use by Christian clerics could undermine the state.

Within the Kahal Kadosh, the *herem* as a political tool was theorized through the lens of the community as a corporate society, as described above in Chapter 1, where I showed how the Kahal Kadosh was atypical in this regard, as it took some contemporaneous tendencies to a logical extreme. The logic of communal authority was based on the idea that the Jewish population had joined together to create an overarching political authority by means of a social contract or covenant. That act was identified with the formation of a *tsibur* or congregation, a group that could establish a ban, so the community as a whole gained exclusive authority to excommunicate. For the community's founders and its later interpreters, as for Christian political thinkers from Althusius to Hobbes and beyond, such a body or 'society'—an organized group of people—was a fundamental political unit. The highly rationalized structure of the Kahal Kadosh was easily interpreted in political terms, making the community seem state-like and the *herem* seem like a state power (as in Christian thought).

In the eighteenth century, when Moses Mendelssohn argued that a Jewish community should be a voluntary association without temporal authority of its own, his argumentation was strikingly consistent with the terms of debate in seventeenth-century Amsterdam. In arguing against Jewish excommunication, he focused on its relationship not to dogma or religious practice but rather to Jewish civic separation. He insisted that 'the most perfect right as well as the ability to [reward and punish] were granted to the state through the social contract . . . Divine religion is far from all this . . . Excommunication and the right to banish, which the state may occasionally permit itself to exercise, are diametrically opposed to the spirit of religion.'[20]

According to Mendelssohn, excommunication (or its analogue, banishment) was a power established by a polity through social contract—just as Aboab and the secessionists alike saw it, as discussed in Chapter 4. What shifted between the Sabbatian period and the period of the Jewish Enlightenment was only the perception of whether a Jewish community should be constituted as such a polity. Mendelssohn wanted to facilitate a new way of being Jewish in community, one limited to the sphere of religion, as opposed to an old way, where the community was state-like. But this study has highlighted that the notion of a state-like Jewish community was itself new, with its origins in particular seventeenth-century ideas and dynamics. Mendelssohn seems to have received such a conception as traditional, without perceiving its recent inception. Further study is needed to examine how ideas were transmitted from the seventeenth-century *nação* to Mendelssohn, especially considering that he was particularly interested in medieval Sephardi Jewish thought. I hypothesize that he (and other modernizers) inherited a late conception of the ban and saw it as a long-standing tradition.

The specific observation about views of excommunication in Jewish community is suggestive of a wider dynamic that mediated the reception of ideas about community from the early modern into the modern age. We might expand our view to include the general early modern phenomenon of the strengthened, formalized, and lay-oriented Jewish community—and even, perhaps, the elevation of exilic communities to a status as theopolitically important. This is not to suggest that earlier Jews did not experience or value strong, established, close-knit, communal organization, or to ignore the robust lineage of the Jewish practices and laws that informed early modern ones. Rather, a new idealization of community *qua* community developed in the early modern period, a perspective that leaned towards a state-like understanding of communal organization. It accompanied changes in the political zeitgeist that allowed for new assumptions about the nature of associations and societies. In Amsterdam's Kahal

[20] Mendelssohn, *Jerusalem*, 72–3.

Kadosh we have observed a new notion of the community as a constituted and bounded entity in which a Jewish government, not a rabbi or other person with independent authority, was said to wield power vested in it by its members. Such a notion was a product of its age. And its external trappings, at least, are similar to those visible in many other Jewish communities.

This claim requires the recognition of local and chronological specificity in the way Jewish people have shaped and interpreted their collective institutions and norms, instead of seeing 'community' as timeless and universal. Legal status, regulatory bodies, private organizations, fiscal administration, theoretical assumptions, halakhah and minhag, sources of power and authority, and other features varied widely among premodern Jewish communities. Jews' associations and mutual obligations included councils and charismatic leaders, rich men and rabbis, guilds and agreements and bans and more. The bonds Jewish people created among themselves, all of which fall under the general idea of 'community', could be formal or informal, highly local or transregional; they could address ritual, charity, family life, taxes, conflicts, and much more, unsystematically and to different degrees. Jews built courts, synagogues, *mikvehs*, offices, and treasure chests. Many also—to be sure—treated a *kehilah* as an important Jewish entity. But we too often take for granted what that was and how it was understood. It is not likely that today's concept of 'community' can be uncomplicatedly applied to the past at all; nor should the seventeenth-century state-like community be taken as identical to what came before.

I have offered a profile of the Kahal Kadosh Talmud Torah that highlights what was distinctive in its structure and its thought. Perception of its distinctiveness, however, is hampered by the prevalence of this particular model of community in the Jewish thought that came after it. What I suggest here is comparable to a historiographical insight about the concept of feudalism: that in the Middle Ages no such system existed by name, or at least that the well-defined idea of it did not play an important cultural role. Just as medieval people did not typically understand themselves to be living in 'the Middle Ages', so they did not think of their social and economic world as a 'feudal system'. Rather, it was later, early modern, English jurists who created the notion in order to justify their own current practices on the grounds that they preserved modes of social and economic organization that they saw as traditional. Their idea of the medieval feudal system, in turn, served as a model of 'traditional' English society against which reformers and social rationalists later inveighed.[21] In parallel, early modern Jews formed a new concept of the institutionalized, all-encompassing, and state-like community, whether as a corporate society (as in Amsterdam) or in any other political form. They set new store by the very concept of community, building it up and changing its profile in the name of continuity.

In typically early modern fashion, the new form of community converted once sprawling, contested, dynamic, and diverse forms of Jewish self-regulation into forms that were more systematic and clear-cut. The new form then stood as 'traditional' for later figures who sought to preserve, alter, or memorialize the premodern Jewish community. In this respect, the state-like community can be compared to another early modern innovation, the ghetto. Daniel Schwartz pointed out that later Jewish thinkers seeking to improve Jewish society adopted the walled ghetto as a symbol of the old Jewish isolation, of everything that characterized the absence of modernity. But, like the idea of the community as a polity, the ghetto actually only arose in the early modern period: 'a secluded yet basically open and legally voluntary Jewish quarter was the normative form of Jewish settlement in medieval Europe before the mandatory ghetto'.[22] In both cases, the new thing represented an incremental change from what preceded it, but also created a new paradigm.

And the state-like community was a powerful paradigm indeed. The afterlives of the Jewish politics of Spinoza's Amsterdam did not end with Mendelssohn and the first fractures of modernity. The seventeenth-century context has visible traces in a much later turn to social history and the history of the community as well. Around the start of the twentieth century scholarly pioneers like Salo Baron, Simon Dubnow, Yitzhak Baer, Benzion Dinur, and Haim Hillel Ben-Sasson ignited interest in new dimensions of Jewish culture as they embraced the worldly affairs that David N. Myers felicitously called the 'corporate and corporeal' aspects of Jewish life.[23]

Myers's phrasing hints at the significance of the consensus among Jewish social historians that the Jewish community of the past could be described as a 'corporate society'. The phrase held within it the sense that Jews were socially separate and also that they had a fully realized world

---

[21] See Davis, *Periodization*.
[22] D. Schwartz, *Ghetto*, 2, 11–13 (quotation from p. 13).
[23] Myers, 'Between Diaspora and Zion', 96.

unto themselves. Robert Bonfil summarized decades of scholarly opinion in 1994: 'By and large, the Jewish community in Italy during the Renaissance was no different from other such communities under the *ancien régime* and may be described as a corporation with social, religious, and ethnic goals.'[24] Note that the Renaissance here is taken as part of what is sometimes called the Jewish 'long Middle Ages', taking the breakdown of communal autonomy beginning mainly in the eighteenth century as the end of an era of continuous tradition—a principle of periodization that was itself centred on social history.

But from what did these scholars derive the idea that traditional community was a corporate society? Broadly, they applied to Jewish culture concepts of 'society' and the 'social' that were themselves distant relatives of the conceptual family of the Hobbesian commonwealth, republic, or polity. The social historiography of the twentieth century was imbued with Weberian terminology wherein a 'society' or 'association' was the fundamental building block of human collectivity, i.e., politics.[25] And Weber's conception of society was informed by Hobbes's treatment of a polity as more than a mere aggregation of individuals, as an encompassing and surpassing entity. The same political theory undergirded the Kahal Kadosh as it was formed in 1639, where individual members' original rights were transferred to the body as an aggregate. A fundamental concept was thus shared between the modern discussion of the Jewish corporate society and the state-like definition of community codified by the Kahal Kadosh.

A striking display of the way specific qualities of the seventeenth-century communal model came to stand in for the structure of Jewish communities across premodernity is found in a quotation from Salo Baron. Baron, who contributed more than any other modern historian to establishing the significance of 'community' in Jewish history, distilled his extensive knowledge about medieval Jewish social and religious life into

[24] He continues, echoing Dubnow's autonomism: 'As such, it constituted a sort of Jewish city within the Christian city, not because the Jews had obtained and established a degree of independence, but because they had always aspired to independence, despite the practical impossibility of achieving it.' Bonfil, *Jewish Life in Renaissance Italy*, 179–80. Baron gives an extensive description of the place of the 'autonomous Jewish corporation' among other corporations in 'Ghetto and Emancipation'.

[25] 'Society', formed by and of the people but not equivalent to the people, is what Weber emphasized was formed by 'rational agreement by mutual consent'. Weber, *Economy and Society*, 41.

a compact description of 'the medieval community' in 1942, as follows:

Over professing Jews the community often exercised more authority than the most powerful secular regimes. Buttressed by the legal recognition of state and church; imbued with the spirit of a nomistic and ethical, i.e., activist religion; bound together by strong economic ties, outside animosity and a communal responsibility both theoretical and practical; permeated with a profound reverence for tradition, it was a sort of little state, interterritorial and non-political, but none the less quasi-totalitarian.[26]

The way Baron described the prototypical Jewish community was as a closed, obligatory system in which Jews were fully ensconced and enchanted. The community of Baron's imagination in this passage is a nostalgic and creative synthesis.

Although it generalizes, however, it is not generic; it is actually quite specific in comparison to the real variety of Jewish communal life. And in its specificity, it accords with the state-like community modelled by the Kahal Kadosh. Rabbinic law and courts are not mentioned; nor are individual leaders. The entity with power over members is the 'community'—the body, the aggregate, the *Gesellschaft*. The 'community' apparently compelled its members, but members were also in some sense willing participants. Like a 'secular regime', or polity, it governed all aspects of the lives of its members, even to the point of being 'quasi-totalitarian', a designation that evokes the supposed autocracy of communal leaders. Baron's caricature of the 'medieval' was, in all likelihood unknowingly, coloured by the legacy of the seventeenth-century Jewish community, filtered through the Western political tradition and later Jewish thought.

Ironically, he—like many others—saw Amsterdam's Spanish and Portuguese Jews not as symbols of the old but as harbingers of the new. He would not have attributed these qualities to the Kahal Kadosh, but rather described it as having left behind the medieval community with its split personality of suffocating inwardness and comforting totality.[27] There is some truth in such a perception of novelty, of course, since members were culturally open, with fluid identity and relatively equitable status as individuals. More than that, they did do something new with the community: they

---

[26] Baron, *The Jewish Community*, i. 208. On the impact of Baron's work and its relevance to today's scholarship, see Carlebach, 'Between Universal and Particular'.

[27] Baron called the Kahal Kadosh a 'new beginning' and a 'fresh start' (*Social and Religious History*, xv. 70). See Sutcliffe, 'Imagining Amsterdam', 79, and Y. Kaplan, 'An Alternative Path'.

sharpened and systematized the very idea of a community as a quasi-state. Even while calling it traditional, they made Jewish community into something that could be understood, mobilized, and eulogized within modern Jewish religious and political discourse, which had likewise assimilated the new European political thought.

Afterlives: Politics

In 1942, a moment when the question of Jewish self-determination was urgent, realistic, and extremely messy, Baron's description of community was deeply meaningful. The characterization of the premodern Jewish community as a totalitarian regime is a fascinating choice that reflected, perhaps, an overarching sense of Jewish modernity as offering only a frustrating sort of freedom. The imagined counterpart of contemporary aspirations and unmooring was unbroken, closed-off, and inescapable belonging.

Like members of the Kahal Kadosh, and other modern historians, Baron situated Jews in a world of polities through the medium of the community. He took a certain model of community as evidence that features of a state such as government, law, economy, unity, and administration were not alien to Judaism. In focusing on the wide array of communal arrangements over the course of Jewish history, including their institutions and structures, affairs and demographics, power dynamics, legal traditions, and economies, he rejected the wholesale negation of the diaspora that some espoused.[28]

Unlike the writers of the Kahal Kadosh, however, Baron and others saw fit to clarify that the 'little state' was nonetheless 'non-political'. David Shohet's description is typical: 'The Jews of the Middle Ages, in so far as the civil authorities would permit, vested in their communal organizations all the powers and functions which among living nations would properly belong to the state.'[29] (Jews as opposed to living nations!) The notion that exilic Jews lacked politics recast a long-standing paradigm of Jewish uniqueness and subjugation with which the members of the Kahal Kadosh had also struggled. The modern historians and the early modern ones adopted contrasting theopolitical stances on the same issue, through the same lens of community.

Did modern Jewish historians avoid the word 'politics' because the

---

[28] See e.g. Baron, 'Ghetto and Emancipation'.   [29] Shohet, *Jewish Court*, 18.

category was foreign to Jewish tradition, representing an imposition of Greek and generally Western ideas, an Athenian category incommensurate with Jerusalem's affairs? If that was the matter, 'society'—not to mention any number of other borrowings from modern European or classical Western political culture, including 'community' itself—should have been equally problematic. No: they avoided it as a result of a conceptual association between politics and sovereignty. Politics within their frame of reference were indelibly linked with governments of sovereign territorial states (in alignment with 'Westphalian' sovereignty, not coincidentally a seventeenth-century concept). Baron accordingly called the community 'inter-territorial', clarifying that Jews lacked one designated territory,[30] and Dubnow listed 'state, territory, army' as the particular elements that apolitical diaspora Jews lacked.[31] What approximated politics in non-sovereign contexts, on the other hand, could be designated as 'social'. In this framing, the social history of the diaspora was theoretically distinguished from politics. Jewish modernity was defined as the acquisition of political life, either individually or collectively.

Today most would see it as self-evident that a sovereign state is not the only site of political thought and practice, that dispersion and subjugation are not the same as a lack of politics, and that Jews never lacked politics in the most general sense of the word as a basic mode of activity.[32] The distinction between social and political is faulty as regards the Middle Ages, when the concepts of 'state' and 'sovereignty' with all of the theoretical accretions of modern political philosophy are not easily applied. The grand narratives of the twentieth century thus come to seem identitarian, ideological, and theologically inflected.

Setting those narratives aside, there is now much excellent research on medieval and early modern Jewish legal and communal cultures. Most also recognize that abstract Jewish political thought was expressed before modernity despite the fact that, as Amos Funkenstein put it, premodern 'Jewish literature lacked a specific genre, a place in which to articulate political

---

[30] Earlier, in 1928, Baron had written that 'the Jew, indeed, had in effect a kind of territory and State of his own throughout the Middle Ages and early modern period'; Baron, 'Ghetto and Emancipation', 55. It is worth thinking about how this critical rephrasing reflected world events in the intervening years.   [31] Dubnow, *Jewish History*, 18–19.

[32] See A. Melamed, 'Is There a Jewish Political Thought?', and Elon, 'Power'. See also Walzer et al. (eds.), *The Jewish Political Tradition*, iii; Elazar was working on these ideas at least from the mid-1970s but first published them in 'Covenant'.

reasoning'.[33] In addition, historians have noted various forms of politics among early modern Jews, mainly but not always in terms of interaction with non-Jewish regimes. From the widest vantage point, there has also been a reconsideration of what politics are and how they are practised, with scholars locating 'higher' forms of political thinking in many 'lower' forms of power relations and associations, including those of unenfranchised minorities.[34] Some have also sought a definition of politics that is truly neutral or universal, beyond the one with its roots in early modern Christian thought.[35]

All of these advances remind us that the European politics of the seventeenth century are not the only possible politics, even though the claim to universality is intrinsic to this particular system of thought. That the generic idea of a polity that emerged in early modern Europe is usefully rendered as 'commonwealth' (as Pocock taught us) is in itself a sign of the historical specificity of the concept. We should not mistake the particular politics of one time and place for an archetype of all politics. This is as true for the Jewish politics of Spinoza's Amsterdam as it is for the Christian politics of the Anglo-Dutch Atlantic.

Still, the particular politics of the seventeenth century happen to inform much of modern Jewish thought, with its governing themes of difference and belonging, loss and continuity, disjunction and universality. The framing of the community as a polity emerged in the defining and transitional time of Sabbatai, Spinoza, and Hobbes. So did another lasting paradigm: the expectation that Jews had or should have some form of polity, as a natural expression of the politicality that they shared with all peoples. Distinct from the earlier notion that Jews lacked a king, the expectation of Jewish politicality was imbued with the very issues of church and state, of biblicism and historical progression, of revelation and realpolitik, of self-determination and dominion, that contributed to the formation of the idea of the state.

The early modern Christians who piloted this new political culture

[33] Funkenstein, *Perceptions*, 167. This comment holds true for the reception of the figures treated here: Isaac Abravanel's politics are most often categorized as commentary and messianism; Simone Luzzatto's as apologetics; Abraham Pereyra's as ethics and pietism; Isaac Orobio's and Isaac Cardoso's as philosophy and polemics.

[34] For example, Collinson, *De Republica*; Griffiths et al. (eds.), *Experience of Authority*; Wrightson, 'Politics'; and Harris, 'Introduction'.

[35] See, for example, Yavari and Forster, 'Introduction'.

were profoundly interested in biblical history and their relationship to it. The new paradigm of Jewish politicality therefore brought along with it the baggage of European Christian attitudes towards Jews, with their odd combination of attentiveness and marginalization. I have suggested, therefore, that the dynamics of early modern theopolitics laid the groundwork for a notable characteristic of later Jewish thought, whereby Jews were seen as political like everyone else but simultaneously lacking true politics or in need of theopolitical remediation. In addition to its evident relationship to Zionism, this stance is important to the historiography of Yerushalmi and Funkenstein, along with figures such as Baron and Dubnow, not to mention Scholem. Modern Jewish historians instinctively turned to the early modern period—and often directly to Amsterdam's Kahal Kadosh—and identified it as a locus of change, in part because this was the period when the paradox of Jewish politicality, which so drove their own intellectual projects, was born.

The largest-scale Jewish historical narratives of our time emerged from and responded to a fundamental question that took on new dimensions in the time of Spinoza and Sabbatai: how to incorporate Jewish biblical and post-biblical history and politics into a meaningful Jewish frame. Looking directly at Spinoza's and Sabbatai's historical moment invites notice of the ways that later efforts to contend with Jewish politics and history were created and conditioned by the setting of seventeenth-century theopolitics. The framework within which Baron and others later operated was built by the introduction into Jewish discourse of the Christian ideas of politics, the polity, and the state—ostensibly generic but actually heavily freighted culturally and religiously. These themes then remained, translated and transposed across different Jewish contexts as if they were universal or eternal.

The dynamics that animated the *nação* during this short period were forgotten, but their traces remained in the theopolitical significance ascribed to the diaspora community. Through its reconceptualization as a commonwealth, the semi-autonomous community became a site not only of Jewish identity but also of much messy entanglement.

This book has focused on ideas that lit up the common intellectual spaces of Jews and Christians at a crucial juncture in both Jewish and European history. Exploring the full breadth and resonance of Jewish politics in Spinoza's Amsterdam, we have seen that members of the Kahal Kadosh Talmud Torah were acutely aware of the new political developments that surrounded them, and they sought to meet the moment. These figures speak in a recognizably modern political language—the language of states, governments, democracies, and constitutions—and yet they tell of a vanished world. Their theopolitical reflections, urgent and nimble in their own day, became heavily encrusted with myth and ideology over time. Recovering their perspectives opens a window onto the deep history of modern Jewish political thought.

BIBLIOGRAPHY

Manuscripts

Bibliotheca Rosenthaliana (Ros.)

MONTALTO, ELIJAH, *Libro feito p[e]lo ilustrissimo Haham Eliau Montalto de g[loriosa] m[emoria]: en que mostra a verdade de diversos textos e cazos, que alegão as gentilidadez para confirmar suas sectas* [Commentary on Isaiah 53], MS Ros. 76.

MORTEIRA, SAUL LEVI, *Preguntas que se hizieron de un clerigo de Ruan a Amsterdam respondidas por el Haham Saul Levi Mortera*, MS Ros. 127.

OROBIO DE CASTRO, ISAAC, *Prevenciones divinas contra la vana idolatria de las gentes*, MS Ros. 631.

Ets Haim Library (EH)

AGUILAR, MOSES RAPHAEL D', *Breve explicação do capitulo 53 de Jesaya*, MS EH 48 A 11, fos. 31^r–38^v.

—— *Explicasão do cap 53 de Yesaias feita no Brazil*, MS EH 48 A 11, fos. 425^r–436^v.

—— *Preguntas que se me fizerão de Anveres*, MS EH 48 A 11, fos. 6^r–24^v.

MORTEIRA, SAUL LEVI, *Obstaculos y opociciones contra la religion [cris]tiana en Amsterdam*, MS EH 48 D3.

—— *Providencia de Dios con Ysrael. Eternidad de la ley de Moseh, y nulidad de las demas leyes, que se atribuyeron divinidad*, MS EH 48 B 16.

SARPHATI, DAVID, 'Sermão que pregou David Sarfattim na Sancta Irmãdade de Abi Yetomim, por mandado dos Senhores Administradores, no ultimo dia de Pascua de Pessah de 5433, em Amsterdam', MS EH 48 C 25, fos. 20^v–26^v.

ZAGACHE, ABRAHAM DE ISRAEL (comp.), 'Libro de los acuerdos de la Nacion', etc., MS EH 48 D 43; listed as 'Collection of historical documents concerning the Sephardic congregation of Amsterdam'.

Stadsarchief Amsterdam (SA)

'Declarasao do modo e forma que se observa no governo da sinagoga e nação ebrea Portugueza em Amsterdam', SA 334, 119AA, 21.

Livro dos acordos da naçam, escamot e eleiçoms do K. K. de T. T. que el Dio augmente [1639–80], SA 334, 19.

Livro dos eleiçoems do K. K. de T. T. Fintas, e repartiçoems de dinheiros para Terra S[anc]ta, e outras resoluçoems dos SSres do Mahamad [1680–1712], SA 334, 20.

Libro dos termos da ymposta da nação [1622–39], SA 334, 13.

Published Sources

ABOAB, IMMANUEL, *Nomologia, o, discursos legales* (Amsterdam, 1629).

ABOAB DA FONSECA, ISAAC, *Exortação, paraque os tementes do Senhor na observança dos preceitos de sua Sancta Ley, não cayão em peccado por falta da conviniente inteligencia* (Amsterdam, 1680).

—— *Parafrasis comentado sobre el pentateuco* (Amsterdam, 1681).

ABRAVANEL, ISAAC, *Perush hatorah*, i, ed. Avishai Shotland (Jerusalem, 1997).

ADLER, JACOB, 'The Zionists and Spinoza', *Israel Studies Forum*, 24/1 (Spring 2009), 25–38.

AGUS, IRVING A., 'Democracy in the Communities of the Early Middle Ages', *Jewish Quarterly Review*, 43 (1952), 153–76.

ALBERT, ANNE ORAVETZ, '"A Civil Death": Sovereignty and the Jewish Republic in an Early Modern Treatment of Genesis 49: 10', in Richard I. Cohen, Natalie B. Dohrmann, Adam Shear, and Elchanan Reiner (eds.), *Jewish Culture in Early Modern Europe: Essays in Honor of David B. Ruderman* (Pittsburgh, Pa., 2014), 63–74.

—— 'On the Possibility of Jewish Politics in Our Time: Scholem, Exile, and Early Modern Transformations', in K. GhaneaBassiri and Paul Robertson (eds.), *All Religion Is Inter-Religion: Engaging the Work of Steven M. Wasserstrom* (London, 2019), 147–58.

—— 'The Rabbi and the Rebels: A Pamphlet on the Herem by Rabbi Isaac Aboab da Fonseca', *Jewish Quarterly Review*, 104 (2014), 171–91.

—— 'Return by Any Other Name: Religious Change among Amsterdam's New Jews', in T. Dunkelgrun and P. Maciejko (eds.), *Bastards and Believers: Jewish Converts and Conversion from the Bible to the Present* (Philadelphia, 2020), 134–55.

ALTHUSIUS, JOHANNES, *Politica: An Abridged Translation of Politics Methodically Set Forth and Illustrated with Sacred and Profane Examples*, ed. and trans. F. S. Carney (Indianapolis, Ind., 1995).

AMUSSEN, SUSAN DWYER, *An Ordered Society: Gender and Class in Early Modern England* (New York, 1988).

APPLEBAUM, SHIM'ON, *Jews and Greeks in Ancient Cyrene* (Leiden, 1979).

ARAD, DOTAN, 'When the Home Becomes a Shrine: Public Prayers in Private Houses among the Ottoman Jews', in Marco Faini and Alessia Meneghin (eds.), *Domestic Devotions in the Early Modern World* (Leiden, 2019), 55–68.

ARMITAGE, DAVID, 'John Locke, Carolina, and the *Two Treatises of Government*', *Political Theory*, 32 (2004), 602–27.

BAER, YITZHAK F., *Galut* (New York, 1947).

—— 'The Origins of Jewish Communal Organization in the Middle Ages', in Joseph Dan (ed.), *Binah: Studies in Jewish History, Thought and Culture*, 1 (1989), 59–82.

BALDWIN, GEOFFREY P., 'The Translation of Political Theory in Early Modern Europe', in Peter Burke and Ronnie Po-Chia Hsia (eds.), *Cultural Translation in Early Modern Europe* (Cambridge, 2007), 101–24.

BARBONE, STEVEN, and LEE RICE, 'Introduction', in Spinoza, *Political Treatise*, trans. Samuel Shirley (Indianapolis, Ind., 2000), 1–30.

BARON, SALO W., 'Azariah de' Rossi's Historical Method', in Baron, *History and Jewish Historians: Essays and Addresses* (Philadelphia, 1964), 205–39.

—— 'Ghetto and Emancipation', in Leo W. Schwarz (ed.), *The Menorah Treasury: Harvest of Half a Century* (Philadelphia, 1964), 50–63.

—— *The Jewish Community: Its History and Structure to the American Revolution*, 3 vols. (Philadelphia, 1942).

—— '"Plenitude of Apostolic Powers" and Medieval "Jewish Serfdom"', in L. A. Feldman (ed.), *Ancient and Medieval Jewish History* (New Brunswick, NJ, 1972), 284–307.

—— *Social and Religious History of the Jews*, 2nd rev. edn. (New York, 1952).

BARRIOS, DANIEL LEVI DE, *Discurso politico, sobre los adversos y prosperos sucessos de las Provincias Unidas desde 23. de Março de 1672. años hasta 12. de Septiembre 1673* (Amsterdam, 1673).

—— *Govierno popular judayco* (Amsterdam, 1684).

—— *Imperio de dios en la harmonia del mundo* (Amsterdam, 1674).

—— *Respuesta panegirica a la carta que escrivio el muy ilustre R. Joseph Penso Vega, al muy sapiente Doctor Ishac Orobio* (Amsterdam, 1677).

—— *Triumpho del govierno popular, y de la antiguedad Holandesa* (Amsterdam, 1683).

BASKIND, SAMANTHA, 'Distinguishing the Distinction: Picturing Ashkenazi and Sephardic Jews in Seventeenth- and Eighteenth-Century Amsterdam', *Journal for the Study of Sephardic and Mizrahi Jewry*, 1 (2007), 1–13.

BASTIN, GEORGES L., 'Adaptation', in Mona Baker (ed.), *Routledge Encyclopedia of Translation Studies* (London, 1998), 3–6.

BATNITZKY, LEORA, *How Judaism Became a Religion: An Introduction to Modern Jewish Thought* (Princeton, 2011).

BELILHOS, DANIEL, 'Sermam funeral por R. Daniel Belilhos. As postumas memorias de seu dignissimo Mestre & sogro, o Señor H. H. Morenu ve Rabenu Ishak Aboab: Ilustre Dayan & Preceptor do K.K. de T.T. em Amsterdam. Pregado na Esnoga, nas exequias do mez. Em 14 Nissan 5453', in *Sermoems pregados por R. Daniel Belilhos na Esnoga da T. T. e dedicados a nobre congrega* (Amsterdam, 1693).

BELINFANTE, JUDITH C. E., et al., *The Esnoga* (Amsterdam, 1991).

BELL, DEAN PHILLIP, 'Jewish Communities in Central Europe in the Sixteenth Century', in M. J. Halvorson and K. E. Spierling (eds.), *Defining Community in Early Modern Europe* (Aldershot, 2008), 143–62.

—— *Jewish Identity in Early Modern Germany: Memory, Power, and Community* (Aldershot, 2007).

BELL, DEAN PHILLIP, *Sacred Communities: Jewish and Christian Identities in Fifteenth-Century Germany* (Boston, Mass., 2001).

BEN-SASSON, HAIM HILLEL, 'The Generation of Spanish Exiles Considers Its Fate', in Joseph Dan (ed.), *Binah: Studies in Jewish History, Thought and Culture*, 1 (1989), 83–98.

BENEDICT, PHILIP, and MYRON P. GUTMANN (eds.), *Early Modern Europe: From Crisis to Stability* (Newark, Del., 2005).

BENOVITZ, MOSHE, *Kol Nidre: Studies in the Development of Rabbinic Votive Institutions* (Atlanta, Ga., 2020).

BENTON, LAUREN, *A Search for Sovereignty: Law and Geography in European Empires, 1400–1900* (Cambridge, 2010).

BERKOVITZ, JAY, 'Crisis and Authority in Early Modern Ashkenaz', *Jewish History*, 26 (2012), 179–99.

—— 'Rabbinic Leadership in Modern France: Competing Conceptions, Paradigms, and Strategies in the Emancipation Era', in Jack Wertheimer (ed.), *Jewish Religious Leadership: Image and Reality*, 2 vols. (New York, 2014), ii. 505–33.

BERKOWITZ, BETH, *Execution and Invention: Death Penalty Discourse in Early Rabbinic and Christian Cultures* (Oxford, 2006).

BERNAND, CARMEN, and SERGE GRUZINSKI, *De l'idolatrie: Une archéologie des sciences religieuses* (Paris, 1988).

BIALE, DAVID, *Gershom Scholem: Kabbalah and Counter-History*, 2nd edn. (Cambridge, Mass., 1982).

—— *Power and Powerlessness in Jewish History* (New York, 1987).

BLACK, ANTONY, *Guilds and Civil Society in European Political Thought from the Twelfth Century to the Present* (Cambridge, 1984).

BLICKLE, PETER, *Communal Reformation: The Quest for Salvation in Sixteenth-Century Germany*, trans. T. Dunlap (Atlantic Highlands, NJ, 1992).

BLIDSTEIN, GERALD J., 'On Political Structures—Four Medieval Comments', *Jewish Journal of Sociology*, 22 (1980), 47–58.

BODIAN, MIRIAM, 'Biblical Hebrews and the Rhetoric of Republicanism: Seventeenth-Century Portuguese Jews on the Jewish Community', *AJS Review*, 22 (1997), 199–221.

—— 'The Biblical "Jewish Republic" and the Dutch "New Israel" in Seventeenth-Century Dutch Thought', *Hebraic Political Studies*, 1 (2006), 186–202.

—— 'The *Escamot* of the Spanish-Portuguese Community of London, 1664', *Michael*, 9 (1985), 9–26.

—— 'Hebrews of the Portuguese Nation: The Ambiguous Boundaries of Self-Definition', *Jewish Social Studies*, 15 (2008), 66–80.

—— *Hebrews of the Portuguese Nation: Conversos and Community in Early Modern Amsterdam* (Bloomington, Ind., 1997).

—— '"Liberty of Conscience" and the Jews in the Dutch Republic', *Studies in Christian-Jewish Relations*, 6 (2011); <https://doi.org/10.6017/scjr.v6i1.1587>.

—— '"Men of the Nation": The Shaping of "Converso" Identity in Early Modern Europe', *Past & Present*, 143 (1994), 48–76.

—— 'The "Portuguese" Dowry Societies in Venice and Amsterdam: A Case Study in Communal Differentiation within the Marrano Diaspora', *Italia*, 6 (1987), 30–61.

—— 'The Portuguese Jews in Amsterdam and the Language of Liberty', *Journal of Levantine Studies*, 6 (2016), 313–32.

—— 'Some Ideological Implications of Marrano Involvement in the International Arena', in Avraham Hayim (ed.), *Society and Community (Proceeding of the Second International Congress for Research of the Sephardi and Oriental Jewish Heritage 1984)* [Ḥevrah ukehilah: midivrei hakongres habeinle'umi hasheni leḥeker moreshet yahadut sefarad vehamizraḥ] (Jerusalem, 1991), 207–17.

BODIN, JEAN, *Six Books of the Commonwealth*, trans. M. J. Tooley (New York, 1955).

BONET CORREA, ANTONIO, 'La ciudad hispanoamericana', in *Gran enciclopedia de España y America* (Madrid, 1986), ix. 25.

BONFIL, ROBERT, 'How Golden Was the Age of the Renaissance in Jewish Historiography?', *History and Theory*, 27/4 (1988), 78–102.

—— *Jewish Life in Renaissance Italy*, trans. A. Oldcorn (Berkeley, 1994).

—— *Rabbis and Jewish Communities in Renaissance Italy* (Oxford, 1990).

BORALEVI, LEA CAMPOS, 'Classical Foundation Myths of European Republicanism: The Jewish Commonwealth', in Martin van Gelderen and Quentin Skinner (eds.), *Republicanism: A Shared European Heritage*, i: *Republicanism and Constitutionalism in Early Modern Europe* (Cambridge, 2002), 247–61.

BOSSUET, JACQUES-BÉNIGNE, *Discourse on Universal History*, trans. Elborg Forster (Chicago, 1976).

—— *Politics Drawn from the Very Words of Holy Scripture*, trans. Patrick Riley (Cambridge, 1990).

BOTERO, GIOVANNI, *The Reason of State*, trans. P. J. and D. P. Waley (New Haven, 1956).

BRAUN, HARALD ERNST, 'The Bible, Reason of State, and the Royal Conscience: Juan Márquez's "El Governador Christiano"', *Renaissance Studies*, 23 (2009), 552–67.

BREGOLI, FRANCESCA, '"Your Father's Interests": The Business of Kinship in a Trans-Mediterranean Jewish Merchant Family, 1776–1790', *Jewish Quarterly Review*, 108 (2018), 194–224.

BRETT, ANNABEL S., *Changes of State: Nature and the Limits of the City in Early Modern Natural Law* (Princeton, 2011).

—— *Liberty, Right, and Nature: Individual Rights in Later Scholastic Thought* (Cambridge, 1997).

BRILLING, BERNHARD, 'An umbekanter document fun Sabbatai Zevi's zayt', in *Yivo-Bletter*, 5 (1933), 41–6.

BURKE, PETER, 'Cultures of Translation in Early Modern Europe', in Peter Burke and R. Po-Chia Hsia (eds.), *Cultural Translation in Early Modern Europe* (Cambridge, 2007), 7–38.

CALABI, DONATELLA, DOROTHEA NOLDE, and RONI WEINSTEIN, 'The "City of Jews" in Europe: The Conservation and Transmission of Jewish Culture', in Donatella Calabi and Stephen Turk Christensen (eds.), *Cultural Exchange in Early Modern Europe*, ii: *Cities and Cultural Exchange in Europe, 1400–1700* (Cambridge, 2007), 87–113.

CAPUTO, NINA, and LIZ CLARKE, *Debating Truth: The Barcelona Disputation of 1263, a Graphic History* (New York, 2017).

CARDOSO, ISAAC, *Las excelencias de los Hebreos* (Amsterdam, 1679).

CARLEBACH, ELISHEVA, 'Between Universal and Particular: Baron's Jewish Community in Light of Recent Research', *AJS Review*, 38 (2014), 417–21.

—— *Divided Souls: Converts from Judaism in Germany, 1500–1750* (New Haven, 2001).

—— 'The Early Modern Jewish Community and Its Institutions', in J. Karp and A. Sutcliffe (eds.), *The Cambridge History of Judaism*, vii: *The Early Modern World, 1500–1815* (Cambridge, 2017), 168–98.

—— *The Pursuit of Heresy: Rabbi Moses Hagiz and the Sabbatian Controversies* (New York, 1990).

—— 'The Sabbatian Posture of German Jewry', *Jerusalem Studies in Jewish Thought*, 16–17 (2001), 1–29.

—— 'Sabbatianism and the Jewish-Christian Polemic', in *Proceedings of the Tenth World Congress of Jewish Studies, Jerusalem, August 16–24, 1989* (Jerusalem, 1990), 1–7.

CARVAJAL, PATRICIO H., 'La teoría de la constitución en la "Politica" de Johannes Althusius', *Revista de estudios histórico-jurídicos* (Sección historia del pensamiento político), 37 (2015), 477–502.

CASTRO TARTAZ, DAVID DE, 'Prologo a o Lector', in *Sermoés que pregarão os doctos ingenios do K.K. de Talmud Torah, desta cidade de Amsterdam, no alegre estreamento, & publica celebridade da fabrica que se consagrou a deos, para caza de oração, cuja entrada se festejou em Sabath Nahamù*, ed. David de Castro Tartaz (Amsterdam, 1675), unpaginated prologue.

CATTERALL, DOUGLAS, *Community without Borders: Scots Migrants and the Changing Face of Power in the Dutch Republic, c.1600–1700* (Leiden, 2002).

CHAZAN, ROBERT, 'Genesis 49: 10 in Thirteenth-Century Christian Missionizing', in Elisheva Carlebach and Jacob Schacter (eds.), *New Perspectives on Jewish–Christian Relations* (Leiden, 2011), 93–108.

COENEN, THOMAS, *Tsipiyot shav shel hayehudim*, trans. Arthur Lagawier and Efraim Shmueli (Jerusalem, 1998).

—— *Ydele werwachtinge der Joden* (Amsterdam, 1669).

COHEN, JEREMY, *A Historian in Exile: Solomon ibn Verga, 'Shevet Yehudah,' and the Jewish-Christian Encounter* (Philadelphia, 2016).

COHEN, MARK R. (trans. and ed.), *The Autobiography of a Seventeenth-Century Venetian Rabbi: Leon Modena's Life of Judah* (Princeton, 1988).

COHEN, RICHARD I., *Jewish Icons: Art and Society in Modern Europe* (Berkeley, 1998).

—— 'Urban Visibility and Biblical Visions: Jewish Culture in Western and Central Europe in the Modern Age', in David Biale (ed.), *Cultures of the Jews: A New History* (New York, 2002), 730–96.

COHEN-SKALLI, CEDRIC, *Don Isaac Abravanel: An Intellectual Biography*, trans. Avi Kallenbach (Waltham, Mass., 2021).

—— 'Don Isaac Abravanel and the Conversos: Wealth, Politics, and Messianism', *Journal of Levantine Studies*, 6 (Summer/Winter 2016), 43–69.

COLLINSON, PATRICK, *De Republica Anglorum: Or, History with the Politics Put Back* (Cambridge, 1990).

CONDREN, CONAL, 'Reason of State and Sovereignty in Early Modern England: A Question of Ideology?', *Parergon*, 28/2 (2011), 5–27.

COOPERMAN, BERNARD, 'Amsterdam from an International Perspective: Tolerance and *Kehillah* in the Portuguese Diaspora', in Y. Kaplan (ed.), *Dutch Intersection: The Jews and the Netherlands in Modern History* (Leiden, 2007), 1–18.

—— 'Ethnicity and Institution Building among Jews in Early Modern Rome', *AJS Review*, 30 (2006), 119–45.

—— 'Portuguese *Conversos* in Ancona: Jewish Political Activity in Early Modern Italy', in B. Cooperman (ed.), *In Iberia and Beyond: Hispanic Jews Between Cultures*, Proceedings of a Symposium to Mark the 500th Anniversary of the Expulsion of Spanish Jewry (Newark, Del., 1998), 297–352.

COUDERT, ALLISON P., and JEFFREY S. SHOULSON (eds.), *Hebraica Veritas? Christian Hebraists and the Study of Judaism in Early Modern Europe* (Philadelphia, 2004).

CUNAEUS, PETRUS, *The Hebrew Republic*, trans. Peter Wyetzner (Jerusalem, 2006).

CURTIS, CATHY, and DAVID MARTIN JONES, 'Reason of State, Natural Law, and Early Modern Statecraft', *Parergon*, 28/2 (2011), 1–4.

DA SILVA ROSA, J. S., *Die spanischen und portugiesischen gedruckten Judaica in der Bibliothek des Jüd. Portug. Seminars 'Ets Haim' in Amsterdam: Eine Ergänzung zu Kayserlings 'Biblioteca española-portugueza-judaica'* (Amsterdam, 1933).

DAM, HARM-JAN VAN, 'Introduction', in Hugo Grotius, *De imperio summarum potestatum circa sacra*, ed. and trans. Harm-Jan van Dam (Leiden, 2001), i. 1–151.

DAN, JOSEPH, *Gershom Scholem and the Mystical Dimension of History* (New York, 1987).

DAUBER, NOAH, *State and Commonwealth: The Theory of the State in Early Modern England, 1549–1640* (Princeton, 2016).

DAVIS, KATHLEEN, *Periodization and Sovereignty: How Ideas of Feudalism and Secularization Govern the Politics of Time* (Philadelphia, 2008).

DEARDORFF, MAX, 'Republics, Their Customs, and the Law of the King: Convivencia and Self-Determination in the Crown of Castile and Its American Territories, 1400–1700', *Rechtsgeschichte—Legal History*, 26 (2018), 162–99.

DELLA ROCCA, MICHAEL, 'Getting His Hands Dirty: Spinoza's Criticism of the Rebel', in Yitzhak Y. Melamed and Michael A. Rosenthal (eds.), *Spinoza's Theological-Political Treatise: A Critical Guide* (Cambridge, 2010), 168–91.

DEMOS, JOHN, *A Little Commonwealth: Family Life in Plymouth Colony* (Oxford, 1970).

DEN BOER, HARM, 'Exile in Sephardic Literature of Amsterdam', *Studia Rosenthaliana*, 35 (2001), 187–99.

—— 'Literature, Politics, Economy: The Spanish and Portuguese Literature of the Sephardic Jews of Amsterdam', in Elliott Horowitz and Moises Orfali (eds.), *The Mediterranean and the Jews: Society, Culture and Economy in Early Modern Times* (Ramat-Gan, 2002), 101–13.

—— (ed.), *Spanish and Portuguese Printing in the Northern Netherlands, 1584–1825* (CD-ROM; Leiden, 2003).

—— and JONATHAN I. ISRAEL, 'William III and the Glorious Revolution in the Eyes of Amsterdam Sephardi Writers: The Reactions of Miguel de Barrios, Joseph Penso de la Vega, and Manuel Leão', in J. I. Israel (ed.), *The Anglo-Dutch Moment: Essays on the Glorious Revolution and Its World Impact* (Cambridge, 1991), 439–61.

DERRIDA, JACQUES, *The Death Penalty*, ed. Geoffrey Bennington, Marc Crépon, and Thomas Dutoit, trans. Peggy Kamuf, 2 vols. (Chicago, 2014).

DESPLAND, MICHEL, *La Religion en Occident: Évolution des idées et du vécu* (Montreal, 1979).

—— and GERARD VALLÉE (eds.), *Religion in History: The Word, the Idea, the Reality* (Waterloo, Ont., 1992).

DÍAZ ESTEBAN, FERNANDO, 'Fanciful Biblical Etymologies', in Miguel (Daniel Levi) de Barrios' Work', in Moshe Bar-Asher (ed.), *Studies in Hebrew and Jewish Languages Presented to Shelomo Morag* (Jerusalem, 1996), 3–14.

DINUR, BEN-ZION, 'Jewish History—Its Uniqueness and Continuity', in H. H. Ben-Sasson and S. Ettinger (eds.), *Jewish Society through the Ages* (New York, 1971), 15–29.

DUBIN, LOIS, 'Yosef Hayim Yerushalmi, the Royal Alliance, and Jewish Political Theory', *Jewish History*, 28 (2014), 51–81.

DUBNOW, SIMON, *Jewish History: An Essay in the Philosophy of History* (Philadelphia, 1903).

DUNKELGRÜN, THEODOR, 'The Christian Study of Judaism in Early Modern Europe', in Jonathan Karp and Adam Sutcliffe (eds.), *The Cambridge History of Judaism*, vii: *The Early Modern World, 1500–1815* (Cambridge, 2017), 316–48.

—— '"Neerlands Israel": Political Theology, Christian Hebraism, Biblical Antiquarianism, and Historical Myth', in Laura Cruz and Willem Frijhoff (eds.), *Myth in History, History in Myth, Proceedings of the Third International Conference of the Society for Netherlandic History (New York: 5–6 June 2006)* (Leiden, 2009), 201–36.

DUNTHORNE, HUGH, 'Resisting Monarchy: The Netherlands as Britain's School of Revolution in the Late Sixteenth and Seventeenth Centuries', in Robert Oresko, G. C. Gibbs, and H. M. Scott (eds.), *Royal and Republican Sovereignty in Early Modern Europe: Essays in Memory of Ragnhild Hatton* (Cambridge, 1997), 125–48.

DWECK, YAACOB, *Dissident Rabbi: The Life of Jacob Sasportas* (Princeton, 2019).

ELAZAR, DANIEL J., 'Communal Democracy and Liberal Democracy in the Jewish Political Tradition', *Jewish Political Studies Review*, 5 (1993), 5–31.

—— 'Covenant as the Basis of the Jewish Political Tradition', in Daniel J. Elazar (ed.), *Kinship and Consent: The Jewish Political Tradition and Its Contemporary Uses* (Washington, DC, 1983), 21–56.

—— 'The Political Theory of Covenant: Biblical Origins and Modern Developments', *Publius*, 10/4 (1980), 3–30.

ELON, MENACHEM, *Jewish Law: History, Sources, Principles*, trans. Bernard Auerbach and Melvin J. Sykes, 2 vols. (Philadelphia, 1994).

—— 'On Power and Authority: The Halakhic Stance of the Traditional Community and Its Contemporary Implications', in Daniel J. Elazar (ed.), *Kinship and Consent: The Jewish Political Tradition and Its Contemporary Uses*, 2nd rev. edn. (New Brunswick, NJ, 1997), 183–213.

ENRÍQUEZ GÓMEZ, ANTONIO, *Política angélica* (Rouen, 1647).

ERASTUS, THOMAS, *Explicatio gravissimae quaestionis utrum excommunicatio . . .* (Basel, 1572); Eng. trans. *A Treatise of Excommunication* (London, 1682).

ESPOSITO, ANNA, *Un'altra Roma: Minoranze nazionali e comunità ebraiche tra Medioevo e Rinascimento* (Rome, 1995).

EYFFINGER, ARTHUR, '"How Wondrously Moses Goes Along with the House of Orange!": Hugo Grotius' "De Republica Emendanda" in the Context of the Dutch Revolt', in Gordon Schochet, Fania Oz-Salzberger, and Meirav Jones (eds.), *Political Hebraism: Judaic Sources in Early Modern Political Thought* (Jerusalem, 2008), 107–47.

FAUR, ABRAHAM J., 'The Status of Communal Oaths in Jewish Law', *Diné Israel*, 13–14 (1988), 111–21.

FEIL, ERNST, 'From the Classical *Religio* to the Modern *Religion*: Elements of a Transformation between 1550 and 1650', in M. Despland and G. Vallée (eds.), *Religion in History: The Word, the Idea, the Reality* (Waterloo, Ont., 1992), 31–44.

FEUER, LEWIS SAMUEL, *Spinoza and the Rise of Liberalism* (Boston, Mass., 1958).

FIELD, SANDRA LEONIE, *Potentia: Hobbes and Spinoza on Power and Popular Politics* (New York, 2020).

FINKELSTEIN, LOUIS, *Jewish Self-Government in the Middle Ages* (Westport, Conn., 1924).

FISHER, BENJAMIN E., *Amsterdam's People of the Book: Jewish Society and the Turn to Scripture in the Seventeenth Century* (Cincinnati, Ohio, 2020).

FISHMAN, TALYA, *Shaking the Pillars of Exile: 'Voice of a Fool,' an Early Modern Jewish Critique of Rabbinic Culture* (Stanford, Calif., 1997).

FORD, RICHARD T., 'Law's Territory (A History of Jurisdiction)', *Michigan Law Review*, 97 (1999), 843–930.

FOUCAULT, MICHEL, *Discipline and Punish: The Birth of the Prison*, trans. Alan Sheridan (New York, 1979).

FRIEDLAND, PAUL, *Seeing Justice Done: The Age of Spectacular Capital Punishment in France* (Oxford, 2012).

FRIJHOFF, WILLEM, and MARIKE SPIES, *Dutch Culture in a European Perspective*, i: *1650: Hard-Won Unity* (Assen, 2004).

FRIJHOFF, WILLIAM, 'Religious Toleration in the United Provinces: From "Case" to "Model"', in R. Po-Chia Hsia and Henk van Nierop (eds.), *Calvinism and Religious Toleration in the Dutch Golden Age* (Cambridge, 2002), 37–62.

FUKUOKA, ATSUKO, *The Sovereign and the Prophets: Spinoza on Grotian and Hobbesian Biblical Argumentation* (Leiden, 2018).

FUKS, LEO, 'The Inauguration of the Portuguese Synagogue in Amsterdam in 1675', in Renate G. Fuks-Mansfeld (ed.), *Aspects of Jewish Life in the Netherlands: A Selection from the Writings of Leo Fuks* (Assen, 1995), 81–99.

—— and R. G. FUKS-MANSFELD, 'The Inauguration of the Portuguese Synagogue of Amsterdam, Netherlands, in 1675', *Arquivos do Centro Cultural Português*, 14 (1979), 489–507.

FUNKENSTEIN, AMOS, 'Basic Types of Christian Anti-Jewish Polemics in the Later Middle Ages', *Viator*, 2 (1971), 373–82.

—— *Perceptions of Jewish History* (Berkeley, 1993).

GARRETT, DON, '"Promising" Ideas: Hobbes and Contract in Spinoza's Political Philosophy', in Yitzhak Y. Melamed and Michael A. Rosenthal (eds.), *Spinoza's Theological-Political Treatise: A Critical Guide* (Cambridge, 2010), 192–209.

GELDEREN, MARTIN VAN, 'The Machiavellian Moment and the Dutch Revolt: The Rise of Neostoicism and Dutch Republicanism', in Giselle Bock, Quentin Skinner, and Maurizio Virolli (eds.), *Machiavelli and Republicanism* (Cambridge, 1990), 205–23.

GIESEY, RALPH E., *If Not, Not: The Oath of the Aragonese and the Legendary Laws of Sobrarbe* (Princeton, 1968).

GIL, XAVIER, 'Republican Politics in Early Modern Spain: The Castilian and Catalano-Aragonese Traditions', in Martin van Gelderen and Quentin Skinner (eds.), *Republicanism: A Shared European Heritage*, i: *Republicanism and Constitutionalism in Early Modern Europe* (Cambridge, 2002), 263–88.

GOLDIE, MARK, 'The Unacknowledged Republic: Officeholding in Early Modern England', in T. Harris (ed.), *The Politics of the Excluded, c.1500–1850* (Basingstoke, 2001), 153–94.

GOLDISH, MATT, 'Jews, Christians and Conversos: Rabbi Solomon Aailion's Struggles in the Portuguese Community of London', *Journal of Jewish Studies*, 45 (1994), 227–57.

—— 'New Approaches to Jewish Messianism', *AJS Review*, 25 (2000), 71–83.

—— 'Orthodoxy and Heterodoxy in the 1689 London Sermons of Hakham Solomon Aailion', in Chanita Goldblatt and Howard Kreisel (eds.), *Tradition, Heterodoxy, and Religious Culture: Judaism and Christianity in the Early Modern Period* (Beer Sheva, 2006), 139–65.

—— 'Patterns in Converso Messianism', in Richard Popkin and Matt Goldish (eds.), *Jewish Messianism in the Early Modern World* (Dordrecht, 2001), 41–63.

—— *The Sabbatean Prophets* (Cambridge, Mass., 2004).

GOLDMAN-IDA, BATSHEVA, 'Synagogues in Central and Eastern Europe in the Early Modern Period', in Steven Fine (ed.), *Jewish Religious Architecture: From Biblical Israel to Modern Judaism* (Leiden, 2020), 184–207.

GOMES SILVEIRA, ABRAHAM, *Sermones compuestos por Abraham Gomes Silveira* (Amsterdam, 1677).

GOODMAN, DENA, 'Public Sphere and Private Life: Toward a Synthesis of Current Historiographical Approaches to the Old Regime', *History and Theory*, 31 (1992), 1–20.

GRAFF, GIL, *Separation of Church and State: Dina de-Malkhuta Dina in Jewish Law, 1750–1848* (University, Ala., 1985).

GRAFTON, ANTHONY, and JOANNA WEINBERG, *'I Have Always Loved the Holy Tongue': Isaac Casaubon, the Jews, and a Forgotten Chapter in Renaissance Scholarship* (Cambridge, Mass., 2011).

GREENBERG, MOSHE, and HAIM HERMANN COHN, 'Herem', in Michael Berenbaum and Fred Skolnik (eds.), *Encyclopaedia Judaica* (Detroit, 2007), ix. 10–16.

GREYERZ, KASPAR VON, *Religion and Culture in Early Modern Europe: 1500–1800*, trans. T. Dunlap (Oxford, 2008).

GRIFFITHS, PAUL, ADAM FOX, and STEVE HINDLE (eds.), *The Experience of Authority in Early Modern England* (New York, 1996).

GROENVELD, SIMON, 'For the Benefit of the Poor: Social Assistance in Amsterdam', in P. van Kessel and E. Schulte (eds.), *Rome and Amsterdam: Two Growing Cities in Seventeenth-Century Europe* (Amsterdam, 1997), 192–208.

GROTIUS, HUGO, *De imperio summarum potestum circa sacra*, ed. and trans. Harm-Jan van Dam (Leiden, 2001).

——*Remonstrantie*, in David Kromhout and Adri Offenberg, *Hugo Grotius's Remonstrantie of 1615: Facsimile, Transliteration, Modern Translations and Analysis* (Leiden, 2019).

GUESNET, FRANÇOIS, 'The Politics of Precariousness—Josel of Rosheim and Jewish Intercession in the Holy Roman Empire in the 16th Century', *Jewish Culture and History*, 19 (2018), 8–22.

GUNNOE, CHARLES D., JR., 'The Evolution of Erastianism: Hugo Grotius's Engagement with Thomas Erastus', *Grotiana*, 34 (2013), 41–61.

GUTWIRTH, ELEAZAR, 'The Expulsion of the Jews from Spain and Jewish Historiography', in Ada Rapoport-Albert and Steven J. Zipperstein (eds.), *Jewish History: Essays in Honour of Chimen Abramsky* (London, 1988), 141–61.

——'Penso's Roots: The Politics and Poetics of Cultural Fusion', *Studia Rosenthaliana*, 35 (2001), 269–84.

HA, POLLY, *English Presbyterianism, 1590–1640* (Stanford, Calif., 2010).

HABERMAS, JÜRGEN, *The Structural Transformation of the Public Sphere: An Inquiry into a Category of Bourgeois Society*, trans. Thomas Burger (Cambridge, Mass., 1989).

HACKER, JOSEPH, and YARON HAREL (eds.), *The Sceptre Shall Not Depart from Judah: Leadership, Rabbinate and Community in Jewish History: Studies Presented to Professor Simon Schwarzfuchs* [Lo yasur shevet miyehudah: hanhagah, rabanut ukehilah betoledot yisra'el] (Jerusalem, 2011).

HAGOORT, LYDIA, 'The Del Sottos, a Portuguese Jewish Family in Amsterdam in the Seventeenth Century', *Studia Rosenthaliana*, 31 (1997), 31–57.

HAITSMA MULIER, ECO O. G., 'A Controversial Republican: Dutch Views on Machiavelli in the Seventeenth and Eighteenth Centuries', in G. Bock, Q. Skinner, and M. Viroli (eds.), *Machiavelli and Republicanism* (Cambridge, 1990), 247–63.

——'The Language of Seventeenth-Century Republicanism in the United Provinces: Dutch or European?', in Anthony Pagden (ed.), *The Languages of Political Theory in Early-Modern Europe* (Cambridge, 1987), 179–96.

HALPERIN, DAVID J. (ed. and trans.), *Sabbatai Zevi: Testimonies to a Fallen Messiah* (Oxford, 2007).

HAMMILL, GRAHAM, and JULIA REINHARD LUPTON, 'Introduction', in Hammill and Lupton (eds.), *Political Theology and Early Modernity* (Chicago, 2012), 1–20.

HARRIS, TIM, 'Introduction', in T. Harris (ed.), *The Politics of the Excluded, c.1500–1850* (Basingstoke, 2001), 1–29.

HARRISON, PETER, *'Religion' and the Religions in the English Enlightenment* (Cambridge, 1990).

HARVEY, WARREN ZEV, 'Spinoza on Ibn Ezra's "Secret of the Twelve"', in Yitzhak Y. Melamed and Michael A. Rosenthal (eds.), *Spinoza's Theological-Political Treatise: A Critical Guide* (Cambridge, 2010), 41–55.

—— 'Spinoza's Counterfactual Zionism', *Iyyun: The Jerusalem Philosophical Quarterly*, 62 (2013), 235–44.

HAZARD, PAUL, *La Crise de la conscience européenne, 1680–1715* (Paris, 1935).

—— *The Crisis of the European Mind: 1680–1715*, trans. J. Lewis May (New York, 2013).

HAZONY, YORAM, 'The Biblical Century', 10 May 2010; <https://jerusalemletters.com/the-biblical-century/>.

HELLER, ENA GIURESCU, 'Western Ashkenazi Synagogues in Medieval and Early Modern Europe', in Steven Fine (ed.), *Jewish Religious Architecture: From Biblical Israel to Modern Judaism* (Leiden, 2020), 169–83.

HERMANN, JACQUELINE, *No reino do desejado: A construção do sebastianismo em Portugal, séculos XVI e XVII* (São Paulo, 1998).

HERRERO SANCHEZ, MANUEL, 'La monarquía hispánica y las repúblicas europeas: El modelo republicano en una monarquía de ciudades', in Manuel Herrero Sanchez (ed.), *Repúblicas y republicanismo en la Europa moderna (siglos XVI–XVIII)* (Madrid, 2017), 273–326.

HILL, CHRISTOPHER, *The English Bible and the Seventeenth-Century Revolution* (London, 1993).

HOBBES, THOMAS, *Leviathan*, ed. Richard Tuck, rev. edn. (Cambridge, 1996).

HONT, ISTVAN, *Politics in Commercial Society: Jean-Jacques Rousseau and Adam Smith*, ed. Béla Kapossy and Michael Sonenscher (Cambridge, Mass., 2015).

HOROWITZ, ELLIOTT, 'Procession, Piety, and Jewish Confraternities', in Robert C. Davis and Benjamin Ravid (eds.), *The Jews of Early Modern Venice* (Baltimore, 2001), 231–47.

—— *Reckless Rites: Purim and the Legacy of Jewish Violence* (Princeton, 2006).

HSIA, R. PO-CHIA, 'Introduction', in R. Po-Chia Hsia and Henk van Nierop (eds.), *Calvinism and Religious Toleration in the Dutch Golden Age* (Cambridge, 2002), 11–17.

HUUSSEN, AREND H., 'The Legal Position of the Sephardi Jews in Holland, c.1600', in Jozeph Michman (ed.), *Dutch Jewish History*, Proceedings of the Fifth Symposium on the History of the Jews in the Netherlands, Jerusalem, 25–28 Nov. 1991 (Assen, 1993), 19–41.

IBN VERGA, SOLOMON, *La vara de yehudah (Sefer sebet yehudah)*, trans. Maria José Cano (Barcelona, 1991).

ISRAEL, JONATHAN I., 'An Amsterdam Merchant of the Golden Age: Jeronimo Nunes da Costa (1620–1697), Agent of Portugal in the Dutch Republic', *Studia Rosenthaliana*, 18 (1984), 21–40.

—— *Diasporas within a Diaspora: Jews, Crypto-Jews and the World Maritime Empires (1540–1740)* (Leiden, 2002).

ISRAEL, JONATHAN I., *The Dutch Republic: Its Rise, Greatness, and Fall 1477–1806* (Oxford, 1995).

—— *European Jewry in the Age of Mercantilism 1550–1750* (London, 1998).

—— 'How Does Spinoza's "Democracy" Differ from That of Hobbes? A Discussion of *Potentia: Hobbes and Spinoza on Power and Popular Politics*', *Hobbes Studies*, 34 (2021), 227–40.

—— 'The Intellectual Debate about Toleration in the Dutch Republic', in C. Berkvens-Stevelinck, J. Israel, and G. H. M. Posthumus Meyjes (eds.), *The Emergence of Tolerance in the Dutch Republic* (Leiden, 1997), 3–36.

—— 'The Intellectual Origins of Modern Democratic Republicanism (1660–1720)', *European Journal of Political Theory*, 3 (2004), 7–36.

—— 'Manuel López Pereira of Amsterdam, Antwerp and Madrid: Jew, New Christian, and Advisor to the Conde-Duque De Olivares', *Studia Rosenthaliana*, 19 (1985), 109–26.

—— *Monarchy, Orangism, and Republicanism in the Later Dutch Golden Age* (Amsterdam, 2004).

—— 'Orobio de Castro and the Early Enlightenment', in Henry Méchoulan and Gérard Nahon (eds.), *Mémorial I.-S. Révah: Études sur le marranisme, l'hétérodoxie juive et Spinoza* (Paris, 2001), 227–45.

—— *Radical Enlightenment: Philosophy and the Making of Modernity 1650–1750* (Oxford, 2001).

—— 'The Republic of the United Netherlands until about 1750: Demography and Economic Activity', in Hans Blom, David J. Wertheim, Hetty Berg, and Bart T. Wallet (eds.), *Reappraising the History of the Jews in the Netherlands* (London, 2021), 75–104.

—— (ed.), *The Anglo-Dutch Moment: Essays on the Glorious Revolution and Its World Impact* (Cambridge, 1991).

JACOBS, MARTIN, 'Joseph ha-Kohen, Paolo Giovio, and Sixteenth-Century Historiography', in David B. Ruderman and Giuseppe Veltri (eds.), *Cultural Intermediaries: Jewish Intellectuals in Early Modern Italy* (Philadelphia, 2004), 67–85.

JOHNSON, JAMES TURNER, *Sovereignty: Moral and Historical Perspectives* (Washington, DC, 2014).

JONES, DAVID MARTIN, 'Aphorism and the Counsel of Prudence in Early Modern Statecraft: The Curious Case of Justus Lipsius', *Parergon*, 28/2 (2011), 55–85.

JUDAH HALEVI, *Kitab al Khazari*, trans. Hartwig Hirschfeld (New York, 1905).

JÜTTE, DANIEL, *The Strait Gate: Thresholds and Power in Western History* (New Haven, 2015).

KAGAN, RICHARD L., *Clio and the Crown: The Politics of History in Medieval and Early Modern Spain* (Baltimore, 2009).

KANARFOGEL, EPHRAIM, 'Unanimity, Majority, and Communal Government in Ashkenaz during the High Middle Ages: A Reassessment', *Proceedings of the American Academy for Jewish Research*, 58 (1992), 79–106.

KAPLAN, BENJAMIN J., *Divided by Faith: Religious Conflict and the Practice of Toleration in Early Modern Europe* (Cambridge, Mass., 2007).

—— '"Dutch" Religious Tolerance: Celebration and Revision', in R. Po-Chia Hsia and H. van Nierop (eds.), *Calvinism and Religious Toleration in the Dutch Golden Age* (Cambridge, 2002), 8–26.

—— 'Fictions of Privacy: House Chapels and the Spatial Accommodation of Religious Dissent in Early Modern Europe', *American Historical Review*, 7 (2002), 1031–64.

KAPLAN, DEBRA, 'Communal Places: Early Modern Jewish Homes and Religious Devotions', in Marco Faini and Alessia Meneghin (eds.), *Domestic Devotions in the Early Modern World* (Leiden, 2019), 315–33.

—— *The Patrons and Their Poor: Jewish Community and Public Charity in Early Modern Germany* (Philadelphia, 2020).

KAPLAN, YOSEF, 'An Alternative Path to Modernity', in Kaplan, *An Alternative Path to Modernity*, 3–13.

—— *An Alternative Path to Modernity: The Sephardi Diaspora in Western Europe* (Leiden, 2000).

—— 'The Attitude of the Sephardi Leadership in Amsterdam to the Sabbatian Movement, 1665–1671', in Kaplan, *An Alternative Path to Modernity*, 211–33.

—— 'Bans in the Sephardi Community of Amsterdam in the Late Seventeenth Century' (Heb.), in Aaron Mirsky, Abraham Grossman, and Yosef Kaplan (eds.), *Exile after Diaspora: Research in the History of the Jewish People Dedicated to Professor Haim Beinart on the Occasion of His Seventieth Birthday* [Galut aḥar golah: meḥkarim betoledot am yisra'el mugashim leprofessor ḥayim beinart limelot lo shivim shanah] (Jerusalem, 1988), 517–40.

—— 'Concealed and Fluid Identities: Conversos and New Christians in the Early Modern Period' (Heb.), in Avi Elqayam and Yosef Kaplan (eds.), *Conceal the Outcasts: Jews with Hidden Identities* [Satri nidaḥim: yehudim im zehuyot ḥavuyot] (Jerusalem, 2016), 47–68.

—— 'Deviance and Excommunication in the Eighteenth Century: A Chapter in the Social History of the Sephardi Community of Amsterdam', in Jozeph Michman (ed.), *Dutch Jewish History*, Proceedings of the Fifth Symposium on the History of the Jews in the Netherlands, Jerusalem, 25–28 Nov. 1991 (Assen, 1993), 103–16.

—— 'Discipline, Dissent, and Communal Authority in the Western Sephardic Diaspora', in Jonathan Karp and Adam Sutcliffe (eds.), *The Cambridge History of Judaism*, vii: *The Early Modern World, 1500–1815* (Cambridge, 2018), 378–406.

KAPLAN, YOSEF, 'El mesianismo en la sociedad Judía de la temprana edad moderna', in A. Alvar Ezquerra, J. Contreras Contreras, and J. I. Ruiz Rodríguez (eds.), *Política y cultura, en la época moderna (cambios dinásticos, milenarismos, mesianismos y utopias)* (Álcala de Henares, 2000), 521–32.

—— 'El perfil cultural de tres rabinos sefardíes a través del análisis de sus bibliotecas', in B. J. García, J. Contrera, and I. Pulido (eds.), *Familia, religión y negocio: El sefardismo en las relaciones entre el mundo ibérico y los Países Bajos en la Edad Moderna* (Madrid, 2002), 269–86.

—— 'For Whom Did Emanuel de Witte Paint His Three Pictures of the Sephardi Synagogue in Amsterdam?', in Kaplan, *An Alternative Path to Modernity*, 29–50.

—— *From Christianity to Judaism: The Story of Isaac Orobio de Castro*, trans. Raphael Loewe (Oxford, 1989).

—— '*Gente Política*: The Portuguese Jews of Amsterdam vis-à-vis Dutch Society', in Chaya Brasz and Yosef Kaplan (eds.), *Dutch Jews as Perceived by Themselves and Others, Proceedings of the Eighth International Symposium on the History of the Jews in the Netherlands* (Leiden, 2001), 21–40.

—— 'Isaac Fernando Cardoso' (Heb.), in Isaac Cardoso, *Ma'alot ha'ivrim* [The Excellencies of the Hebrews], trans. Yosef Kaplan (Jerusalem, 1971), 7–28.

—— 'On the Relation of Spinoza's Contemporaries in the Portuguese Jewish Community of Amsterdam to Spanish Culture and the Marrano Experience', in C. de Deugd (ed.), *Spinoza's Political and Theological Thought, International Symposium under the Auspices of the Royal Netherlands Academy of Arts and Sciences Commemorating the 350th Anniversary of the Birth of Spinoza (Amsterdam: 24–27 Nov. 1982)* (Amsterdam, 1984), 82–94.

—— 'Order and Discipline in the Portuguese Synagogue of Amsterdam', in Albert van der Heide and Irene E. Zwiep (eds.), *Jewish Studies and the European Academic World* (Paris, 2005), 1–14.

—— 'Political Concepts in the World of the Portuguese Jews of Amsterdam during the Seventeenth Century: The Problem of Exclusion and the Boundaries of Self-Identity', in Yosef Kaplan, Henry Méchoulan, and Richard Popkin (eds.), *Menasseh ben Israel and His World* (Leiden, 1989), 45–62.

—— 'The Portuguese Community of Amsterdam in the 17th Century between Tradition and Change', in Avraham Hayim (ed.), *Society and Community (Proceeding of the Second International Congress for Research of the Sephardi and Oriental Jewish Heritage 1984)* [Ḥevrah ukehilah: midivrei hakongres habeinle'umi hasheni leḥeker moreshet yahadut sefarad vehamizraḥ] (Jerusalem, 1991), 141–71.

—— 'Preface', in Yosef Kaplan (ed.), *Religious Changes and Cultural Transformations in the Early Modern Western Sephardic Communities* (Leiden, 2019), pp. ix–xxxii.

——'The Social Functions of the Herem', in Kaplan, *An Alternative Path to Modernity*, 108–42.

——'Wayward New Christians and Stubborn New Jews: The Shaping of a Jewish Identity', *Jewish History*, 8/1–2 (1994), 27–41.

KASHER, ASA, and SHLOMO BIDERMAN, 'Why Was Baruch de Spinoza Excommunicated?', in David S. Katz and Jonathan I. Israel (eds.), *Sceptics, Millenarians and Jews* (Leiden, 1990), 98–141.

KATCHEN, AARON, *Christian Hebraists and Dutch Rabbis: Seventeenth-Century Apologetics and the Study of Maimonides' Mishneh Torah* (Cambridge, Mass., 1984).

KATZ, DANA E., *The Jewish Ghetto and the Visual Imagination of Early Modern Venice* (Cambridge, 2017).

KATZ, DAVID S., *Philo-semitism and the Readmission of the Jews to England, 1603–1655* (Oxford, 1982).

KATZ, JACOB, *Tradition and Crisis: Jewish Society at the End of the Middle Ages* (New York, 1961).

KAYSERLING, MEYER, *Biblioteca espanola-portugueza-judaica* (Strasbourg, 1890).

KIMELMAN, REUVEN, 'Abravanel and the Jewish Republican Ethos', in Daniel H. Frank (ed.), *Commandment and Community: New Essays in Jewish Legal and Political Philosophy* (Albany, NY, 1995), 195–214.

KISCH, GUIDO, *The Jews in Medieval Germany: A Study of Their Legal and Social Status* (Chicago, 1949).

KLEIN, ELKA, *Jews, Christian Society, and Royal Power in Medieval Barcelona* (Ann Arbor, 2006).

KNIGHTS, MARK, et al., 'Commonwealth: The Social, Cultural, and Conceptual Contexts of an Early Modern Keyword', *Historical Journal*, 54 (2011), 659–87.

KOOI, CHRISTINE, *Calvinists and Catholics during Holland's Golden Age: Heretics and Idolaters* (Cambridge, 2012).

——'Paying Off the Sheriff: Strategies of Catholic Toleration in Golden Age Holland', in R. Po-Chia Hsia and Henk van Nierop (eds.), *Calvinism and Religious Toleration in the Dutch Golden Age* (Cambridge, 2002), 87–101.

KOSSMANN, E. H., 'The Course of Dutch Political Theory in the Seventeenth Century', in Kossman, *Political Thought in the Dutch Republic: Three Studies* (Amsterdam, 2000), 25–129.

——'The Development of Dutch Political Theory in the Seventeenth Century', in J. S. Bromley and E. H. Kossmann (eds.), *Britain and the Netherlands*, i (London, 1960), 91–110.

——'Dutch Republicanism', in *Politieke theorie en geschiedenis: Verspreide opstellen en voordrachten* (Amsterdam, 1987), 211–33.

——*Political Thought in the Dutch Republic: Three Studies* (Amsterdam, 2000).

KRAVSTOV, SERGEY, 'Juan Bautista Villalpando and Sacred Architecture in the Seventeenth Century', *Journal of the Society of Architectural Historians*, 64 (2005), 312–39.

KRINSKY, CAROL HERSELLE, *Synagogues of Europe: Architecture, History, Meaning* (Cambridge, Mass., 1985).

LARA, JAIME, *City, Temple, Stage: Eschatological Architecture and Liturgical Theatrics in New Spain* (Notre Dame, Ind., 2004).

LASKER, DANIEL J., 'Reflections of the Medieval Jewish–Christian Debate in the Theological-Political Treatise and the Epistles', in Yitzhak Y. Melamed and Michael A. Rosenthal (eds.), *Spinoza's Theological-Political Treatise: A Critical Guide* (Cambridge, 2010), 56–71.

LAZIER, BENJAMIN, *God Interrupted: Heresy and the European Imagination between the World Wars* (Princeton, 2010).

LAZZERI, CHRISTIAN, 'Le Gouvernement de la raison d'état', in Christian Lazzeri and Dominique Reynié (eds.), *Le Pouvoir de la raison d'état* (Paris, 1992), 91–134.

LEE, DANIEL, *Popular Sovereignty in Early Modern Constitutional Thought* (Oxford, 2016).

LEEUWEN, TH. MARIUS VAN, 'Philippus van Limborch's *Amica Collatio* and Its Relation to Grotius's *De veritate*', *Grotiana*, 35 (2014), 158–67.

LEHMANN, MATTHIAS, *Ladino Rabbinic Literature and Ottoman Sephardic Culture* (Indianapolis, Ind., 2005).

LEIBMAN, LAURA, 'Sephardic Sacred Space in Colonial America', *Jewish History*, 25/1, Special Issue on Synagogue Architecture in Context (2011), 13–41.

LEVENE, NANCY, *Spinoza's Revelation: Religion, Democracy, and Reason* (Cambridge, 2004).

LEVIE BERNFELD, TIRTSAH, 'Financing Poor Relief in the Spanish-Portuguese Jewish Community in Amsterdam in the Seventeenth and Eighteenth Centuries', in J. I. Israel and R. Salverda (eds.), *Dutch Jewry: Its History and Secular Culture* (Leiden, 2002), 63–102.

—— *Poverty and Welfare among the Portuguese Jews in Early Modern Amsterdam* (Oxford, 2012).

LIBERLES, ROBERT, 'On the Threshold of Modernity: 1618–1780', in Marion A. Kaplan (ed.), *Jewish Daily Life in Germany, 1618–1945* (Oxford, 2005), 9–92.

LIEBERMAN, JULIA REBOLLO, *El teatro alegórico de Miguel (Daniel Leví) de Barrios* (Newark, Del., 1996).

LIEBES, YEHUDA, 'Sabbatean Messianism', in *Studies in Jewish Myth and Messianism* (Albany, NY, 1992), 93–106.

LIFSHITZ, JOSEPH ISAAC, *Rabbi Meir of Rothenburg and the Foundation of Jewish Political Thought* (New York, 2016).

LIPIS, MIMI LEVY, *Symbolic Houses in Judaism: How Objects and Metaphors Construct Hybrid Places of Belonging* (Farnham, Surrey, 2011).

LIPSIUS, JUSTUS, *Politica: Six Works of Politics or Political Instruction*, ed. Jan Waszink (Assen, 2004).

LIPTON, SARA, *The Dark Mirror: The Medieval Origins of Anti-Jewish Iconography* (New York, 2014).

LITT, STEFAN, *Pinkas, Kahal, and the Mediene: The Records of the Dutch Ashkenazi Communities in the Eighteenth Century as Historical Sources* (Leiden, 2008).

LLOYD, HOWELL A., 'Constitutionalism', in J. H. Burns (ed.), *The Cambridge History of Political Thought, 1450–1700* (Cambridge, 1991), 254–97.

LOCKE, JOHN, *Second Treatise of Government*, ed. C. B. Macpherson (Indianapolis, Ind., 1980).

—— *Two Treatises of Government: A Critical Edition with an Introduction and Apparatus Criticus*, ed. Peter Laslett, student edn. (Cambridge, 1988).

LOPES, ELIYAHU, 'Sermão Quinto', in *Sermoés que pregarõo os doctos ingenios do K.K. de Talmud Torah, desta cidade de Amsterdam, no alegre estreamento, & publica celebridade da fabrica que se consagrou a deos, para caza de oração, cuja entrada se festejou em Sabath Nahamù*, ed. David de Castro Tartaz (Amsterdam, 1675), 77–98.

LORBERBAUM, MENACHEM, *Politics and the Limits of the Law* (Stanford, Calif., 2001).

LUZZATTO, SIMONE, *Discorso circa il stato degli Hebrei et in particolar dimoranti nell'inclita citta di Venetia* (Venice, 1638).

—— *Discourse on the State of the Jews: Bilingual Edition*, ed. and trans. Giuseppe Veltri and Anna Lissa (Berlin, 2019).

MACHIAVELLI, NICCOLÒ, *The Prince*, ed. Q. Skinner and R. Price (Cambridge, 1988).

MACIEJKO, PAWEL (ed.), *Sabbatian Heresy: Writings on Mysticism, Messianism, and the Origins of Jewish Modernity* (Waltham, Mass., 2017).

McCLINTOCK, MATT, 'Johannes Althusius' *Politica*: The Culmination of Calvin's Right of Resistance', *European Legacy: Toward New Paradigms*, 11 (2006), 485–99.

McILWAIN, CHARLES HOWARD, *Constitutionalism, Ancient and Modern* (Ithaca, NY, 1940).

MACPHERSON, C. B., 'Introduction', in John Locke, *Second Treatise of Government*, ed. C. B. Macpherson (Indianapolis, Ind., 1980), pp. vii–xxi.

MAGNIER, GRACE, *Pedro de Valencia and the Catholic Apologists of the Expulsion of the Moriscos* (Leiden, 2010).

MALCOLM, NOEL, *Aspects of Hobbes* (Oxford, 2002).

MALKIEL, DAVID, 'The Ghetto Republic', in Robert C. Davis and Benjamin Ravid (eds.), *The Jews of Early Modern Venice* (Baltimore, 2001), 117–42.

—— *A Separate Republic: The Mechanics and Dynamics of Venetian Jewish Self-Government, 1607–1624* (Jerusalem, 1991).

MANDELBROTE, SCOTT, and JOANNA WEINBERG, *Jewish Books and Their Readers: Aspects of the Intellectual Life of Christians and Jews in Early Modern Europe* (Leiden, 2016).

MANN, VIVIAN B., 'Synagogues of Spain and Portugal during the Middle Ages', in Steven Fine (ed.), *Jewish Religious Architecture: From Biblical Israel to Modern Judaism* (Leiden, 2020), 151–68.

—— 'Towards an Iconography of Medieval Diaspora Synagogues', in Christoph Cluse (ed.), *The Jews of Europe in the Middle Ages (Tenth to Fifteenth Centuries), Proceedings of the International Symposium held at Speyer, 20–25 Oct. 2002* (Turnhout, 2004), 341–52.

MÁRQUEZ, JUAN, *El governador christiano: Deducido de las vidas de Moysen, y Josue, principes del pueblo de Dios* (Amsterdam, 1664).

MARX, ALEXANDER, *Studies in Jewish History and Booklore* (New York, 1944).

MÉCHOULAN, HENRY, 'Abraham Pereyra, juge des marranes et censeur de ses coreligionnaires à Amsterdam au temps de Spinoza', *Revue des études juives*, 138 (1979), 391–400.

—— 'Diego de Estella, une source espagnole de l'oeuvre d'Abraham Pereyra', *Studia Rosenthaliana*, 15 (1981), 178–87.

—— 'Le *Herem* à Amsterdam et "l'excommunication" de Spinoza', *Cahiers Spinoza*, 3 (1979), 117–34.

—— *Hispanidad y Judaismo en tiempos de Espinoza: Edición de La Certeza del Camino de Abraham Pereyra* (Salamanca, 1987).

—— 'The Importance of Hispanicity in Jewish Orthodoxy and Heterodoxy in Seventeenth-Century Amsterdam', in Bernard Dov Cooperman (ed.), *In Iberia and Beyond: Hispanic Jews between Cultures* (Newark, Del., 1998), 353–72.

—— 'La Pensée d'Abraham Pereyra dans *La Certeza del Camino*', in Jozeph Michman and Tirtsah Levie (eds.), *Dutch Jewish History, Proceedings of the Symposium on the History of the Jews in the Netherlands, 28 Nov.–2 Dec. 1982* (Jerusalem, 1984).

—— 'La Raison d'état dans la pensée espagnole au siècle d'or (1550–1650)', in Yves-Charles Zarka (ed.), *Raison et déraison d'état: Théoriciens et théories de la raison d'état aux XVIe et XVIIe siècles* (Paris, 1994), 245–64.

—— and GÉRARD NAHON (eds.), *Menasseh ben Israel: The Hope of Israel. The English Translation by Moses Wall, 1652* (Oxford, 1987).

MEGIVERN, JAMES J., *The Death Penalty: An Historical and Theological Survey* (New York, 1997).

MEIJER, JACOB, 'Hugo Grotius' "Remonstrantie"', *Jewish Social Studies*, 17/2 (1955), 91–104.

MEINSMA, K. O., *Spinoza en zijn kring: Historisch-kritische studiën over Hollandsche vrijgeesten* (The Hague, 1896).

MELAMED, ABRAHAM, 'The Attitude toward Democracy in Medieval Jewish Philosophy', in Daniel H. Frank (ed.), *Commandment and Community: New Essays in Jewish Legal and Political Philosophy* (Albany, NY, 1995), 173–94.

—— 'Is There a Jewish Political Thought? The Medieval Case Reconsidered', *Hebraic Political Studies*, 1 (2005), 24–56.

—— *Wisdom's Little Sister: Studies in Medieval and Renaissance Jewish Political Thought* (Boston, Mass., 2012).

MELAMED, YITZHAK Y., *Spinoza's Metaphysics: Substance and Thought* (New York, 2013).

—— and MICHAEL A. ROSENTHAL (eds.), *Spinoza's Theological-Political Treatise: A Critical Guide* (Cambridge, 2010).

MENASSEH BEN ISRAEL, *Conciliador: O de la conveniencia de los lugares de la s[agrada] escriptura que repugnantes entre si parecen*, 4 vols. (Amsterdam, 1632–51).

—— *De la fragilidad humana, y inclinacion del hombre al peccado* (Amsterdam, 1642).

—— '*Even yeqarah. Piedra gloriosa; o de la estatua de Nebuchadnesar* (Amsterdam, 1655).

—— *Hope of Israel*, 2nd English edn. (Amsterdam, 1652).

—— *The Humble Addresses of Menasseh Ben Israel, a Divine, and Doctor of Physick, in Behalfe of the Jewish Nation* (London, 1655).

MENDELSSOHN, MOSES, *Jerusalem: Or, On Religious Power and Judaism*, trans. Allan Arkush (Waltham, Mass., 1983).

Midrash Rabbah, trans. H. Freedman and Maurice Simon, 10 vols. (London, 1939).

MIGLIETTI, SARA, 'Sovereignty, Territory, and Population in Jean Bodin's *République*', *French Studies*, 72/1 (2018), 17–34.

Mikraot gedolot haketer, ed. Menachem Cohen (Ramat Gan, 1993), ii.

MILTON, JOHN R., 'Dating Locke's *Second Treatise*', *History of Political Thought*, 16 (1995), 356–90.

MITTLEMAN, ALAN, *The Scepter Shall Not Depart from Judah: Perspectives on the Persistence of the Political in Judaism* (Lanham, Md., 2000).

MORENO-CARVALHO, FRANCISCO, 'Yaacov Rosales: Medicine, Astrology, and Political Thought in the Works of a Seventeenth-Century Jewish-Portuguese Physician', *Korot*, 10 (1993/4), 143–56.

MOSS, ANN, 'The *Politica* of Justus Lipsius and the Commonplace-Book', *Journal of the History of Ideas*, 59 (1998), 421–36.

MYERS, DAVID N., 'Between Diaspora and Zion: History, Memory, and Jerusalem Scholars', in David N. Myers and David B. Ruderman (eds.), *The Jewish Past Revisited* (New Haven, 1998), 88–103.

—— and ALEXANDER KAYE (eds.), *The Faith of Fallen Jews: Yosef Hayim Yerushalmi and the Writing of Jewish History* (Boston, Mass., 2013).

NADLER, STEVEN, *Menasseh ben Israel: Rabbi of Amsterdam* (New Haven, 2018).

—— *Spinoza: A Life* (Cambridge, 1999).

NADLER, STEVEN, *Spinoza's Heresy: Immortality and the Jewish Mind* (Oxford, 2001).

NAHMANIDES (RAMBAN), 'Mishpat haherem', in *Hidushei haramban*, ed. Moshe Hershler (Jerusalem, 1970), 281–304.

—— *Perushei hatorah*, ed. C. B. Chavel, i (Jerusalem, 1960).

—— 'Vikuah haramban', in *Kitvei rabenu mosheh ben nahman*, ed. C. B. Chavel (Jerusalem, 1964), 302–20.

—— *Writings & Discourses*, trans. and annot. Charles B. Chavel, 2 vols. (New York, 1978).

NAJMAN, HINDY, 'Introduction' to Ezra and Nehemiah, in Adele Berlin and Marc Zvi Brettler (eds.), *The Jewish Study Bible* (Oxford, 2004), 1666–71.

NELSON, ERIC, *The Hebrew Republic: Jewish Sources and the Transformation of European Political Thought* (Cambridge, Mass., 2010).

NETANYAHU, BENZION, *Don Isaac Abravanel: Statesman and Philosopher*, 5th rev. edn. (Ithaca, NY, 1998).

NETTO, ISAAC, 'Sermão Quarto', in *Sermoés que pregarão os doctos ingenios do K.K. de Talmud Torah, desta cidade de Amsterdam, no alegre estreamento, & publica celebridade da fabrica que se consagrou a deos, para caza de oração, cuja entrada se festejou em Sabath Nahamù*, ed. David de Castro Tartaz (Amsterdam, 1675), 59–74.

NEUMAN, KALMAN, 'Political Hebraism and the Early Modern "Respublica Hebraeorum": On Defining the Field', *Hebraic Political Studies*, 1/1 (2005), 57–70.

NEWEY, GLEN, *Routledge Guidebook to Hobbes' Leviathan* (London, 2008).

NIEROP, HENK VAN, 'Sewing the Bailiff in a Blanket: Catholics and the Law in Holland', in R. Po-Chia Hsia and Henk van Nierop (eds.), *Calvinism and Religious Toleration in the Dutch Golden Age* (Cambridge, 2002), 102–11.

NONGBRI, BRENT, *Before Religion: A History of a Modern Concept* (New Haven, 2015).

NOVAK, DAVID, *Covenantal Rights: A Study in Jewish Political Theory* (Princeton, 2000).

OELMAN, TIMOTHY, *Marrano Poets of the Seventeenth Century: An Anthology of the Poetry of João Pinto Delgado, Antonio Enríquez Gomez, and Miguel de Barrios* (London, 1982).

OFFENBERG, ADRI, 'Dirk van Santen and the Keur Bible: New Insights into Jacob Judah (Arye) Leon Templo's Model Temple', in *Jewish Ceremonial Objects in Transcultural Context = Studia Rosenthaliana*, 37 (2004), 401–22.

—— 'Jacob Jehuda Leon (1602–1675) and His Model of the Temple', in J. van den Berg and Ernestine van der Wall (eds.), *Jewish-Christian Relations in the Seventeenth Century: Studies and Documents* (Dordrecht, 1988), 95–115.

OLIEL-GRAUSZ, ÉVELYNE, 'Résolution des litiges commerciaux et circulations transnationales au début du XVIIIe siècle: L'affaire Pimenta-Nunes Pereira', *Archives Juives*, 47/2 (2014), 77–90.

Oz-Salzberger, Fania, 'The Jewish Roots of the Modern Republic', *Azure*, 13 (2002), 88–132.

Paraira, David P. Cohen, 'A Jewel in the City: The Architectural History of the Portuguese-Jewish Synagogue', in Martine Stroo and Ernest Kupershoek (eds.), *The Esnoga: A Monument to Portuguese-Jewish Culture* (Amsterdam, 2001), 41–5.

Parker, Charles H., 'Paying for the Privilege: The Management of Public Order and Religious Pluralism in Two Early Modern Societies', *Journal of World History*, 17 (2006), 267–96.

Parker, Geoffrey, *Sovereign City: The City-State through History* (London, 2004).

Pedro de Valencia, *Tratado acerca de los moriscos de España*, ed. Rafael González Cañal, *Obras completas*, iv (León, 1999).

Perelis, Ronnie, 'Jewish Sacred Architecture in the Spanish and Portuguese Diaspora', in Steven Fine (ed.), *Jewish Religious Architecture: From Biblical Israel to Modern Judaism* (Leiden, 2020), 221–37.

Pereyra, Abraham, *La certeza del camino* (Amsterdam, 1666), ed. and annotated with introd. by H. Méchoulan in *Hispanidad y Judaismo en tiempos de Espinoza: Edición de* La Certeza del Camino *de Abraham Pereyra* (Salamanca, 1987).

—— *Espejo del vanidad del mundo* (Amsterdam, 1671).

Pieterse, Wilhelmina C., *Daniel Levi de Barrios als Geschiedschrijver van de Portugees-Israelietische Gemeente te Amsterdam in zijn 'Triumpho del Govierno Popular'* (Amsterdam, 1968).

Pineda, Juan de, *Los treynta libros de la monarchia ecclesiastica o historia universal del mundo* (Barcelona, 1606).

Pines, Shlomo, 'Spinoza's *Tractatus Theologico-Politicus* and the Jewish Philosophical Tradition', in Isidore Twersky and Bernard Septimus (eds.), *Jewish Thought in the Seventeenth Century* (Cambridge, Mass., 1987), 499–521.

Pipkin, Amanda C., *Rape in the Republic, 1609–1725: Formulating Dutch Identity* (Leiden, 2013).

Pocock, J. G. A., 'The Dutch Republican Tradition', in Margaret C. Jacob and Wijnand W. Mihnhardt (eds.), *The Dutch Republic in the Eighteenth Century: Decline, Enlightenment, and Revolution* (Ithaca, NY, 1992), 188–93.

—— *The Machiavellian Moment: Florentine Political Thought and the Atlantic Republican Tradition* (Princeton, 1975).

—— *Politics, Language, and Time: Essays on Political Thought and History* (Chicago, 1960).

Popkin, Richard, 'Christian Jews and Jewish Christians in the 17th Century', in Richard Popkin and Gordon Weiner (eds.), *Jewish Christians and Christian Jews: From the Renaissance to the Enlightenment* (Dordrecht: Kluwer, 1994), 57–72.

POPKIN, RICHARD, 'Three English Tellings of the Sabbatai Zevi Story', *Jewish History*, 8/1–2 (1994), 43–54.

—— 'Two Unused Sources about Sabbatai Zevi and His Effect on European Communities', in Jozeph Michman (ed.), *Dutch Jewish History, Proceedings of the Fourth Symposium on the History of the Jews in the Netherlands, 7–10 Dec. 1986, Tel Aviv–Jerusalem*, 2 vols. (Maastricht, 1989), ii. 67–74.

—— and MATT GOLDISH (eds.), *Millenarianism and Messianism in Early Modern European Culture*, 4 vols. (Dordrecht, 2001).

POSNANSKI, ADOLF, *Schiloh: Ein Beitrag zur Geschichte der Messiaslehre* (Leipzig, 1904).

PRICE, J. L., *Holland and the Dutch Republic in the Seventeenth Century: The Politics of Particularism* (Oxford, 1994).

PRIOR, CHARLES W. A., 'Hebraism and the Problem of Church and State in England, 1642–1660', *The Seventeenth Century*, 28/1 (2013), 37–61.

PROKHOVNIK, RAIA, *Spinoza and Republicanism* (Basingstoke, 2004).

PUFENDORF, SAMUEL, *The Political Writings of Samuel Pufendorf*, ed. Craig L. Carr, trans. Michael J. Seidler (New York, 1994).

RABINOWITZ, LOUIS I., *The Herem Hayyishub: A Contribution to the Medieval Economic History of the Jews* (London, 1945).

RAVID, BENJAMIN, '"How Profitable the Nation of the Jewes Are": The "Humble Addresses" of Menasseh ben Israel and the "Discorso" of Simone Luzzatto', in Y. Reinharz and D. Swetschinski (eds.), *Mystics, Philosophers, and Politicians: Essays in Jewish Intellectual History in Honor of Alexander Altmann* (Durham, NC, 1982), 159–80.

RAVVEN, HEIDI M., and LENN E. GOODMAN (eds.), *Jewish Themes in Spinoza's Philosophy* (Albany, NY, 2002).

RAY, JONATHAN, *After Expulsion: 1492 and the Making of Sephardic Jewry* (New York, 2013).

—— *The Sephardic Frontier: The Reconquista and the Jewish Community in Medieval Iberia* (Ithaca, NY, 2006).

REINDERS, MICHEL, *Printed Pandemonium: Popular Print and Politics in the Netherlands, 1650–72* (Leiden, 2013).

REMER, GARY, 'After Machiavelli and Hobbes: James Harrington's Commonwealth of Israel', in Gordon Schochet, Fania Oz-Salzberger, and Meirav Jones (eds.), *Political Hebraism: Judaic Sources in Early Modern Political Thought* (Jerusalem, 2008), 207–30.

RÉVAH, I. S., 'Un pamphlet contre l'inquisition d'Antonio Enriquez Gómez: La seconde partie de la "Politica Angélica" (Rouen, 1647)', *Revue des études juives*, 121 (1962), 81–168.

RIBADENEIRA, PEDRO DE, *Tratado de la religion y virtudes que deve tener el principe christiano, para governar y conservar sus estados, contra lo que Nicolas Machiavelo y los politicos deste tiempo enseñan* (Antwerp, 1597).

ROBLES CARCEDO, LAUREANO, 'Abraham Pereyra y "La Certeza del Camino"', in Fernando Díaz Esteban (ed.), *Los Judaizantes en Europa y la literatura Castellana del siglo de oro* (Madrid, 1994), 321–33.

ROITMAN, JESSICA VANCE, *The Same But Different? Inter-cultural Trade and the Sephardim, 1595–1640* (Leiden, 2011).

ROODEN, P. T. VAN, 'Jews and Religious Toleration in the Dutch Republic', in R. Po-Chia Hsia and Henk van Nierop (eds.), *Calvinism and Religious Toleration in the Dutch Golden Age* (Cambridge, 2002), 132–47.

—— and J. W. WESSELIUS, 'The Early Enlightenment and Judaism: The "Civil Dispute" between Philippus van Limborch and Isaac Orobio de Castro (1687)', *Studia Rosenthaliana*, 21/2 (1987), 140–53.

ROSENAU, HELEN, 'Jacob Judah Leon Templo's Contribution to Architectural Imagery', *Journal of Jewish Studies*, 23/1 (1972), 72–81.

—— 'The Synagogue and Protestant Church Architecture', *Journal of the Warburg and Courtauld Institutes*, 4/12 (1940–1), 80–5.

ROSENBLATT, JASON P., *Renaissance England's Chief Rabbi: John Selden* (Oxford, 2006).

ROSENSTOCK, BRUCE, 'Abraham Miguel Cardoso's Messianism: A Reappraisal', *AJS Review*, 23/1 (1998), 63–104.

—— *New Men: Conversos, Christian Theology, and Society in Fifteenth-Century Castile* (London, 2002).

ROTH, CECIL, *A Life of Menasseh ben Israel, Rabbi, Printer, and Diplomat* (Philadelphia, 1934).

RUDERMAN, DAVID B., *Early Modern Jewry: A New Cultural History* (Princeton, 2010).

SAASTAMOINEN, KARI, 'Hobbes and Pufendorf on Natural Equality and Civil Sovereignty', in Ian Hunter and David Saunders (eds.), *Natural Law and Civil Sovereignty: Moral Right and State Authority in Early Modern Political Thought* (New York, 2002).

SAAVEDRA FAJARDO, DIEGO DE, *Idea de un príncipe político-cristiano representada en cien empresas* (Monaco, 1640).

SACKS, DAVID HARRIS, *The Widening Gate: Bristol and the Atlantic Economy, 1450–1700* (Berkeley, 1993).

SARNA, JONATHAN, 'Jewish Prayers for the United States Government: A Study in the Liturgy of Politics and the Politics of Liturgy', in Ruth Langer and Steven Fine (eds.), *Liturgy in the Life of the Synagogue: Studies in the History of Jewish Prayer* (Winona Lake, Ind., 2005), 205–24.

SARPHATI, DAVID, 'Sermão Septimo', in *Sermoés que pregarão os doctos ingenios do K.K. de Talmud Torah, desta cidade de Amsterdam, no alegre estreamento, & publica celebridade da fabrica que se consagrou a deos, para caza de oração, cuja entrada se festejou em Sabath Nahamù*, ed. David de Castro Tartaz (Amsterdam, 1675), 133–55.

SASPORTAS, JACOB, *Tsitsat novel tsevi* (Jerusalem, 1954).

SCHAUB, JEAN-FRÉDÉRIC, *Le Portugal au temps du Comte-Duc D'Olivares (1621–1640): Le Conflit de juridictions comme exercice de la politique* (Madrid, 2001).

SCHOCHET, GORDON, FANIA OZ-SALZBERGER, and MEIRAV JONES (eds.), *Political Hebraism: Judaic Sources in Early Modern Political Thought* (Jerusalem, 2008).

SCHÖFFER, IVO, 'Did Holland's Golden Age Coincide with a Period of Crisis?', in Geoffrey Parker (ed.), *The General Crisis of the Seventeenth Century* (London, 1978), 78–109.

SCHOLBERG, KENNETH, 'Miguel de Barrios and the Amsterdam Sephardic Community', *Jewish Quarterly Review*, 53/2 (1962), 120–59.

SCHOLEM, GERSHOM, 'The Crisis of Tradition in Jewish Messianism', in id., *The Messianic Idea in Judaism and Other Essays on Jewish Spirituality* (New York, 1971), 49–77.

—— 'Isaac Luria and His School', in id., *Major Trends in Jewish Mysticism* (New York, 1946), 244–86.

—— 'On the Possibility of Jewish Mysticism in Our Time', in A. Shapira (ed.), *On the Possibility of Jewish Mysticism in Our Time and Other Essays*, trans. J. Chipman (Philadelphia, 1997).

—— 'Redemption through Sin', in id., *The Messianic Idea in Judaism and Other Essays on Jewish Spirituality* (New York, 1971), 78–141.

—— *Sabbatai Ṣevi: The Mystical Messiah*, trans. R. J. Zwi Werblowsky (Princeton, 1993).

—— 'Sabbatianism and Mystical Heresy', in id., *Major Trends in Jewish Mysticism* (New York, 1946), 287–324.

SCHRIER, GERARD VAN DER, and ROB GROENLAND, 'A Reconstruction of 1 August 1674 Thunderstorms over the Low Countries', *Natural Hazards and Earth System Sciences*, 17 (2017), 157–70.

SCHWARTZ, BARRY, '*Hanoten Teshua*': The Origin of the Traditional Jewish Prayer for the Government', *Hebrew Union College Annual*, 57 (1986), 113–20.

SCHWARTZ, DANIEL B., *The First Modern Jew: Spinoza and the History of an Image* (Princeton, 2012).

—— *Ghetto: The History of a Word* (Cambridge, Mass., 2019).

—— (ed.), *Spinoza's Challenge to Jewish Thought: Writings on His Life, Philosophy, and Legacy* (Waltham, Mass., 2019).

SELDEN, JOHN, *Table-Talk*, ed. S. W. Singer (London, 1890).

SENELLART, MICHEL, 'La Raison d'état antimachiavélienne: Essai de problématisation', in Christian Lazzeri and Dominique Reynié (eds.), *La Raison d'état: Politique et rationalité* (Paris, 1992), 15–32.

SEPTIMUS, BERNARD, 'Biblical Religion and Political Rationality in Simone Luzzatto, Maimonides and Spinoza', in Isadore Twersky and Bernard Septimus (eds.), *Jewish Thought in the Seventeenth Century* (Cambridge, Mass., 1987), 399–433.

SHEAR, ADAM, *The Kuzari and the Shaping of Jewish Identity: 1167–1900* (New York, 2008).

SHELFORD, APRIL, 'Of Sceptres and Censors: Biblical Interpretation and Censorship in Seventeenth-Century France', *French History*, 20 (2006), 161–81.

—— *Transforming the Republic of Letters: Pierre-Daniel Huet and European Intellectual Life* (Rochester, NY, 2007).

SHOHAM-STEINER, EPHRAIM, and ELISABETH HOLLENDER, 'Beyond the Rabbinic Paradigm', *Jewish Quarterly Review*, 111 (Spring 2021), 236–64.

SHOHET, DAVID, *The Jewish Court in the Middle Ages* (New York, 1931; repr. New York, 1974).

SHOULSON, JEFFREY, *Fictions of Conversion: Jews, Christians, and Cultures of Change in Early Modern England* (Philadelphia, 2013).

SIEGMUND, STEFANIE, 'Communal Leaders (*rashei qahal*) and the Representation of Medieval and Early Modern Jews as "Communities"', in Jack Wertheimer (ed.), *Jewish Religious Leadership: Image and Reality*, i (New York, 2014), 333–70.

—— *The Medici State and the Ghetto of Florence: The Construction of an Early Modern Jewish Community* (Stanford, Calif., 2006).

SILVERA, MIRIAM, 'Contribution à l'examen des sources de *L'Histoire des Juifs* de Jacques Basnage: *Las Excelencias de los Hebreos* de "Ysaac Cardoso"', *Studia Rosenthaliana*, 25/1 (Spring 1991), 42–54.

SIMONSOHN, SHLOMO, *History of the Jews in the Duchy of Mantua* (Jerusalem, 1977).

SKINNER, QUENTIN, *The Foundations of Modern Political Thought*, 2 vols. (Cambridge, 1978).

—— 'Hobbes's Changing Conception of Civil Science', in id., *Visions of Politics*, iii: *Hobbes and Civil Science* (Cambridge, 2002), 66–86.

SMITH, JONATHAN Z., 'Religion, Religions, Religious', in M. C. Taylor (ed.), *Critical Terms for Religious Studies* (Chicago, 1998), 269–84.

SMITH, STEVEN B., *Spinoza, Liberalism, and the Question of Jewish Identity* (New Haven, 1997).

—— 'Spinoza's Democratic Turn: Chapter 16 of the "Theologico-Political Treatise"', *Review of Metaphysics*, 48 (1994), 359–88.

—— 'Spinoza's Paradox: Judaism and the Construction of Liberal Identity in the Theologico-Political Treatise', *Journal of Jewish Thought and Philosophy*, 4 (1995), 203–25.

SMITH, THOMAS, *De republica anglorum: The maner of gouvernement or policie of the realme of England* (London, 1583).

SMITH, WILFRED CANTWELL, *The Meaning and End of Religion: A New Approach to the Religious Traditions of Mankind* (New York, 1963).

SNYDER, SASKIA COENEN, *Building a Public Judaism: Synagogues and Jewish Identity in Nineteenth-Century Europe* (Cambridge, Mass., 2012).

SOMMERVILLE, JOHANN P., 'Hobbes, Selden, Erastianism, and the History of the Jews', in G. A. J. Rogers and T. Sorell (eds.), *Hobbes and History*, i (London, 2000), 176–204.

SORKIN, DAVID, 'Beyond the East–West Divide: Rethinking the Narrative of the Jews' Political Status in Europe, 1600–1750', *Jewish History*, 24 (2010), 247–56.

——*Jewish Emancipation: A History across Five Centuries* (Princeton, 2019).

SPAANS, JOKE, 'Religious Policies in the Seventeenth-Century Dutch Republic', in R. Po-Chia Hsia and Henk van Nierop (eds.), *Calvinism and Religious Toleration in the Dutch Golden Age* (Cambridge, 2002), 82–96.

SPICER, ANDREW, *Calvinist Churches in Early Modern Europe* (Manchester, 2007).

SPIERLING, KAREN E., and MICHAEL J. HALVORSON, 'Introduction: Definitions of Community in Early Modern Europe', in M. J. Halvorson and K. E. Spierling (eds.), *Defining Community in Early Modern Europe* (Aldershot, 2008), 1–23.

SPINOZA, BENEDICT DE, *A Theologico-Political Treatise; A Political Treatise*, trans. R. H. M. Elwes (New York, 1951).

SPRUNGER, KEITH L., *Trumpets from the Tower: English Puritan Printing in the Netherlands, 1600–1640* (Leiden, 1994).

STEINBERG, JUSTIN, 'Spinoza's Political Philosophy', in E. N. Zalta (ed.), *The Stanford Encyclopedia of Philosophy* (Summer 2019 edn.); <https://plato.stanford.edu/archives/sum2019/entries/spinoza-political/>.

STIEFEL, BARRY, 'The Architectural Origins of the Great Early Modern Urban Synagogue', *Leo Baeck Institute Year Book*, 56 (2011), 105–34.

STRAUMANN, BENJAMIN, *Crisis and Constitutionalism: Roman Political Thought from the Fall of the Republic to the Age of Revolution* (New York, 2016).

STRAUSS, LEO, *Spinoza's Critique of Religion* (New York, 1965).

STUCZYNSKI, CLAUDE B., 'From Polemics and Apologetics to Theology and Politics: Alonso de Cartagena and the Conversos within the "Mystical Body"', in Israel Jacob Yuval and Ram Ben-Shalom (eds.), *Conflict and Religious Conversation in Latin Christendom: Studies in Honour of Ora Limor* (Turnhout, 2014), 253–77.

——'Harmonizing Identities: The Problem of the Integration of the Portuguese Conversos in Early Modern Iberian Corporate Polities', *Jewish History*, 25 (2011), 229–57.

——'Pro-Converso Apologetics and Biblical Exegesis', in Jonathan Decter and Arturo Prats (eds.), *The Hebrew Bible in Fifteenth-Century Spain: Exegesis, Literature, Philosophy, and the Arts* (Leiden, 2012), 151–75.

——'Toward a Repolitization of the Converso Phenomenon in Portugal and Beyond', *Journal of Levantine Studies*, 6 (2016), 5–12.

SUTCLIFFE, ADAM, 'The Boundaries of Community: Urban Space and Intercultural Interaction in Early Modern Sephardi Amsterdam and London', in Yosef Kaplan (ed.), *The Dutch Intersection: The Jews and the Netherlands in Modern History* (Boston, Mass., 2008), 19–31.

——'Imagining Amsterdam—The Dutch Golden Age and the Origins of Jewish Modernity', *Simon Dubnow Institute Yearbook*, 6 (2007), 79–98.

——'Sephardi Amsterdam and the European Radical Enlightenment', in Judit Targarona Borrás and Angel Sáenz-Badillos (eds.), *Jewish Studies at the Turn of the Twentieth Century: Proceedings of the 6th EAJS Congress* (Leiden, 1999), 399–405.

——'Sephardic Amsterdam and the Myths of Jewish Modernity', *Jewish Quarterly Review*, 97 (2007), 417–37.

SWETSCHINSKI, DANIEL, 'The Portuguese Jews of Seventeenth-Century Amsterdam: Cultural Continuity and Adaptation', in Frances Malino and Phyllis Cohen Albert (eds.), *Essays in Modern Jewish History: A Tribute to Ben Halpern* (London, 1982), 56–80.

——*Reluctant Cosmopolitans: The Portuguese Jews of Seventeenth-Century Amsterdam* (Oxford, 2000).

——'The Spanish Consul and the Jews of Amsterdam', in Michael Fishbane and Paul Flohr (eds.), *Texts and Responses: Studies Presented to Nahum N. Glatzer on the Occasion of His Seventieth Birthday by His Students* (Leiden, 1975), 158–72.

——'Un refus de mémoire: Les Juifs portugais d'Amsterdam et leur passé Marrane', in Esther Benbassa (ed.), *Mémoires juives d'Espagne et du Portugal* (Paris, 1996), 69–77.

Talmud Bavli: The Schottenstein Edition (Brooklyn, 1990–2005), xxi: *Tractate Moed Katan*.

The Targums of Onkelos and Jonathan ben Uzziel on the Pentateuch, with the Fragments of the Jerusalem Targum from the Chaldee, trans. J. W. Etheridge (London, 1862–5; repr. New York, 1968).

TELLER, ADAM, 'The Laicization of Early Modern Jewish Society: The Development of the Polish Communal Rabbinate in the 16th Century', in M. Graetz (ed.), *Schoepferische Momente des europaischen Judentums in der fruhen Neuzeit* (Heidelberg, 2000), 333–49.

——'Rabbis without a Function: The Polish Rabbinate and the Council of Four Lands in the Sixteenth to Eighteenth Centuries', in Jack Wertheimer (ed.), *Jewish Religious Leadership: Image and Reality*, i (New York, 2004), 371–400.

TEPLITSKY, JOSHUA, 'Messianic Hope in Hamburg, 1666', in *Key Documents of German-Jewish History*; <https://dx.doi.org/10.23691/jgo:article-195.en.vi>.

TISHBY, ISAIAH, 'The Letters of Rabbi Jacob Sasportas against the *Parnasim* of Livorno in 1681' (Heb.), *Kovets al yad*, NS 4 (1946), 143–60.

TITTLER, ROBERT, *Architecture and Power: The Town Hall and the English Urban Community, c.1500–1640* (Oxford, 1991).

TOAFF, ALFREDO S., 'The Controversy between R. Sasportas and the Jewish Community in Livorno (1681)' (Heb.), *Sefunot*, 9 (1964), 169–91.

TÖNNIES, FERDINAND, *Community and Society (Gemeinschaft und Gesellschaft)*, trans. Charles P. Loomis (East Lansing, Mich., 1957).

TREVOR-ROPER, HUGH, 'The General Crisis of the Seventeenth Century', *Past & Present*, 16 (1959), 31–64.

TRIVELLATO, FRANCESCA, *The Familiarity of Strangers: The Sephardic Diaspora, Livorno, and Cross-Cultural Trade in the Early Modern Period* (New Haven, 2009).

TUCK, RICHARD, 'Introduction', in Thomas Hobbes, *Leviathan*, ed. R. Tuck, rev. edn. (Cambridge, 1996), pp. ix–xlv.

—— *Philosophy and Government 1572–1651* (Cambridge, 1993).

TURNER, HENRY S., *The Corporate Commonwealth: Pluralism and Political Fictions in England, 1516–1651* (Chicago, 2016).

TURNIANSKY, CHAVA (ed.), *Glikl: Memoirs 1691–1719*, trans. Sara Friedman (Waltham, Mass., 2019).

USQUE, SAMUEL, *Samuel Usque's Consolation for the Tribulations of Israel*, trans. Martin Cohen, 2nd edn. (Philadelphia, 1977).

VALLANCE, EDWARD, *Revolutionary England and the National Covenant: State Oaths, Protestantism and the Political Nation, 1553–1682* (Woodbridge, 2005).

VAN PRAAG, J. A., 'Almas en litigio', *Clavileño*, 1 (1950), 13–26.

VELEMA, WYGER R. E., '"That a Republic Is Better than a Monarchy": Anti-monarchism in Early Modern Dutch Political Thought', in Martin van Gelderen and Quentin Skinner (eds.), *Republicanism: A Shared European Heritage*, i: *Republicanism and Constitutionalism in Early Modern Europe* (Cambridge, 2002), 9–26.

VELLOZINO, ISAAC, 'Sermão Sexto', in *Sermoés que pregarão os doctos ingenios do K.K. de Talmud Torah, desta cidade de Amsterdam, no alegre estreamento, & publica celebridade da fabrica que se consagrou a deos, para caza de oração, cuja entrada se festejou em Sabath Nahamù*, ed. David de Castro Tartaz (Amsterdam, 1675), 101–29.

VELTRI, GIUSEPPE, *Renaissance Philosophy in Jewish Garb: Foundations and Challenges in Judaism on the Eve of Modernity* (Leiden, 2009).

VIROLI, MAURIZIO, *From Politics to Reason of State: The Acquisition and Transformation of the Language of Politics 1250–1600* (Cambridge, 1992).

VLAARDINGERBROEK, PIETER (ed.), *The Portuguese Synagogue in Amsterdam* (Amsterdam, 2013).

VLESSING, ODETTE, 'The Excommunication of Baruch Spinoza: A Struggle between Jewish and Civil Law', in Jonathan I. Israel and Reinier Salverda (eds.), *Dutch Jewry: Its History and Secular Culture (1500–2000)* (Leiden, 2002), 141–72.

—— 'New Light on the Earliest History of the Amsterdam Portuguese Jews', in Jozeph Michman (ed.), *Dutch Jewish History, Proceedings of the Fifth Symposium on the History of the Jews in the Netherlands, Jerusalem, 25–28 Nov. 1991* (Assen, 1993), 43–75.

VRIES, JAN DE, 'The Economic Crisis of the Seventeenth Century after Fifty Years', *Journal of Interdisciplinary History*, 40 (2009), 151–94.

WACKS, DAVID, *Double Diaspora in Sephardic Literature: Jewish Cultural Production before and after 1492* (Bloomington, Ind., 2015).

WALFISH, BARRY DOV, *Esther in Medieval Garb: Jewish Interpretation of the Book of Esther in the Middle Ages* (Albany, NY, 1993).

WALSHAM, ALEXANDRA, 'The Social History of the Archive: Record-Keeping in Early Modern Europe', *Past & Present*, Supplement 11 (2016), 9–48.

WALUCHOW, WIL, 'Constitutionalism', in Edward N. Zalta (ed.), *The Stanford Encyclopedia of Philosophy* (Spring 2018 edn.); <https://plato.stanford.edu/archives/spr2018/entries/constitutionalism/>.

WALZER, MICHAEL, MENACHEM LORBERBAUM, and NOAM J. ZOHAR (eds.), *The Jewish Political Tradition*, i: *Authority* (New Haven, 2000).

—— —— —— and MADELINE KOCHEN (eds.), *The Jewish Political Tradition*, iii: *Community* (New Haven, 2018).

WARSHAWSKY, MATTHEW D., '"All True, All Holy, All Divine": Jewish Identity in the Polemics and Letters of Isaac Orobio de Castro, a Former Portuguese New Christian in 1600s Amsterdam', *Journal of Jewish Identities*, 11 (2018), 267–87.

WASZINK, JAN, 'Introduction', in Justus Lipsius, *Politica: Six Works of Politics or Political Instruction*, ed. Jan Waszink (Assen, 2004), 3–203.

WEBER, MAX, *Economy and Society: An Outline of Interpretive Sociology*, ed. Guenther Roth and Claus Wittich (Berkeley, 2013).

WERBLOWSKY, R. J. ZWI, 'Messianism in Jewish History', in H. H. Ben-Sasson and Shmuel Ettinger (eds.), *Jewish Society through the Ages* (New York, 1971), 30–45.

WESTSTEIJN, ARTHUR, *Commercial Republicanism in the Dutch Golden Age: The Political Thought of Johan and Pieter de la Court* (Leiden, 2012).

—— 'Why the Dutch Didn't Read Harrington: Anglo-Dutch Republican Exchanges, c.1650–1670', in Gaby Mahlberg and Dirk Wiemann (eds.), *European Contexts for English Republicanism* (Farnham, 2012), 105–20.

WILDE, MARC DE, 'Offering Hospitality to Strangers: Hugo Grotius's Draft Regulations for the Jews', *Tijdschrift voor rechtsgeschiedenis/The Legal History Review*, 85 (2017), 391–433.

WILENSKY, MORDECHAI, 'Four English Pamphlets on the Sabbatian Movement' (Heb.), *Zion*, 17 (1952), 157–72.

WILKE, CARSTEN, 'La *Trompette du jugement* de Miguel de Barrios: Essai de déchiffrement', in Henry Méchoulan and Gérard Nahon (eds.), *Mémorial I. S. Révah: Études sur le marranisme, l'hétérodoxie juive et Spinoza* (Paris, 2001), 515–27.

—— 'Semi-Clandestine Judaism in Early Modern France: European Horizons and Local Varieties of a Domestic Devotion', in Yosef Kaplan (ed.), *Religious Changes and Cultural Transformations in the Early Modern Western Sephardic Communities* (Leiden, 2019), 113–36.

WILLET, ANDREW, *Hexapla in Genesin: That Is, a Sixfold Commentarie upon Genesis* (Cambridge, 1605).

WINSHIP, MICHAEL P., *Godly Republicanism: Puritans, Pilgrims, and a City on a Hill* (Boston, Mass., 2012).

WITHINGTON, PHIL, *The Politics of Commonwealth: Citizens and Freemen in Early Modern England* (Cambridge, 2005).

WIZNITZER, ARNOLD, *Jews in Colonial Brazil* (New York, 1960).

—— 'The Merger Agreement and Regulations of Congregation Talmud Torah of Amsterdam (1638–9)', *Historia Judaica*, 20 (1958), 109–32.

WOOLF, JEFFREY R., *The Fabric of Religious Life in Medieval Ashkenaz (1000–1300): Creating Sacred Communities* (Leiden, 2015).

WRIGHTSON, KEITH, 'The Politics of the Parish in Early Modern England', in Paul Griffiths, Adam Fox, and Steve Hindle (eds.), *The Experience of Authority in Early Modern England* (New York, 1996), 10–46.

YAARI, ABRAHAM, 'The Pereyra Yeshivot in Jerusalem and Hebron' (Heb.), in M. Ish-Shalom, M. Benayahu, and A. Shohet (eds.), *Yerushalayim: Review for Erets Yisra'el Research* [Yerushalayim: meḥkerei erets yisra'el] (Jerusalem, 1953), 185–202.

YAVARI, NEGUIN, and REGULA FORSTER, 'Introduction', in R. Forster and N. Yavari (eds.), *Global Medieval: Mirrors for Princes Reconsidered* (Cambridge, Mass., 2015).

YERUSHALMI, YOSEF HAYIM, 'Clio and the Jews: Reflections on Jewish Historiography in the Sixteenth Century', *Proceedings of the American Academy for Jewish Research*, 46–7/2 (1979–80), 607–38.

—— 'Exile and Expulsion in Jewish History', in Benjamin R. Gampel (ed.), *Crisis and Creativity in the Sephardic World* (New York, 1997), 3–22.

—— *From Spanish Court to Italian Ghetto: Isaac Cardoso. A Study in Seventeenth-Century Marranism and Jewish Apologetics* (New York, 1971).

—— *The Lisbon Massacre of 1506 and the Royal Image in the 'Shebet Yehudah'* (Cincinnati, 1976).

—— *Servants of Kings and Not Servants of Servants* (Atlanta, Ga., 2005); repr. in David N. Myers and Alexander Kaye (eds.), *The Faith of Fallen Jews: Yosef Hayim Yerushalmi and the Writing of Jewish History* (Boston, Mass., 2013), 245–76.

——*Zakhor: Jewish History and Jewish Memory* (Seattle, 1996).

YISRAELI, YOSI, 'Were God's People Destined to be Ruled by a Mortal King? A Judeo-Converso-Christian Tradition', *Journal of Levantine Studies*, 6 (2016), 13–41.

YOVEL, YIRMIYAHU, *The Other Within: The Marranos. Split Identity and Emerging Modernity* (Princeton, 2009).

ZARKA, YVES-CHARLES (ed.), *Raison et déraison d'état: Théoriciens et théories de la raison d'état aux XVIe et XVIIe sieècles* (Paris, 1994).

ZIMMER, ERIC, *Harmony and Discord: An Analysis of the Decline of Jewish Self-Government in Fifteenth-Century Europe* (New York, 1970).

——*Jewish Synods in Germany during the Late Middle Ages (1286–1603)* (New York, 1978).

ZOHAR, NOAM, 'Civil Society and Government: Seeking Judaic Insights', in N. L. Rosenblum and R. C. Post (eds.), *Civil Society and Government* (Princeton, 2002), 265–79.

ZUCKERMAN, MICHAEL, *Peaceable Kingdoms: New England Towns in the Eighteenth Century* (New York, 1970).

INDEX

revived 17, 19–21, 72, 94
see also community, concepts of
responsa, *see* rabbis
Revolt of the Netherlands 34, 40, 97
revolution, right to 159, 174, 178–9
rights, natural 178, 180–4
ritual 13, 45, 51, 54, 124, 161, 234, 241,
    312, 316
  conditions for 92
  innovations 29, 304
  observances 22
  role of rabbis in 197
  slaughter, *see* butchers
  synagogue as site of 119, 120, 128
  texts of 108
  transgression of 26
  see also *ḥerem*; *kashrut*; *mikveh*
Roman empire 93, 276, 293
Rome 75, 76, 127, 134
rule (*mando*), concepts of 102, 216, 256,
    275, 279
  Cardoso on 264, 266
  of Judah 261, 268–9
  Orobio de Castro on 105, 210, 212,
    217, 267, 271
  Pereyra on 111

S
Sabbatai Zevi 3, 5, 9, 15, 33, 83, 305, 322,
    323
  celebration of the Ninth of Av 149, 304
  conversion to Islam 25–6, 29–30, 150
  death 10, 26, 289, 298
  as 'king' 147–8
  letters of 116, 266
  prayers for 27–8
  return of 248, 290
Sabbatianism 25–31, 86, 89, 103, 144,
    188, 192, 302
  in Amsterdam 10, 86, 299
  displays of 234
  end of 37, 144, 235, 297–8
  and the Esnoga 133–5, 151–2
  historiography of 26–7, 306
  ideas of democracy in 36, 283–5,
    289–90
  opposition to 168, 266, 304–5

political expectations in 24, 26–32, 234,
    248–9, 255, 311
  responses to 34, 116, 147–52, 202, 235,
    246–50, 304, 305
  in Smyrna 150
  Spinoza and 25, 304–7, 308
Salonika (Thessaloniki), Greece 39, 156,
    165
Sanhedrin 166, 205, 206, 208, 212, 213,
    218, 258, 274
Sarphati, David 59, 100–1, 240–1, 252,
    301, 309
  political thought of 24, 36, 228–33, 239,
    242, 243–7, 249–51
  as a 'politico' 233–7, 305
  sermon at dedication of Esnoga 5–7, 10,
    12, 35, 117, 149–51, 220–4
Sasportas, Jacob 28, 168–9, 188, 192, 201,
    203, 289, 298, 305
scepticism, religious 12, 16, 22, 86, 155
scholasticism 100, 240
Scottow, Joshua 303
Sebastianism 30
secularization 31, 142, 155, 188, 295, 310
Selden, John 18, 84, 184, 205, 206, 207
self-determination 10, 131, 262, 320, 322
separation, Jewish 62, 71, 77, 130, 131,
    271, 300, 301, 309, 310, 314
Sephardim 74, 107, 201, 257, 263
  Amsterdam 12, 24, 25, 30, 41, 55, 108,
    112, 132, 243
  medieval 51, 195, 315
  terms of 13, 38
sermons 1, 35, 148, 198, 199, 222, 223,
    229, 234, 245, 247
  Christian 277
  dedicatory 5–6, 12, 18, 100, 118, 119,
    135, 150, 244, 256
  printed 231
  rabbinic 58, 130
shamta, see *ḥerem*
shevet, *see* Judah, sceptre of
Shiloh, *see* messianism
Silveira, Abraham Gomes 82
Sirkes, Joel 192, 201–2, 203
Solomon, king 108, 117, 120, 225, 283
Solon 287